T0182901

Lecture Notes in Computer Science 10442

Commenced Publication in 1973
Founding and Former Series Editors:
Gerhard Goos, Juris Hartmanis, and Jan van Leeuwen

More information about this series at http://www.springer.com/series/7410

Javier Lopez · Simone Fischer-Hübner
Costas Lambrinoudakis (Eds.)

Trust, Privacy and Security in Digital Business

14th International Conference, TrustBus 2017
Lyon, France, August 30–31, 2017
Proceedings

Editors
Javier Lopez
University of Malaga
Malaga
Spain

Costas Lambrinoudakis
University of Piraeus
Piraeus
Greece

Simone Fischer-Hübner
Karlstad University
Karlstad
Sweden

ISSN 0302-9743 ISSN 1611-3349 (electronic)
Lecture Notes in Computer Science
ISBN 978-3-319-64482-0 ISBN 978-3-319-64483-7 (eBook)
DOI 10.1007/978-3-319-64483-7

Library of Congress Control Number: 2017947504

LNCS Sublibrary: SL4 – Security and Cryptology

Printed on acid-free paper

This Springer imprint is published by Springer Nature
The registered company is Springer International Publishing AG
The registered company address is: Gewerbestrasse 11, 6330 Cham, Switzerland

Preface

New computing paradigms, such as cloud computing, big data, and the Internet of Things, openup new horizons to businesses by making possible the provision of high-quality services all over the world. All these developments ultimately aim at improving our quality of life, at making it easier to generate wealth, and at ensuring that businesses remain competitive in the global marketplace. These developments have been made possible in a remarkably short time span, by virtue of the fact that information and communication technologies move fast; sometimes they move too fast for society and for governments. This explains why such rapid technological evolutions cannot be problem-free. In the domain of digital businesses, concerns are raised regarding the lack of trust in electronic procedures and the extent to which information security and user privacy can be ensured.

In answer to these concerns, the 14th International Conference on Trust, Privacy and Security in Digital Business (TrustBus 2017), held in Lyon/France, August 30–31 2017, provided an international forum for researchers and practitioners to exchange information regarding advancements in the state of the art and practice of trust and privacy in digital business. The program included papers describing advances in all areas of digital business applications related to trust and privacy focusing on security and privacy in mobile environments, cloud, IoT, transparency and privacy-enhancing technologies, policy languages, security measures, social engineering, and security awareness.

TrustBus 2017 received 40 paper submissions, which were all reviewed by at least two, and most of them by three or four members of the international Program Committee (PC). Based on the reviews and discussions between PC chairs and PC members, 15 full papers were finally accepted for presentation at the conference. An invited keynote talk was given by Dr. Nora Cuppens, Telecom Bretagne, on "Detecting Privacy Violations in Android-Like Systems."

We would like to thank all authors, especially those, who presented their work selected for the program. Moreover, we are very grateful to all PC members and additional reviewers, who contributed with thorough reviews and participated in PC discussions ensuring a high quality of all accepted papers. We also owe special thanks to Nora Cuppens for contributing with her keynote talk.

Last but not least, we gratefully acknowledge the valuable help by the local DEXA organizer Gabriela Wagner for her outstanding support.

August 2017

Simone Fischer-Hübner
Costas Lambrinoudakis

Organization

General Chair

Javier Lopez	University of Malaga, Spain

Program Committee Co-chairs

Simone Fischer-Hübner	Karlstad University, Sweden
Costas Lambrinoudakis	University of Piraeus, Greece

Program Committee

Aggelinos George	University of Piraeus, Greece
Aimeur Esma	University of Montreal, Canada
Chadwick David W.	University of Kent, UK
Clarke Nathan	University of Plymouth, UK
Cuppens Frederic	ENST Bretagne, France
De Capitani di Vimercati Sabrina	Università degli Studi di Milano, Italy
Domingo-Ferrer Josep	Universitat Rovira i Virgili, Spain
Drogkaris Prokopios	University of the Aegean, Greece
Fernandez Eduardo B.	Florida Atlantic University, USA
Ferrer Josep L.	University of Balearic Islands, Spain
Foresti Sara	Università degli Studi di Milano, Italy
Furnell Steven	University of Plymouth, UK
Fuss Juergen	University of Applied Science in Hagenberg, Austria
Geneiatakis Dimitris	Aristotle University of Thessaloniki, Greece
Gritzalis Dimitris	Athens University of Economics and Business, Greece
Gritzalis Stefanos	University of the Aegean, Greece
Kalloniatis Christos	University of the Aegean, Greece
Karyda Maria	University of the Aegean, Greece
Katos Vasilios	Bournemouth University, UK
Katsikas Sokratis	University of Piraeus, Greece
Kokolakis Spyros	University of the Aegean, Greece
Krenn Stephan	AIT Austrian Institute of Technology GmbH, Austria
Markowitch Olivier	Università Libre de Bruxelles, Belgium
Martin S. Olivier	University of Pretoria, South Africa
Martinelli Fabio	National Research Council, C.N.R, Italy
Martucci Leonardo	Karlstad University, Sweden
Megias David	Universitat Oberta de Catalunya, Spain
Mouratidis Haris	University of Brighton, UK
Nieto Ana	University of Malaga, Spain

Oppliger Rolf	eSECURITY Technologies, Switzerland
Papadaki Maria	University of Plymouth, UK
Pashalidis Andreas	BSI, Germany
Pernul Günther	University of Regensburg, Germany
Posegga Joachim	Institute of IT-Security and Security Law, Passau, Germany
Rizomiliotis Panagiotis	University of the Aegean, Greece
Ruben Rios	University of Malaga, Spain
Rudolph Carsten	Monash University, Australia
Samarati Pierangela	Università degli Studi di Milano, Italy
Teufel Stephanie	University of Fribourg, Switzerland
Tsohou Aggeliki	Ionian University, Greece
Vashek Matyas	Masaryk University and Red Hat Czech, Czech Republic
Weippl Edgar	SBA, Austria
Xenakis Christos	University of Piraeus, Greece

Additional Reviewers

Dritsas Stelios	Athens University of Economics and Business, Greece
Kunz Michael	University of Regensburg, Germany
Mylonas Alexis	Bournemouth University, UK
Rakotondravony Noelle	University of Passau, Germany
Richthammer Christian	University of Regensburg, Germany
Simou Stavros	University of the Aegean, Greece
Striecks Christoph	AIT Austrian Institute of Technology GmbH, Austria
Taubmann Benjamin	University of Passau, Germany
Tsoumas Bill	Athens University of Economics and Business, Greece
Vielberth Manfred	University of Regensburg, Germany

Contents

Privacy in Mobile Environments

FAIR: Fuzzy Alarming Index Rule for Privacy Analysis in Smartphone Apps

Majid Hatamian[1(✉)], Jetzabel Serna[1], Kai Rannenberg[1], and Bodo Igler[2]

[1] Chair of Mobile Business and Multilateral Security, Goethe University Frankfurt, Frankfurt am Main, Germany
{majid.hatamian,jetzabel.serna,kai.rannenberg}@m-chair.de

[2] RheinMain University of Applied Sciences, Wiesbaden, Germany
bodo.igler@hs-rm.de

Abstract. In this paper, we introduce an approach that aims at increasing individuals' privacy awareness. We perform a privacy risk assessment of the smartphone applications (apps) installed on a user's device. We implemented an app behaviour monitoring tool that collects information about access to sensitive resources by each installed app. We then calculate a privacy risk score using a fuzzy logic based approach that considers type, number and frequency of access on resources. The combination of these two concepts provides the user with information about the privacy invasiveness level of the monitored apps. Our approach enables users to make informed privacy decisions, i.e. restrict permissions or report an app based on resource access events. We evaluate our approach by analysing the behaviour of selected apps and calculating their associated privacy score. Initial results demonstrate the applicability of our approach, which allows the comparison of apps by reporting to the user the detected events and the resulting privacy risk score.

Keywords: Smartphone apps · Privacy · Usability · Beacon alarming · Privacy risk score · Fuzzy logic

1 Introduction

Security and privacy have always been a serious concern in the field of information technology in diverse applications such as computer networks, wireless communications, etc. [1]. This is even more serious when it comes to smartphone apps since they provide context-sensitive services to the users. The impressive prosperity of the Android Operating System (OS) has become even more evident with its domination over the smartphone market (with a share of 87.6% in 2016 Q2 [2]). Its prevalence, and openness characteristics have facilitated the development of apps with access to a multiplicity of sensitive resources, resulting in highly personalised and context-sensitive services that benefit users' online interactions and consequently their daily lives. However, and not surprisingly, it has also become the main target of a number of security and privacy related attacks (e.g., 97% of malicious mobile malware [3] targets Android). Furthermore, the

J. Lopez et al. (Eds.): TrustBus 2017, LNCS 10442, pp. 3–18, 2017.
DOI: 10.1007/978-3-319-64483-7_1

huge proliferation of over-privileged apps also poses important privacy risks on the users, who are often unaware of such risks [4].

In this regard, Android's permission model has evolved from a binary one to a more advanced one, which is based on the principle of least privilege [5]; this model enables users to selectively grant/deny specific permissions to each of the installed apps even in run time. However, despite the recent advances, many users continue to ignore those warnings and blindly grant most permissions to apps as they request them [6]. Paradoxically, they continue to express discomfort once they realise that their data are being collected without their informed consent. As shown in [4], this behavior is mostly because of users not being fully aware of the associated privacy risks, partly because of the lack of appropriate information about the use of resources; i.e. which resources are being accessed by which apps and with which frequency; and secondly, a poor understanding of what the privacy consequences are. Thus, in this paper, we propose an app behaviour monitoring tool called *'Beacon Alarming'* system, which makes users aware of the extent to which an app is accessing sensitive resources. In particular, it shows which resources are accessed with what frequency, and whether the user was actually interacting with the app or not. Contrary to the state-of-the-art approaches based on static analysis of code, our system does not require the instrumentation of the Android OS. Secondly, we propose *'FAIR'* as a new method for privacy risk assessment in smartphone apps by using fuzzy logic while considering resource access. FAIR relies on the existence of the beacon alarming system. To the best of our knowledge, this is the first time that fuzzy logic is used as a decision-making method for privacy risk assessment in smartphone apps. We further elaborate the proposed approach with a user-friendly GUI by mapping the Android sensitive resources name to a more descriptive definition to make it more persuasive and easy to understand for the users. Additionally, once users are aware of the privacy issues, the GUI allows users to perform two different actions, either block permissions, or report an app. Finally, we empirically validate the functionality of our proposed approach through initial experiments that monitor real apps behaviour.

The rest of this paper is organized as follows. In Sect. 2 we review the existing work in the literature. Section 3 introduces the proposed architecture of the monitoring tool called beacon alarming. In Sect. 4 we introduce the proposed method for privacy risk assessment of smartphone apps called FAIR. Section 5 examines and evaluates the functionality of the proposed approach. Finally, we present the main conclusions and point out our future research direction in Sect. 6.

2 Related Work

Several efforts have been done to improve the user awareness of privacy and help them to make informed decisions [7–9]. These approaches are based on the advantages of including privacy facts in app descriptions in the app stores. Although, it was believed that this would enable users to make more rational decisions before downloading an app. These approaches could not efficiently operate. This is due to the fact that, during installation, users usually pay limited attention to permission screens and have poor understanding of what the permissions mention. In [10], the authors introduced a method to make smartphone apps more privacy-friendly through automated testing, detecting and analysing privacy violations. They suggested the use of an automated privacy-testing system to efficiently explore an app's functionality, logging relevant events at multiple levels of abstraction as the app executes, and using these logs to accurately characterise app behavior. Although this is an interesting method, there is no fine-grained formulation for their proposed privacy-testing system, as well as no practical implementation. There are also some approaches based on fine-grained control over permissions and majority voting recommendations [11–13]. These approaches enable users to turn on and off the access to sensitive data or functionality (e.g. SMS, camera, microphone, contacts, etc.) on an app-by-app basis to determine whether they feel comfortable granting it or not. In fact, in such solutions, a privacy control approach is provided to enable selectively granting, denying or confining access to specific permissions on a certain app. This of course is inline with our research and as well with the most recent Android's permission model. Nevertheless, such solutions must be complemented with additional mechanisms that will first enable users to better understand the behavior of apps and the privacy implications. Following this direction, the authors in [14], proposed to identify permission hungry apps by considering the set of permissions declared by apps in the Apps store, and making a comparison of the commonly used permission in order to make users aware of apps asking for rare or too many permissions. Authors in [15] explored the privacy behavior of apps based on the analysis of data flows which required the instrumentation of Android.

Our approach complements previous research in the sense that, the beacon alarming component analyses app privacy-related behaviour providing more scalability as it does not require to modify the Android OS, therefore, no re-distribution/installation of a customise OS is required. Our component is privacy-preserving as all information is processed locally (rule-based engine) and does not leave the user's device. Furthermore, our approach does not analyse the data flows, therefore, mechanisms, such as proxies monitoring users communications are not required. We, in turn, focus on providing users with only relevant privacy-related information of apps using more understandable indicators. We encourage users to report privacy aggressive practices of apps based on access to individual resources. The FAIR component advances the state of the art in the calculation of a privacy score using fuzzy logic as a decision-making approach and additionally improves the scalability.

3 Beacon Alarming: Log Monitoring Tool

In this section we introduce the methodology that we followed for the implementation of our proposed monitoring tool called *Beacon Alarming* [16]. This tool reads the logs generated by AppOps - a privacy manager tool which was introduced by Google in Android 4.3 and which is now inaccessible, unless the device is rooted [17]. We monitored the permission requests done by each selected app. Afterwards, we implemented a user awareness component. The access events were analysed and communicated to the user by our awareness module. The outcome of the monitoring tool (it is worth mentioning that our monitoring tool does not require any root access, modification to the Android OS, etc. See Sect. 3.1). We also use the results obtained from beacon alarming as the input for FAIR component which is described in detail in Sect. 4.

3.1 Data Collection

The goal of this process was to collect data about the accesses to the device resources that each of the selected apps had done, in particular those privacy related. To this end, we focused on the Android permissions classification. Generally, permissions are classified as 'normal' and 'dangerous' [5].

1. Normal: There are permissions that do not pose much risk to the user's privacy or the device's operation. Thus, the system *automatically grants* these permissions.
2. Dangerous: There are permissions that could potentially affect the user's privacy or the device's normal operation. Therefore, the system asks the user to *explicitly grant* these permissions.

We implemented a module that is able to monitor access events to both normal and dangerous permissions. Our tool was designed in such a way that we could select which app to be monitored. Thus, the data collection was done by our tool which read the logs generated by the Android's AppOps manager and collected those entries related to the selected apps and privacy related permissions. As an important note, we identified that the root access is only needed to access the AppOps management system, e.g. to tell the system to deny access to one of the operations that is controlled by AppOps. As a result, we found that in order to view the AppOps logs, there is no need to root the device, and they are accessible to any app with debugging privilege. In order to collect the logs, a timer event is sent to the `PermissionUsageLogger` service periodically. When it is received, the logger queries the AppOps service running on the device for a list of apps that have used any of the operations we are tracking. We then check through that list and for any selected app that has used an operation recently, we store the time at which that operation was used in a local data base. These entries are also used to get a usage count.

3.2 User Interface and Communication

In order to provide users with a better understanding of which resources were accessed with what frequency by different apps, we implemented a privacy awareness module (See Fig. 1). In this module users could select which apps

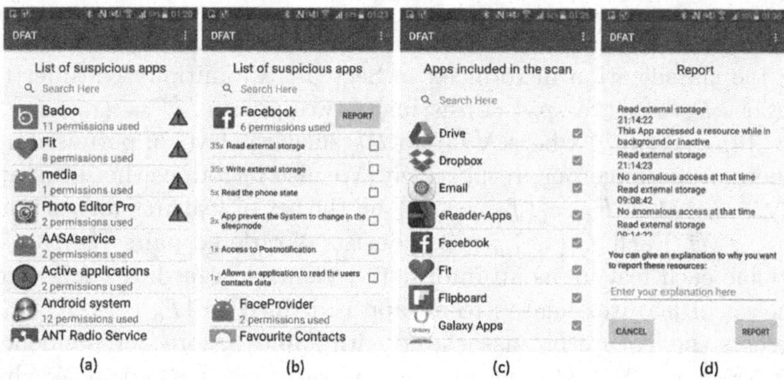

Fig. 1. The proposed beacon alarming (a) list of suspicious apps (b) details of accesses (c) selectively choosing apps to be monitored, and (d) reporting based on the app's behaviour.

```
#When the display is off and critical resource was used, but
    without the case of taking a phone call
if((criticalRecources.contains(resource)) && (screenState ==
    0) && !(closeToObject == 0) && !(resource.equals("
    RECORD_AUDIO"))){
     results.add("1");
     results.add("Screen was off and critical Resource was used
     ");
     return results;
}
```

Fig. 2. An example of rules for app privacy invasiveness detection.

to be monitored, and as a result the module displays a summary of apps and resources accessed including the corresponding timestamps. To increase the usability aspects, we mapped/translated the permissions from those defined by Android to a common language definition. Furthermore, we implement a rule-based mechanism that analysed the behaviour of the app in order to inform the user about unexpected behaviours. An example of these rules can be seen in Fig. 2 (due to space limitations, we refrained from representing of all the rules). Finally, to encourage users to take actions when potential privacy risks were detected, our module provided the interfaces to either restrict a permission or to report a resource and therefore, raise awareness of misconduct behaviors and access to sensitive data.

Restrict Permissions. We provided the interface for direct access to the permission manager system in Android, which allows users to revoke/grant permissions for any app.

Report Permissions. We developed a semi-automatic reporting tool, where users could select to report an app based on the resource that implied privacy risks. With this tool we aim to simplify the app reporting task and encourage users to report privacy related issues.

3.3 Formalisation of Resource Accesses

Based on the classification introduced in Sect. 3.1, we initially consider the set of permissions $\mathcal{P} = \{p_1, \ldots, p_n\}$ consisting of two subsets $\mathcal{NP} = \{np_1, \ldots, np_m\}$ and $\mathcal{DP} = \{dp_1, \ldots, dp_u\}$ where $\mathcal{NP}$ and $\mathcal{DP}$ show the level of permission which is either normal or dangerous, respectively. We also introduce the set of apps by $\mathcal{A} = \{a_1, \ldots, a_w\}$. Let $F_{a_i} = \{f_1, \ldots, f_e\}$ be the set of features for each app a_i, where $1 \leq i \leq w$. Each f_j $(1 \leq j \leq e)$ consists of ordered pairs $\{(p_j, np_k|dp_l)\}$. We determine each feature as an informative element regarding each app. As a result, the set of features related to all app is defined as $\{F_{a_1}, \ldots, F_{a_w}\}$, where F_{a_1} represents the feature F_{a_1} associated with app a_1. Moreover, we denote the used permission p_k $(1 \leq k \leq n)$ in $\mathcal{P}$ by app a_i $(1 \leq i \leq w)$ in $\mathcal{A}$ while the level of permission $np_g \in \mathcal{NP}$ $(1 \leq g \leq m)$ or $dp_f \in \mathcal{DP}$ $(1 \leq f \leq u)$ by $\mathcal{L}_{a_i,p_k} = (a_i, p_k)$. Additionally, we formulate the problem by x_{a_i,p_k} as follows:

$$x_{a_i,p_k} = \begin{cases} 1 & \text{if } \mathcal{L}_{a_i,p_k} = (a_i, p_k). \\ 0 & \text{otherwise,} \end{cases} \tag{1}$$

where if there permission p_k is used by app a_i $(\mathcal{L}_{a_i,p_k})$, then $x_{a_i,p_k} = 1$, otherwise $x_{a_i,p_k} = 0$.

4 FAIR: Fuzzy Alarming Index Rule

This section introduces FAIR, a novel approach which uses fuzzy logic in order to provide a privacy risks assessment of selected apps. The FAIR approach benefits from the beacon alarming system introduced in Sect. 3, as shown in Fig. 3 and detailed in Algorithm 1. We exploit fuzzy logic as an appropriate method that is widely adopted in a mixed variety of IT systems such as wireless networks, intrusion detection systems, etc. [18–20], especially, as it has been extensively employed as the core of decision-making systems [21]. The output of a fuzzy controller is obtained from the fuzzification of inputs using the associated membership functions (MFs). A crisp input is then converted into different members of the associated MFs (based on its value). MF maps the elements of a crisp input into numerical values in the interval [0, 1] and it represents the membership degrees of a variable to a given set. In the following, the expected inputs and output are described.

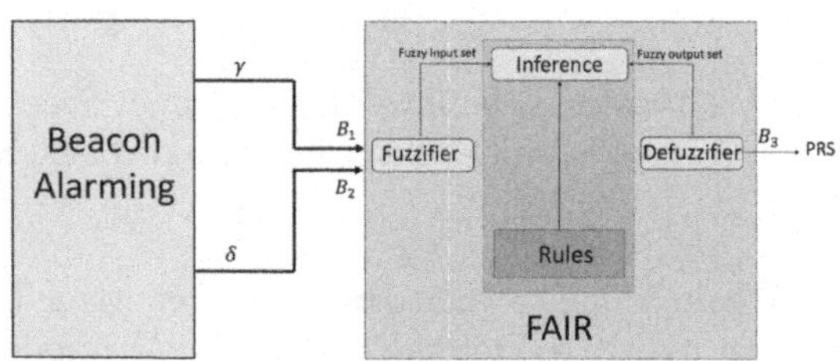

Fig. 3. A high level architecture of FAIR.

Algorithm 1. Pseudo-code of all steps in FAIR.

Procedure FAIR
START
  Define linguistic variables and terms
  Construct membership functions **AND** rule base
  START Fuzzification
    Calculate $\gamma = T^t_{a_i}|^t_{\mathcal{DP}} \setminus N^t_{a_i}$ **AND** $\delta = D^t_{a_i}|_{\mathcal{NP}} \setminus N^t_{a_i}$
    Convert crisp input data to fuzzy values using MFs
  START Inference
    Evaluate rules in the rule base
      Combine results of each rule
    START Defuzzification
    Calculate $B^* = \sum_{i=1}^{5} \text{COA}_i.\text{Area}_i \setminus \sum_{i=1}^{5} \text{Area}_i$
      Convert output data to non-fuzzy values
      END Defuzzification
    END Inference
 END Fuzzification
 END Procedure

4.1 Fuzzification

The fuzzification process converts crisp data (inputs) into MFs (fuzzy data).

Definition 1. Let γ indicate the first input of FAIR. γ is then defined as follows:

$$\gamma = \frac{T^t_{a_i}|_{\mathcal{DP}}}{N^t_{a_i}}, \tag{2}$$

where $T^t_{a_i}|_{\mathcal{DP}}$ represents the total number of accesses that app a_i has (in time t) to the dangerous privacy sensitive permissions ($\mathcal{DP}$s), e.g. `READ_CONTACTS`, etc., and $N^t_{a_i}$ shows the total number of accesses that app a_i has to the permissions (both $\mathcal{DP}$s and $\mathcal{NP}$s). It is evident that, the value of γ is always in the range [0, 1]. γ at its worst case is 1, which means that the app only accesses $\mathcal{DP}$s. The rationale behind this formulation is to investigate the impact of the access frequency to privacy sensitive $\mathcal{DP}$s.

Definition 2. Let δ indicate the second input of FAIR. δ is then defined as follows:

$$\delta = \frac{D^t_{a_i}|_{\mathcal{NP}}}{N^t_{a_i}}, \tag{3}$$

where $D^t_{a_i}|_{\mathcal{NP}}$ represents the total number of accesses that a given app a_i has to privacy sensitive $\mathcal{NP}$s (discussed in Sect. 3.1, such as `ACCESS_WIFI_STATE`. The main idea behind this mathematical model is to evaluate the importance of accesses to privacy sensitive $\mathcal{NP}$s. Because of the capability of fuzzy logic in supporting and implementing decision making systems, it enables us to figure out the impact of both γ and δ on the overall evaluation of privacy risk scores (PRSs) simultaneously.

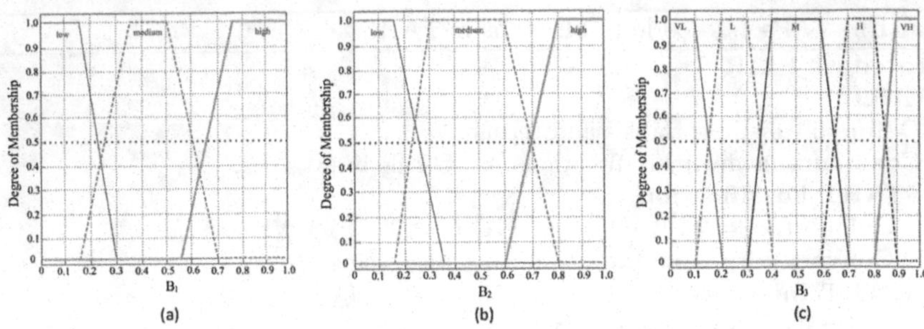

Fig. 4. Fuzzy membership functions (a) B_1 (γ), (b) B_2 (δ), and (c) B_3 (PRS).

Definition 3. Let A_1, A_2, and A_3 represent the crisp sets. Then, $\mu_{B_1} : A_1 \rightarrow [0,1]$, $\mu_{B_2} : A_2 \rightarrow [0,1]$ and $\mu_{B_3} : A_3 \rightarrow [0,1]$ are called the MFs of B_1, B_2 and B_3, which define the fuzzy sets B_1, B_2 and B_3 of A_1, A_2 and A_3. To perform fuzzification process, we should map crisp sets into fuzzy sets as follows (B_1 and B_2 indicate the inputs, and B_3 shows the output):

$$B_1 = \gamma \in \{\text{low}, \text{medium}, \text{high}\}, B_2 = \delta \in \{\text{low}, \text{medium}, \text{high}\}. \tag{4}$$

$$B_3 = \text{Privcy Risk Score} \in \{\text{VL}, \text{L}, \text{M}, \text{H.VH}\}. \tag{5}$$

Remark 1. The fuzzy variable γ has three fuzzy states including: low, medium and high, and its MFs are shown by Fig. 4(a).

Remark 2. The fuzzy variable δ has three fuzzy states including: low, medium and high, and its MFs are shown by Fig. 4(b).

Remark 3. The output represents the privacy risk score (PRS) and has five fuzzy states including: VL (Very Low), L (Low), M (Medium), H (High), and VH (Very High). Also, its MFs are shown by Fig. 4(c).

As it was previously mentioned, the fuzzy rules are directly obtained based on the number of states defined for the inputs, i.e. the more states we define for the inputs, the more fuzzy rules we need to initiate. Thus, to keep the implementation overhead of our fuzzy inference system (FIS) low [21], three states for each input and five states for the output have been defined with respect to the expert knowledge.

4.2 Fuzzy Controller Rules

The control rule is the core of every FIS. To obtain the fuzzy output, a combination of MFs with the control rules is required. In this paper, we use a standard Mamdani type fuzzy system [21] using a bipartite fuzzifier (since we have two inputs). We show the collection of R fuzzy IF-THEN rules as follows:

$$\forall\, R^i : \exists\, b_1 \text{ AND } b_2 \mid \text{IF } \; b_1 \text{ is } B_1^i,\; b_2 \text{ is } B_2^i,\; \text{THEN } b_3 \text{ is } B_3^i, \tag{6}$$

where B_1^i, B_2^i, and B_3^i are fuzzy states which were defined in the previous section, respectively. To obtain the fuzzy system output, we should define the fuzzy rules. In a Mamdani fuzzy system, the number of possible rules is defined as $N_{\text{inputs}} \times N_{\text{mf}}$, where N_{inputs} is the number of inputs, and N_{mf} is the number of MFs. As a result, we have nine fuzzy rules ($3^2 = 9$) which are shown in Table 1.

Table 1. FIS rules

No.	B_1	B_2	B_3
1	Low	Low	VL
2	Low	Medium	L
3	Low	High	H
4	Medium	Low	M
5	Medium	Medium	M
6	Medium	High	H
7	High	Low	VH
8	High	Medium	VH
9	High	High	VH

For the sake of simplicity, we used a trapezoidal function to model the fuzzy sets. So that, the calculations of MFs are simpler, as opposite to other functions such as Sigmoidal, Guassian, etc. The trapezoidal function T is defined as below:

$$T(b_1; \varepsilon, m_1, m_2, \zeta) = \begin{cases} \frac{b_1-\varepsilon}{m_1-\varepsilon}, & \text{if } b_1 \in [\varepsilon, m_1]. \\ 1, & \text{if } b_1 \in [m_1, m_2]. \\ \frac{\zeta-b_1}{\zeta-m_2}, & \text{if } b_1 \in [m_2, \zeta]. \\ 0, & \text{otherwise.} \end{cases} \tag{7}$$

In (7), ε and ζ, and m_1 and m_2 are the valleys and climaxes, respectively. This trapezoidal function maps b_1 to a value between $[0, 1]$ and the degree of membership called $\mu(b_1)$ is then generated. In fact, we should use (7) to obtain the membership degrees of B_1, B_2 and B_3 ($\mu_{B_1}(b_1), \mu_{B_2}(b_2)$, and $\mu_{B_3}(b_3)$). In other words, $\mu_{B_1}(b_1), \mu_{B_2}(b_2), \mu_{B_3}(b_3) \in [0, 1]$, and $B_1 = (b_1, \mu_{B_1}(b_1)|b_1 \in A_1)$, $B_2 = (b_2, \mu_{B_2}(b_2)|b_2 \in A_2)$, and $B_3 = (b_3, \mu_{B_3}(b_3)|b_3 \in A_3)$.

4.3 Defuzzification

Defuzzification is aimed to discover the numerical result of our fuzzy system and calculate the crisp output B^*. We use the center of areas (COA) method for defuzzification [21]. In this method, the fuzzy logic controller first calculates the area under the scaled MFs and within the range of the output variable. Then, it uses the following equation to calculate the geometric center of this area:

$$\text{COA} = \frac{\int \mu_z(z) z \text{d}z}{\int \mu_z(z) . \text{d}z}. \tag{8}$$

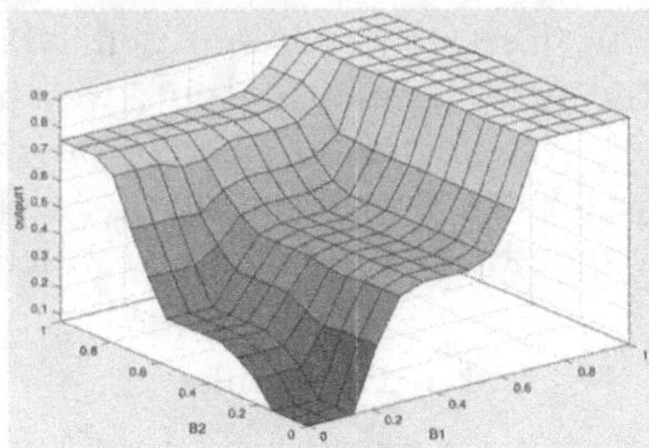

Fig. 5. The graphical structure of the proposed FIS for privacy risk assessment.

5 Analysis and Results

In this section, we evaluate the functionality of our proposed approach. In our experimental setup, we have chosen three sets (categories) of apps in which, each set comprises five apps (in total 15 apps). The rationale behind the selection of those apps is as follows: we selected those apps resulting from the first search result page when the user type a certain keyword. The keywords were selected from the most popular app categories. The selected apps were chosen from the top charts in Google Play store, i.e. apps with more than one million downloads. Figure 5 depicts a graphical representation of the proposed FIS that lets us examine the output surface of the FIS for any one or two inputs. In other words, this graphical interface simply shows us how γ (B_1) and δ (B_2) are mapped to the output (B_3). The colors change according to the output values.

5.1 Theoretical Analysis

In this subsection, we mathematically analyse the functionality of FAIR in estimating privacy risk scores (B^*). Figure 6 re-illustrates the MFs for the output

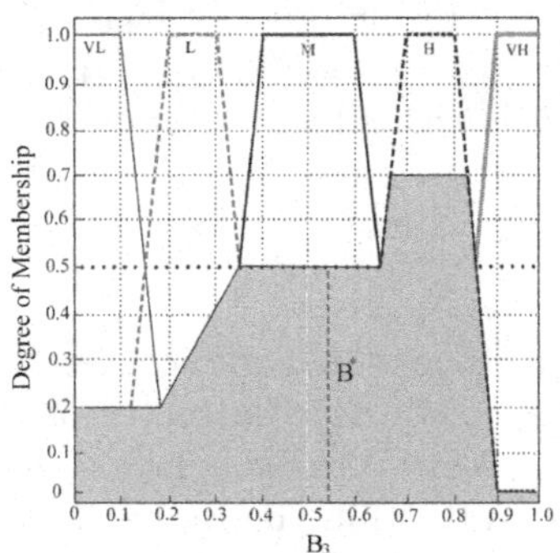

Fig. 6. Calculation of B^*.

which were previously shown by Fig. 4(c). Let N and D be the numerator and denominator of (8), respectively. Then, we have:

$$\begin{aligned} N = & \left[\int_{0}^{0.18} (0.2) z \mathrm{d}z + \int_{0.18}^{0.35} \left(\frac{z-0.18}{3} \right) z \mathrm{d}z + \int_{0.35}^{0.65} (0.5) z \mathrm{d}z \right. \\ & \left. + \int_{0.65}^{0.68} \left(\frac{z-0.65}{2} \right) z \mathrm{d}z + \int_{0.68}^{0.83} (0.7) z \mathrm{d}z + \int_{0.83}^{0.9} (0.9-z) z \mathrm{d}z \right]. \end{aligned} \tag{9}$$

$$\begin{aligned} D = & \left[\int_{0}^{0.18} (0.2) \mathrm{d}z + \int_{0.18}^{0.35} \left(\frac{z-0.18}{3} \right) \mathrm{d}z + \int_{0.35}^{0.65} (0.5) \mathrm{d}z \right. \\ & \left. + \int_{0.65}^{0.68} \left(\frac{z-0.65}{2} \right) \mathrm{d}z + \int_{0.68}^{0.83} (0.7) \mathrm{d}z + \int_{0.83}^{0.9} (0.9-z) \mathrm{d}z \right]. \end{aligned} \tag{10}$$

If we show the crisp output by B^*, then:

$$B^* = \frac{N}{D} = \frac{0.16153}{0.2984917} \simeq 0.54. \tag{11}$$

The value of B^* (0.54) belongs to membership function M (Medium), where γ (B_1) is whether low (when the number of accesses to normal permissions is negligible), medium (when the number of accesses to normal permissions is moderate, which is between [0.3, 0.6]), or high (when the number of accesses to normal permissions is remarkable, which is between [0.7, 1.0]), and δ (B_2) is whether high (when the number of accesses to dangerous permissions is significantly high), medium (when the number of access to dangerous permissions is average, which is between [0.3, 0.6]), or low (when the number of access to dangerous permissions is too less). This value means that the combination of dangerous accesses and normal accesses w.r.t the associated fuzzy rules, leads to the situation in which FAIR decides that the overall PRS is M (Medium).

5.2 Experimental Analysis

In the first phase of the experiment, we only granted the permissions which are necessary for these 15 apps to work properly. Accordingly, we opened them once and allowed to run in the background without user interaction. Afterwards, we collected and analysed the resources that all these 15 apps were accessing (i.e. permission requests). Figure 7 shows the results of our analysis (the numbers in each cell show the times that each app had accessed a given permission).

In the second phase of the experiment, we granted as many permissions as possible to the apps (both normal and dangerous). Afterwards, we monitored them to investigate which one is extensively accessing permissions, even when there is no apparent reason for accessing that permission. It is worth to mention that, during the second phase the only interaction was creating an account in the corresponding apps. The results of this phase is shown in Fig. 8.

Permissions	Health & Fitness					Social Networks					Dating & Friends				
	S Health	Google Fit	Lifesum	Pedometer	Calorie Counter	Facebook	Twitter	Instagram	LinkedIn	Pinterest	LOVOO	OkCupid	Tinder	Badoo	SayHi
READ_EXTERNAL_STORAGE	594	10	2	5	6	35	16	427	3	14	21	8	14	50	5
WRITE_EXTERNAL_STORAGE	594	10	2	5	6	35	16	427	3	14	21	8	14	50	5
READ_PHONE_STATE	–	–	–	–	–	5	–	–	–	–	–	–	4	35	–
ACCESS_WIFI_STATE	–	–	–	–	–	–	–	–	–	–	–	–	–	57	–
ACCESS_FINE_LOCATION	–	130	–	–	7	–	–	–	–	–	–	–	–	395	–
ACCESS_COARSE_LOCATION	–	–	–	–	–	–	–	–	–	–	–	–	–	5	2
READ_CONTACTS	–	–	–	–	–	1	–	–	–	–	–	–	–	–	–
WRITE_CONTACTS	–	–	–	–	–	–	–	–	–	–	–	–	–	–	–
RECORD_AUDIO	–	–	–	–	–	–	–	–	–	–	–	–	–	–	–
CAMERA	–	–	–	–	–	–	–	–	–	–	–	–	–	–	–
BODY_SENSORS	425	–	–	–	–	–	–	–	–	–	–	–	–	–	–

Fig. 7. Result of app monitoring for the first phase of the experiment.

Permissions	Health & Fitness					Social Networks					Dating & Friends				
	S Health	Google Fit	Lifesum	Pedometer	Calorie Counter	Facebook	Twitter	Instagram	LinkedIn	Pinterest	LOVOO	OkCupid	Tinder	Badoo	SayHi
READ_EXTERNAL_STORAGE	1067	18	44	1	43	1531	63	580	28	54	143	41	212	349	27
WRITE_EXTERNAL_STORAGE	1067	18	42	1	43	1375	49	583	27	51	118	41	196	343	29
READ_PHONE_STATE	–	–	–	–	–	4	–	–	–	–	–	–	4	176	–
ACCESS_WIFI_STATE	–	–	–	–	–	39	–	–	–	–	–	–	–	170	–
ACCESS_FINE_LOCATION	3	452	–	–	123	346	43	31	–	–	37	35	37	599	–
ACCESS_COARSE_LOCATION	–	–	–	–	16	381	–	–	–	–	4	3	–	47	29
READ_CONTACTS	–	–	–	–	2	5	14	–	6	6	–	–	–	1	–
WRITE_CONTACTS	–	–	–	–	–	–	–	–	1	–	–	–	–	–	–
RECORD_AUDIO	–	–	–	–	–	1	8	2	–	–	–	–	–	1	–
CAMERA	4	–	4	–	4	15	16	27	–	5	–	–	–	10	8
BODY_SENSORS	465	–	–	–	–	–	–	–	–	–	–	–	–	–	–

Fig. 8. Result of app monitoring for the second phase of the experiment.

5.3 Initial Results

Figure 9 shows the main results of the two phase experiment. As we can observe, all the PRSs associated with each app has been measured by FAIR based on the resources that they have accessed. It is important to note that we only focused on the resource accesses that are directly related to the users' privacy, e.g. an app which had accessed `WAKE_LOCK` permission was not considered while calculating PRS since this resource access is hardware-oriented.

Figure 10 shows all the changes that we observed during performing both phases of the experiment regarding each app. This is a sensible way to figure out the variations of PRSs for each installed app to imagine a general overview regarding the privacy invasive behaviours of the apps. It is evident that the invasiveness degree of Social Networks and Dating & Friends apps has tangibly increased since they have unreasonably accessed dangerous permissions even if the user does nothing with the smartphone, e.g. our findings showed that

	First Phase		Second Phase	
App	B_3	PRS	B_3	PRS
S Health	1	VH	1	VH
Google Fit	0.51	M	0.53	M
Lifesum	0	VL	0.93	VH
Pedometer	0	VL	0	VL
Calorie Counter	0.24	L	0.51	M
Facebook	0.07	VL	0.92	VH
Twitter	0	VL	0.81	H
Instagram	0	VL	0.94	VH
LinkedIn	0	VL	0.29	L
Pinterest	0	VL	0.71	H
LOVOO	0	VL	0.50	M
OkCupid	0	VL	0.62	M
Tinder	0.11	VL	0.91	VH
Badoo	0.92	VH	0.89	VH
SayHi	0.14	VL	0.85	VH

Fig. 9. Associated PRSs with each app calculated by FAIR.

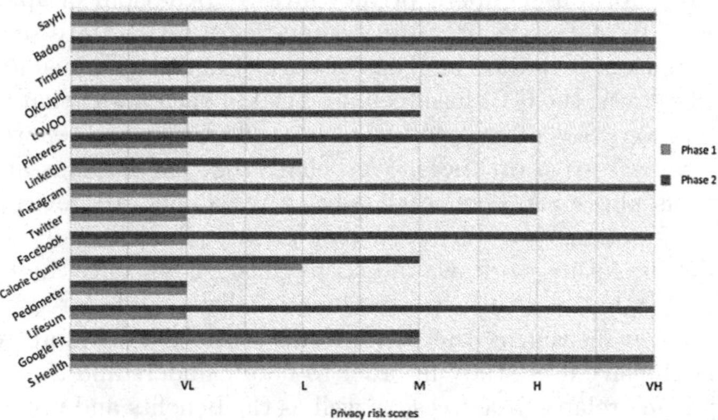

Fig. 10. A comparison between results obtained from both phases of the experiment.

some apps of these two categories had accessed to certain kinds of dangerous permissions (e.g. Camera) even if the smartphone was not being used.

5.4 Discussion

Our findings confirm a considerable difference between the PRSs in both phases of the experiment. This backs up the point that users must pay careful attention while they grant a dangerous permission to an app. This is why we implemented beacon alarming in such a way as to support users for granting/limiting permissions that they feel they might be offended. Moreover, in calculating PRSs, we neglected accesses to the external storage. The logic behind this is twofold. First, in Android there is no way to discriminate different accesses to storage, e.g. we cannot find whether the app accessed photo, video, etc. Second, all apps can read and write files placed on the external storage. It means, this is the basic permissions for every app. Moreover, we have categorised all the resource accesses, and we only focus on the resources that are directly related to the users' privacy.

The scope of this paper comprises Android OS. Regardless of the choice of the research area, the proposed approach for monitoring resources cannot be applied to other smartphone platforms (e.g. iOS). Furthermore, integrating additional methods of data collection (e.g. user perceptions) could have increased the scope and depth of analyses.

6 Conclusions and Future Work

In this paper, we proposed a new paradigm towards protecting privacy in smartphone ecosystems. FAIR provides a high flexible architecture by applying fuzzy logic to measure the privacy risk score of apps; thanks to the monitoring tool, FAIR is able to inform users about privacy invasive behaviour of apps installed on their devices. To realise the promising properties of FAIR, the essential mathematical formulation, including analysis of normal and dangerous accesses was introduced. Moreover, the GUI has been designed in such a way that we tried to encourage users to review their permissions more efficiently and report apps that showed privacy aggressive practices. We believe that the findings and insights discussed in this paper can encourage privacy researchers to devise more and better privacy functions to address current privacy challenges in smartphone ecosystems. In our future work, we intend to consider not only the behavior of each installed app, but also the expected functionality and declared permissions requirements when measuring the privacy risk score. Furthermore, we aim to carry out an extensive user study in order to better understand the importance of different privacy related resources, as well as the benefits and potential needs of FAIR from the user perspective.

Acknowledgments. The authors would like to thank: A. Paterno, D. Mattes, D. Wowniuk, M. Duchmann, M. Krapp, and R. Dieges for providing the app. This research work has received funding from the H2020 Marie Skłodowska-Curie EU project "Privacy&Us" under the grant agreement No. 675730.

References

1. Naghizadeh, A., Razeghi, B., Meamari, E., Hatamian, M., Atani, R.E.: C-trust: a trust management system to improve fairness on circular P2P networks. Peer-to-Peer Netw. Appl. **9**(6), 1128–1144 (2016)
2. Smartphone OS Market Share, 2016 Q2. https://www.idc.com/prodserv/smartphone-os-market-share.jsp. Accessed 6 Dec 2016

3. 97% of malicious mobile malware targets Android. http://www.scmagazineuk.com/updated-97-of-malicious-mobile-malware-targets-android/article/422783/. Accessed 6 Dec 2016
4. Bal, G., Rannenberg, K.: User control mechanisms for privacy protection shouldgo hand in hand with privacy-consequence information: the case of smartphone apps. In: Proceedings of W3C Workshop on Privacy and User-Centric Controls, pp. 1–5, Germany (2014)
5. Android Developers. https://developer.android.com/index.html. Accessed 6 April 2017
6. Felt, A.P., Ha, E., Egelman, S., Haney, A., Chin, E., Wagner, D.: Android permissions: user attention, comprehension, and behavior. In: Proceedings of the Symposium on Usable Privacy and Security (SOUPS), pp. 1–14, USA (2012)
7. Kelley, P.G., Cranor, L.F., Sadeh, N.: Privacy as part of the app decision-making process. In: Proceedings of the SIGCHI Conference on Human Factors in Computing Systems, pp. 3393–3402, France (2013)
8. Kelley, P.G., Consolvo, S., Cranor, L.F., Jung, J., Sadeh, N., Wetherall, D.: A conundrum of permissions: installing applications on an android smartphone. In: Proceedings of the 26th International Conference on Financial Cryptography and Data Security, pp. 68–79, Bonaire (2012)
9. Nauman, M., Khan, S., Zhang, X.: Apex: extending android permission model and enforcement with user-defined runtime constraints. In: Proceedings of the 5th ACM Symposium on Information, Computer and Communications Security, pp. 328–332, China (2010)
10. Gilbert, P., Chun, B.G., Cox, L., Jung, J.: Automating privacy testing of smartphone applications. Technical report CS-2011-02. Duke University (2011)
11. Beresford, A., Rice, A., Sohan, N.: MockDroid: trading privacy for applica-tion functionality on smartphones. In: Proceedings of the 12th Workshop on Mobile Computing Systems and Applications, pp. 49–54, USA (2011)
12. Zhou, Y., Zhang, X., Jiang, X., Freech, V.W.: Taming information-stealing smartphone applications (on Android). In: Proceedings of the 4th International Conference on Trust and Trustworthy Computing, pp. 93–107, USA (2011)
13. Pearce, P., Felt, A.P., Nunez, G., Wagner, D.: AdDroid: privilege separation for applications and advertisers in Android. In: Proceedings of the 7th ACM Symposium on Information, Computer and Communications Security, pp. 71–72, South Korea (2012)
14. Taylor, V.F., Martinovic, I.: SecuRank: starving permission-hungry apps using contextual permission analysis. In: Proceedings of the 6th Workshop on Security and Privacy in Smartphones and Mobile Devices, pp. 43–52, Austria (2016)
15. Felt, A.P., Chin, E., Hanna, S., Song, D., Wagner, D.: Android permissions demystied. In: Proceedings of the 18th ACM Conference on Computer and Communications Security, pp. 627–638, USA (2011)
16. Hatamian, M., Serna, J.: Informed decision-making supporter and privacy risk analyser in smartphone applications. In: Proceedings of the 35th IEEE International Conference on Consumer Electronics (ICCE), pp. 468–471, USA (2017)
17. Google removes vital privacy feature from Android, claiming its release was accidental. https://www.eff.org/deeplinks/2013/12/google-removes-vital-privacy-features-android-shortly-after-adding-them/. Accessed 17 July 2016
18. Razeghi, B., Hatamian, M., Naghizadeh, A., Sabeti, S., Hodtani, G.A.: A novel relay selection scheme for multi-user cooperation communications using fuzzy logic. In: Proceedings of the 12th IEEE International Conference on Networking, Sensing and Control (ICNSC), pp. 241–246, Taiwan (2015)

19. Berenjian, S., Shajari, M., Farshid, N., Hatamian, M.: Intelligent automated intrusion response system based on fuzzy decision making and risk assessment. In: Proceedings of the 8th IEEE International Conference on Intelligent Systems (IS), pp. 709–714, Bulgaria (2016)
20. Tavakkoli, P., Souran, D.M., Tavakkoli, S., Hatamian, M., Mehrabian, A., Balas, V.E.: Classification of the liver disorders data using multi-layer adaptive neuro-fuzzy inference system. In: Proceedings of the 6th International Conference on Computing, Communication and Networking Technologies (ICCCNT), pp. 1–4, USA (2015)
21. Chen, G., Pham, T.T.: Introduction to Fuzzy Sets, Fuzzy Logic, and Fuzzy Control Systems. CRC Press, Boca Raton (2001)

Mobile Personal Identity Provider Based on OpenID Connect

Luigi Lo Iacono[1], Nils Gruschka[2(✉)], and Peter Nehren[1]

[1] Cologne University of Applied Sciences, Betzdorfer Str. 2, 50679 Cologne, Germany
{luigi.lo_iacono,peter.nehreng}@th-koeln.de
[2] Kiel University of Applied Sciences, Grenzstr. 5, 24149 Kiel, Germany
nils.gruschka@fh-kiel.de

Abstract. In our digital society managing identities and according access credentials is as painful as needed. This is mainly due to the demand for a unique password for each service a user makes use of. Various approaches have been proposed for solving this issue amongst which Identity Provider (IDP) based systems gained most traction for Web services. An obvious disadvantage of these IDPs is, however, the level of trust a user requires to place into them. After all, an IDP stores a lot of sensitive information about its users and is able to impersonate each of them.

In the present paper we therefore propose an architecture that enables to operate a personal IDP (PIDP) on a mobile device owned by the user. To evaluate the properties of our introduced mobile PIDP (MoPIDP) we analyzed it by means of a prototype. Our MoPIDP architecture provides clear advantages in comparison to classical IDP approaches in terms of required trust and common threats like phishing and additionally regarding the usability for the end user.

1 Introduction

In the last decade, the Web has become an essential part of human society. Nearly every aspect of our daily life is infused by Web services (e.g. news reading, travel booking, shopping etc.) and in some areas the digital services have partly or completely eliminated the traditional services by now. In the recent years, this trend was further pushed with the ubiquitous usage of Internet service on mobile devices. With the increasing number of services used also the number of user accounts is rising, which leads to one of the main open issues of digital services: identity management [20].

Identity management (IDM) typically includes two aspects. The first is authentication, a basic security control required in any application that interacts with a user. The user claims his identity by presenting an identifier and then giving some proof for this identity. The proof can be realized in many different forms (e.g. fingerprint, cryptographic protocol), but the most widespread authentication factor by far is the password. Password authentication can be easily implemented by a service and does not require any special software or

J. Lopez et al. (Eds.): TrustBus 2017, LNCS 10442, pp. 19–31, 2017.
DOI: 10.1007/978-3-319-64483-7_2

hardware on the user side. However, passwords are prone to many attacks and misuses. Further, password authentication burdens the user the task of password management, leading very often to simple passwords or reusing the same password for different services. Another problem of authentication is the linkability of identities across distinct services. Most services require a valid email address as identifier, leading the user to use the same identifier with different services.

The second aspect of identity management is management of attributes. For performing its service, the service provider needs a number of attributes from the user (e.g. address, birthday, credit card number). Nowadays, a service asks the user during the registration to enter all attributes which the service might need eventually. This creates some privacy problems. First, most services request more attributes than necessary. Second, the user has to update attribute changes (e.g. after moving houses) at multiple places. Finally, the distributed storage increases the danger of unwanted attribute disclosure.

IDM systems aim to solve the issues presented before. The typical IDM architecture includes a third party, the so-called Identity Provider (IDP). The user authenticates directly only to the IDP. The IDP than creates authentication assertions which can be used to authenticate to services (also called *relying party* (RP) in this context), this requires obviously a trust relationship between the service and the IDP. Now the user only needs authentication credentials to the IDP, i.e., in the case of password authentication, only one (complex and unique) password. This enables also a single sign-on (SSO) functionality. Once the user has logged into the IDP he can access multiple services without entering her credentials again even when provided by distinct service providers.

Further, the IDP can also operate as attribute provider. In that case, services are not supposed to store user attributes locally, but request attributes on demand at the IDP and get the current values (if the user has granted access to the attribute). To increase privacy, the assertions given to the service might even masquerade confidential attributes. For example: if a service requires legal age of costumers, instead of sending the birth date the IDP can send an assertion "is older than 21 years". Finally, the IDP can create assertions for authorization delegation, e.g. authorizing service A to access the users pictures stored at service B.

Despite the mentioned benefits of IDM systems, some problems remain. First, the user must completely trust the IDP, as it can impersonate the user to the services. This can be solved by operating a personal identity provider. In this paper, we present a personal IDP, which can be self hosted on the user's mobile device. Second, most existing IDM systems are not very widespread and very often are discontinued after a while. In order to ease the distribution, our system is based on OAuth and OpenID Connect, two protocols which are already used by a number of large Internet companies. Further, a self hosted IDP usually induces the problem of discovering it. We overcame this by triggering the OpenID protocol flows from the IDP (instead of from the service). This solves finally also the problem of phishing attack, i.e. redirecting the user to a spoofed IDP site and phishing the user's IDP password.

The paper is organized as follows: the next section gives an overview of the related work on authentication and identity management. Section 3 presents our solution for a Mobile Personal Identity Provider. In Sect. 4 the security and privacy properties of our solution is discussed and compared to other solutions. Finally, Sect. 5 concludes the paper.

2 Related Work

2.1 Authentication and Identity Management

Since more than 20 years efforts are undertaken to replace the simple (static) password as authentication method to Internet and especially Web services. One possibility is using different passwords for every authentication action, named *one-time passwords (OTP)*, e.g. the well known S/Key from Leslie Lamport [15]. However, OTP requires either manual password lists for every service or special hardware tokens, which is unhandy or rather expensive. A further possibility are authentication methods based on cryptographic protocol, e.g. TLS client authentication [9]. However, this typically requires complex management of cryptographic credentials at the user side (e.g. transferring private keys from one computer to another one). Further, biometric attributes (e.g. fingerprint, face, voice) can be used for user recognition and authentication [17]. However, until a few years ago, this required special hardware attached to the computer.

With the wide spread of mobile phones the situation has changed. Mobile devices can act as credential storage, password generator and even as biometric recognition sensor. Thus, it comes as little surprise, that a number of authentication systems have emerged, which use a mobile phone as primary or secondary authentication factor. Examples are the FIDO UAF system [2], which combine strong local authentication at the smart phone (e.g. fingerprint recognition) with cryptographic authentication protocols, or Google Authenticator [13], a mobile application for creating OTPs with limited lifetime [22]. However, these systems only support the authentication aspect of identity management (IDM), lacking authorization, delegation and attribute management.

The most known IDM protocols are SAML, OpenID and OAuth. The Security Assertion Markup Language (SAML) [19] is a full-fledged IDM system, offering data formats and communication patterns for all IDM functionalities presented in the previous section. However, due to the high complexity, SAML was only disseminated in special areas (e.g. as Shibboleth [21] in higher education facilities or in SOA environments [25]).

OpenID [12] is a simpler identity provider (IDP) based authentication protocol specially for Web use cases. OpenID also did not find the broad adoption its creators have hoped for. Finally, OAuth [16] is a protocol especially for authorization delegation. OAuth was widely adopted for API authorization e.g. at Google [14], Facebook [10], Twitter [26] etc. As authorization requires prior authentication, some API provider "misused" OAuth for pseudo-authentication to avoid the additional implementation of OpenID, leading to proprietary OpenID extensions. To overcome this issue, OpenID Connect [23] was proposed, extending the OAuth protocol and workflow with OpenID authentication.

Some security and usability problems remain also in OpenID Connect which where known from OpenID [8]: (1) The user has to trust the IDP with his data. (2) When redirected to the IDP for authentication, the user has to check carefully, that it is really the IDP and not a phishing site. (3) The user has to remember and enter her OpenID URI at the service provider.

To overcome problem (1) the user can host her own IDP, also called a *Personal IDP (PIDP)*. Further, problem (2) can at least be mitigated, if the PIDP is running of the users mobile devices. In this case the user is not interacting with a (probably spoofed) Web site, but with a local application on her mobile phone. The idea of a personal mobile is not new, examples are can be found in [11] or [1]. However, these systems have been developed for the outdated OpenID 2.0 and additionally still lack from problem (3).

This paper introduces a mobile personal identity provider (MoPIDP) which eliminates the above mentioned problems. First of all, it is—to the best of our knowledge—the first PIDP based on the current OpenID Connect standard. Also, as a personal IDP, impersonation by the IDP is not a problem. Further, we invert the flow control in the beginning of the protocol: instead of redirecting the user from the RP to IDP, the MoPIDP gets the required information for the first protocol step via a barcode from the RP and the MoPIDP contacts the RP. This eliminates the phishing problem. Further, this increases the usability of the overall process, as the user does not need to remember and enter her IDP's URI.

2.2 OpenID Connect

To illustrate the differences to our MoPIDP architecture we present how OpenID Connect works. In this paper we will solely regard the *Authorization Code Flow*, as other OpenID flows have been proven to be insecure [24].

Before a service application can use OpenID authentication with a certain IDP, it is required to register the service at the IDP. The standard way for this is that developers register their application once at the IDP out of band. As part of this process, the application gets a `client_id` and a `client_secret` to make authenticated requests to the IDP.

Once this step is completed, OpenID Connect Authentication like shown in Fig. 1 is possible. Here, the user (using a Web browser) accesses a restricted resource at the service, which requires authentication. The user enters her OpenID URI and the service redirects the user to the appropriate IDP. The redirect contains an authentication request, which holds a number of parameters including the service's `client_id` and a redirect url for returning to the service. The user has to authenticate to the IDP. This can be done in different ways, e.g. by user name and password. If the user has authenticated before and still has an active session with the IDP, this step is omitted. Then the user is redirected to the service (using the redirect URL from the authentication request).

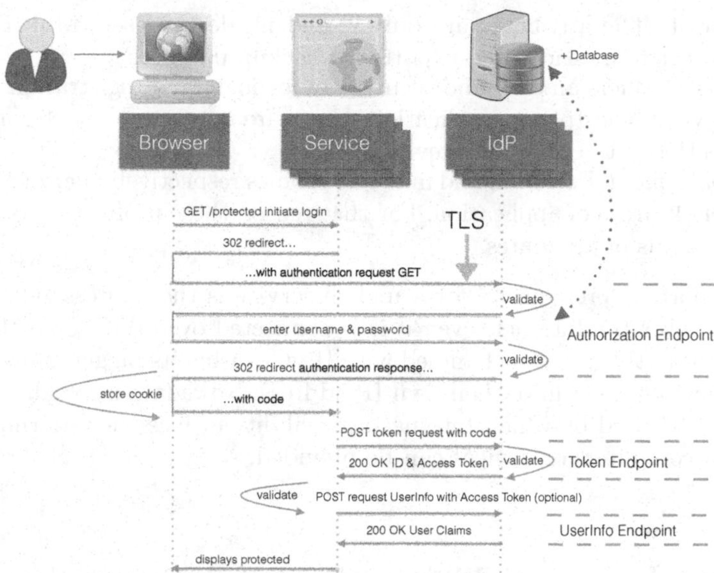

Fig. 1. OpenID connect authentication

The redirect to the service contains the authentication response, which again contains a `code` parameter, the authorization code.

This authorization code can be used by the service in a token request to the IDP. If the code is correct, the IDP returns an access token[1] and an ID token. The access token can be used to access further services, e.g. requesting detailed user info or (which is the standard OAuth use case; not shown in the figure) invoking an external service on behalf of the user. The ID token is the most relevant extension in OpenID connect compared to OAuth 2.0. It contains information on the authenticated user like a subject identifier and an expiration time stamp.

Now finally, the service returns the restricted resource to the user's Web client.

3 Mobile Personal Identity Provider

3.1 Requirements and Preconditions

From the aspects discussed in the previous section we derive the following requirements for our Mobile Personal Identity Provider (MoPIDP):

Self-control. Only users themselves have full control over the MoPIDP and no other third party is involved into the whole process. This control contains all kind of information stored securely inside the application and who gets

[1] Until here the protocol is identical to OAuth 2.0.

access to it. The attributes are only stored inside the users MoPIDP. The only exception are encrypted exports for backup purposes.

Convenience. It offers an easy and secure way for login and registration on Web services via a smartphone application. Users are not forced to enter any kind of credential to the computer keyboard.

Profile Management. Users can add multiple profiles respectively digital identities for different areas of application. For that reason these profiles are connected to other kinds of attributes.

One important prerequisite for a mobile service is the addressability of the smartphone over the Internet, even if it is connected over WiFi or mobile networks. In future this could be handled with IPv6 causing its bigger address room where all devices could have their own IP address. Nowadays a so called reverse proxy could be used by which Internet accessibility of local servers running on any kind of computers or devices can be provided.

3.2 Overview

The architecture of the MoPIDP is based on OpenID Connect. However, due to the requirements stated before the architecture has to be modified slightly. In OpenID Connect an IDP is always on-line, hosted at the same domain and accessible every time. The MoPIDP is always with the user and just on-line if the user wants to make use of it. Another difference is, that an normal MoPIDP is responsible for multiple users. In the new system every user owns his own personal MoPIDP.

As every user has her own IDP, a static out of band registration like in OpenID Connect is not reasonable. Instead, applications register dynamically with the user's MoPIDP on their first use. Such an use case is supported by OpenID Connect with its specification of dynamic client registration.

Like shown above, an OpenID Connect authentication process usually starts with the service redirecting to the IDP for entering the user's credentials. With their own IDP in hand users are now able to start the process right from the device. For starting the authentication process with a smartphone, the application on the phone needs the information where the user wants to login to. In our implementation an unique QR code on the service's website is used for that purpose. The QR code is easy to create for service providers and as well easy to scan and evaluate for smartphone applications. When the user scans it to use the service authenticated, she gets an overview on her smartphone on the service and the kind of information the service is requesting. After that the user has the possibility to decide whether she wants to login respectively register with the service or not. If she agrees a specific protocol flow starts between the service and the MoPIDP which results in an successful authenticated user.

3.3 Protocol

In this section the protocol flow between a service and a MoPIDP will be explained in detail. The user needs to have the application installed on his

response_type=code
&scope=openid%20name%20email%20picture
&state=af0ifjsldkj
&redirect_uri=https://client.example.com/authorize

Fig. 2. MoPIDP QR code example

smartphone and the service provider has to support authentication over the MoPIDP. The QR code displayed on the website contains the content of the query string which is used in OpenID Connect for the authentication request. Only the `client_id` is not included because it differs for every MoPIDP. An example QR code is displayed in Fig. 2.

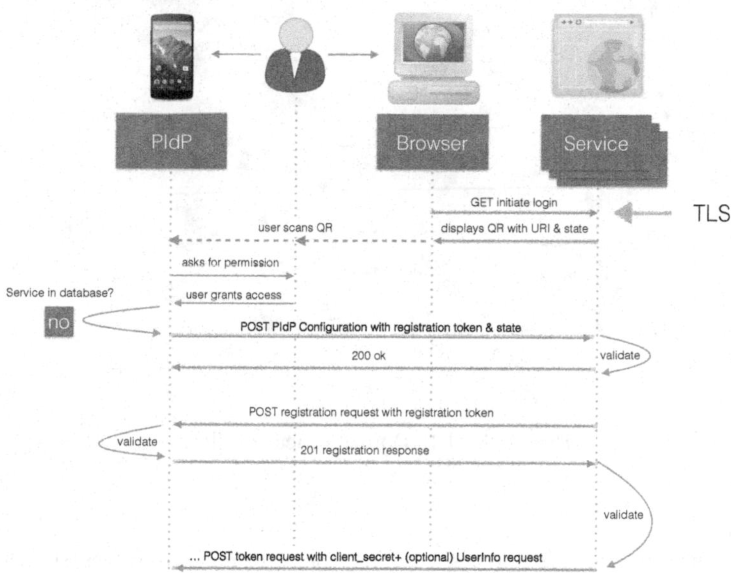

Fig. 3. MoPIDP registration flow

Registration. The user starts the MoPIDP application and selects one of her digital identities. After scanning the QR code the application checks if the service has been visited before with this selected identity. If not, the MoPIDP registration flow illustrated in Fig. 3 starts after a user consent. The MoPIDP sends its own configuration data to the registration endpoint of the service. It is the same configuration data which is placed at `/.well-known/openid-configuration` in

OpenID Connect. So the service gets informcation about endpoints, public key location, algorithms and much more. Also the `state` parameter from the QR code and an access token for future requests to the MoPIDP registration endpoint is included. The service has to check if there is an running session for this incoming `state` parameter. If it is valid the service stores the configuration data for this user temporally. With this information the service can make a default registration request to the MoPIDP registration endpoint. Also the answer from the MoPIDP is OpenID Connect standard and includes the parameters `client_id` and `client_secret`. This happens once for every service registering with an digital identity from an MoPIDP.

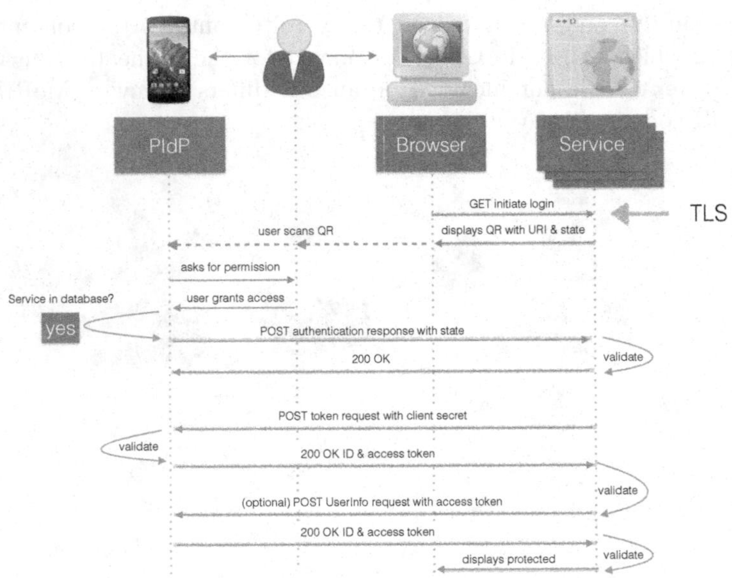

Fig. 4. MoPIDP authentication flow

Authentication. When the user scans the QR code and registration with the used digital identity was already performed, the MoPIDP authentication flow starts which is shown in Fig. 4. This happens without any user interaction because the application records all visited services. The MoPIDP sends an requests to the service which contains the same parameters as they where in the OpenID Connect authentication response. In addition to these parameters it includes the `client_id` so the service can assign the right user data out of its database.

Our system does not use redirects and also does not transfer any kind of sensible data over Web browsers. That is the reason why there is no temporary `code` required like in the OpenID Connect Authorization Code Flow. After a token request, tokens can be send back to the service directly. This token request contains `client_id` and `client_secret` for trust reasons. This client authentication method is called `client_secret_post` in OpenID Connect.

As soon as the service validated the tokens, the user is successfully authenticated. If additional user data is needed, there can be made another request with the just received access token. The structure of this UserInfo request is the same as in OpenID Connect. This mostly happens just once after initial registration because it could replace usual registration forms.

3.4 Implementation

To demonstrate the feasibility of this approach, a functional prototype of the system has been developed. One part of it is a dummy Web application in which potential users want to register via the MoPIDP protocol. On the start page of the service the unique QR code required for authentication is displayed. The QR code includes the above mentioned information like `scopes`, `state` and `redirect uri`. Further, the service includes a protected area with user-specific data.

The MoPIDP application shown in Fig. 5 has been implemented for the Android operation system and offers the possibility to register and log on to MoPIDP-instrumented Web applications with different user-profiles respectively digital identities. It includes the necessary scanning mechanism for reading the QR code, a simple web server for handling requests made to the MoPIDP application and cryptographic libraries for signing and encrypting responses. Firstly, the scanning of QR codes was implemented by an external application installed on the smartphone. However, as little information as possible should leave the MoPIDP application sandbox, which is why this functionality was integrated to the application afterwards.

Another problem which had to be addressed was the continuous connection between the web page opened in a browser and the web server. This connection is necessary for the automatic authentication or registration process, since the server must tell that the QR code has been scanned and the user is successfully authenticated. The problem could be solved by polling, which however leads to a permanent reloading of the page. A more efficient solution is to use WebSockets, a TCP-based protocol that enables bi-directional connections between a web page rendered inside a browser and a web server. The client establishes a TCP connection to the server, which remains open unlike in the HTTP protocol. From then on, both parties can exchange data without new HTTP requests whereby the server can tell the client that an authentication has taken place.

As is also the case with OpenID Connect, tokens are represented as JSON Web Tokens (JWT) [5]. JWT is an open standard for representing and sharing claims for e.g. authorization purposes. JSON Object Signing and Encryption (JOSE) [3] is used for signing or encrypting such JWTs to ensure integrity, confidentiality and authenticity of the contained data. Frameworks for implementing JWT and JOSE are available in many programming languages such as Java [7], C/C++ [6] and Ruby [4]. The Java library of the JWT and JOSE is used for the prototype, both for the service, as well as for the Android application.

In order to be able to sign and encrypt tokens required by the protocol, keys must be known by the parties. Therefore, the service hosts a so called JSON Web Key Set (JWKS) [18] on a specified `.well-known` location to synchronize information about supported algorithms and the service's public key. During the Registration Flow, the MoPIDP application temporary hosts a JWKS too, containing the public key of the chosen identity. Both public keys are used to build so called `Nested JWTs` for the MoPIDP Flows. For example the ID Token is such a Nested JWT since the PIDP signs the requested claims with the identity's private key and subsequently encrypts it with the services public key which was pulled from the `.well-known` JWKS source. So indeed the ID Token is a signed JSON nested inside an encrypted JSON.

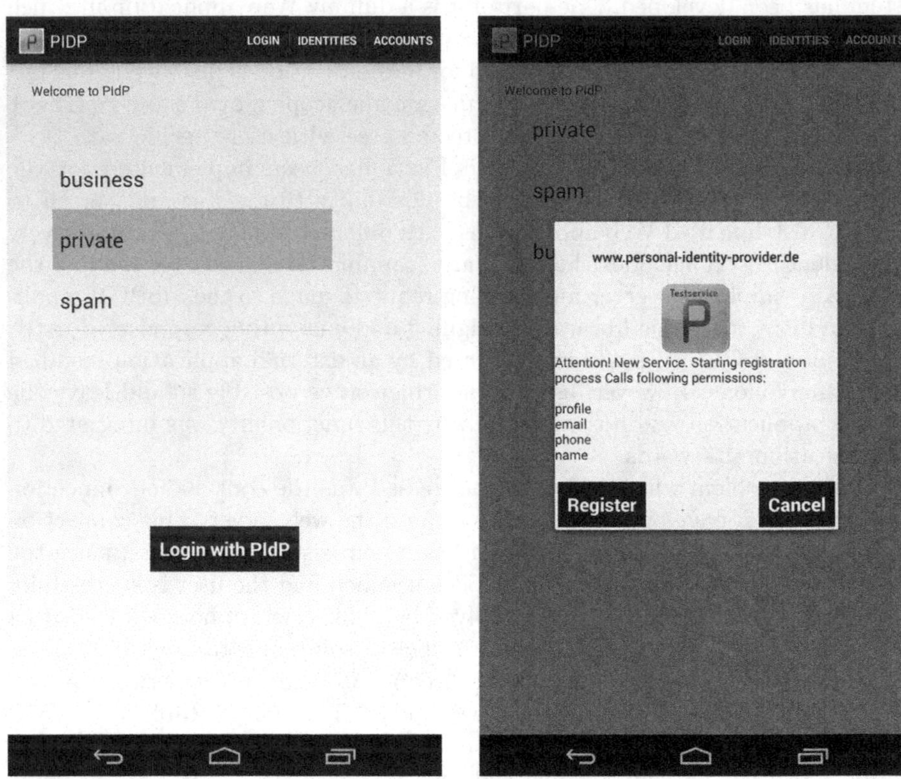

Fig. 5. MoPIdP android application

4 Security and Privacy Considerations

Our approach obviously inherits most security properties of OAuth/OpenID Connect. For example, authentication and confidentiality between the peers is performed by the underlying TLS protocol. This means, the transport security relies on the security of TLS and in extend on certificate and PKI security. However, the use of TLS also eases the deployment as no additional exchange of keys is required.

One desired property for IDP systems is the possibility of using different identifiers for different services and prohibiting the linkability of different accounts. Here, a personal IDP has disadvantages, as there is a one-to-one mapping between IDP and user. Thus, even when using different identifiers, these ids can be easily linked. However, as the different identifiers are rather rarely used, this disadvantage is probably not very relevant in practice.

In identity management systems, a high level of trust in the IDP is required, because it can completely impersonate the user. A personal IDP (fixed or mobile) has a huge advantage compared to a (traditional) external IDP, as the user itself is the operator of the IDP.

However, the most severe security threat for IDP based authentication is phishing. Usually, the user accesses the RP and is forwarded by the RP to the IDP. A rogue RP can easily redirect the user to a phishing IDP instead of the correct IDP. Therefore, the user must very carefully check the IDP before authenticating. However, most users neglect this level of caution. As soon as the phisher has gained the IDP authentication token (usually just a password), he can completely impersonate the user on all of the connected sites. With a personal IDP the phishing threat is slightly reduced, but still feasible. With our MoPIDP, however, phishing is not possible, as the redirection step is omitted. Instead the (personal) IDP communicates from the beginning directly to the RP.

Table 1. Comparison of security and privacy aspects

	IDP	PIDP	MoPIDP
Impersonation	−	+	+
Phishing	− −	−	+
Identity linkability	+	o	o
Transport security (TLS)	o	o	o

Table 1 summarizes the above described security and privacy properties. It compares a "standard" OpenID Connect deployment (IDP) with a personal IDP (PIDP) and with our mobile personal IDP (MoPIDP).

Finally, the security of MoPIDP obviously depends on the security of the mobile device. Access to the MoPIDP app and the database must be restricted, e.g. by a PIN or a fingerprint. This prohibits misuse by an adversary in case of lost or stolen device. In that case also the legitimate user looses the credentials stored in the MoPIDP database. This is a standard problem of authentication systems which are based on tokens stored on a mobile device. To solve this issue, either an additional mechanism for account recovery at the service provider must be added or regular backups of the MoPIDP database to a secure location must be created.

5 Conclusion

Authentication and identity management are still open issues in our world of online services. Despite their obvious disadvantages, password authentication and "manual" management of identities by the end user are still the predominant solutions.

In this paper, we presented an approach using a smart phone as personal Identity Provider. This solution exceeds usual identity management solutions with regards to security and usability. As discussed above, a personal IDP has small privacy disadvantages compared to standard IDP deployments (i.e. the possibility of identity linkability). However, our solution is still a major improvement compared to current authentication schemes using an email address (with most people: always the same address) as identifier.

References

1. Abe, T., Itoh, H., Takahashi, K.: Implementing identity provider on mobile phone. In: Proceedings of the 2007 ACM Workshop on Digital Identity Management, DIM 2007, pp. 46–52. ACM, New York (2007). http://doi.acm.org/10.1145/1314403.1314412
2. Alliance, F.: FIDO UAF Architectural Overview (2016). https://fidoalliance.org/specs/fido-uaf-v1.1-rd-20161005/fido-uaf-overview-v1.1-rd-20161005.html
3. Barnes, R., Mozilla: Use Cases and Requirements for JSON Object Signing and Encryption (JOSE) (2014). https://tools.ietf.org/html/rfc7165
4. Bennett, A.: Jose library for ruby. https://github.com/potatosalad/ruby-jose
5. Bradley, J., Sakimura, N., Jones, M.: JSON Web Token (JWT) (2015). https://tools.ietf.org/html/rfc7519
6. Cisco Systems: cjose - jose library for c/c++. https://github.com/cisco/cjose
7. Connect2id: JOSE + JWT library for Java. https://connect2id.com/products/nimbus-jose-jwt
8. Dhamija, R., Dusseault, L.: The seven flaws of identity management: usability and security challenges. IEEE Secur. Priv. **6**(2), 24–29 (2008)
9. Dierks, T.: The Transport Layer Security (TLS) Protocol Version 1.2 (2008). https://tools.ietf.org/html/rfc5246
10. Facebook: Access Tokens - Facebook Login - Documentation (2017). https://developers.facebook.com/docs/facebook-login/access-tokens/
11. Ferdous, M.S., Poet, R.: Portable personal identity provider in mobile phones. In: 2013 12th IEEE International Conference on Trust, Security and Privacy in Computing and Communications (TrustCom), pp. 736–745. IEEE (2013). http://ieeexplore.ieee.org/abstract/document/6680909/
12. Foundation, O.: OpenID Authentication 2.0 (2007). http://openid.net/specs/openid-authentication-2_0.html
13. Google: Google Authenticator (2016). https://github.com/google/google-authenticator
14. Google: Using OAuth 2.0 to Access Google APIs | Google Identity Platform (2016). https://developers.google.com/identity/protocols/OAuth2
15. Haller, N.: The S/KEY One-Time Password System (1995). https://tools.ietf.org/html/rfc1760

16. Hardt, D.: The OAuth 2.0 authorization framework (2012). https://tools.ietf.org/html/rfc6749.txt
17. Jain, A.K., Ross, A., Prabhakar, S.: An introduction to biometric recognition. IEEE Trans. Circuits Syst. Video Technol. **14**(1), 4–20 (2004)
18. Jones, R., Microsoft: JSON Web Key (JWK) (2015). https://tools.ietf.org/html/rfc7517
19. Lockhart, H., Campbell, B.: Security assertion markup language (SAML) V2.0 technical overview. OASIS Comm. Draft **2**, 94–106 (2008). https://www.oasis-open.org/committees/download.php/14360/sstc-saml-tech-overview-2.0-draft-08-diff.pdf
20. Lopez, G., Canovas, O., Gomez-Skarmeta, A.F., Girao, J.: A SWIFT take on identity management. Computer **42**(5), 58–65 (2009)
21. Morgan, R.L., Cantor, S., Carmody, S., Hoehn, W., Klingenstein, K.: Federated security: the shibboleth approach. Educ. Q. **27**(4), 12–17 (2004). http://eric.ed.gov/?id=EJ854029
22. Rydell, J., M'Raihi, D., Pei, M., Machani, S.: TOTP: Time-based One-time Password Algorithm (2011). https://tools.ietf.org/html/rfc6238
23. Sakimura, N., Bradley, J., Jones, M., de Medeiros, B., Mortimore, C.: Openid connect core 1.0. The OpenID Foundation p. S3 (2014). http://openid.net/specs/openid-connect-core-1_0-final.html
24. Sun, S.T., Beznosov, K.: The devil is in the (implementation) details: an empirical analysis of OAuth SSO systems. In: Proceedings of the 2012 ACM Conference on Computer and Communications Security, pp. 378–390. ACM (2012). http://dl.acm.org/citation.cfm?id=2382238
25. Thomas, I., Meinel, C.: An identity provider to manage reliable digital identities for SOA and the web. In: Proceedings of the 9th Symposium on Identity and Trust on the Internet, IDTRUST 2010, pp. 26–36. ACM, New York (2010). http://doi.acm.org/10.1145/1750389.1750393
26. Twitter: OAuth Twitter Developers (2017). https://dev.twitter.com/oauth

A Middleware Enforcing Location Privacy in Mobile Platform

Asma Patel(✉) and Esther Palomar

School of Computing and Digital Technology,
Birmingham City University, Birmingham, UK
{asma.patel,esther.palomar}@bcu.ac.uk
http://www.bcu.ac.uk/

Abstract. Emerging indoor positioning and WiFi infrastructure enable building apps with numerous Location-based Services (LBS) that represent critical threats to smartphone users' location privacy provoking continuous tracking, profiling and unauthorized identification. Currently, the app eco-system relies on permission-based access control, which is proven ineffective at controlling how third party apps and/or library developers use and share users' data. In this paper we present the design, deployment and evaluation of PL-Protector, a location privacy-enhancing middleware, which through a caching technique minimises the interaction and data collection from wireless access points, content distributors and location providers. PL-Protector also provides a new series of control settings and privacy rules over both, the information and control flows between sources and sinks, to prevent user information disclosure during LBS queries. We implement PL-Protector on Android 6, and conduct experiments with real apps from five different categories of location-based services such as instant messaging and navigation. Experiments demonstrate acceptable delay overheads (lower than 22 ms) within practical limits; hence, our middleware is practical, secure and efficient for location-demanding apps.

Keywords: Location privacy · Location-based services · Smartphones · Caching · Location-based applications · Android · Mobile platforms

1 Introduction

The explosive growth of Internet of Things, Smart Cities and Smart-Home application frameworks, e.g., Samsung SmartThing [23] and Google Weave/Android of Things [12], leverage third party developers to build apps that compute on user's sensitive data. For instance, emergent context-aware mobile apps bring about tremendous opportunities for a whole new class of Location-Based Services (LBS) [21]. Geo-marketing and geo-social networking, location-based games, and assisted eHealth represent a small subset of these opportunities that can certainly pose a serious threat to the users' privacy [17,24].

J. Lopez et al. (Eds.): TrustBus 2017, LNCS 10442, pp. 32–45, 2017.
DOI: 10.1007/978-3-319-64483-7_3

Currently, privacy settings of user location on smartphones[1] are modeled after existing permission controls that are based on a binary process[2]. In general, apps use permission-based access control for data sources and sinks, but they do not control flows between the authorised sources and sinks. Besides, users are forced to rely on third party service providers/sinks that in many cases continuously collect, use and share their location data, and in some cases even prompt the user to give away their position on page load [1,24]. Moreover, both academia and industry agree on the urgent need of adopting a Privacy-by-Design (PbD) approach for the development of more user-friendly and socially-accepted solutions to privacy preservation on their mobile products and services [6].

To encounter this challenge, our approach campaigns new design principle and privacy policy recommendation that forces the smartphone app ecosystem to make location data use patterns explicit, while preventing all other sensitive data flows. In this paper, we present the design, deployment and evaluation of the middleware called *Private Location Protector* (PL-Protector), which implements the LP-Caché model introduced in [20]. PL-Protector envisions beyond the simple grant/deny access method and provides the user with advanced mechanisms to decide the extent of disclosing location data with service providers. It also incorporates caching technique to determine users' geographical location in a privacy preserving manner by means of wireless access points, and with minimum cache storage requirements. The contributions of this work are as follows:

- To identify the required functionality goals that protect users from location-demanding apps through the analysis of location privacy specific challenges and security design issues within the existing mobile platforms.
- Design of the on-device location computation model that enables robust and efficient source to sink (unauthorised apps and third party app providers) flow control. We present implementation details of the PL-Protector middleware for mobile platforms. Our prototype runs on a Nexus 6p with Android that acts as platform's location privacy knob. PL-Protector only requires process isolation and IPC services from the underlying operative system (OS); thus, minimizing the requirements placed on the hardware/OS.
- Evaluation of PL-Protector in terms of Quality of Service (QoS), communication and computational overheads. We ported five real location-based apps to PL-Protector. Macro-benchmarks of these apps (latency) and our empirical settings indicate that PL-Protector performance overheads are acceptable, and it is practical, secure, and efficient middleware for location-demanding apps.

The rest of the paper is organized as follows. Section 2 outlines the background and related work. Section 3 overviews PL-Protector's privacy model.

[1] Throughout this paper, we use the terms Smartphone and Mobile interchangeably.

[2] Data protection directives and acts [8,15] across the globe state that personal data should not be disclosed or shared with third parties without consent from subject(s). Such a consent is typically obtained by mandatory acceptance of the conditions mentioned in the End User License Agreement (EULA), or through opt-out possibilities and other regulations [16].

Section 4 fully elaborates on the design decisions, architecture and implementation of the middleware. We evaluate PL-Protector's performance overheads in Sect. 5. Finally, Sect. 6 concludes and sets future plans.

2 Background

In this section we analyze the location privacy threats within the smartphone app ecosystem. This includes studying how the location calculation process works in smartphones and how LBS apps collect the user location data. We also justify our decision on implementing PL-Protector as middleware for Android platforms. Nonetheless, our results can be extrapolated to other permission-based mobile platforms such as iOS.

2.1 Location Sources

To understand location privacy specific challenges and security design issues, we start analysing the process of location calculation in smartphones when using LBS. Based on our prior study [20], we understand that the three major existing mobile platforms, namely *Android*, *Windows* and *iOS* that span the domains of smartphones, follow common patterns of location data retrieval. Basically, the standard architecture of using LBS on a mobile platform comprises of four main entities: (1) User Device i.e. installed apps, (2) App Provider, (3) Network Infrastructure, and (4) Location Provider. The user device collects the unique identifiers from the surrounding network access points along with GPS data, and sends these over to the location provider to get the exact device location. Calculation[3] of the user device's actual position is then performed at the location provider who sends it back to the user device in the shape of a location object containing geo-coordinates. At the device, this location object is shared amongst apps, and then, it is transmitted to app providers along with LBS query via the standard programming interface/API [3].

Simple eavesdropping on this location object is a major threat to this architecture even if users put in place the corresponding location sharing preferences[4], which generally are highly context sensitive and use dependent [26]. Moreover, existing OS's location access controls by system services respond inadequately to major privacy threats [1,10].

2.2 Operating System Controls and Apps' Location Access

In Android, apps can only access sensitive resources through the official APIs once the corresponding permissions declared at the manifest files are granted and

[3] i.e., WiFi Triangulation and Cell-tower Triangulation, GPS Mapping, etc.

[4] Types and levels of controls for user location privacy settings depend on the OS and apps. In some cases, apps do not allow users to control others' access to their location data.

authorised by the user. Since Android 6.0 (API level 23), users grant permissions to apps while the app is running, not when they install the app. However, in both cases, a positive user authorisation might result in other remote third parties and external sources benefiting from this information made available in ad-libraries for commercial purposes and/or untrusted code execution [7,9]. These existing studies and reports of data-stealing malware on smartphones clearly show the need of a better run-time permission method regulating the way apps and ad libraries are integrated into Android and other permission based platforms.

2.3 Middleware

Privacy Enhancing Techniques (PETs) and other cryptographic schemes [19,25] have been proposed to the location query formation and privacy preservation between the app/LBS providers in the different architectures and settings. Besides, several proposals apply caching scheme, along with PETs, to address location privacy challenges. Most of these techniques, however, rely on a series of theoretical assumptions such as the existence of a trusted infrastructure providing privacy protection, a group of similar app users being at the same time and same place, or a data collection servers complying with location privacy regulations, e.g., *MobiCaché* [4,18,27].

Caché [2] maintains an on-device cache to store entire location based queries contents and data-types to be re-used in future LBS queries that increases the cache storage requirements. Besides the storage overhead, Caché also requires the abilities of app developer to modify the way app access location data. PL-Protector only caches the network fingerprints and mapped geo-coordinates, which reduces the memory requirements significantly. Our middleware, PL-Protector, considers installed apps as black boxes; this way, it does not require app developer to modify the app code.

The service called *Koi* in [13] is cloud-based and demands numerous changes in the existing smartphone ecosystem. It requires developers to use a different API for the local access to the device location and implements a comparison mechanism and location criteria. Similar to ours, solution proposed in [11] does not rely neither on the adaptation of the apps code nor on the existence of theoretically trusted infrastructure. However, it does not allow the user to control wireless and location data that is shared with the location provider and/or the app provider. This issue is mainly due to considering the location provider as the only source of the user location when developing location-based apps. Moreover, it applies *indistinguishability* on the location data, which increases the computational overhead over time.

LP-Caché introduced in [20] and its implementation as the middleware PL-Protector are, to our knowledge, first working prototype leading the new design principles and policy recommendations to secure the computation and transmission of user location data within the existing mobile ecosystem. Main achievements lead to a minimisation of the wireless AP data collection by both, the wireless content distributors and location providers, and the provision of the control settings preventing user information disclosure from the generated LBS queries (e.g., points of interests (PoIs) and nearest neighbors).

3 Privacy Model

We characterize PL-Protector's privacy model considering the threat model and evaluation metrics for both app usage and privacy protection.

3.1 Threat Model

We consider two different threat scenarios to PL-Protector mainly caused by the level of access to user location in and out the device, as follows:

Android's Middleware Layer Threats. A series of attacks operates at Android's middleware layer [5]. PL-Protector mitigates the location privacy attacks coming from over-privileged and malicious 3rd party apps and libraries.

Privacy Threats. User tracking, identification and profiling (i.e., personal habits, movement patterns, etc.) are fundamental threats to location privacy [25]. Without PL-Protector, the continuous flow of LBS queries between user devices and service providers, that include device's exact geo-coordinates information, leverages malicious misuse of the user location data, especially in the presence of a malicious location provider, app provider and via advanced network sniffing practices.

PL-Protector computes the exact location within the user device, without the location provider's involvement, whilst trusting the device on the storage of sensitive data. However, the user has still the option of giving consent for app providers and/or location providers to access location data. Mobile network providers might, however, collect user location data via cellular clients. It is also excluded from our work the option of manually inserting the location data (e.g., street name and post code) within the LBS query.

3.2 Preliminaries

We now model the user mobility and app usage (specifically at private places) as a series of privacy evaluation metrics that will be used to validate PL-Protector's working assumptions.

Mobility Model. We formulate users' points of interests (PoIs), (e.g., Home or Work) as private places that users frequently visit. Hence, p_i represent ith private place identification, which is derived from a series of scanned beacons n_x and the representative location l_r for that private place, and P_l is a set of user's total private places, as shown in Eqs. 1 and 2.

$$p_i = [n_1], [n_2], \ldots, [n_x] \rightarrow [l_r] \tag{1}$$
$$P_l = [p_i], [p_j], \ldots, [p_n] \tag{2}$$

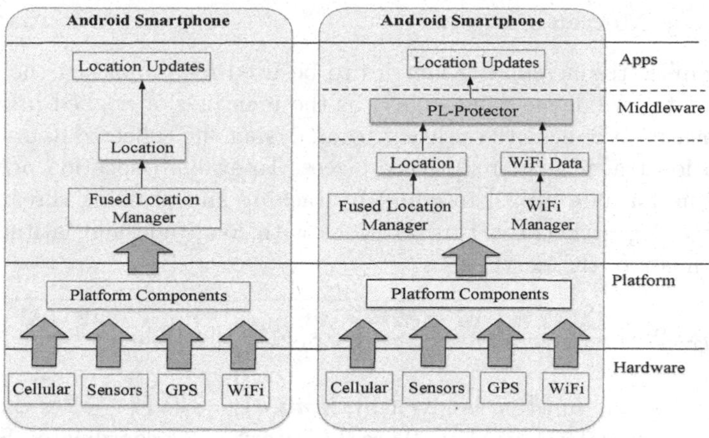

Fig. 1. Mechanism to access user's location in Android (left), and PL-Protector's deployment in Android (right).

At location p_i, the user can then visit a subset of private places $U_{p_i} \subseteq p_1, p_2, \cdots, p_j$, running the different LBS apps on his device. PL-Protector relies on the user input to define the set of private places that are distinct for every user mobility profile. Moreover, to set up network fingerprints at p_i, we measure the response rate as the ratio of detection count and the total number of scans for each beacon as follows:

$$R_{n_c,x} = \frac{\sum_{i=1}^{n_c} b_{x,i}}{n_c}, b_{x,i} = \begin{cases} 1 & \text{if beacon } x \text{ found in } i\text{th scan} \\ 0 & \text{otherwise} \end{cases} \quad (3)$$

where $R_{n_c,x}$ is the response rate of beacon x at p_i and n_c is the total scan count since the private place was entered. The detection count of each beacon is maintained to identify the frequently occurring beacons. Beacons with higher response rate are used to create the network fingerprint for that p_i. $R_{n_c,x}$ will be maintained in the PL-Protector database to update the response rate of every detected beacon during a specified time interval t spent at private place p_i.

App-Usage Model. We will apply privacy rules to the app sessions taking place at private places. We define "app session" as the duration of the app usage. In Android, according to the execution status, an app can run in three different states: foreground, background and perceptible. In general, apps get access to the user's location in foreground. When the user exits an app, this is cached and moved to background state for faster execution. Persistent status is informed by notifications. Background state allows prolonged location access; therefore, tracking threats are more harmful here.

3.3 Privacy Metrics

Table 1 compiles the hereinafter metrics to be used for evaluating the location privacy threats. We define value of Pl_s as the identifier of applied privacy setting and measure the achieved privacy by analysing the collected dataset of the actual location traces at user's private places. To evaluate location privacy, we use Haversine formula in [22] to quantify tracking and profiling threats as the distance Pl_d (Eq. 4) between two positions with longitude and latitude (ϕ, λ) and the radius r of the Earth:

$$Pl_d = 2r\sin^{-1}(\sqrt{\sin^2(\frac{\phi1-\phi2)}{2} + \cos(\phi1)\cos(\phi2)\sin^2(\frac{\lambda2-\lambda1}{2}))} \quad (4)$$

where the haversine function is given by $Hsin(\theta) = sin^2(\frac{\theta}{2})$, $\phi1$ & $\phi2$ are the original geo-coordinates, and $\lambda1$ & $\lambda2$ are the observed geo-coordinates. Secondly, the privacy rules (see more details in Sect. 4.1) pre-set by user will, later, be used to measure achieved privacy using the distance scale $\langle P_{high}, P_{medium}, P_{low}\rangle$.

Table 1. The evaluation metrics for the location privacy threats.

Metric	Description
Pl_s	Unique value to identify applied privacy settings
Pl_d	Distance between two points with longitude and latitude
P_{high}	Distance is >111.32 km
P_{medium}	Distance is >11.132 km
P_{low}	Distance is >1.1132 km

4 PL-Protector on Android

In this section we describe the architecture and implementation decisions for PL-Protector middleware on Android.

4.1 Architecture

PL-Protector enables users to control per-location access sessions.

App-Session Handler component is responsible of intercepting location access events so to lead the LBS apps' control flow to our middleware. It first pauses the requesting app and, retrieves the newly acquired location object to be sent to the *Private Location Manager* component for rule checking. Once the privacy policy rules are applied, the App-Session Handler will receive the anonymised/transformed location and resume the requesting app's control flow.

The **Private Location Manager** is the central component that receives both events (actions) and data from the different components as well as it maintains

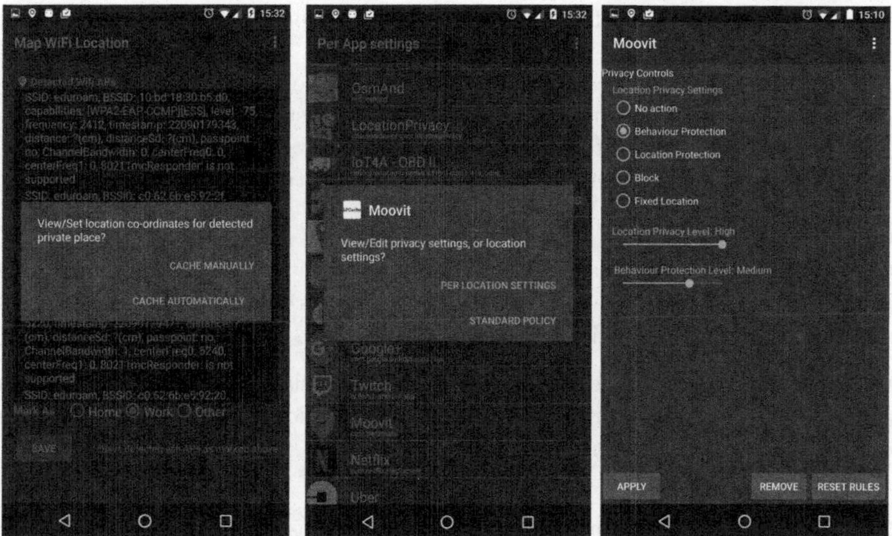

Fig. 2. User interface: (left) WiFi settings screen, and (middle and right) screens to manage per-app/location rule settings

the *Cache DB* database. User inputs via user interface (UI) are used to create privacy rules for specific private locations and network fingerprints. Moreover, the Private Location Manager detects unique identifiers of the surrounding wireless APs and maintains a binary flag to detect private places. When the flag is ON, the location data is retrieved from the *Cache DB* and sent to the *Policy Controller*. In case of an unmatched query on the cached locations, and the user do not want to input geo-coordinates manually (via maps provided in UI) the location data is received by location providers from the *Location Receiver*.

The **Policy Controller** gathers the location objects from the *Private Location Manager* as to apply the corresponding user permissions on the location coordinates, altering them if needed, and transferring the processed location to the *App Session Handler* module. The two privacy policies that the User can set per-app/place basis are the *Standard Policy* and *Per-location Policy* (see Fig. 2), as follows:

1. The Standard Policy consists of three location settings as follow:
   (a) The *Behaviour Protection* setting implements the geo-coordinate obfuscation equation defined in [20] to generate transformed/obfuscated geo-coordinates (l', l'_g) for every app session. The behaviour protection level is defined by a scale (Low, Medium, and High) that determines randomness of the obfuscation equation's parameters $\langle s, \theta, (l, l_g)\rangle$, where s is the scaling factor, θ is the random rotation angle, and (l, l_g) are the original coordinates.
   (b) The *Location Protection* setting implements the geo-coordinate truncation equation defined in [20] and follows a location granularity scale like

(Low, Medium, and High) to adjust the location precision level for every app session.

(c) The *Block/Fixed Location* setting picks high behaviour and location protection level by default and determines a constant value of altered geo-coordinates for every app session.

2. The Per-location policy allows the User to apply standard policy settings for each pre-marked private places that are displayed on the map.

Once processed geo-coordinates (l' l'_g) that comply with pre-set privacy rule are generated, we measure achieved level of privacy on per-session basis using values of both Pl_d and Pl_s (as defined in Sect. 3.3).

The **Location Receiver** component receives a location object, which includes the user device's geo-coordinates from location providers, and sends it over to the *Private Location Manager* for further processing.

4.2 Middleware Implementation

PL-Protector orchestrates a mobile platform based location protection service on Android to modify the location resource handling process. The middleware communication requires process isolation and IPC services; hence, minimising the requirements placed on hardware or OS modifications.

PL-Protector Life Cycle. In Android, there are two methods to access user's location: (1) Location Manager Service (Old), and (2) Fused Location Manager Service (New) that are part of Google Play Services. However, both methods require the app to request a callback function to get regular updates by registering a location listener. The app receives a new location object when a new location is available, the callback function is invoked (Fig. 1 (left)). Modifying these two Google services is complicated, but we make PL-Protector communicate with the location requesting apps by intercepting the location object before it reaches requesting apps (Fig. 1-(right)). One of the main task is to add a system

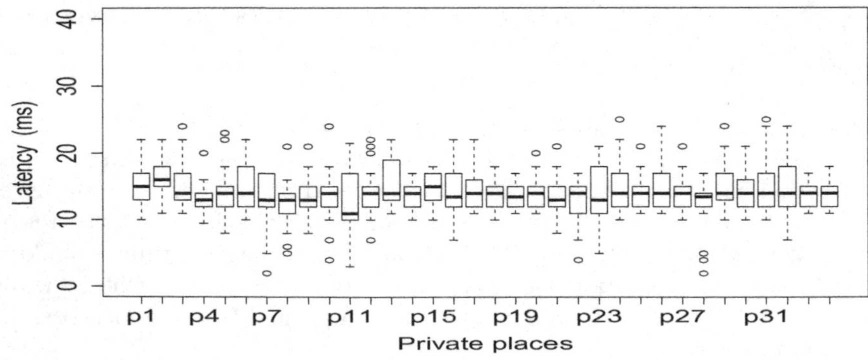

Fig. 3. PL-Protector's overall computation latency caused at 34 distinct private places.

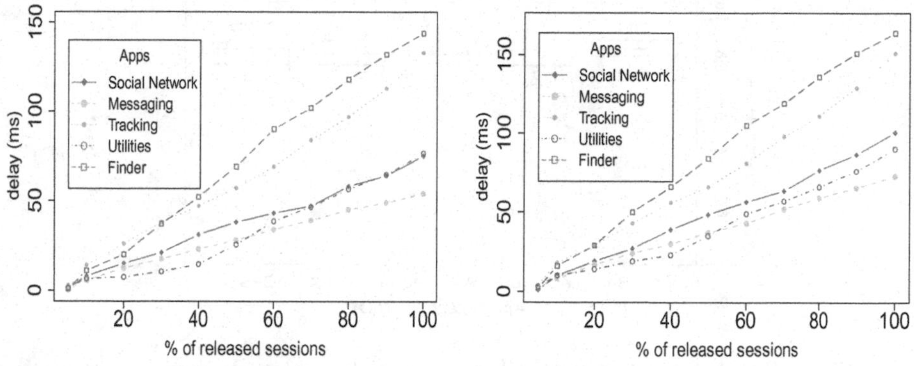

Fig. 4. Apps communication overhead without (left) and with (right) PL-Protector.

service, where the class belongs to the location APIs. Thus, the PL-Protector's service is placed in the `android.location package`, which detects private locations via WiFi APs and can also be used by other components when calling context. In Android, a context allows an app to interact with the OS resources. Similar to [11], we add a static context field to the location class, which will be populated when the app is invoked; this enables PL-Protector to know which app is currently requesting the location object, and also communicate with the OS. Besides, `Fused Location Manager` combines sensors, GPS, Wi-Fi, and cellular data into a single API for location-based applications [14], hence separating data from `GPS_PROVIDER` and `NETWORK_PROVIDER` is no longer straight forward. PL-Protector addresses this issue by preventing app's location request to reach the `Fused Location Manager` that collects and sends the network session data to the location provider. Instead, the requested location is retrieved from the on-device cache, and then, it is sent to the requesting app (with privacy rules applied).

Bootstrapping. When PL-Protector first boots and before turning 'ON' the location sharing setting, the user will have to perform an initial setup. This will allow WiFi AP scanning, input geo-coordinates and set privacy choices using *User Interfaces* (UI) (Fig. 2 - left). PL-Protector's UI incorporates a map to get the corresponding geo-coordinates so achieving an effective privacy without affecting the location accuracy. At the same time, this prevents non-authorised sharing of device's exact location and network session data. The UI (Fig. 2 - middle and right) enables users to set and manage their private locations and apps distinctly.

5 Evaluation

We evaluate PL-Protector in terms of QoS, communication and computational overheads.

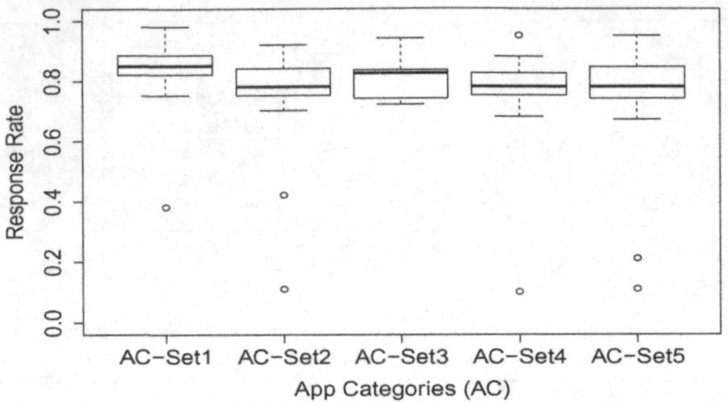

Fig. 5. Total response rate by PL-Protector when interacting with apps

5.1 Experimental Setup

We deployed PL-Protector middleware on a Nexus 6 with Android 6.0 (API 23) and ported apps of five different LBS queries categories namely (1) Social Networking (e.g., Facebook), (2) Instant Messaging/chatting (e.g., Whatsapp), (3) Tracking (e.g., Fitness), (4) Utilities (e.g., Weather, Alarm, etc.) and (5) Finder (PoI Finder/Geo-search). Based on app operations, we assume that both types (1) and (3) require continuous access to location data; whereas, types (2), (4) and (5) involve sporadic access. We have collected empirical data from a number of sessions running at different time intervals over a period from 1 to 6 months. We then created two datasets at 34 selected private places. In the first dataset, we include the ported apps' session data running over the conventional Android environment without interacting with PL-Protector. The second dataset consists of the same apps running in the presence of PL-Protector.

5.2 Impact on the Quality of Service

Crucial for its functionality, we measure latency as the time PL-Protector takes to interact with the app and perform an entire computational cycle, i.e., to compute the location on-device and to apply the privacy rules. On average, PL-Protector presents a latency lower than 22 ms upon all the location-access calls executing PL-Protector's privacy controls at runtime (as shown in Fig. 3). The reason for increased latency is due to PL-Protector's load time, and cross-process/IPC service transfers of location updates. However, this latency is smaller than 100 ms and, thus, small enough to not cause user-noticeable delays while utilising apps on the device. Furthermore, Fig. 4 show the communication overhead for the 5 app categories and compares both execution environments. In per-location access sessions, we found <19 ms delays when continuous location updates, and <8 ms delay for sporadic location updates. Thus, PL-Protector is suitable to run all the existing apps of aforementioned five LBS categories since their core functionality already accepts delays in this range.

5.3 Cache Accuracy

To analyse the accuracy of the on-device cache method at runtime, we measure cache hits and misses that includes three possible outcomes: 1. *The location is cached and up-to-date*, 2. *The location is cached but is out-of-date*, and 3. *The location is not cached*. The total observed response rates range between 70% to 90% accuracy (Fig. 5) that demonstrates the suitability of PL-Protector's on-device location computation process with types of apps requiring both sporadic and continuous location-updates. This indicates PL-Protectors's on-device cache update frequency is within practical limits, and it provides accurate location data at runtime.

6 Conclusion

In this paper, we have presented the design, deployment and evaluation of PL-Protector, a location privacy-enhancing middleware, which minimises the interaction and data collection from wireless access points, content distributors and location providers. The middleware also provides a new series of control settings to prevent user information disclosure during formation of LBS queries. PL-Protector enforces these privacy rules over both the information and control flows occurred between sources and sinks. We have fully implemented PL-Protector on Android 6 and validated with real apps from five different LBS queries categories. Experiments demonstrated acceptable delay overheads and within efficient and practical limits. Immediate future work pursues analysis on the threat model to read its compliance with the three privacy settings and measure achieved level of privacy. Additionally, we plan deployment improvements related to the on-device computation and cache storage, i.e., by incorporating PL-Protector as a part of Android custom Read-Only-Memory. We are also planning to conduct a usability study that will allow us to enhance PL-Protector's privacy and usability rates.

References

1. Almuhimedi, H., Schaub, F., Sadeh, N., Adjerid, I., Acquisti, A., Gluck, J., Cranor, L.F., Agarwal, Y.: Your Location has been Shared 5,398 Times! A Field Study on Mobile App Privacy Nudging. In: Proceedings of the 33rd Annual ACM Conference on Human Factors in Computing Systems, pp. 787–796. ACM (2015)
2. Amini, S., Lindqvist, J., Hong, J., Lin, J., Toch, E., Sadeh, N.: Caché: caching location-enhanced content to improve user privacy. In: Proceedings of ACM International Conference on Mobile Systems, Applications, and Services, pp. 197–210. ACM (2011)
3. Android Developer Reference: March 2016. http://developer.android.com/reference/
4. Ardagna, C.A., Livraga, G., Samarati, P.: Protecting privacy of user information in continuous location-based services. In: 2012 IEEE 15th International Conference on Computational Science and Engineering (CSE), pp. 162–169. IEEE (2012)

5. Bugiel, S., Heuser, S., Sadeghi, A.R.: Flexible and fine-grained mandatory access control on android for diverse security and privacy policies. In: Usenix Security, pp. 131–146 (2013)
6. Cranor, L.F., Sadeh, N.: A shortage of privacy engineers. IEEE Secur. Priv. **2**, 77–79 (2013)
7. Enck, W., Gilbert, P., Han, S., Tendulkar, V., Chun, B.G.: Others: TaintDroid: an information-flow tracking system for realtime privacy monitoring on smartphones. TOCS **32**(2), 5 (2014)
8. European Commission: Protection of personal data (2016). http://ec.europa.eu/justice/data-protection/
9. Faruki, P., Bharmal, A., Laxmi, V., Ganmoor, V., Gaur, M.S., Conti, M., Rajarajan, M.: Android security: a survey of issues, malware penetration, and defenses. IEEE Commun. Surv. Tutor. **17**(2), 998–1022 (2015)
10. Fawaz, K., Feng, H., Shin, K.G.: Anatomization and protection of mobile apps' location privacy threats. In: 24th USENIX Security Symposium (USENIX Security 15), pp. 753–768. USENIX Association (2015)
11. Fawaz, K., Shin, K.G.: Location privacy protection for smartphone users. In: Proceedings of ACM Conference on Computer and Communications Security, pp. 239–250. ACM (2014)
12. Google Weave: Weave. https://developers.google.com/weave/
13. Guha, S., Jain, M., Padmanabhan, V.N.: Koi: a location-privacy platform for smartphone apps. In: Proceedings of the 9th USENIX conference on Networked Systems Design and Implementation, pp. 14–14. USENIX Association (2012)
14. Hellman, E.: Android Programming: Pushing the Limits. Wiley, Hoboken (2013)
15. IETF: Geographic Location Privacy, March 2016. http://datatracker.ietf.org/wg/geopriv/charter/
16. Michael, K., Clarke, R.: Location and tracking of mobile devices: Überveillance stalks the streets. Comput. Law Secur. Rev. **29**(3), 216–228 (2013)
17. Muslukhov, I., Boshmaf, Y., Kuo, C., Lester, J., Beznosov, K.: Understanding users' requirements for data protection in smartphones. In: IEEE International Conference on Secure Data Management on Smartphones and Mobiles, pp. 228–235. IEEE (2012)
18. Niu, B., Li, Q., Zhu, X., Cao, G., Li, H.: Enhancing privacy through caching in location-based services. In: Proceedings of IEEE INFOCOM (2015)
19. Patel, A., Palomar, E.: Privacy preservation in location-based mobile applications: research directions. In: Proceeings of IEEE International Conference on Availability, Reliability and Security (ARES), pp. 227–233. IEEE (2014)
20. Patel, A., Palomar, E.: LP-Caché: Privacy-aware cache model for location-based apps. In: Proceedings of the 13th International Conference on Security and Cryptography (SECRYPT), pp. 183–194 (2016)
21. Pontes, T., Vasconcelos, M., Almeida, J., Kumaraguru, P., Almeida, V.: We know where you live: privacy characterization of foursquare behavior. In: Proceedings of ACM Conference on Ubiquitous Computing, pp. 898–905. ACM (2012)
22. Robusto, C.C.: The cosine-haversine formula. Am. Math. Mon. **64**(1), 38–40 (1957)
23. Samsung: smartthings. http://www.samsung.com/uk/smartthings/
24. Shklovski, I., Mainwaring, S.D., Skúladóttir, H.H., Borgthorsson, H.: Leakiness and creepiness in app space: perceptions of privacy and mobile app use. In: Proceedings of ACM Conference on Human factors in computing systems, pp. 2347–2356. ACM (2014)

25. Wernke, M., Skvortsov, P., Dürr, F., Rothermel, K.: A classification of location privacy attacks and approaches. Pers. Ubiquit. Comput. **18**(1), 163–175 (2014)
26. Xie, J., Knijnenburg, B.P., Jin, H.: Location sharing privacy preference: analysis and personalized recommendation. In: Proceedings of the 19th International Conference on Intelligent User Interfaces, pp. 189–198. ACM (2014)
27. Zhu, X., Chi, H., Niu, B., Zhang, W., Li, Z., Li, H.: Mobicache: when k-anonymity meets cache. In: GLOBECOM, pp. 820–825. IEEE (2013)

Transparency and Privacy Enhancing Technologies

Pattern-Based Representation of Privacy Enhancing Technologies as Early Aspects

Rene Meis(✉) and Maritta Heisel

paluno - The Ruhr Institute for Software Technology, University of Duisburg-Essen, Duisburg, Germany
{rene.meis,maritta.heisel}@paluno.uni-due.de

Abstract. Several regulations and standards emphasize that privacy shall already be considered from the very beginning in software development. A crucial point during the development of a privacy-friendly software is the selection and integration of measures that implement specific privacy requirements or mitigate threats to these. These measures are called privacy enhancing technologies (PETs). PETs have a cross-cutting nature. That is, a PET needs often to be integrated into several base functionalities of the software-to-be. For example, anonymization techniques need to be integrated into functionalities that shall reveal originally identifiable information in an anonymized form to others. One possibility to handle cross-cutting concerns already on the requirements level is aspect-oriented requirements engineering. In this paper, we show how PETs can be represented as early aspects and how these can be integrated into a given requirements model in problem frames notation. Furthermore, we show how PETs can be represented as patterns to help requirements engineers to identify and select appropriate PETs that address the privacy requirements they have to satisfy. We use the PET Privacy-ABCs (Attribute-Based Credentials) to illustrate our approach.

1 Introduction

Regulations, such as the EU General Data Protection Regulation [1], and industrial standards, such as ISO 29100 [2], emphasize that privacy shall already be considered from the very beginning in software development. To realize the privacy requirements of the software-to-be, privacy enhancing technologies (PETs) may be used at different stages. First, the selection of a PET can emerge from the given requirements. For example, it could be an initial requirement that an anonymous authentication scheme shall be used to ensure the authenticity and correctness of personal information (PI) provided by data subjects (DS), e.g., end-users, without revealing too much information to the software-to-be and consequently its controller. Second, during a privacy risk analysis it can become apparent that the integration of PETs is necessary to mitigate unacceptable privacy risks. For example, it could be identified that specific data needs first to be anonymized before it is transmitted, or that a mechanism needs to be integrated to inform end-users about the controller's privacy policy.

J. Lopez et al. (Eds.): TrustBus 2017, LNCS 10442, pp. 49–65, 2017.
DOI: 10.1007/978-3-319-64483-7_4

In both situations, requirements engineers face the following questions. (1) How to find out whether and which PETs exist with the needed properties? (2) How to select from a set of PETs addressing a privacy requirement the most appropriate for the system-to-be? (3) How to align the selected PET with the other requirements? That is, the selected PET needs to be integrated into one or more other functional requirements to satisfy the desired privacy requirement.

In this work, we propose a pattern-based representation of PETs that aims at assisting in answering questions (1) and (2) by providing a common structure to describe PETs. This structure shall help requirements engineers to assess whether a PET can be integrated into their software system (question (1)) and to compare the benefits and liabilities of different PETs to select the best-fitting PET (question (2)). To support question (3), we propose the consideration of PETs as early aspects. PETs (or parts of it) describe *cross-cutting functionality* that is integrated into the *base functionality* of the software-to-be to ensure certain privacy properties, e.g., anonymity and transparency, or to mitigate specific privacy threats, e.g., eavesdropping and unawareness. The cross-cutting functionalities are also called *aspects* in aspect-oriented requirements engineering. Aspects are described independently from the base functionality they shall be integrated into. Additionally, it needs to be described how an aspect is integrated into the base functionality. This integration is also called *weaving*.

The rest of the paper is structured as follows. Section 2 provides the background of this paper. The pattern format to represent PETs is introduced in Sect. 3. An example instantiation of the format for the PET Privacy-ABCs follows in Sect. 4. We discuss the contribution of this paper in Sect. 5. Related work is presented in Sects. 6 and 7 concludes the paper.

2 Background

In this paper, we use context and problem diagrams to illustrate the software systems a PET shall be integrated into and the PET itself. Jackson [3] introduced these diagrams as part of his problem frames notation. A context diagram shows the software system consisting of the software-to-be, called *machine* (represented by the symbol ◫), in its environment, which consists of *domains*. A domain can either be biddable 🄱 (a human), causal 🄲 (a technical device with a predictable behavior), or lexical ☒ (a physical representation of data). The domains and machines are connected by *interfaces* that consist of *phenomena* (e.g., events, actions, operations, and data) the domains and machines share with each other. A phenomenon is always controlled by exactly one of the connected domains and machines and observed by the others. A problem diagram shows a part of the context diagram that is responsible to address a certain *functional requirement*. Hence, it consists of the machine that is responsible to satisfy the requirement, the domains relevant for the requirement, the interfaces between them, and the requirement itself with its references to the domains. These references can either just *refer to* phenomena of a domain, or *constrain* a domain to cause specific phenomena or a modification of its phenomena's states.

Figure 2 shows a simple problem diagram. It consists of the machine Base Machine, the biddable domain User, and the domain Resource depicted as rectangles. Note that the type of the domain Resource is left open, i.e., it can be of an arbitrary type. The problem diagram also contains two interfaces. One connects the User with the Base Machine and one connects the Base Machine with the Resource. At the interface between the User and the Base Machine, the User is able to issue the phenomenon requestResource. This is expressed using the notation U!, where U is the abbreviation for the domain User. Furthermore, the problem diagram contains the requirement Provide Service depicted as dashed oval. This requirement refers to the request of the User (dashed line without arrowhead) and constrains the Resource to provide its service (dashed line with arrowhead).

We extended Jackson's notation in previous work [4] to model cross-cutting functional requirements (called *aspects*). For this purpose, we introduce the concept of *join points*. A join point is a placeholder for a domain or machine of a *base problem* (i.e., a not cross-cutting functional requirement) the aspect shall be integrated into. This allows to describe the aspect independently from a concrete base problem it shall be integrated into. For the integration of the aspect, the join points are instantiated. In this paper, we represent join points as rectangles with gray background and "normal" domains as rectangles with white background. Figure 5 shows an aspect diagram with the Verifier Machine, Presentation Policy, and User Agent as "normal" domains, the Base Machine, Resource, and User as join points, and the cross-cutting requirement Request Policy which states that if a User requests access to the Resource, the User Agent first requests the Presentation Policy. In consequence, the Base Machine shall request the Presentation Policy from the Verification Machine and provide it to the User Agent.

In addition to the structural view provided by the above-mentioned diagrams, we use UML sequence diagrams to provide a behavioral view on the base problems, aspects, and their integration, which is also called *weaving*. In the sequence diagrams, we also highlight the elements related to join points with gray background (cf. Fig. 6). How context, problem, aspect, and sequence diagrams are created is out of the scope of this paper. Details on this can be found in [3,4].

3 Pattern Format for PET Patterns

Table 1 shows the pattern format that we propose to represent PETs. The audience of the PET patterns are requirements engineers that want to identify, select, and integrate PETs that address certain privacy requirement they have to consider. The patterns themselves can be created by anyone who is familiar with the respective PET and the aspect-oriented problem frames notation (see Sect. 2). The pattern format is based on the suggestions of Harrison [5].

The pattern sections **Motivation**, **Context**, **Problem**, **Privacy Forces**, and **General Forces** are concerned with the kind of software system the PET can be integrated into. These pattern sections can be used by requirements engineers to assess whether they can use the PET or not. We propose to describe

Table 1. The pattern format for PET patterns

1 Name	All known names of the PET
2 Motivation	Example scenarios that show the necessity of the PET
3 Context	Description of the software systems the PET can be integrated into
4 Problem	Description of the software system's base problems with privacy requirements the PET shall address
5 Privacy Forces	Privacy requirements in the Problem the PET addresses
5.1 Confidentiality	PI shall be kept secret
5.2 Integrity	PI shall be correct and up-to-date
5.3 Availability	PI shall be accessable
5.4 Anonymity	PI shall not be linkable to the data subject (DS)
5.5 Data Unlinkability	PI shall not be linkable to each other
5.6 Undetectability	Existence or occurrence of PI shall not be recognizable
5.7 Pseudonymity	Only pseudonyms shall be linkable to the PI
5.8 Collection Information	DS shall be informed about data collection
5.9 Storage Information	DS shall be informed about storage procedures
5.10 Flow Information	DS shall be informed about flows of PI to others
5.11 Exceptional Information	DS and authorities shall be informed about breaches
5.12 Data Subject Intervention	DS shall be able to intervene into the processing
5.13 Authority Intervention	Authorities shall be able to intervene into the processing
6 General Forces	Other issues making it difficult to address the Problem
6.1 End-user friendliness	The PET's influence on the user experience
6.2 Performance	The PET's impact on the system's performance
6.3 Costs	Costs and effort to be spent emerging from the PET
6.4 Impact on functionality	Potential effects of the PET on the software system
6.5 Abuse of PET	Unintended usage of the PET
6.6 Revocation	Possibilities to abolish privacy properties of the PET
7 Solution	Description of the PET and how it can be integrated into base problems fitting to the Context and Problem
7.1 General Overview	Overview of the domains involved in the PET
7.2 Assumptions	Assumptions on which the PET relies
7.3 Aspects	Description of the PET's cross-cutting functionality
7.4 Weaving	Explains how Aspects are integrated into the Problem
7.5 Base Problems	Not cross-cutting functionality introduced by the PET
8 Design Issues	Discussion of specific design and implementation details
9 Privacy Benefits	The PET's positive consequences on the Privacy Forces
10 General Benefits	The PET's positive consequences on the General Forces
11 Privacy Liabilities	The PET's negative consequences on the Privacy Forces
12 General Liabilities	The PET's negative consequences on the General Forces
13 Examples	Applications of the PET (e.g., on the Motivation)
14 Related Patterns	A list of patterns describing related PETs

the **Context** using a high-level context diagram that contains the machines, domains, and interfaces that such a software system typically has as join points. The base problems in section **Problem** shall be presented as high-level problem diagrams using the machines, domains, and interfaces of the context diagram provided in the **Context**. Additionally, a behavioral view on the base problems shall be specified for the later description of the *Weaving*.

We suggest to describe the *forces* that make it difficult to address the existing privacy requirements of the software system in two pattern sections. First, the **Privacy Forces** shall be documented, i.e., the privacy requirements that the PET shall address. We propose to consider the privacy requirements that we also use in the Problem-based Privacy Analysis (ProPAn) method [6,7] (cf. Table 1), but the list can also be extended with further privacy requirements if appropriate. Second, **General Forces** shall be discussed. We identified six generic general forces that should be considered (cf. Table 1), but others may be added.

The PET itself and its consequences are considered in the pattern sections **Solution**, **Design Issues**, **Privacy Benefits**, **General Benefits**, **Privacy Liabilities**, **General Liabilities**, and **Examples**. The **Solution** is structured into five subsections. First, it contains a *General Overview* of the domains involved in the PET (including the join points of the **Context**) and the interfaces between them in the form of a context diagram. It is also important to document the *Assumptions* on which the functionality of the PET and its proposed privacy-enhancing properties rely. The PET's cross-cutting functionality shall be described as *Aspects* providing both a structural and a behavioral view. The *Weaving* explains how the aspects can be integrated into the base problems that are described in the pattern section **Problem**. The weaving shall combine the behavioral views of the base problems and the PET's aspects. Finally, a PET can introduce additional *Base Problems*, i.e., functionality that is not cross-cutting. These base problems are mostly concerned with the configuration of the PET.

To describe the consequences of a PET, we distinguish, as usual, between positive consequences, called *benefits*, and negative consequences, called *liabilities*. We further differentiate between **Privacy Benefits/Liabilities** and **General Benefits/Liabilities**, as we also did for the forces. The documented consequences shall help requirements engineers to compare different PETs that fit to their software system with each other and to finally select a PET.

4 A PET Pattern for Privacy-ABCs

In this section, we show how the pattern format described in the previous section can be used to present the PET Privacy-ABCs (Attribute-Based Credentials). As source for this PET pattern, we took the description [8] from the ABC4Trust project. The rest of this section shows the PET Pattern for Privacy-ABCs.

1 Name. Privacy-ABCs, Attribute-Based Credentials.

2 Motivation. A cigarette vending machine shall only provide cigarettes to adults. Hence, the machine has to check whether a customer is adult before cigarettes are provided to him or her. The cigarette vending machine shall not be able to gain more information about the customer or to learn that a certain customer already purchased cigarettes from it.

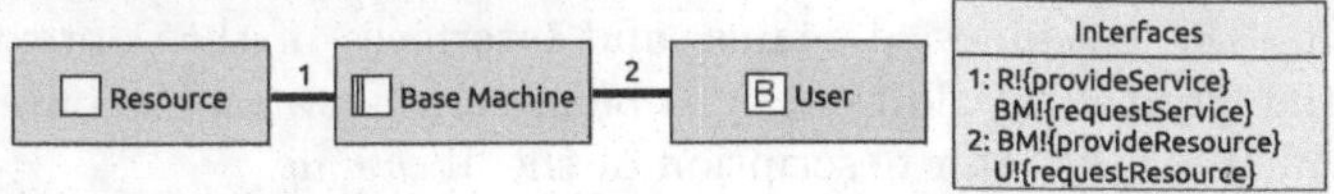

Fig. 1. Context of Privacy-ABCs

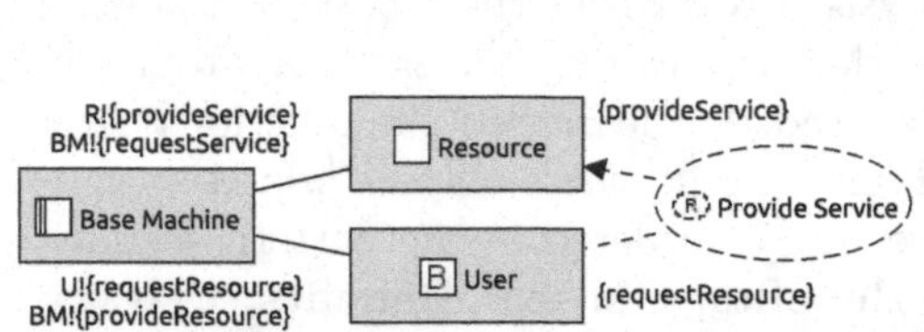

Fig. 2. Basic structure of base problems addressed by Privacy-ABCs

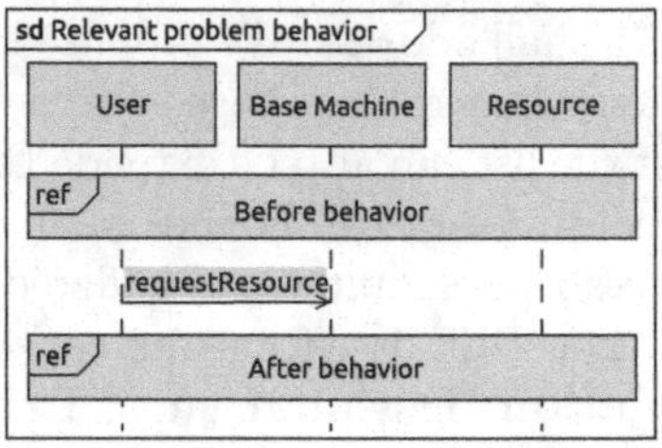

Fig. 3. Behavior of base problems addressed by Privacy-ABCs

3 Context. A software shall be developed that processes personal information (PI) of its users in order to provide a service using an additional resource. It shall be ensured that certain PI provided by the user is correct and authentic. That is, users shall not be able to input incorrect data about them. Figure 1 shows a context diagram that consists of the core elements of systems the PET shall be integrated into. The context diagram shows the User that can request the service of the Resource from the Base Machine that manages this Resource.

4 Problem. A mechanism is needed to prove that a user's PI has a certain property or to provide parts of the PI while as little PI as necessary is revealed to the software. Figure 2 shows the kind of base problems Privacy-ABCs might be integrated into. The problems have in common that a User requests a Resource's service from a Base Machine. The Base Machine processes the request and shall only provide under specific circumstances the requested service of the Resource to the User. Figure 3 shows the relevant behavior of the base problems. The behavior consists of an arbitrary Before behavior, the request of the User and an arbitrary After behavior. The request is the relevant behavior because the Base Machine shall only execute the After behavior if the information provided with the request is authentic, correct, and satisfies certain properties, e.g., it contains a proof that the user's age is above 18.

5 Privacy Forces

5.1 Confidentiality: Only partial PI or the proof that the PI satisfies a certain property is needed. The actual PI shall not be disclosed at all.

5.2 Integrity: The provided information shall be authentic and correct.

5.4 Anonymity: The service provider shall not be able to link the data collected during an interaction with the user to him or her.

5.5 Data Unlinkability: The service provider shall not be able to link the data collected during an interaction with the user to the data collected during other interactions of him or her.

5.7 Pseudonymity: Transaction pseudonyms are needed. That is, for each interaction with a user, a new pseudonym is created that is neither linkable to the user nor to other actions of him or her (for details see [9]).

5.8 Collection Information: Users shall be informed about the PI to be collected.

6 General Forces

6.1 End-User Friendliness: The mechanism to check the authenticity and correctness of the user's request and the provided data shall not introduce much inappropriate effort that needs to be spent by users in comparison to the sensitivity of the PI that is needed to provide the requested service.

6.2 Performance: The mechanism to check the authenticity and correctness of the user's request and his or her data shall not unnecessarily reduce the response time of the software-to-be or slow down the overall software system.

6.3 Costs: The costs, also in the sense of effort, to implement, integrate, deploy, and maintain the PET shall be appropriate in comparison to its benefits.

6.4 Impact on Software System's Functionalities: The integration of a solution into the base problems shall not negatively influence other system functionality.

6.5 Abuse of PET: It shall not be possible to get access to the service by providing incorrect data.

6.6 Revocation: In certain situations, e.g., abuse of the service, it may be wished to be able to re-identify the individual user that performed certain actions that led to that certain situation.

7 Solution

7.1 General Overview: Figure 4 shows the context diagram for a basic Privacy-ABCs system derived from [8]. The gray domains originate from the base problem Privacy-ABCs shall be integrated into and the white domains are introduced by Privacy-ABCs. The machine that needs to be built is the Verifier Machine. This machine is operated by the Verifier (service provider) who is able to manage the Presentation Policy. The Presentation Policy describes which information a User has to disclose in order to get access to the Resource. To create a Presentation Policy, the Credential Specification and Issuer Parameters provided by an Issuer are used. The Issuer's task is to provide Credentials to Users and to ensure that these Credentials contain only valid information about the respective User. Which information can be stored in a Credential is defined in the Credential Specification. The Issuer Parameters specify how Presentation Tokens generated from User's Credentials can be verified to satisfy or to not satisfy certain properties. To generate Credentials, the Issuer uses his or her Issuance Key. The Verifier Machine represents the software part of Privacy-ABCs that needs to be integrated into

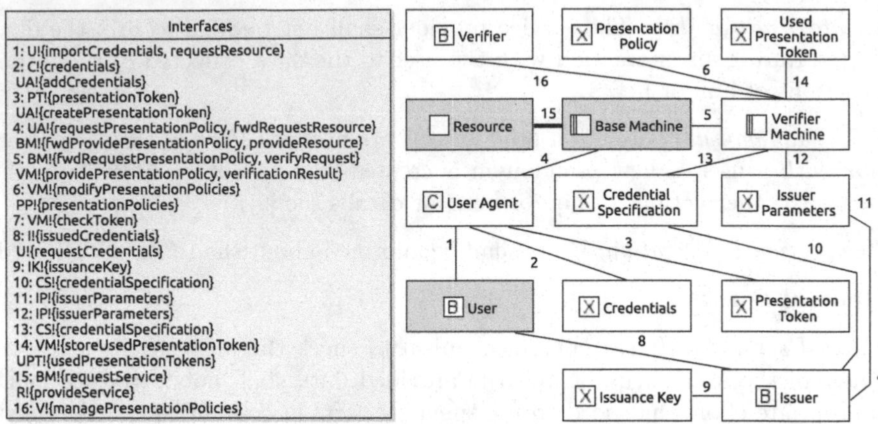

Fig. 4. Context diagram of Privacy-ABCs

the software-to-be. It receives requests from the Base Machine to provide the Presentation Policy and to check whether a User is allowed to access the Resource by verifying a provided Presentation Token using the Presentation Policy and the Credential Specification. The Verifier Machine may store these Used Presentation Tokens. Instead of receiving the requests directly from the User, the Base Machine receives the User's request from his or her User Agent. The User Agent manages the User's Credentials and generates on demand Presentation Tokens based on a Presentation Policy and the Credentials to request access to a Resource. A User can request Credentials from an Issuer and import these to his or her User Agent.

7.2 Assumptions: We have to consider some assumptions for the issuing of credentials. The Issuer shall create only authentic and correct Credentials for Users using the Credential Specification and Issuance Key. The Issuer needs to be trusted by the User and the Verifier. Furthermore, we assume that the User will add the Credentials provided by the Issuer to his or her User Agent and is not able to modify them. For the generation of Presentation Tokens, we have to assume that a User's User Agent is able to properly generate Presentation Tokens for the Resource the User requests based on the User's Credentials and the Verifier's Presentation Policy. Furthermore, we have to assume that User Agent and Base Machine use an anonymous communication channel, e.g., using Tor[1]. Otherwise, it could be possible for the Base Machine to use meta-data, e.g., the User's IP address, to link Presentation Tokens to each other.

7.3 Aspects: Privacy-ABCs contain three aspects that need to be integrated into base problems which are concerned with requests of a User to a Resource that shall be protected. (1) The Presentation Policy that specifies the information a Presentation Token shall contain to get access to the requested Resource needs to be provided to the User Agent. The aspect diagram for this cross-cutting concern

[1] https://www.torproject.org/ Accessed 21 Mar 2017.

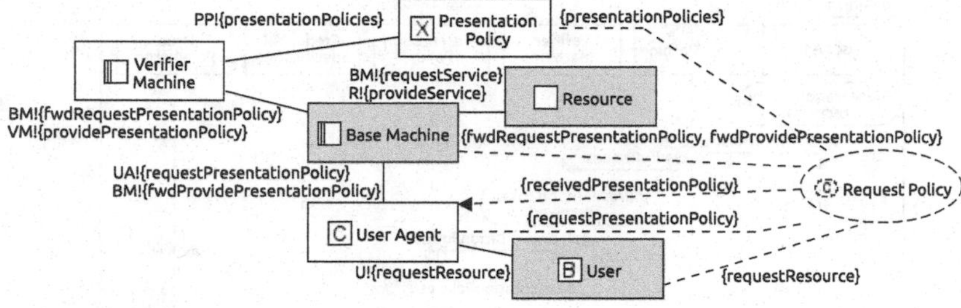

Fig. 5. Aspect diagram for providing the presentation policy

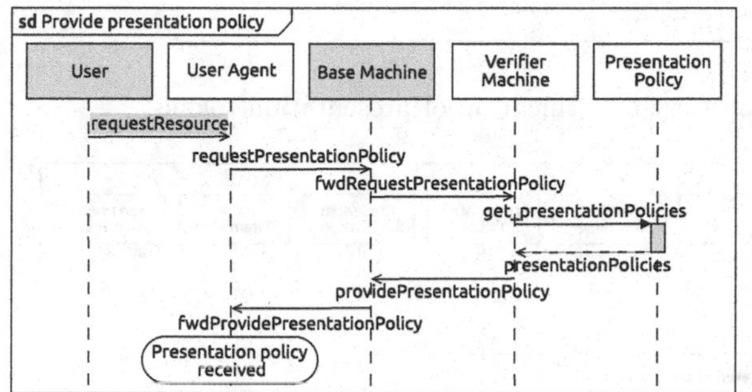

Fig. 6. Sequence diagram for providing the presentation policy

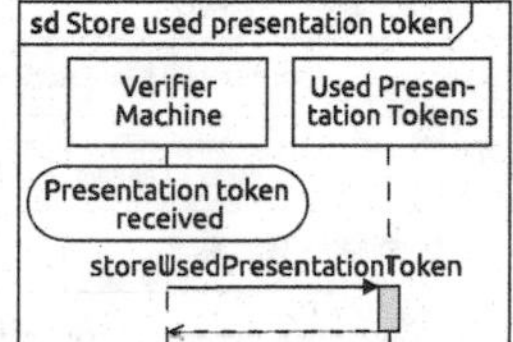

Fig. 7. Sequence diagram for the storage of used presentation tokens

is shown in Fig. 5. The behavioral view to address the aspect is shown in Fig. 6. The sequence diagram shows that if the User requests a resource via his or her User Agent, the User Agent first requests the Presentation Policy from the Base Machine. The Base Machine forwards the request to the Verifier Machine that retrieves the Presentation Policy and provides it to the Base Machine. Finally, the Base Machine provides the Presentation Policy to the User Agent, which then consequently received the presentation policy. (2) The Presentation Token provided by the User Agent needs to be verified to check whether the User is allowed to access the requested Resource using the Presentation Policy, Credential Specification, and Issuer Parameters. The result of the verification is sent to the Base Machine that then denies or provides access to the Resource for the User. For the sake of simplicity, we omit the corresponding aspect diagram. The necessary interaction between the domains to achieve the aspect is shown in Fig. 8. The interaction can be started if the User Agent received the Presentation Policy. The User Agent then generates a respective presentation token (see Assumptions) for the user's request of a resource and requests the resource from the Base Machine using the generated Presentation Token. The Base Machine asks then the Verifier Machine to verify the received request. To do this, the Verifier Machine needs to retrieve the Presentation Policy, Credential Specification, and Issuer Parameters.

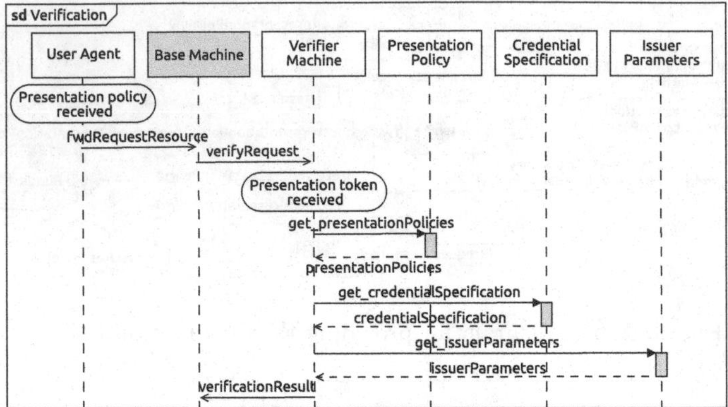

Fig. 8. Sequence diagram for the verification of presentation tokens

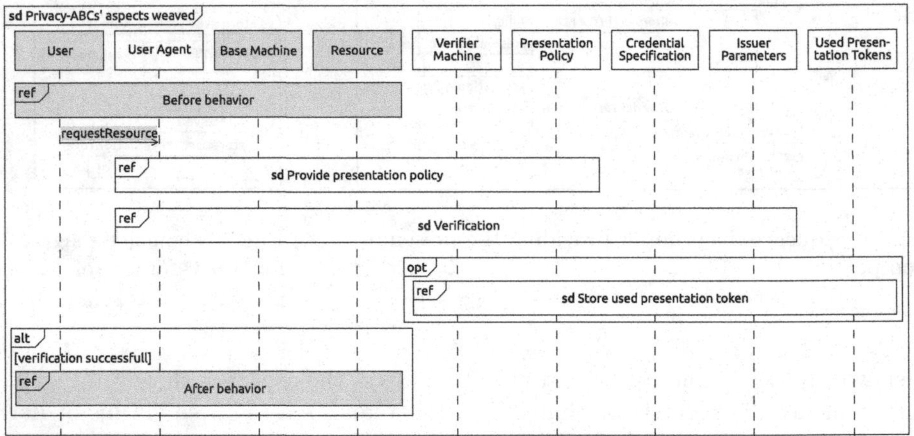

Fig. 9. Weaving of Privacy-ABCs' aspects into base problems

The result of the verification is finally returned to the Base Machine. (3) The Presentation Tokens used by Users to request access to a Resource may be stored, e.g., for statistical or maintenance reasons. We left out the corresponding aspect diagram for the sake of simplicity. Figure 7 provides the behavioral view on this aspect. It specifies that if the Verifier Machine received a presentation token, then the machine can store that token in the lexical domain Used Presentation Tokens.

7.4 Weaving: The sequence diagram shown in Fig. 9 shows how the three aspects are weaved into the base problem (see Fig. 3). First, the arbitrary Before behavior of the base problem takes place and the User requests a Resource via his or her User Agent. The User Agent then requests the Presentation Policy (see Fig. 6) to be able to generate the presentation token. Thereafter, the User Agent sends the generated presentation token that the Verifier Machine shall verify (see Fig. 8). Optionally, the used presentation token, can be stored by the Verifier Machine

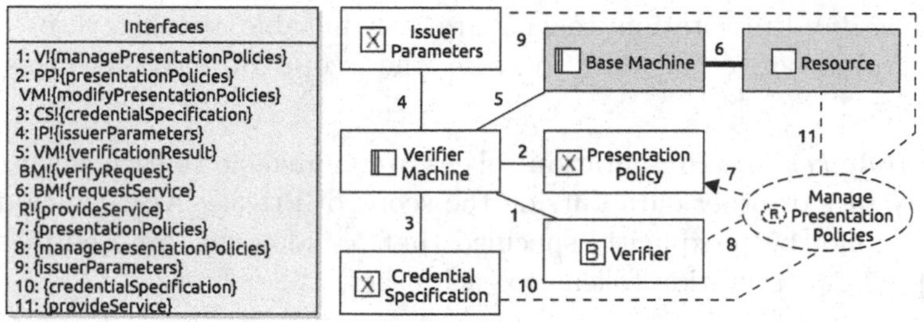

Fig. 10. Problem diagram for the management of presentation policies

(see Fig. 7). Iff the Verifier Machine reports a successful verification, the Base Machine executes the After behavior, i.e., the User gets access to the requested Resource.

7.5 Base Problems: Privacy-ABCs introduce an additional requirement that does not cross-cut functionalities of the software-to-be. This is, the Verifier shall be able to specify his or her Presentation Policy that specifies which properties a User's Presentation Token must have to get access to a specific Resource. The Presentation Policy is based on the Credential Specification and the Issuer Parameters. The problem diagram for this additional base problem is shown in Fig. 10. If it is expected that further Issuer Parameters and Credential Specification from other Issuers need to be added or that the Issuer changes these in the future, then similar base problems need to be introduced that are concerned with the management of the lexical domains Issuer Parameters and Credential Specification. For the sake of simplicity, we omit the behavioral views for these base problems.

8 Design Issues. If an existing Privacy-ABCs' infrastructure is used, there are not many design issues because most algorithms, protocols, and formats are prescribed. Only the presentation policy needs to be specified properly and the interface between the User and the Base Machine has to be refined with the User Agent (cf. Fig. 4). If an own infrastructure shall be developed, several design decisions concerning algorithms, protocols, and formats have to be made. For the sake of simplicity, we omit the details on these issues.

9 Privacy Benefits

9.1 Confidentiality: ABCs can be used to reveal PI that shall be kept confidential only partially or to prove that the PI satisfy a certain condition without revealing it. For example, it could be proved that a user is older than 18 without revealing his or her exact age or date of birth.

9.2 Integrity: Issuers guarantee that the credentials they issue contain only authentic and correct data (with respect to the date these where issued). It is cryptographically ensured that (1) no entities except the issuers can create credentials, (2) the credentials cannot be modified to contain other data, and (3) the presentation tokens created from a credential can contain only information from this credential or proofs about its properties.

9.4 Anonymity: Presentation tokens are not linkable to their user (unless attribute values or other data outside the scope of Privacy-ABCs allow linking).

9.5 Data Unlinkability: Presentation tokens are unlinkable to each other (unless attribute values or other data outside the scope of Privacy-ABCs allow linking and if it has not been explicitly specified that pseudonyms are used to be able to link specific presentation tokens to each other).

9.7 Pseudonymity: Privacy-ABCs can be used to implement transaction pseudonyms for presentation tokens, i.e., a new pseudonym is created for each presentation token. The presentation policy can also specify that specific presentation tokens are linkable to each other if the issuer parameters allow that. Hence, it is possible to implement other kinds of pseudonyms, e.g., role pseudonyms [9].

9.8 Collection Information: The service provider has to specify a presentation policy that is used to generate the user's presentation tokens. This policy specifies which information needs to be encoded into the presentation tokens. The presentation policy can be assessed by the user via his or her user agent before a respective token is created. Note that if the revealed attributes do not allow the verifier to link them back to the individual they belong to, then the elicited information is not considered as PI and needs no further protection according to the EU General Data Protection Regulation [1].

9.12 Data Subject Intervention: If the revealed attributes do not allow the verifier to link them back to the individual they belong to, then the verifier does not need to provide specific intervention options to users.

10 General Benefits

10.1 End-User Friendliness: If an existing Privacy-ABCs infrastructure can be used and the potential users already have appropriate credentials, then users do not need to explicitly register to use the software and they do not have to input their PI explicitly again. Users have to register only once at the issuer.

10.3 Costs: A Privacy-ABCs' infrastructure can be shared among several controllers that need to process the same or similar PI, or an existing infrastructure provided by an identity provider may be used. For example, the German eID card can be used by authorized and certified controllers to check whether a user's age is below or above a specified value [10].

10.4 Impact on Software System's Functionalities: It is possible that Privacy-ABCs replace another planned authentication mechanism and hence, make it unnecessary to manage user accounts and the like.

10.5 Abuse of PET: It is cryptographically ensured that corrupted tokens can be detected. Furthermore, the issuer guarantees that the data contained in the issued credentials are correct and belong to the user.

11 Privacy Liabilities

11.1 Confidentiality: The presentation policy specifies which information can be accessed by the verifier. It has to be specified in a way that only those PI is revealed that is necessary to carry out the verifier's duties.

11.2 Integrity: Some PI may change overtime, e.g., contact address. Hence, it may be necessary for users to request new credentials from an issuer and to invalidate the old credential. This issue is addressed by Privacy-ABCs with Revocation Authority [8].

11.4 Anonymity: The presentation policy specifies which information can be accessed by the verifier. If some provided information or other data outside the scope of Privacy-ABCs allow for linking, then anonymity may be broken.

11.5 Data Unlinkability: The presentation policy specifies which information can be accessed by the verifier and whether the verifier is able to link presentation tokens to each other. The policy has to be specified in a way that presentation tokens can be linked to each other only if this is necessary.

11.7 Pseudonymity: The needed kind of pseudonym has to be specified in the verifier's presentation policy.

11.8 Collection Information: The presentation policy specifies which PI is collected, however, verifiers may still need to inform users about the purpose for which the revealed information is used.

11.12 Data Subject Intervention: Under specific circumstances, it may be necessary to integrate a mechanism that allows users to order the deletion of presentation tokens or to restrict the processing of them (cf. Article 11 of the EU General Data Protection Regulation [1]).

12 General Liabilities

12.1 End-User Friendliness: The usage of Privacy-ABCs has some issues concerning the end-user friendliness. First, users need to get credentials from an issuer that they need to trust. Second, users have to use a user agent for managing their credentials and generating presentation tokens. Hence, the perceived user-friendliness strongly depends on the properties of this user agent.

12.2 Performance: Depending on the complexity of the properties that need to be proved, the response time for the user could be higher than with a classical authentication mechanism.

12.3 Costs: The creation of an own Privacy-ABCs infrastructure, including issuing credentials and the development of user agents that generate presentations tokens, will be too expensive in most cases. If an existing infrastructure is used instead, it is possible that certain parts of the software need to be certified. Such a certification also raises costs.

12.4 Impact on Software System's Functionalities: It has to be ensured that the PI necessary to provide the requested services is collected and that (if necessary) users' interactions can be linked to each other.

12.5 Abuse of PET: If the software-to-be can be misused, e.g., to commit a crime or to damage the service provider, it is hardly possible to identify the malicious user (cf. **Privacy Benefits**). This threat can be mitigated by the Privacy-ABCs variant with Inspector.

12.6 Revocation: The basic Privacy-ABCs implementation provides no revocation options, but there are two extensions that provide different revocation options. The first extension allows revocation of credentials. That is, once issued credentials can be made invalid by a revocation authority. The second extension introduces the role of an inspector. The inspector is able to reveal the exact PI contained in a credential from a given presentation token or to uncover the individual to whom the presentation token belongs. The verifier shall only be allowed to request this inspection under specified circumstances that are also part of the verifier's presentation policy.

13 Examples. If we apply Privacy-ABCs to the cigarette vending machine example, then the join point Base Machine (cf. Fig. 2) would be instantiated with the vending machine, the Resource with the cigarettes, and the User with the customer who wants to buy cigarettes. In Germany, the existing Privacy-ABCs infrastructure of the German eID card [10] can be used. In this case the Issuer (cf. Fig. 4) is the German state and the User Agent is the eID card. The Credential contains information such as the customer's name, address, date and place of birth. The Presentation Policy of the vending machine specifies that the generated Presentation Token only needs to contain a proof that the customer is older than 18.

14 Related PET Patterns. Privacy-ABCs with Revocation Authority, Privacy-ABCs with Inspector.

5 Discussion

Harrison states in [5]: *"The patterns community has been justly criticized for rehashing previously published material."* With this work, we want to emphasize that *"rehashing previously published material"* is necessary if the audience of the material is changed from researchers to practical requirements engineers, and beneficial if the rehashing leads to a homogeneous representation of PETs which makes it easier to identify and compare different solutions for the same privacy requirements with each other. However, our work yet lacks evidence that the proposed presentation of PETs as patterns using an aspect-oriented notion really helps requirements engineers to address questions (1)–(3) introduced in Sect. 1. In future work, we plan to empirically evaluate how much requirements engineers benefit from a catalog of PET patterns. We also expect that we get valuable feedback from the participants of the experiments to further improve the pattern format, e.g., by adding further pattern (sub)sections to it, and to improve the presentation of PETs as early aspects.

In addition to the question whether requirements engineers are willing to use a catalog of PET patterns, the question arises who will provide the PET patterns and maintain such a catalog. We would prefer an open platform, similar to existing platforms for privacy patterns (cf. Sect. 6), to which people who have experience with a certain PET can add a respective PET pattern.

In this paper, we have shown how Privacy-ABCs can be presented as PET pattern supported by an aspect-oriented notation. We additionally created PET patterns for K-Anonymity [11], P3P[2], Privacy-ABCs with Revocation Authority and Inspector, and the cryptosystem RSA [12]. These initial results have shown that both simple and more complex PETs can be represented as early aspects in the proposed pattern format.

Actually, the proposed pattern format is independent of the problem frames notation and aspect-orientation. That is, any other notation or only plain text may be used to describe the **Context**, **Problem**, and **Solution**. But we believe that the provided context, problem, aspect, and sequence diagrams help to illustrate the **Context**, **Problem**, and **Solution** of a PET. Especially, the *Weaving* shall support requirements engineers to understand into which base problems of the software-to-be a PET needs to be integrated and how.

Our proposed representation of PETs is dedicated to the requirements engineering phase, to support an early consideration of PETs and an integration of these into the other requirements of the software-to-be. Hence, our proposed pattern for Privacy-ABCs lacks information concerning concrete algorithms and other implementation details, e.g., in which format presentation tokens or policies are stored. This is intended, because the focus in the requirements engineering phase should be on understanding the problem of building the software-to-be rather than on implementation details [3]. Hence, we want to understand which additional entities (domains) have to be considered if a PET is selected, how these entities are related to each other and the software-to-be, how the software-to-be needs to be adapted to integrate the PET, under which assumptions does the PET function, and with which benefits and liabilities does the PET come.

6 Related Work

Hafiz [13] presents a pattern language for developing PETs consisting of 12 patterns. Each pattern describes a solution to achieve a certain privacy property. The goal of the pattern language is to assist developers of PETs. Lobato et al. [14] propose patterns that support the presentation of privacy policies to users. Schumacher [15] presents two privacy patterns that describe best-practices for end-users to protect their privacy. Romanosky et al. [16] identified three privacy patterns for online interactions. These contain patterns for best-practices for end-users and best-practices for the design of privacy-friendly software. Porekar et al. [17] propose organizational privacy patterns. These privacy patterns shall help to address privacy issues already on the organizational level by providing corresponding solutions. The solution description is enhanced with Secure Tropos diagrams. In addition to the previously mentioned works, there are two websites[3]

[2] http://w3c.p3p.com Accessed 21 Mar 2017.

[3] https://privacypatterns.org and https://privacypatterns.eu.

that provide catalogs of privacy patterns similar to the mentioned works. In contrast to these works, we propose to express PETs themselves as patterns to support requirements engineers to select appropriate PETs and to integrate them into the software-to-be to address identified privacy requirements. The consideration of PETs as early aspects is a novel contribution of this paper.

7 Conclusions

In this paper, we have proposed a pattern format to represent PETs as early aspects. We have illustrated how a PET pattern shall look like using the rather complex PET Privacy-ABCs. Initial results have shown that a variety of PETs can be expressed as PET patterns. The PET patterns shall help requirements engineers to identify the PETs that address the privacy requirements that they need to integrate into the software-to-be, then to select the PET that best fits to the needs without having too much impact on the software-to-be, and finally to integrate the PET's requirements into the requirements of the software-to-be.

In future work, we want to set up a larger catalog of PET patterns. Using this catalog, we want to empirically evaluate how much requirements engineers benefit from PET patterns. This is, we want to assess whether the catalog helps them to identify, select, and integrate PETs into a software system.

References

1. European Commission: Regulation (EU) 2016/679 of the european parliament and of the council (general data protection regulation), April 2016
2. ISO/IEC: ISO/IEC 29100:2011 information technology - security techniques - privacy framework. Technical report (2011)
3. Jackson, M.: Problem Frames. Analyzing and Structuring Software Development Problems. Addison-Wesley, Boston (2001)
4. Faßbender, S., Heisel, M., Meis, R.: A problem-, quality-, and aspect-oriented requirements engineering method. In: Holzinger, A., Cardoso, J., Cordeiro, J., Libourel, T., Maciaszek, L.A., Sinderen, M. (eds.) ICSOFT 2014. CCIS, vol. 555, pp. 291–310. Springer, Cham (2015). doi:10.1007/978-3-319-25579-8_17
5. Harrison, N.B.: Advanced pattern writing - patterns for experienced pattern authors. In: Manolescu, D., Voelter, M., Noble, J. (eds.) Pattern Languages of Program Design 5. Addison-Wesley, Boston (2006)
6. Meis, R., Heisel, M.: Computer-aided identification and validation of privacy requirements. Information **7**, 28 (2016)
7. Meis, R., Heisel, M.: Computer-aided identification and validation of intervenability requirements. Information **8**, 30 (2017)
8. Camenisch, J., Krontiris, I., Lehmann, A., Neven, G., Paquin, C., Rannenberg, K., Zwingelberg, H.: D2.1 architecture for attribute-based credential technologies – version 1. Technical report, ABC4Trust (2011)
9. Pfitzmann, A., Hansen, M.: A terminology for talking about privacy by data minimization: anonymity, unlinkability, undetectability, unobservability, pseudonymity, and identity management, August 2010. v0.34

10. Bundestag, D.: Gesetz über Personalausweise und den elektronischen Identitätsnachweis sowie zur Änderung weiterer Vorschriften. Bundesgesetzblatt **I**(33) (2009)
11. Sweeney, L.: K-anonymity: a model for protecting privacy. Int. J. Uncertain. Fuzziness Knowl.-Based Syst. **10**(5), 557–570 (2002)
12. Rivest, R.L., Shamir, A., Adleman, L.: A method for obtaining digital signatures and public-key cryptosystems. Commun. ACM **21**(2), 120–126 (1978)
13. Hafiz, M.: A pattern language for developing privacy enhancing technologies. Softw.: Pract. Exp. **43**(7), 769–787 (2013)
14. Lobato, L.L., Fernandez, E.B., Zorzo, S.D.: Patterns to support the development of privacy policies. In: Proceedings of the 1st International Workshop on Organizational Security Aspects (OSA) (2009)
15. Schumacher, M.: Security patterns and security standards - with selected security patterns for anonymity and privacy. In: European Conference on Pattern Languages of Programs (EuroPLoP) (2003)
16. Romanosky, S., Acquisti, A., Hong, J., Cranor, L.F., Friedman, B.: Privacy patterns for online interactions. In: Proceedings of the 2006 Conference on Pattern Languages of Programs. PLoP 2006, pp. 12:1–12:9. ACM, New York (2006)
17. Porekar, J., Jerman-Blazic, A., Klobucar, T.: Towards organizational privacy patterns. In: Second International Conference on the Digital Society, pp. 15–19, February 2008

Iron Mask: Trust-Preserving Anonymity on the Face of Stigmatization in Social Networking Sites

Hamman Samuel(✉) and Osmar Zaïane

University of Alberta, Edmonton, Canada
{hwsamuel, zaiane}@ualberta.ca

Abstract. Social networking sites are pervasively being used for seeking advice, asking questions, giving answers, and sharing experiences on various topics including health. When users share content about sensitive health topics, such as sexual dysfunction, infertility, or STDs, they may wish to do so anonymously to avoid stigmatization and the associated negative effects on mental health. However, a user masking their name with a pseudonym may still be inadvertently exposing their identity because of various quasi-identifiers present in their profile. One such quasi-identifier that has not been investigated in literature is the content itself, which could be used for authorship identification. Moreover, an anonymous user's credibility cannot be established because their profile is no longer linked with their reputation. This study proposes the Iron Mask algorithm for providing enhanced anonymity while preserving trust. Iron Mask improves anonymity by using a probabilistic machine learning approach based on whiteprint identification and inclusion of content as a quasi-identifier. Iron Mask also introduces the concept of a trust-preserving pseudonym which masks user identity without loss of credibility. We evaluate the proposed algorithm using datasets from Quora, a question-answering social networking site, and demonstrate the efficacy of our algorithm with satisfactory recall and survey feedback results.

Keywords: Anonymity · Pseudonymity · Trust

1 Introduction

Social Networking Sites (SNS) provide various mechanisms to facilitate sharing of information, advise, questions and answers related to various topics. Different types of actions are available on various instances of SNS such as Quora, Stack Exchange, Facebook, and Twitter. Users can "friend" or "follow" other users, thereby creating connections. Different types of content can be created and shared on SNS, including text-based articles, blogs, microblogs, or multimedia content such as pictures and videos, or links to other users' postings and external websites. Users can also subscribe to topics of interest, thereby creating online communities of like-minded individuals. Normally, the user who is sharing a posting is identified as the author of the post by displaying their registered user name or full name. However, situations can arise in which the user does not want to be identified.

J. Lopez et al. (Eds.): TrustBus 2017, LNCS 10442, pp. 66–80, 2017.
DOI: 10.1007/978-3-319-64483-7_5

If a user shares a link with connections about sexual dysfunction or infertility, the user may wish to do so anonymously to avoid any potential stigmatization which may result from the assumption that the user sharing the content suffers from the condition [1]. Pseudonyms have proven effective within online forum communities for supporting stigmatized issues and people tend to discuss and learn more openly about stigmatized issues when the perceived risk of being publicly associated with the issue is taken away [2]. On the other hand, the negative effects of users experiencing social stigma can be severe, with outcomes ranging from poorer mental health to increased risk behaviors [3]. It is known that users have been increasingly using the internet for sharing personal experiences and seeking advice about various personal issues, which increases the likelihood of stigmatization from online activities [4].

Despite the potential severity of online social stigma, options and controls to anonymously post content are not well-supported in most SNS. Users on SNS may hide their real identity by creating a new account with a fake name or pseudonym, thereby duplicating the SNS user base. This is not ideal and unnecessarily complicates the process of information sharing. From the list of popular social media websites such as Facebook, Twitter, LinkedIn, YouTube, Google+, Stack Exchange and Quora, only the latter allows asking questions anonymously without needing to create a new account.

There are also potential drawbacks with the approach to replace the user's real identity with the generic pseudonym "anonymous". Firstly, despite their name being replaced by "anonymous", users may be inadvertently releveling their identity because of the similarities between the content they have posted in the past. Phrases, wordings, topics and other nuances about the writing style in the user's past postings may constitute a quasi-identifier that can be associated to a specific user. Secondly, the generic anonymous pseudonym also eliminates the user's associated credibility, thereby motivating the need for trust-preservation during anonymization. Information from a known source is easier to identify as being either more or less trustworthy than if it is coming from an unknown source [5]. For example, someone unknown suggesting in a post to take a certain medication will be less credible than a person who is known to be a medical expert. At the same time, advise from a person confirmed to have little knowledge of medicine would give a clearer indication of distrust, in contrast with when an unknown person gives similar advice.

The notions of credibility and trust are homonyms related to the belief that a person's actions during an interaction will be beneficial rather than detrimental [6]. Credibility of a user in SNS is often expressed using a reputation system based on an aggregate of positive and negative feedback received from other users. This mechanism is used by Quora and Stack Exchange, where the aggregate points received can be used to determine a user's level of expertise. The assumption, barring Sybil attacks, is that the higher a user's aggregate points, the more knowledgeable they are, given that they have received more positive than negative feedback. Another form of trustworthiness is based on the personalized grouping of connections based on closeness of relationship. This strategy is available in Facebook, where connections are categorized as "family", "close friends", "friends", "acquaintances", "friends of friends". This hierarchy of closeness can be interpreted as being directly proportional to trustworthiness, the closer the user, the more trustworthy.

Our proposed algorithm, Iron Mask, uses the whiteprint or authorship identification approach to take into account the user's historical content, thereby enhancing anonymity by minimizing the risk of re-identification and decreasing the likelihood of online stigma. Iron Mask also provides trust-preservation to balance the social network's needs to generate credible content with the user's need for optional yet reliable anonymity. The naïve approach of explicitly revealing information related to user credibility would constitute a quasi-identifier, and could lead to identity being compromised through correlations [7], so a more sophisticated approach is required. To achieve this, Iron Mask introduces the concept of the Trust-Preserving Pseudonym (TPP), which provides a broader range of pseudonym labels, in addition to the generic "anonymous" pseudonym to mask or cover up the user's actual account name identity while appropriately summarizing credibility information.

The scope of our work is on self-contained SNS, and adversaries external to the social network are not considered. External adversaries would have additional information that is outside the network, while internal adversaries would be registered users within the SNS. Two aspects of the Iron Mask algorithm need to be evaluated. Firstly, the whiteprint identification approach is tested using datasets from the Quora question answering community. The evaluation demonstrates the accuracy of predicting the author of a post even when their user name is hidden. Secondly, the trust-preservation approach and TPP are evaluated using a survey-based approach to demonstrate usefulness and applicability.

The rest of the paper is organized as follows. Section 2 presents related work on anonymity in SNS, while Sect. 3 gives an outline of the Iron Mask algorithm. Section 4 provides details of our experimental design and evaluation results, including identification of content dealing with sensitive topics, while Sect. 5 concludes with comparative analysis and commentary on future directions.

2 Literature Review

Narayanan et al. [8] investigated different de-anonymization attacks on social networks such as Twitter. Their study looked at possible re-identification risks involved with user information available on more than one social network, i.e. Twitter and Flickr, and how intersection of common information could lead to re-identification. A similar study by Beach et al. [9] also looked at anonymity in social networks and the disadvantages of using traditional anonymization methods such as *k*-anonymity on SNS like Facebook. However, these studies focused on partial anonymization where some properties of the user are hidden, such as name, while others are visible, like gender or location. Our research looks at the scenario where the user's identity is completely hidden via full anonymization. Also, the adversaries considered in these studies had information that was external to the target SNS, while our study focuses on information being exclusively within the network.

The veiled viral marketing approach was suggested by Hansen and Johnson for sending anonymized messages to friends within Facebook [1]. In the study, research on an awareness campaign for Human Papilloma Virus (HPV) showed that people who knew HPV is a sexually transmitted were more likely to feel shame and stigma, and less likely to share or post information about it on their Facebook profiles. Moreover, people were willing to share links to websites about social causes like breast cancer awareness, but were unlikely to do likewise for links to syphilis or gonorrhea websites. The proposed veiled viral marketing approach allowed sending of anonymous "veiled" messages to friends, which essentially substituted the user's identity with the "friend" pseudonym. Users would know that the message came from one of their friends, but would not know which friend actually sent the message. However, this study did not take into account any risk of de-anonymization from the content being a quasi-identifier. In addition, no exploration was made on any relationships between credibility of information and anonymity, although it was implied that users trusted their friends' shared content more than that of strangers.

The relationship between historical posted content and user identity was partially investigated by Milhail and Ilya as a side effect of their study [10]. They looked into the situation where the same person had several different accounts on the same web portal, potentially for manipulation of feedback, ratings and Sybil attacks on the web portal. The study proposed a solution to short messages text authorship determination using a naive Bayesian classifier. The classifier was trained using short messages from known users. This classifier was then used to determine if a new post belonged to an existing user. One drawback of the study was the low accuracy of 50%, which could be attributed to the selection of features, size of the training data, or the classifier used. Another similar study was conducted by Keretna et al. on whiteprint identification in Twitter to recognize multiple accounts being created by the same user [11].

The relationship between anonymity and trust has also been explored in peer-to-peer networks for providing ratings and feedback anonymously [12], which also has applications in e-governance and online voting [13]. The proposed approaches focus on the anonymized reporting of aggregated results. This relationship is also important to dematerialized money and cryptocurrencies, where the emphasis is on completing trustworthy transactions while maintaining anonymity of the agents involved [14]. In contrast with these domains, to the best of our knowledge, there has not been much direct work done on enhancing the relationship between trust and anonymity in SNS. There are various SNS that have either internal or external anonymity controls. The former, such as Quora, allow users to anonymously post content without revealing their actual registered account's user name. The latter includes SNS that let anyone with an internet connection post content without having to register an account. Pseudo-accounts are a third option in which users register fake accounts to hide their real identities, and subsequently do not require additional anonymity controls or options [15].

3 Methodology

The general workflow of anonymization is summarized in Fig. 1, where the user is provided a choice of using anonymity. If the user selects in the affirmative, then the author of the posting is reported with the generic label of "anonymous", and no hyperlinks or internal associations to the actual user are maintained. Consequently, anyone viewing the content will see the content's author as anonymous. Otherwise, the actual identity of the user is displayed. These two binary choices are available on SNS such as Quora. Our proposed approach using the Iron Mask algorithm provides an alternative route for anonymity.

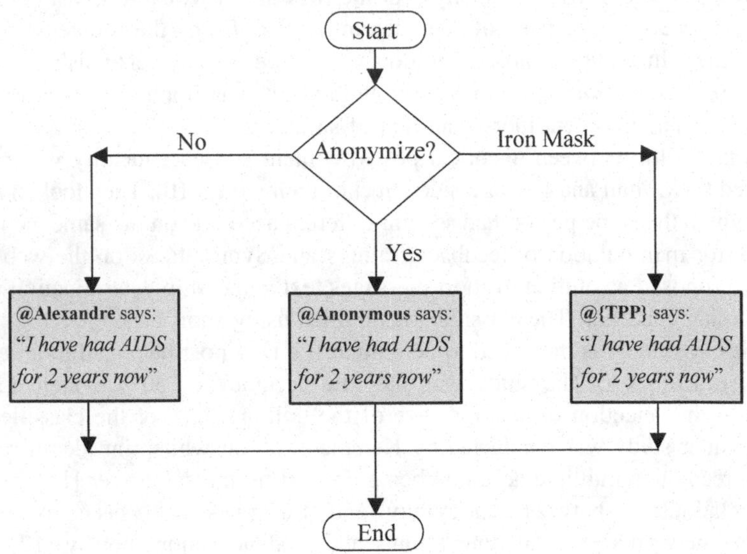

Fig. 1. Overview of anonymization approaches and trust-preserving pseudonyms.

Iron Mask assigns a pseudonym using a two-stage approach: firstly, the content to be posted is scrutinized to determine the probability of de-anonymization. Secondly, a trust-preserving pseudonym is assigned based on the SNS characteristics and the user's profile. For example, the TPP assigned could be "close friend", which would let the reader know that a close friend of theirs has made this posting, which could be better received than a posting from a stranger or casual acquaintance. The TPP could also be "competent" based on a combination of the Dreyfus model of skill acquisition and the user's reputation points on the SNS. This would let the reader know that the user' is knowledgeable or not based on other users' feedback on previous postings.

Programmatically, the procedure for posting new content with options for anonymization with Iron Mask is abstracted in Algorithm 1. If there is a risk of re-identification, then the user is warned of this before proceeding. It is up to the user to take the risk or not. The user's pseudonym is determined by the `TPP()` function. The generic `SAVE()` procedure is dependent on the SNS to save the content to the appropriate persistent storage such as a database.

Algorithm 1. `POST` (*user, content, anon*)

Require: *user*: the posting's author, *content*: the content to be posted, *anon*: option to anonymize or not

```
if anon is False then
    SAVE (user, content)
    return
if IRONMASK(user, content) is False then
    WARN ()
else
    pseudonym = TPP (user)
    SAVE (pseudonym, content)
return
```

3.1 Whiteprint Identification Using Probabilistic Classification

Algorithm 2 outlines the Iron Mask step-by-step procedure using a probabilistic classifier. Probabilistic classification is able to predict a probability distribution over a set of classes. In essence, probabilistic classifiers provide the degree of confidence of a sample belonging to a class [16]. To initialize, a probabilistic classifier is trained using existing users and their postings from Quora, where the user name is the class, and the content is converted to *n*-grams as features. Training computes a score for how strongly classes and attributes are associated, and the trained model can then be used for making predictions on new data, while probability calibration converts the scores to probabilities [17]. All possible combinations of adjacent words of length *n* within a posting are referred to as *n*-grams. For instance, a posting containing words [w_1, w_2, …, w_n] would yield bigrams as [w_1w_2, w_1w_3, $\ldots w_{n-1}w_n$]. For our implementation, we use naïve Bayes with isotonic regression as the probability calibration in the Scikit-Learn library [18]. We used a combination of uni-, bi- and tri-grams as features.

Essentially, the probabilistic classifier is performing whiteprint identification by associating content and user identity [11]. The content is also being used as a quasi-identifier. More formally, user names and historically posted content can be expressed as the traditional database table defined in *k*-anonymization with *n* rows and *m* columns, with the rows representing each user's previously posted content, and the columns representing *n*-grams from the content, along with the user name. This database table also maps to the classification problem model, where each row comprises a complete tuple, and, in our case, the user name column is the identified class [19].

A new posting is input to the trained probabilistic classifier to get a set of predicted candidate users. On the trained probabilistic classifier, two thresholds are available for making a decision: top-*n* and τ. The top-*n* threshold returns the top candidate users based on the sorted degree of confidence. If the actual author is found within these top-n candidates, then the Iron Mask algorithm returns a warning status. On the other hand, if the confidence level for predicting the actual author is greater than a given threshold, τ, then Iron Mask also returns a warning status. The thresholds can be used concurrently or separately based on how they are configured. For instance, configuring $\tau = 1$ or $n = 0$ would disable either threshold.

Algorithm 2. IRONMASK (*user*, *content*)

Require: *user*: the posting's author, *content*: the content to be posted, τ: internal threshold for determining risk of re-identification, n: internal threshold for choosing number of predicted candidates

1. *candidates* = PROBCLASSIFIER (*content*)
2. *top_candidates* = *candidates*[:*n*]
3. *user_prob* = *candidates*.FIND (*user*).*probability*
4. **if** *user* **in** *top_candidates* **or** *user_prob* $\geq \tau$ **then**
5.   **return False**
6. **else**
7.   **return True**

3.2 TPP Algorithm

In addition to the generic "anonymous" pseudonym, additional pseudonyms can be assigned to a user to preserve information about their credibility, based on level of expertise or level of relational closeness.

Level of Expertise. We use the Dreyfus model of skill acquisition as a reference for anonymizing a user's online reputation on the SNS [20]. The Dreyfus model specifies five categories of expertise: novice, advanced beginner, competent, proficient, and expert. Depending on the SNS, there are various reputation attributes available. Quora allows users to "Upvote" or "Downvote" postings based on the voter's perceptions of quality. This feedback, along with general interaction statistics such as number of postings and comments, can be aggregated as a reputation score for each user to determine the user's level of expertise on the Dreyfus hierarchical scale, with pre-configured mappings of reputation scores to each level. Algorithm 3 outlines this approach as an implementation of TPP using expertise and reputation. The scoring function incorporates the number of upvotes and downvotes received, as well as the total number of postings, while penalizing downvotes. The severity and effect of downvotes on reputation can be adjusted using a weighting factor. The reputation score aggregation formulation can be customized to fit the needs of the SNS. Moreover, if there is not enough data available to define level of expertise, the "anonymous" label can be used.

Algorithm 3. TPP (*user*)

Require: *user*: the posting's author, t_i: values for Dreyfus levels, where $t_{i-1} < t_i$, w: weighting factor to adjust severity effect of downvotes

rep = GETREPUTATION(*user*)
$score = (rep.upvotes + rep.num\_postings) / (w * rep.downvotes + 1)$
if $score \geq t_1$ **then**
    return EXPERT
else if $score < t_1$ **and** $score \geq t_2$ **then**
    return PROFICIENT
else if $score < t_2$ **and** $score \geq t_3$ **then**
    return COMPETENT
else if $score < t_3$ **and** $score \geq t_4$ **then**
    return ADVANCED_BEGINNER
else if $score < t_4$ **and** $score \geq t_5$ **then**
    return NOVICE
else if $score < t_5$ **then**
    return ANONYMOUS

Level of Relational Closeness. For SNS that do not use reputation metrics, the type of ties or connections and their relative perception of relational closeness can be used as an indicator of trustworthiness. For instance, Facebook is not designed as question answering community, and there is no explicit notion of reputation. Algorithm 4 outlines the approach for determining a TPP based on a hierarchy of relational closeness. At each level of the hierarchy, starting from the more intimate, for instance family, the connections of the user posting the new content are enumerated. Each connection's number of connections are then determined, and a probability of re-identification solely based on the number of connections is computed. As an example, a user named D'Artagnan has three "close friends" connections named, Aramis, Athos and Porthos. For each of the three connections, their number of "close friend" connections are computed in turn. Aramis may have only one close connection, D'Artagnan himself. Hence, Aramis will surely guess the identity of D'Artagnan if he were to be labelled with the pseudonym "close friend". In this situation, a pseudonym that is higher in the hierarchy is then attempted recursively. If no suitable pseudonym is found, then the "anonymous" label is used. Hence, the possibility of de-anonymization when using a TPP is also covered by incorporating the probability of re-identification at each stage of the TPP hierarchy. For social networks without hierarchical relationships, such as Twitter, a TPP would not capture trustworthiness due to lack of differentiation between connections.

The proposed approaches for TPP are meant to cover characteristics of different variations of SNS. For Quora, the level of expertise is more appropriate. Another aspect to consider when selecting either TPP approach is the nature of the posting. For instance, a posting about a user sharing their experiences on a sensitive topic does not necessarily require knowledge about their reputation, but their relational connection would help. On the other hand, a user giving an anonymous answer or advise about a sensitive health topic would need some validation of credibility in order to ensure no harm is done.

Algorithm 4. TPP (*user*)

Require: *user*: the posting's author, *connection_hierarchy*: hierarchy of connection types based on level of relational closeness, τ: minimal connections threshold

```
pseudonym = ANONYMOUS
for each type in connection_hierarchy
    connections = GETCONNECTIONS (user, type)
    pseudonym = type
    for each connection in connections
        num_connections = GETCONNECTIONS(connection, type).COUNT ()
        if num_connections ≤ τ then
            pseudonym = ANONYMOUS
            break
return pseudonym
```

4 Evaluation

For evaluation of the proposed methodology, we retrieved datasets from Quora via unofficial APIs that have been approved by Quora, and in line with Quora's terms of use on web scraping and rate limits. A summary of the number of subsets retrieved is given in Table 1, along with the topics used for filtering the postings. The topics were selected in line with the focus of our research on sensitive health content.

Table 1. Quora dataset for evaluation, filtered by topics. A: Men's sexual health, B: Women's sexual health, C: Sexuality, D: HIV, E: Mental health

Subset	A	B	C	D	E	Total
Initial profiles retrieved	58	48	110	56	122	394
Questions retrieved	179	122	300	151	300	1,072
Answers retrieved	895	488	1,500	302	960	4,145
Additional profiles	358	97	750	30	348	1,619

The retrieval process involved accessing a topic's list of questions, then retrieving the list of followers of the topic. Each follower's profile was then programmatically accessed, and questions they have posted were retrieved, as well as upvotes and downvotes on each question. Users are also allowed to post questions anonymously, in which case the questions do not appear on their profile's listing of questions asked.

Next, for each question retrieved, the corresponding answers were also enumerated, including the associated upvotes and downvotes, as well as additional profiles of users who authored the answers.

4.1 Accuracy of Content as Quasi-Identifier

In order to determine the accuracy of whiteprint identification, a sample of users were arbitrarily selected from the Quora dataset. Various iterations of this process were performed using different configurations of threshold, while the number of users selected was kept constant for all iterations. The sample dataset was then split into two parts for training and testing. The training set *Tr* was used for building the probabilistic classifier model. Next, the trained model was used with the other half of the sample dataset, i.e. the test set *Ts*, to predict user identity. Both the test and training sets were split such that the users in the test dataset were also in the training dataset. However, the content within the test dataset was not in the training counterpart. More formally, if u_i represents users and c represents content of the users, then $u_i \in Tr$, $c_i \in Tr$, $u_j \in Ts$, and $c_j \in Ts$, but $u_j \subset u_i$ and $c_j \not\subset c_i$.

The recall measure was used to determine the effectiveness of the trained model. Probabilistic classifiers are traditionally evaluated using root mean square error, but since we are evaluating the Iron Mask algorithm and various threshold configurations for top-n and τ, the recall metric is best to achieve our evaluation goals as well as capture the classifier's accuracy. As an illustrative example of our evaluation strategy, if top-$n = 1$, that implies that Iron Mask would only detect the user's correct identity and give a warning if the trained model ranked that identity with the highest probability. In other words, if a given user's identity was correctly predicted within the top-n, the recall score was recorded as 1, else it was recorded as 0. An average of the recall was taken for the various users selected for each iteration, shown in Fig. 2 for different values of top-n. Similarly, for different values of τ, recall was recorded based on whether Iron Mask gave a warning or not, and the results are summarized in Fig. 3.

For top-n, the recall and hence the prediction of Iron Mask gets better with larger values of n. This is expected, because the larger the options to choose from, the higher the likelihood of discovering the item being searched. Similar results are also observed with τ, where lower values result in a much higher recall. These results demonstrate that Iron Mask is able correlate identity with historical postings to a fairly satisfactory level of performance. Even with tighter constraints of $n = 1$ or $\tau = 0.90$, the algorithm performs reasonably well and demonstrates that there is indeed a correlation between historical postings and user identity.

To reiterate, τ is used to control the level of confidence that Iron Mask can work with; false positives are prevented by setting a high level, which prevents Iron Mask from warning users of re-identification if the probability is low. On the other hand, top-n allows whiteprint identification without explicitly considering confidence; as long as the user's identity is among the most likely candidates, the Iron Mask algorithm warns the user. Ultimately, the Iron Mask algorithm can successfully predict the user's identity ahead of any re-identification attacks using either metric.

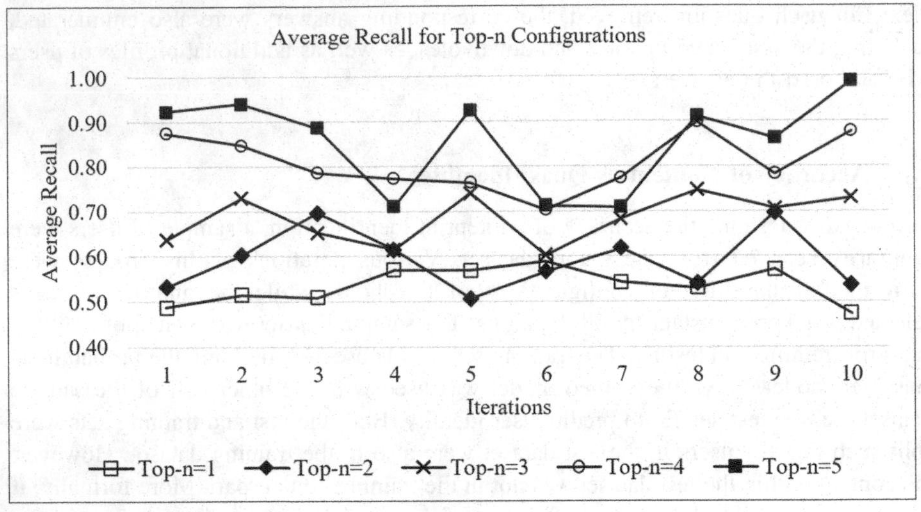

Fig. 2. Average recall for Top-*n* configurations

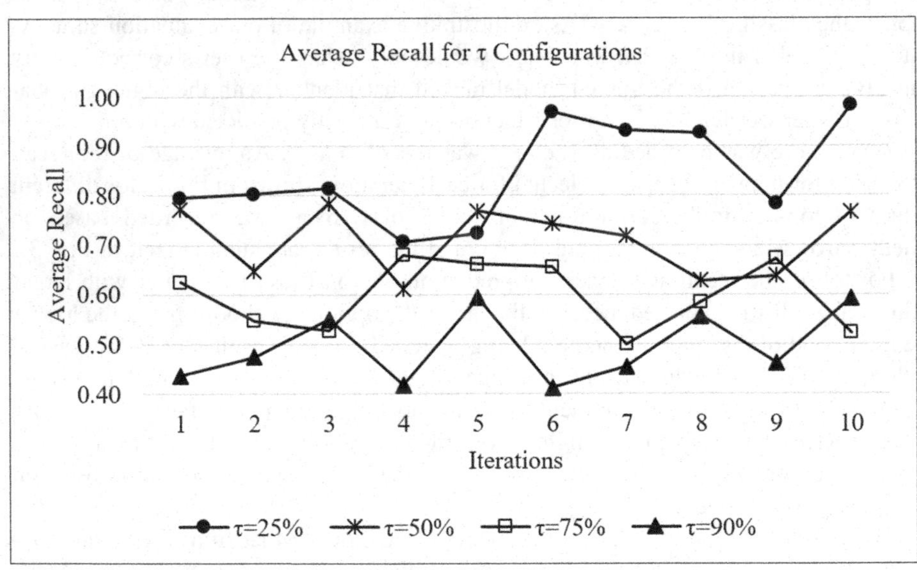

Fig. 3. Average recall for τ configurations

4.2 Effectiveness of TPP

To evaluate the effectiveness of TPP, we designed an online questionnaire-based survey. A total of 46 responses were recorded for the survey, and there were no specific user profile criteria for participation. The survey starts with displaying an arbitrarily selected question from the Quora database. Users are then asked to read the question, and then for the first input step, they are shown one of the answers for the question. Two versions of the answer are shown: one with the generic "anonymous" label, and the other with a TPP determined from level of expertise. Users are asked to select the answer format that they find more credible from the two choices; a binary comparative choice. In the second input step, users are shown a different answer to the question and asked to select if the answer is trustworthy or not; a binary affirmative yes/no selection. The user label for this step is either "anonymous" or TPP, so some users see the "anonymous" label while others are shown a TPP label based on level of expertise.

Figure 4 presents a summary of the results from step 1, showing the total number of labels presented over the course of the survey, the number of positive selections for each label, and the number of negative selections as well. At first glance, it may look like the "anonymous" label was selected as the majority but this is actually not the case. Relatively, the generic label was selected by 17 out of the 46 users, while 29 users selected one of the TPP labels. In the breakdown shown for TPP labels, negative selections imply the "anonymous" label was preferred. Likewise, for the "anonymous"

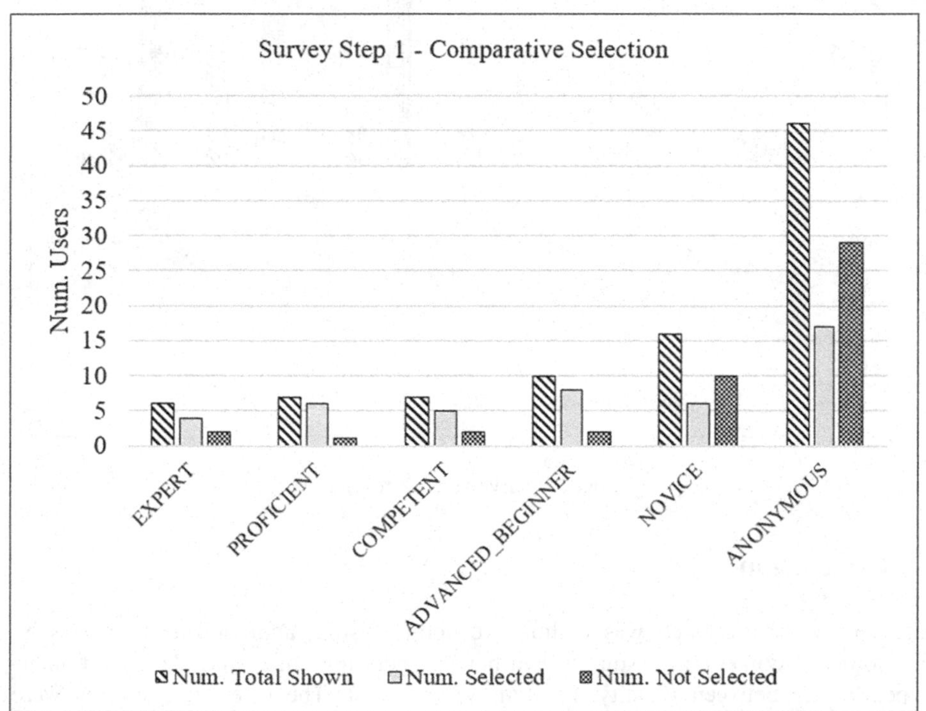

Fig. 4. Survey step 1 results

label, non-selection implies that one of the TPP labels were preferred. Further analysis reveals that out of the 17 selections, 10 were when the "novice" label was presented alongside with "anonymous". This might be due to the surveyors perceiving "novice" and "anonymous" being relatively similar in terms of trustworthiness.

Figure 5 shows the results of step 2 of the survey, displaying the total number of instances of the labels presented, the number of "yes" selections implying the label was trustworthy, and the number of "no" selections when surveyors disagreed with the labels conveying trustworthiness. The results show that when the "novice" label was used, the users were more likely to disagree with the label conveying trustworthiness. As with step 1, the users seemed equally likely to select between "anonymous" and "novice". For the questions showing the higher-level expertise labels, the users agreed in the majority with the label being correlated with trustworthiness. This can be seen in both steps 1 and 2, implying there was a general consensus within the sample population about the effectiveness of the TPP labels.

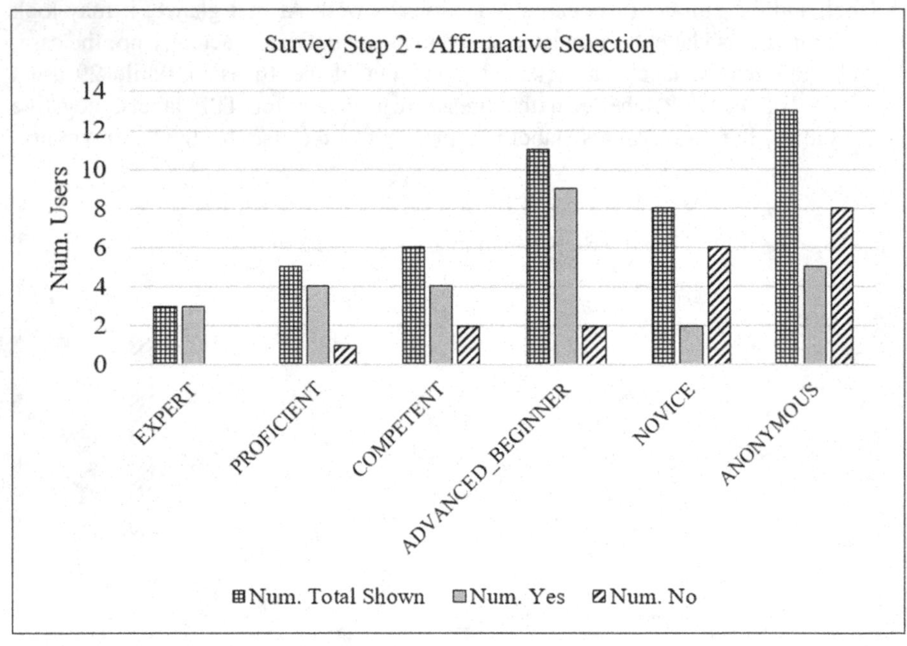

Fig. 5. Survey step 2 results

5 Conclusion

The aim of this research was to improve upon existing anonymization options by investigating content as a quasi-identifier. In addition, this study explored interdependencies between identity, anonymity, and trust. The research questions were motivated by the need to provide anonymity for avoiding social stigmatization when users discuss about sensitive topics. Our results provide a satisfactory baseline for concluding that content created by users can reveal their identity, evaluated via machine learning methods. Moreover, our proposed trust-preserving pseudonyms have shown potential for providing a balance between credibility and anonymity based on user surveys.

For future work, there is room for improvement in the evaluation of trust-preserving pseudonyms within real social networks. Furthermore, one potential drawback of the whiteprint identification evaluation is the *cold-start problem*, where newly registered users may not have enough data to be classified using the trained probabilistic model. In this case, the naïve approach is to use the default "anonymous" label. Additional exploration can be done regarding how much data is necessary to tackle the cold-start issue and maintain the effectiveness of Iron Mask and TPPs. In other words, one research question we intend to explore in future research is how much data is too little. Moreover, we plan to incorporate Iron Mask into a health social network under construction, code named Cardea, which allows patients and medics to communicate with each other online within specialized, secure, private, and trusted areas for patient-patient, patient-medic and medic-medic conversations. Within Cardea, users can also create support groups based on mutual topics of interest and develop hierarchical connections with other users. We also plan to investigate alternative machine learning approaches to authorship identification, such as clustering and deep neural networks. Another area of interest is the contextualization of credibility by topic, whereby users' level of expertise could be granularized to topical expertise.

Acknowledgements. The authors would like to thank the Alberta Machine Intelligence Institute (Amii) for funding this research. Amii is a research lab at the University of Alberta, Edmonton, Canada, working to enhance understanding and innovation in machine intelligence, existing at the intersection of machine learning and artificial intelligence.

References

1. Hansen, D.L., Johnson, C.: Veiled viral marketing: disseminating information on stigmatized illnesses via social networking sites. In: 2nd ACM SIGHIT International Health Informatics Symposium, pp. 247–254. ACM, Miami (2012)
2. White, M., Dorman, S.M.: Receiving social support online: implications for health education. Health Educ. Res. **16**(6), 693–707 (2001)
3. Frost, D.M.: Social stigma and its consequences for the socially stigmatized. Soc. Pers. Psychol. Compass **5**(11), 824–839 (2011)
4. Hong, Y., Patrick, T.B., Gillis, R.: Protection of patient's privacy and data security in e-health services. In: 1st International Conference on Biomedical Engineering and Informatics, pp. 643–647. IEEE, Sanya (2008)
5. Cofta, P.: Confidence, trust and identity. BT Technol. J. **25**(2), 173–178 (2007)
6. Child, J.: Trust - the fundamental bond in global collaboration. Org. Dyn. **29**(4), 274–288 (2001)

7. Dwork, C.: Differential privacy: a survey of results. In: Agrawal, M., Du, D., Duan, Z., Li, A. (eds.) TAMC 2008. LNCS, vol. 4978, pp. 1–19. Springer, Heidelberg (2008). doi:10.1007/978-3-540-79228-4_1
8. Narayanan, A., Shmatikov, V.: De-anonymizing social networks. In: 30th IEEE Symposium on Security and Privacy, pp. 173–187. IEEE Computer Society, Washington, DC (2009)
9. Beach, A., Gartrell, M., Han, R.: q-Anon: rethinking anonymity for social networks. In: 2nd International Conference on Social Computing, pp. 185–192. IEEE, Minneapolis (2010)
10. Milhail, S., Ilya, L.: Methodologies of internet portals users' short messages texts authorship identification based on the methods of mathematical linguistics. In: 8th International Conference on Application of Information and Communication Technologies, pp. 1–6. IEEE, Astana (2014)
11. Keretna, S., Hossny, A., Creighton, D.: Recognising user identity in Twitter social networks via text mining. In: International Conference on Systems, Man, and Cybernetics, pp. 3079–3082. IEEE Computer Society, Washington, DC (2013)
12. Johnson, A.M., Syverson, P., Dingledine, R., Mathewson, N.: Trust-based anonymous communication: adversary models and routing algorithms. In: 18th Conference on Computer and Communications Security, pp. 175–186. ACM, Chicago (2011)
13. Sassone, V., Hamadou, S., Yang, M.: Trust in anonymity networks. In: Gastin, P., Laroussinie, F. (eds.) CONCUR 2010. LNCS, vol. 6269, pp. 48–70. Springer, Heidelberg (2010). doi:10.1007/978-3-642-15375-4_5
14. Maurer, F.K.: A survey on approaches to anonymity in bitcoin and other cryptocurrencies. In: Mayr, H.C., Pinzger, M. (eds.) INFORMATIK 2016. LNI, vol. 259, pp. 2145–2150. Gesellschaft für Informatik, Bonn (2016)
15. Bernstein, M.S., Monroy-Hernández, A., Harry, D., André, P., Panovich, K., Vargas, G.G.: 4chan and /b/: an analysis of anonymity and ephemerality in a large online community. In: 5th International Conference on Weblogs and Social Media, pp. 50–57. AAAI, Barcelona (2011)
16. Taskar, B., Segal, E., Koller, D.: Probabilistic classification and clustering in relational data. In: International Joint Conference on Artificial Intelligence, pp. 870–878. Lawrence Erlbaum Associates Ltd., Seattle (2001)
17. Zadrozny, B., Elkan, C.: Transforming classifier scores into accurate multiclass probability estimates. In: 8th International Conference on Knowledge Discovery and Data Mining, pp. 694–699. ACM, New York (2002)
18. Pedregosa, F., Varoquaux, G., Gramfort, A., Michel, V., Thirion, B., Grisel, O., Blondel, M., Prettenhofer, P., Weiss, R., Dubourg, V., Vanderplas, J., Passos, A., Cournapeau, D., Brucher, M., Perrot, M., Duchesnay, E.: Scikit-learn: machine learning in python. J. Mach. Learn. Res. **12**, 2825–2830 (2011)
19. Kameya, Y., Hayashi, K.: Bottom-up cell suppression that preserves the missing-at-random condition. In: Katsikas, S., Lambrinoudakis, C., Furnell, S. (eds.) TrustBus 2016. LNCS, vol. 9830, pp. 65–78. Springer, Cham (2016). doi:10.1007/978-3-319-44341-6_5
20. Dreyfus, S.E., Dreyfus, H.L.: A five-stage model of the mental activities involved in directed skill acquisition. California University Berkeley Operations Research Center (1980)

Modelling Metrics for Transparency in Medical Systems

Dayana Spagnuelo(✉), Cesare Bartolini, and Gabriele Lenzini

Interdisciplinary Centre for Security Reliability and Trust (SnT), University of Luxembourg, Luxembourg, Luxembourg
dayana.spagnuelo@uni.lu

Abstract. Transparency, a principle advocated by the General Data Protection Regulation, is usually defined in terms of properties such as availability, auditability and accountability and for this reason it is not straightforwardly measurable. In requirement engineering, measuring a quality is usually implemented by defining a set of metrics for its composing properties, but conventional approaches offer little help to achieve this task for transparency. We therefore review requirements for availability, auditability and accountability and, with the help of a meta-model used to describe non-functional properties, we discuss and advance a set of metrics for them. What emerges from this study is a better justified and comprehensive tool which we apply to measure the level of transparency in medical data-sharing systems.

Keywords: Transparency · Metrics · Availability · Auditability · Accountability

1 Introduction

Transparency is a principle that can be embraced to prove honesty and therefore trustworthiness. Applied in distributed data management systems, such as cloud computing, electronic banking, or medical data-sharing, transparency is also a strategic element in business. Personal data are an asset [16,17] and the data providers which monetise on them may suffer the mistrust of data subjects (e.g., users, clients, patients) who, aware of the risks to expose personal information [8], can be reluctant to consent to the processing of their personal data. Transparency here can help build and preserve trust: providers that offer detailed information about their policies and practices, express them in a clear and readable manner, and have easily-accessible documents and histories of processing operations, will also have a better chance to gain their client's trust and stay in business.

There are also other reasons to implement transparency. The importance of being transparent has being spurred by the recent legal reform on data protection

D. Spagnuelo—Supported by FNR/AFR project 7842804 TYPAMED.

J. Lopez et al. (Eds.): TrustBus 2017, LNCS 10442, pp. 81–95, 2017.
DOI: 10.1007/978-3-319-64483-7_6

in the European Union[1]. In this context, transparency is intended to guarantee that the systems are processing personal data in a lawful and fair manner.

But how can transparency be modelled and implemented, and how to measure the amount of transparency that a system is able to guarantee?

The problem of *modelling and implementing transparency* in terms of a Requirements Engineering (RE) approach has been already explored [4,20]. Transparency is described as a Non-Functional Requirement (NFR) that offers some degree of monitoring over the systems by providing the users with *information* and *mechanisms*. Both intended to impart knowledge on how the user's data has been or will be processed.

The problem of *measuring transparency* can also be tackled by following a RE approach. Assuming that transparency is translated into a set of specific requirements, measuring transparency means defining *metrics* to evaluate to what degree the requirements are met in a system. This is exactly what this paper does, specifically focusing on the domain of medical data-sharing systems.

Medical data are very sensitive data and are subject to exceptional protection measures[2]. Even though transparency is not meant to provide such measures, it allows the patients to verify that the system is taking or has taken the necessary precautions to protect their privacy.

Metrics for transparency in the medical domain have been studied in the past [19]. Those metrics are tailored to measure aspects of the information and mechanisms provided to endow a given system with transparency. However, the number of metrics proposed is heavily uneven: out of a total of eight metrics, only two were proposed for mechanisms, with one being shared with information. This might be due to fact that the methodology used to compose the set of metrics was not tailored to transparency and oversaw some aspects of it.

This is the motivation for this work. It aims at further investigating the problem of modelling transparency and defining metrics. We do so by adopting a methodology presented in [6], which proposes a meta-model to define metrics for NFRs in cloud computing. In here we slightly adapted this model to make it better represent the peculiarities of transparency in medical systems. This work completes our previous research [19]: here we propose a Model-Driven Engineeing (MDE) representation of the requirements, and on that representation we clarify and extend the metrics for transparency.

The remaining of this work is structured as follows: Sect. 2 presents the literature related to this work. In Sect. 3 the details about transparency, its requirements and metrics are described. In Sect. 4 the high-level components of the model for transparency are explained, while Sects. 5 and 6 present the components focusing in the sub-properties of transparency. Finally, Sect. 7 concludes this work and presents future research directions.

[1] Regulation (EU) 2016/679 of the European Parliament and of the Council of 27 April 2016 on the protection of natural persons with regard to the processing of personal data and on the free movement of such data, and repealing Directive 95/46/EC (General Data Protection Regulation). See in particular Article 5.1(a).

[2] *Ibid.*, Art. 9.

2 Related Works

Transparency is a multi-faceted non-functional property. In the context of medical systems it is defined in terms of *availability*, *auditability*, *accountability* and *verifiability* [20]. Availability is discussed as a property that ensures the users are able to obtain and use information related to their personal data whenever needed. Auditability is the property that allows users to verify what happened to their personal data. Accountability enables users to monitor the usage of their data and hold a person accountable in case of misuse. Auditability and accountability are related to verifiability: the first is equivalent to it when applied to personal data, while the second is a more specific interpretation of verifiability.

The multi-faceted structure that characterizes transparency poses challenges to model and measure it. Conventional modelling and measuring approaches are not suited to represent its peculiarities, and methodologies focused on transparency, to the best of our knowledge, only cover part of the problem. A model for transparency, for example, has been proposed in [12]. The authors propose a model for representing transparency requirements and their relationship with other requirements, and extend an existing methodology to encompass the identification and validation of those requirements. Even though this work presents a valid approach for modelling transparency requirements, it does not consider the problem of measuring the quality of its implementation.

However, there are other relevant works on the properties composing transparency. Accountability, for example, has been systematically analysed [6] proposing a UML meta-model for defining metrics. This model helps reasoning on complex properties, structuring them into more basic ones whose metrics are simpler to define. Though designed with the purpose of measuring accountability, the model is not strictly tailored for it and can be generalised for other properties.

There are other works proposing approaches to express requirements based on MDE techniques (e.g., [2,5]). However, with respect to the previously-mentioned work on accountability, these meta-models seemed less fit to model transparency.

Metrics for transparency have also been studied from the point of view of RE. In [19] metrics are proposed to measure the quality of a transparent implementation. That work defines the qualities a transparent system should present: *informativeness*, *understandability*, *accessibility* and *validity*. Those qualities are later decomposed into eight sub-qualities, each associated with a metric to measure it. The metrics produce normalised results (ranging from 0 to 1, where 0 is the worst grade and 1 is the best). The interpretation proposed by [19] is similar to the benchmarking strategy, in which each metric is an indicator of the degree to which the properties that compose transparency are present. The metrics indicate the possibility for improvement of each property and, therefore, guide a better implementation of transparent systems.

Here, by reviewing the meta-model proposed in [6] for transparency we validate those previous metrics and we enrich them giving a more solid, model-driven, justification.

3 On Transparency Requirements and Metrics

As mentioned in Sect. 2, a previous work [20] classifies transparency according to RE techniques. The classification operates under two separate viewpoints. On one side, a macroscopic classification defines the relationship between transparency and other related properties. The diagram in Fig. 1 shows a visual description of this classification, pointing out how transparency is composed by the other properties (displayed as blocks).

On the other side, transparency and its sub-properties were partitioned identifying the essential requirements, extending upon previous literature [4]. These properties have been decomposed into a total of thirty-six technical requirements [20] that indicate what a medical system should do to be deemed transparent. Each of these requirements encourages the system governance to share relevant bits of knowledge about the stored data with the respective users.

This can be accomplished either by providing the users with general *information* (all kinds of "communication or reception of knowledge or intelligence"[3]) regarding the usage of data, policies and regulations, the system practices, or extraordinary events; or by offering the users *mechanisms*, that are instruments with which the user can perform operations on the data stored in the system, such as filter, select, digest, or process them, in support to some conclusion that he or she intends to take. Figure 1 outlines how the previously-mentioned properties relates to information (area in blue) and mechanisms (area in green).

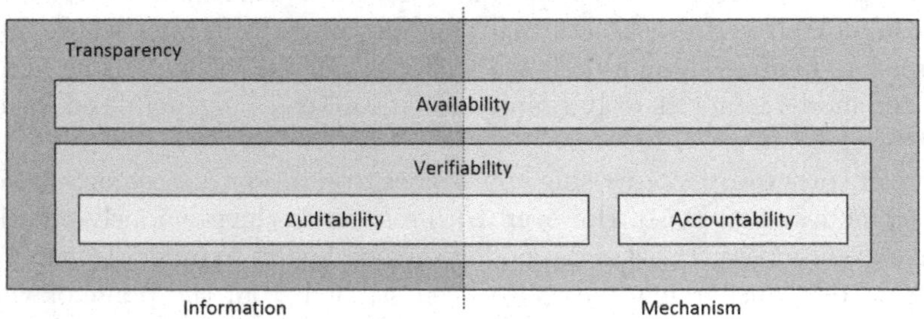

Fig. 1. Transparency and its relations with other properties. (Color figure online)

To measure the compliance with these requirements, [19] defines eight metrics, each relating to a specific quality of the properties: *accuracy, currentness, conciseness, detailing, readability, portability, reachability*[4] and *effectiveness.* The metrics apply according to the features of each requirement. Those requirements that mandate the system to inform the user about its practices are easier to measure, and share the first seven metrics. Requirements that mandate the

[3] Definition extracted from the Merriam-Webster Dictionary.

[4] Reachability was originally presented as *availability* in [19]. Here it has been renamed to avoid confusion with the transparency sub-property availability.

system to provide a mechanism to the users are measured only by the last two metrics, with *reachability* being shared among the two families of requirements.

4 Modelling Transparency Properties and Metrics

For the sake of simplicity, transparency is discussed and modelled with regard to five requirements, specifically the ones shown in the excerpt contained in Table 1. Even though this set may seem small, the requirements were carefully selected. Examples of each type of information-based and mechanism-based requirements, and the relevant characteristic for selecting metrics, are shown. The first three requirements demonstrate how to attain to the transparency sub-property of *availability* by providing *information* (AV.1–3), while the last two entail a *mechanism* for the transparency sub-properties of *auditability* (AU.1) and *accountability* (AC.1) respectively.

Table 1. Excerpt from the transparency requirements.

ID	Description
AV.1	The system must inform the user about who is responsible for handling owned data
AV.2	The system must inform the user on how to protect data or how data are protected
AV.3	The system must notify the user in case the policy is overridden (break the glass)
AU.1	The system must provide the user with audit mechanisms
AC.1	The system must provide the user with accountability mechanisms

Hereby two models explore and define the metrics for transparency and its requirements. These models also help understand the relationship between the different elements and facets of transparency (see Figs. 2 and 3). Details that are not immediately needed to model and validate transparency and its metrics, the goal of this work, are not shown.

The original meta-model [6] presents several elements: *Property*, *BaseProperty* and *CompoundProperty*, the objects of study; *Goal*, the high-level description of the property; *Entity*, responsible for realising the property; *Action*, representing what is executed by, or has an effect on, the entity; *Evidence* and *EvidenceProcessing*, the tangible and observable elements of the property; *Criterion*, a constraint to what should be measured; and *Metric*, *BaseMetric* and *CompoundMetric*, the methods that measures the property.

In the meta-model, the process responsible for collecting and processing the evidence is as important as the evidence itself. Hence, another evidence is proposed in association with each process to explain how it works. We slightly adapt this in our work. We accept a requirement may be implemented in several different ways, depending on the business model of each system. However, regardless of the actual implementation, the bottom line is that the user must be able to observe the evidence in the system. This approach is alike to the software engineering technique of black-box testing, whose purpose is to test a piece of software in the absence of any knowledge of its internal structure, and based solely on the observation of its inputs and outputs [3]. Since this approach was not completely aligned to what is defined in the original meta-model [6], we slightly adapted it. This is referred throughout this paper as the "black-box approach" and is further explained in Sects. 5 and 6.

In the following we present how the elements proposed in the original meta-model are interpreted and adapted to transparency in medical systems. We first present the elements common to the two models (elements in yellow), and later, in Sects. 5 and 6, we present the remaining ones (elements in blue).

Properties. The central component of these models is the *Property*, which represents what is being described. We put *Transparency* as the central property. Its composing sub-properties *Availability*, *Auditability*, *Accountability* and *Verifiability*, are represented by elements inheriting from *BaseProperty*.

In addition to transparency, two other properties are presented in this model: *Privacy* and *Usability*. They have been introduced as secondary properties that influence and need to be considered in order to provide a fair transparency. However, even in a condition of very low privacy and usability, the system may not fail to be transparent. The two properties are, therefore, not analysed in the perspective of defining metrics. This viewpoint is in accordance to what has been proposed in the literature [20], which provides more details about the relationship between those properties and transparency.

Entity and Action. The properties are realised by the *Entity* element. An entity also performs or is affected by an *Action* that happens over a period of time. As transparency aims at sharing knowledge with users about how a system processes their personal data, and the system is managed by a data controller, *DataController* and *Processing* components are used.

Goal. The *Goal* is the component that provides a high-level description of the purpose for which the property is being modelled, and contains a reference to the stakeholder for which the goal is oriented. The proposed model does not adopt a goal to leave the possibility of exploring all the possible facets of transparency. This element might be defined at a later stage, when applying the model to a specific scenario, in order to select the transparency requirements deemed relevant to achieve a given goal, and the metrics suited to measure them.

Criterion. Any constraint that may refine the aspects of the property that should be measured is modelled by the *Criterion* component. This includes regulations, guides, stakeholders' preferences and the alike. As the current work is focused on the requirements for transparency, they were composed considering the regulations and standards for data protection, and especially those relevant to medical systems. Any other constrain are not regarded in the model as they are beyond the scope of this work. This component is associated with the goal and, therefore, should be modelled together with it when needed.

5 Availability

The model presented in Fig. 2 describes the three requirements of availability (AV.1–3). These requirements are all information-based and were selected in a way to represent every possible evidence. Because of that, Fig. 2 also hints how a model of any other information-based requirement would look like.

5.1 Evidences and Evidence Processing

The characteristics of each requirement are represented by the *Evidence*. It captures the elements a user can observe with respect to the property of interest.

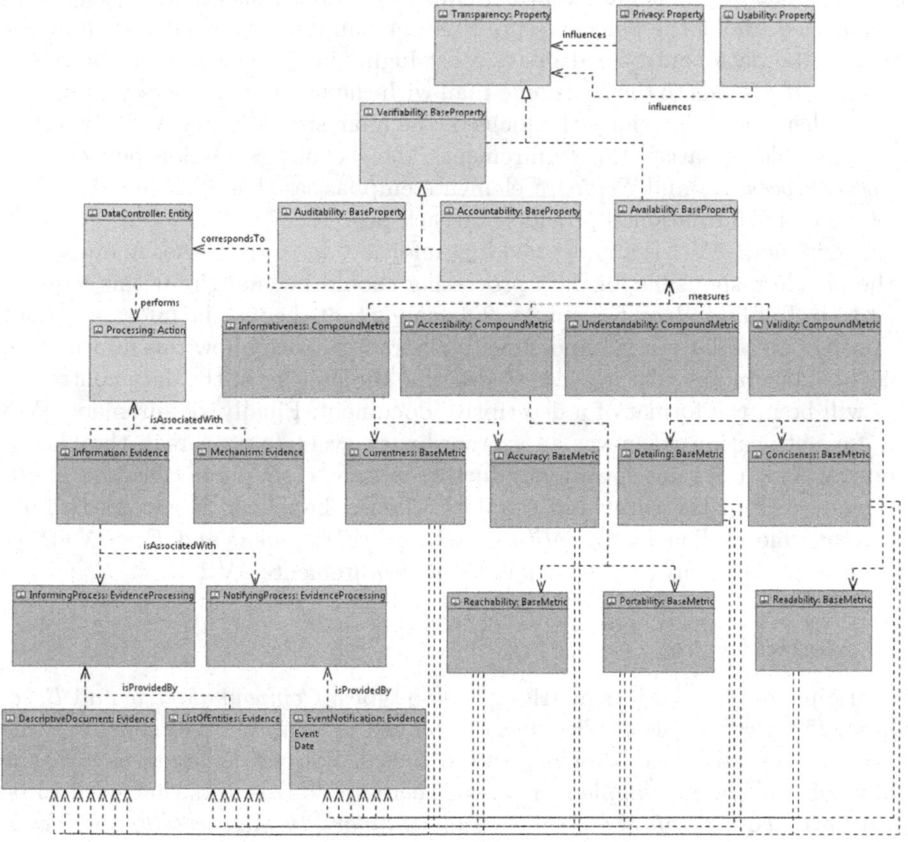

Fig. 2. Model of availability requirements.

Transparency is a high-level concept, difficult to observe and measure. However, whenever the requirements for transparency are properly implemented (and therefore transparency is as well), the users must have access to pieces of information regarding the processing of their personal data. In other words, a sufficient amount of information provided to the user is a concrete indication that a system is actually transparent. Consequently, in this model, the *Information* component is the evidence associated with the *Processing* action.

The *EvidenceProcessing* component helps modelling the fact that the evidence, although associated with the action performed by the entity, is not produced by it. In the current model, *Information* is evidence of the fact that the *Action* of data processing is undergoing, but it is generated by other processes, which are solely responsible for informing and notifying the user. These processes are represented by the *InformingProcess* and *NotifyingProcess* elements.

According to the black-box approach described in Sect. 4, the analysis is centred on the evidence itself, rather than the process that collects the evidence. For example, in the requirement AV.1, "The system must inform the user about who is responsible for handling owned data", the important aspect is that users are informed about the person responsible for handling their data. It does not matter if the data controller displays a list highlighting each responsible in the system, or if it sends to the users an e-mail with the name of the person in charge of his or her data. Therefore, the focus of the analysis is on how well this information is able to satisfy the requirement. The second association between the *EvidenceProcessing* and *Evidence* elements emphasises this, it better describes what type of information is provided by each process.

Requirement AV.1 is about providing information to the users. A simple list of the people responsible for data processing should be enough for this requirement to be fulfilled. Requirement AV.2 demands that the user be informed about the protection of data. It is impossible to abstractly specify how this information looks like, but in any case it needs to describe the policies of the data controller, so it will be in the format of a descriptive document. Finally, requirement AV.3 asks for notification whenever an extraordinary event (e.g., "break the glass") happens. As it does not specify any further details, a simple notification about the occurrence of the event and the date when it happened is enough to fulfil this requirement. The *ListOfEntities*, *DescriptiveDocument* and *EventNotification* components represent the evidences in requirements AV.1–3.

5.2 Metrics

The original model classifies metrics into two types: *CompoundMetric* and *BaseMetric*. The first models metrics that are defined in terms of other metrics, while the second actually uses the evidences for the calculations. When measuring the quality of transparency implementations, there are four factors that need to be taken into account: *Informativeness*, *Understandability*, *Accessibility* and *Validity* [19]. The four factors are represented as compound metrics in this work. Whenever the data controller declares to have provided some kind of information to the users, that information is expected to have the following features:

1. to convey the precise knowledge (informativeness); 2. a comprehensible meaning (understandability); 3. the users must be able to easily obtain it (accessibility). Validity is a quality that only concerns mechanisms for transparency, and it is about their precision and correctness of their results. Validity is presented in this model to depict the entire scenario, but will be better explored in Sect. 6.

Previous works [19] have defined seven metrics (represented in this model) to measure the quality of information-based requirements. *Accuracy* and *Currentness* are related to the informativeness of the evidence. *Conciseness*, *Detailing* and *Readability* concern the understandability of the evidence. Finally, *Reachability* and *Portability* refer to the accessibility of the evidence. These metrics, and a short description for each, are summarised in Table 2.

Table 2. Metrics for information-based requirements.

Metric	Compound	Description
Accuracy	Informativ.	How much the information matches the real process of the system
Currentness	Informativ.	How timely is the information
Conciseness	Understand.	How straightforward is the information
Detailing	Understand.	Whether the information is detailed enough for the general understanding of its subject
Readability	Understand.	How easy it is for a user to read and understand a text
Reachability	Accessibility	How easy it is for a user to reach the information
Portability	Accessibility	How easy it is to transfer and use an information in different systems

By highlighting the specific pieces of evidence that are used to model transparency and its sub-properties, it is possible to refine the metrics and define which ones are suitable to be applied to each type of information. In particular, *Accuracy*, as a metric intended to compare statements about the data controller process and intentions to its actual practice, is not suitable for measuring events notification. That is because the events are considered as extraordinary occurrences, such as overriding an access control policy, or a security breach. Since they are unexpected, the user might not find any further information apart from the mere notification to compare them against. *Conciseness* and *Readability* are also not suitable for application to all kinds of information. The reason is that these metrics operate on a piece of information in the form of a text made up of sentences. As such, evidence in other forms, e.g., a list, might not be evaluated using those metrics. Apart from these, the other metrics remain applicable to all kinds of information-based evidences.

6 Auditability and Accountability

The model in Fig. 3 describes the requirements for Auditability and Accountability (AU.1 and AC.1 respectively). These requirements are highly representative

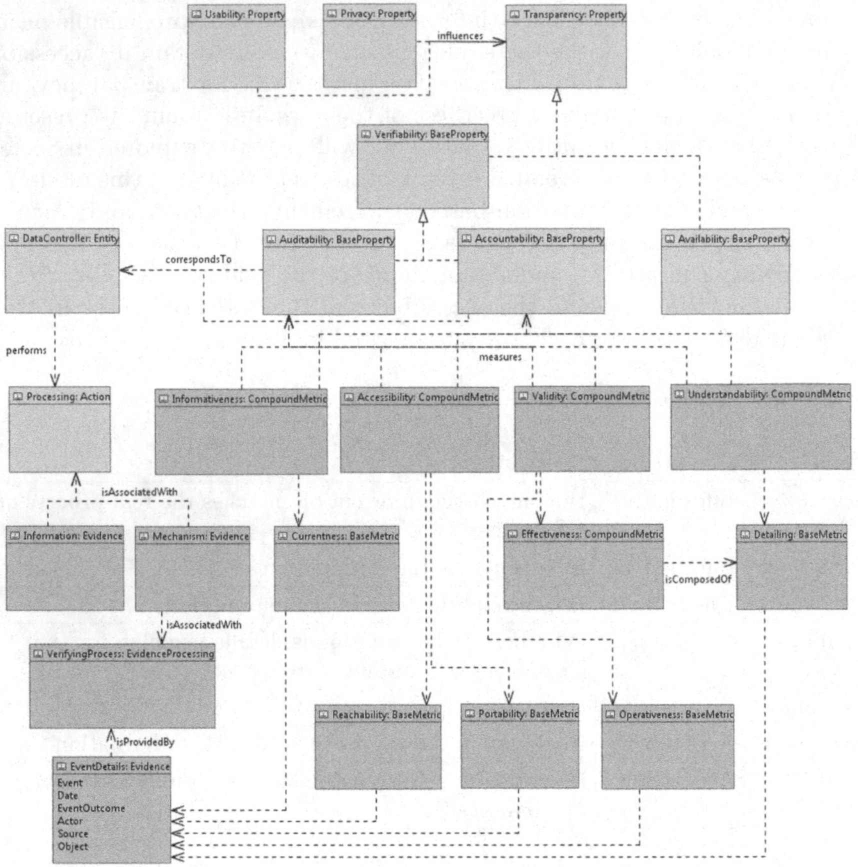

Fig. 3. Model of auditability and accountability requirements.

for the mechanism-based family: all evidence is represented therein and, we think, any other mechanism-based requirements can be modelled in a similar way. Since the model overlaps with that depicted in Sect. 5 we will discuss only the part that is new.

6.1 Evidences and Evidence Processing

Using an argument similar to that we used in Sect. 5, a system that complies with AU.1 and AC.1 must give users access to some sort of mechanism to verify how their data have been processed. In the model, this is represented by the evidence component *Mechanism*, and by the associated evidence processing component *VerifyingProcess.*

In the domain of medical systems, auditability and accountability are commonly interpreted as properties about access control (e.g., [7,10,22]). As such, they allow the users to monitor how and by whom their data has been accessed, used, and modified[5]. The concepts of "access", "usage" and "modification" are interpreted in this work as the basic actions for persistent storage: CRUD (create, read, update and delete). In the following, auditability and accountability will be regarded as mechanisms with respect to those actions.

As each requirement may be implemented in several different ways, depending on the business model of the system implementing it, the analysis is based on the evidence they produce (as explained in Sect. 4). The question, then, is how the evidence of auditability and accountability mechanisms should be structured.

RFC 3881 [11] defines the format and minimum attributes that need to be captured in order to provide auditability and accountability for health systems. This document describes the data to be collected for four different events, among which patient's data events. It states that the system should document "what was done, by whom, using which resources, from what access points, and to whose medical data". On this basis, the mechanism's output should contain the following event details: 1. event identification: description of the action performed; 2. date and time; 3. event outcome: whether it was successful or not; 4. actor identification: who performed the event; 5. source: details from where the event was performed (user interface, application, etc.); 6. object identification: the data that suffered the actions. These details are abstracted in our model by the evidence component *EventDetails*.

6.2 Metrics

In the previous literature [20], only two metrics were defined to measure mechanisms-based requirements: *Effectiveness* (how satisfactory the mechanisms is by checking whether or not its goal has been reached) and *Reachability* (how easy it is for the users to reach the mechanism). The new perspective of this work resulted in the definition of one new metric and the redefinition of four other. Table 3 summarises the result of this analysis. Apart from the new metric defined, the other four are not going to be thoroughly discussed here, as they were analysed in due detail in a previous work [20].

Table 3. Metrics for mechanism-based requirements.

Metric	Compound	Description
Reachability	Accessibility	How easy it is for a user to reach the mechanism
Portability	Accessibility	How easy it is to transfer/use the mechanism output in different systems
Currentness	Informativ.	How up-to-date is the mechanism
Effectiveness	Validity	How satisfactory is the mechanism provided
Operativeness	Validity	Whether the mechanism functions and produces an appropriate effect

[5] The interpretation adopted here also seems to be the one followed by ISO/TS 18308:2004. See in particular Sect. 5.4.6 [9].

Reachability. This metric has been defined in the previous work [20] as a function of the number of interaction necessary to reach the mechanism, but no strategy was presented to help the evaluator identify a mechanism. That was a weakness as many possible implementation are acceptable. In this work, a mechanism is considered in place whenever users can reach its output, even if a tool or plug-in is not visible to them. As such, the reachability of the mechanism has been redefined. It is measured with the same function as the previous metric, but instead it considers the number of interactions until its output is reached. The metric is represented in the model by the *Reachability* base metric.

Portability and Currentness. The same reasoning applies to portability and currentness. They were originally conceived to measure the quality of information, but with the new black-box approach it is possible to apply them to the mechanism by considering its output. These metrics measure to which extent the mechanism provides information that could be easily used in other systems, and how up-to-date it is. They are represented in the model by the *Portability* and *Currentness* base metrics.

Effectiveness. This metric is also being redefined here with respect to the previous work [20]. It was originally considered as a base metric that evaluated whether the mechanism was providing the expected result. By decomposing the mechanism into evidences, effectiveness can be defined in terms of the output. The new metric partly overlaps with the previously-defined *Detailing* metric. In other words, a mechanism is effective if the output it provides contains enough details to understand whether and by whom the personal data has been accessed and used (i.e., the goal of the mechanisms in requirements AU.1 and AC.1). As a consequence, in the new model *Effectiveness* is a compound metric element by the *Detailing* base metric.

Operativeness. Something is said to be operative if it is functioning and "producing an appropriate effect"[6]. This metric proposes a strategy for defining whether or not a mechanism is operative. It is inspired by the black-box tests of the audit type [18] and uses the technique of equivalence partitioning [14]. It consists in partitioning the input domain of a mechanism into equivalence classes, in such a way that it is reasonable to assume that testing a value in a given class is equivalent to testing any other value in the same class. In this context, the equivalence classes are based on the actions executed in the system that a mechanism should process, and the test consists on executing these actions and observing the output to verify if they were processed by the mechanism.

For requirements AU.1 and AC.1, a reasonable set of equivalence classes can be the CRUD actions. This set of equivalence classes can be expressed as $E = C \cup R \cup U \cup D$, the union of all possible actions, where C contains create actions, R contains read actions, and so on. Measuring the operativeness metric requires to select a sub-set of actions $A = \{a_0, a_1, \ldots, a_{k-1}\} : (A \subseteq E)$, that contains at least one action of each equivalence class (i.e., $(A \cap C \neq \emptyset) \wedge (A \cap R \neq \emptyset) \wedge (A \cap U \neq \emptyset) \wedge (A \cap D \neq \emptyset))$ and test it. The test consists in verifying if

[6] Definition extracted from the Merriam-Webster Dictionary.

the actions were correctly processed and reported in the mechanism's output. If one action is not reported, or it is not possible to verify (e.g., deceptive or inconsistent information provided as output), the entire test fails. In particular, if the set of actions A contains k actions, and the number of actions that can be verified is represented by n, the result of test $\mathcal{T}_A$ can be expressed as shown in Eq. (1). The result of the operativeness metric $\mathcal{O}$ is the tuple of all actions tested and the result of the test, as shown in Eq. (2). This metric is represented in the model with the *Operativeness* base metric element.

$$\mathcal{T}_A = \lfloor n/k \rfloor \tag{1}$$

$$\mathcal{O} = (A, \mathcal{T}_A) \tag{2}$$

The operativeness metric presents a strategy to rationally reason about a mechanism's functioning, without delving into subjective aspects, such as whether or not the mechanism's output conveys satisfactory knowledge. This metric is conservative, meaning that it considers that one counter-example is enough to show that a mechanism is not properly functioning (this is represented by the floor function in Eq. (1)). The output of 1 can be interpreted as an indication that the mechanism has performed as expected, supporting and inspiring a sense of confidence. Although, it must be noted that the operativeness of a mechanism is always measured with regard to one specific set of actions (here represented by A). Its result is therefore always accompanied by the set of actions tested, lest the result be meaningless and the test not be replicable. Each equivalence class should be measured, so it is necessary to select at least one action from each of those. If it is not possible to select one action from a particular class, it means that it is not possible to verify that class, and the test should be considered unsuccessful. The metric is flexible and allows the evaluator to decide how to couple the actions into classes, so it is possible to decide on the granularity of the test. The most suitable equivalence classes and granularity strictly depend on the peculiarities of the system implementing the mechanism. Discussing what classes can be the most appropriate for a specific system, is outside the scope of this work.

7 Discussion and Conclusions

This paper proposes a MDE approach to the transparency of a system, introducing a UML model for transparency and its metrics based on a meta-model previously used in RE. The model unfolds transparency into basic and concrete elements, much easier to measure than the high-level property of transparency itself. Through the use of this model, metrics for transparency undergo a significant uplift, with a refinement of those already defined and the introduction of new ones, and with the evidence at the centre of the analysis. By regarding accountability as one of the building blocks for transparency, the meta-model (which was tailored to model accountability) is applicable to the domain of transparency in general.

This work contributes to the understanding of transparency. It sheds a light on how to decide if a solution is in compliance with the data protection regulation and the dramatic changes it will bring about when it finally becomes applicable, on 25 May 2018[7]; it does so by improving and extending the set of metrics that can be used to measure transparency.

Previously, the transparency analysis comprehensively embraced the information-based requirements, but it fell severely short on the mechanisms. The MDE approach presented in this paper allows to fill in that gap. The methodology clarifies that the implementation of transparency mechanisms is not so much relevant as the output they deliver to the users. Under this new perspective, it is possible to gather how well implemented a transparency mechanism is by looking at its output. Three new metrics were defined and adapted for mechanism-based requirements, and the two already-existing ones were fine-tuned.

A future research direction that stretches along the line of this work is to define a methodology to assess the trustworthiness of the transparency mechanism. Trustworthiness has several interpretations, but one that seems to be well accepted is that it is related to the assurance the system will perform as expected (e.g., [1,13,15]). In this sense, trustworthiness can be presented as a more complex metric that builds on top of the operativeness metric, using a well defined methodology to select the actions tested in that metric. Such a methodology, when implemented in a simple and streamlined software tool, could be independently run by any user with access to the transparency mechanisms, providing grounds to reinforce the trust framework of the system.

This work also calls for some development on the technical side. The models introduced herein could be implemented using some modelling support tool and meta-model such as Ecore [21] or some other formalism that integrates seamlessly with the formalism used in software engineering tools. By integrating transparency requirements into tools used in software engineering, such tools would allow to design and develop software services addressing transparency throughout all the software development life-cycle.

References

1. Alhadad, N., Serrano-Alvarado, P., Busnel, Y., Lamarre, P.: Trust evaluation of a system for an activity. In: Furnell, S., Lambrinoudakis, C., Lopez, J. (eds.) TrustBus 2013. LNCS, vol. 8058, pp. 24–36. Springer, Heidelberg (2013). doi:10.1007/978-3-642-40343-9_3
2. Baudry, B., Nebut, C., Le Traon, Y.: Model-driven engineering for requirements analysis. In: Proceedings of the 11th IEEE International Enterprise Distributed Object Computing Conference, pp. 459–466. IEEE (2007)
3. Beizer, B.: Black-box Testing: Techniques for Functional Testing of Software and Systems. Wiley, Hoboken (1995)
4. Cruzes, D.S., Jaatun, M.G.: Cloud provider transparency: a view from cloud customers. In: 5th International Conference on Cloud Computing and Services Science, pp. 30–39 (2015)

[7] Regulation (EU) 679/2016, Article 99.2.

5. Denger, C., Berry, D.M., Kamsties, E.: Higher quality requirements specifications through natural language patterns. In: Proceedings of the IEEE International Conference on Software: Science, Technology and Engineering, pp. 80–90. IEEE (2003)
6. Fernández-Gago, C., Nuñez, D.: Metrics for accountability in the cloud. In: Felici, M., Fernández-Gago, C. (eds.) A4Cloud 2014. LNCS, vol. 8937, pp. 129–153. Springer, Cham (2015). doi:10.1007/978-3-319-17199-9_6
7. Flores, A.E., Vergara, V.M.: Functionalities of open electronic health records system: a follow-up study. In: 6th International Conference on Biomedical Engineering and Informatics, pp. 602–607. IEEE (2013)
8. Hildebrandt, M.: Defining profiling: a new type of knowledge? In: Hildebrandt, M., Gutwirth, S. (eds.) Profiling the European Citizen, pp. 17–45. Springer, Dordrecht (2008). doi:10.1007/978-1-4020-6914-7_2
9. International Organization for Standardization: ISO/TS 18308: 2004 Health informatics - Requirements for an electronic health record architecture (2004)
10. King, J.T., Smith, B., Williams, L.: Modifying without a trace: general audit guidelines are inadequate for open-source electronic health record audit mechanisms. In: Proceedings of the 2nd ACM SIGHIT International Health Informatics Symposium, pp. 305–314. ACM (2012)
11. Marshall, G.: RFC 3881 - Security Audit and Access Accountability Message XML Data Definitions for Healthcare Applications. Request for comments, Internet Engineering Task Force (IETF) (2004)
12. Meis, R., Heisel, M.: Computer-aided identification and validation of intervenability requirements. Information **8**(1), 30 (2017)
13. Mohammadi, N.G., Heisel, M.: A framework for systematic analysis and modeling of trustworthiness requirements using i* and BPMN. In: Katsikas, S., Lambrinoudakis, C., Furnell, S. (eds.) TrustBus 2016. LNCS, vol. 9830, pp. 3–18. Springer, Cham (2016). doi:10.1007/978-3-319-44341-6_1
14. Myers, G.J., Sandler, C., Badgett, T.: The Art of Software Testing. Wiley, Hoboken (2011)
15. Pavlidis, M., Mouratidis, H., Kalloniatis, C., Islam, S., Gritzalis, S.: Trustworthy selection of cloud providers based on security and privacy requirements: justifying trust assumptions. In: Furnell, S., Lambrinoudakis, C., Lopez, J. (eds.) TrustBus 2013. LNCS, vol. 8058, pp. 185–198. Springer, Heidelberg (2013). doi:10.1007/978-3-642-40343-9_16
16. Schwab, K., Marcus, A., Oyola, J.O., Hoffman, W., Luzi, M.: Personal data: the emergence of a new asset class (2011). https://www.weforum.org/reports/personal-data-emergence-new-asset-class. Accessed Apr 2017
17. Schwartz, P.M.: Property, privacy, and personal data. Harvard Law Review **117**(7), 2056–2128 (2004)
18. Smith, B.: Systematizing security test case planning using functional requirements phrases. In: Proceedings of the 33rd International Conference on Software Engineering, pp. 1136–1137. ACM (2011)
19. Spagnuelo, D., Bartolini, C., Lenzini, G.: Metrics for transparency. In: Livraga, G., Torra, V., Aldini, A., Martinelli, F., Suri, N. (eds.) DPM/QASA -2016. LNCS, vol. 9963, pp. 3–18. Springer, Cham (2016). doi:10.1007/978-3-319-47072-6_1
20. Spagnuelo, D., Lenzini, G.: Transparent medical data systems. J. Med. Syst. **41**(1), 8 (2016)
21. Steinberg, D., Budinsky, F., Paternostro, M., Merks, E.: EMF: Eclipse, 2nd edn. Addison-Wesley, Boston (2009)
22. Tong, Y., Sun, J., Chow, S.S., Li, P.: Cloud-assisted mobile-access of health data with privacy and auditability. IEEE J. Biomed. Health Inform. **18**(2), 419–429 (2014)

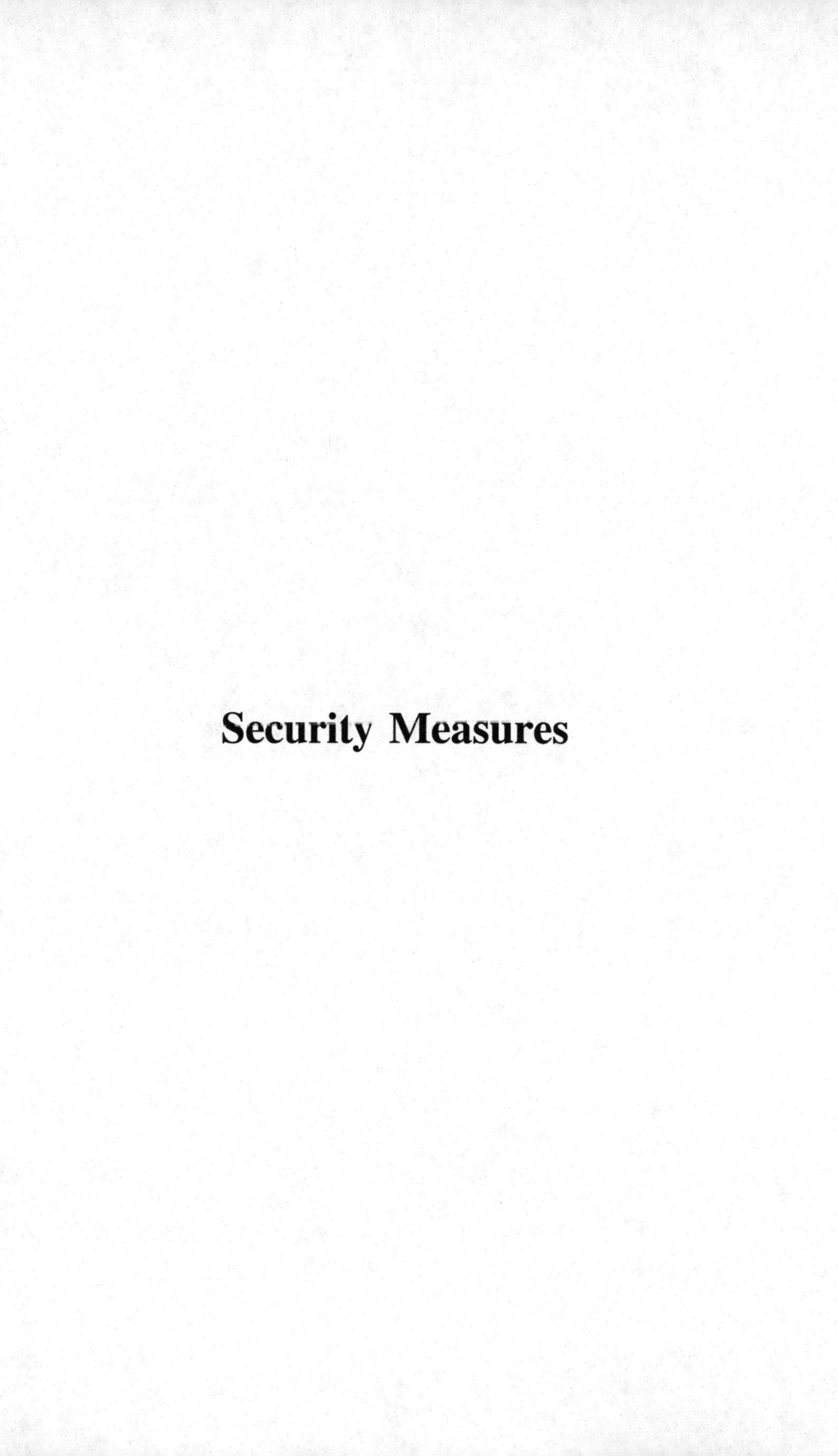

Security Measures

Selecting Security Mechanisms in Secure Tropos

Michalis Pavlidis(✉), Haralambos Mouratidis, Emmanouil Panaousis, and Nikolaos Argyropoulos

University of Brighton, Brighton, England
{m.pavlidis,h.mouratidis,e.panaousis,n.argyropoulos}@brighton.ac.uk

Abstract. As security is a growing concern for modern information systems, Security Requirements Engineering has been developed as a very active area of research. A large body of work deals with elicitation, modelling, analysis, and reasoning about security requirements. However, there is little evidence of efforts to align security requirements with security mechanisms. This paper extends the Secure Tropos methodology to enable a clear alignment, between security requirements and security mechanisms, and a reasoning technique to optimise the selection of security mechanisms based on these security requirements and a set of other factors. The extending Secure Tropos supports modelling and analysis of security mechanisms; defines mathematically relevant modelling concepts to support a formal analysis; and defines and solves an optimisation problem to derive optimal sets of security mechanisms. We demonstrate the applicability of our work with the aid of a case study from the health care domain.

Keywords: Security modelling · Secure Tropos

1 Introduction

Security is an important aspect of modern information systems and it is widely accepted that it should be treated from the early stages of the information system development process, and not as an afterthought [1–4]. As a result, during the last fifteen years the research community has witnessed a significant amount of works [5,6], which deal with the definition, elicitation, analysis, and reasoning of security requirements. We have contributed to this body of literature, with our work on *Secure Tropos* [7], which is a security requirements engineering methodology that supports elicitation and analysis of security requirements.

Ideally, enough security countermeasures (also known as security mechanisms or security safeguards) should be applied to a system to satisfy those security requirements. However, in practice, there is usually a trade-off between security measures and other factors such as cost and time. The literature from the security engineering community has proposed a number of works that focus on security countermeasures selection usually in relation to vulnerabilities [8–10], investment costs [11,12] or risks [13,14]. However, such approaches have ignored the relationship between security mechanisms and security requirements.

J. Lopez et al. (Eds.): TrustBus 2017, LNCS 10442, pp. 99–114, 2017.
DOI: 10.1007/978-3-319-64483-7_7

We believe, this is an important parameter, especially in the current era of information systems, where security requirements can frequently evolve, and there is a plethora of available security mechanisms. It is only when there is a clear relationship between security requirements, security mechanisms, and potential trade-off factors (such as cost and benefit of such mechanisms) that the decision is fully supported with the right evidence.

On the other hand, despite the impressive amount of work in the (Security) Requirements Engineering area, the literature provides little evidence of works that provide a clear relationship between security requirements and potential security mechanisms, and it lacks automated approaches to optimise the selection of security mechanisms based on security requirements and a set of other factors, such as cost.

In this paper, we address this gap by extending our previous work on Secure Tropos.

The specific contributions of our work can be summarised as follows:

- Extension of a security requirements engineering methodology to support a clear alignment of security requirements and security mechanisms through a well defined process;
- Definition of benefit, cost, satisfiability, satisfiability weight, non-functional requirements (NFR) cost, financial cost in the context of security requirements analysis, and a clear relationship with related concepts of the Secure Tropos methodology;
- Mathematical representation/formulation of the relevant modelling concepts and relations, along with a definition of a graph data structure to support their modelling;
- Computation of an optimal set of security mechanisms in relation to security requirements, given certain criteria about maximum NFR costs, minimum satisfiability levels for each security requirement, and an available monetary budget, by solving a multi-objective optimisation problem;
- Application and evaluation of the work to a real-case study.

The next section provides an overview and comparison with related work, while Sect. 3 provides a summary of Secure Tropos. Section 4 introduces our extensions and Sect. 5 introduces a case study from the health care domain, and it discusses the application of our approach to the case study. Section 6 concludes the paper.

2 Related Work

The domain of requirements engineering is already rich in terms of decision making techniques, which reason about the selection of alternative design options in order to satisfy requirements that are represented as goals in Goal Oriented Requirements Engineering GORE approaches [15–22].

However, all these works have not been developed with security in mind. As such, on a conceptual level they lack a clear definition of security requirements and security related concepts such as security mechanisms, while on a process level they lack structured methods and processes to support the identification of security mechanisms and the selection of security packages (set of security mechanisms) to satisfy the elicited security requirements.

The literature also provides a large body of work from the security requirements engineering area [3,6]. Mellado et al. [23] introduced the Security Requirements Engineering Process (SREP), which is based on several Common Criteria constructs to elicit and analyse security requirements. The Security Quality Requirement Engineering Methodology (SQUARE) [24] is another security requirements engineering approach similar to SREP. Both SREP and SQUARE are asset-based and risk-driven methods that follow a number of steps, for eliciting, categorising, and prioritising security requirements. Sindre and Opdahl [25] have developed a misuse case driven approach to establish visual link between use cases and misuse cases for eliciting security requirements at an early stage of the development. McDermott and Fox [1] adapt use cases to capture and analyse security requirements, and they call the adaption an abuse case model. Liu et al. [26] analyse security requirements as relationships amongst strategic actors by proposing different kinds of analysis techniques to model potential threats and security measures. Paja et al. [27] provide reasoning techniques for detecting inconsistencies among security requirements. [9,10], base their work on security problem frames, which are patterns that classify security software development problems related to security and support developers in analyzing them. Lamsweerde [28] provides an extension of the KAOS approach, where security goals are refined until they become precise and represent security requirements. Then, once alternative countermeasures have been identified the NFR qualitative framework is employed to support the selection process according to how critical the security goal been threatened is and how well the countermeasure meets the other non-functional requirements. However, these approaches focus on the elicitation and analysis of security requirements and they do not explicitly consider the concept of security mechanism. As such, they lack a clear definition between the security requirements/security mechanisms relationship and lack support in attributing financial cost. In contrast, our selection algorithm has been integrated into the security requirements engineering process, and as such, derives a set of security mechanisms that satisfy identified security requirements based on preferable criteria, which are set by the requirements engineer. As discussed in the introduction, we believe that such alignment is very important where security requirements can frequently evolve, and there is a plethora of available security mechanisms. It is only when there is a clear relationship between security requirements, security mechanisms, and potential trade-off factors (such as cost and benefit of such mechanisms) that the decision is fully supported with the right evidence. Our approach not only provides an alignment between the what and why (security requirements) with the how (security mechanisms), but also a quantitative method that enables requirements engineers to cope with the complexity of selecting the optimal combination of security countermeasures in a systematic way.

In addition, there is a line of research in the area of security risk assessment [29–31] where there is identification, assessment, and mitigation of risks to security mechanisms that will endanger the satisfaction of security requirements. However, the risk are investigated in isolation with limited support for cost/benefit trade-off analysis. In [32] although the security solution design trade-off is addressed, there is no clear alignment of the security solutions with the security requirements. The literature also provides research related to the selection of security mechanisms during the run-time of a system, such as (e.g. [20, 33]) as well as from the Decision support area, such as [11–14]. However, these works are heavily based on risk management and in most cases, the selection criteria are the financial cost of a mechanism and its effectiveness in blocking an attack, the potential impact (i.e. risk) and the attack success likelihood. However, they offer limited support to identify security requirements, and most importantly the security mechanisms are not linked to the security requirements. Therefore, the selection algorithms do not consider which security requirement a security mechanism satisfies and also what the importance of that requirement is. Moreover, although useful during run time, such approaches entail that a wide range of security mechanisms are acquired and implemented without considering their financial cost.

3 Secure Tropos

The Secure Tropos methodology [7] is based on the principle that security should be analysed and considered from the early stages of the software system development process, and not added as an afterthought. To support that approach, the methodology provides a modelling language, a security-aware process, and a set of automated processes to support the analysis and consideration of security from the early stages of the development process. The Secure Tropos language consists of a set of concepts from the requirements engineering domain, and in particular Goal-Oriented Requirements Engineering [34, 35], such as actor, goal, plan, and dependency, which are enriched with concepts from security engineering, such as security constraint, secure plan, and attacks. An actor [35], represents an entity that has intentionality and strategic goals within the software system or within its organisational setting. Within a network of actors, which is usually the case in large software systems with multiple stakeholders, one actor might depend on another actor for a goal, a plan or a resource. A goal [35] represents a condition in the world that an actor would like to achieve. In other words, goals represent actor's strategic interests. A plan represents, at an abstract level, a way of doing something [35]. The fulfilment of a plan can be a means for satisfying a goal. As such, different alternative plans, that actors might employ to achieve their goals, are modelled to enable software engineers to reason about the different ways that actors can achieve their goals, and decide upon the optimal way. A resource [35] presents a physical or informational entity that one of the actors requires. The main concern when dealing with resources is whether the resource is available, and who is responsible for its delivery.

In line with existing literature [6,36,37], we define security requirements as constraints on specific functions of a system. Towards this end, security requirements are represented, in Secure Tropos, as *Security Constraints*. A Security Constraint is defined as a security condition imposed to an actor that restricts the achievement of an actor's goals, the execution of plans or the availability of resources. To support the analysis and evaluation of the developed security solution, the modelling language supports the modelling of security attacks. An attack is an action that might cause a potential violation of security in the system (this definition has been adopted by Matt Bishop's definition of a computer attack). Within the context of an attack, an attacker represents a malicious actor that is interested in attacking the system. As described above, an actor has intentionality and strategic goals within the system. In the case of an attacker, these are related to breaking the security of a system, and identifying and executing malicious goals. To support the modelling of an actor by depending on another actor for a security constraint, Secure Tropos introduces the idea of Secure Dependency. A Secure Dependency introduces one or more Security Constraints that must be fulfilled for the dependency to be valid. *Vulnerabilities* are defined as weaknesses or flaws, in terms of security, that exist from a resource, an actor and/or a goal. Vulnerabilities are exploited by threats, as an attack or incident within a specific context. It is worth stating that legitimate actors might unintentionally introduce vulnerabilities to a system due to failure or mistakes. Threats pose potential loss or indicate problems that can put the system at risk. On the other hand, actors within the system environment have single or multiple goals. The *process* in Secure Tropos is one of analysing the security needs of the stakeholders and the system in terms of security constraints, imposed on the stakeholders and the system, identifying relevant security threats and attacks and analyse and identify potential countermeasures against those attacks.

4 Proposed Extensions

In this section we discuss how we have extended the Secure Tropos methodology. We first discuss the extensions to the modelling language, we then mathematically formulate some of the Secure Tropos components, and finally, we present a new Secure Tropos process.

The modelling language of Secure Tropos, as briefly described in the previous section, is extended with concepts and links required to model and analyse security countermeasures, but also to create models that have a clear explicit alignment between security constraints and security countermeasures. The updated meta-model of the Secure Tropos language is shown in Fig. 1.

When a Security Constraint is introduced, further analysis is required to establish if and how this constraint can be satisfied. A Security Objective represents an objective that is assigned to an actor, and it indicates a course of action that the actor needs to follow to satisfy one or more security constraints, whose satisfaction by a security objective is defined through a `Satisfies` relationship. Countermeasures are defined in our approach in terms of security mechanisms.

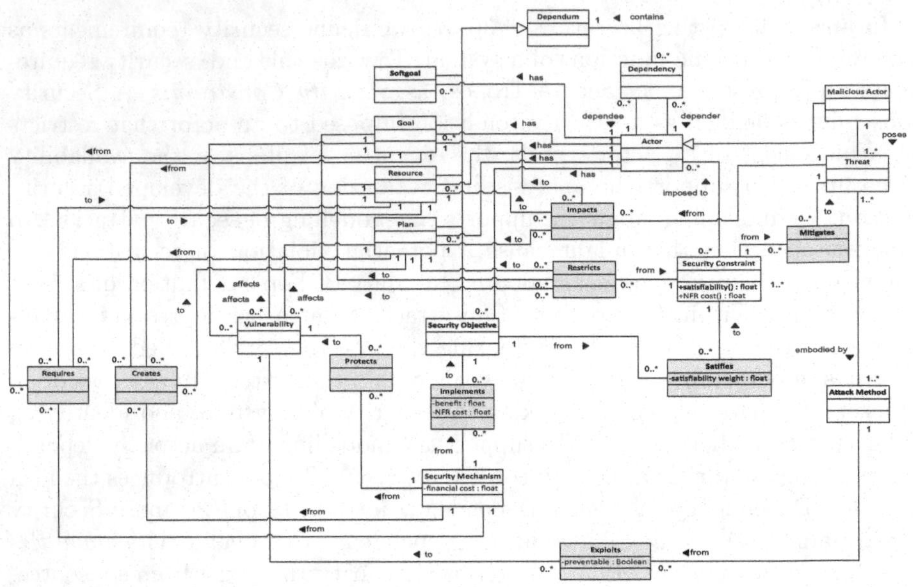

Fig. 1. A part of the secure tropos metamodel.

These represent standard security methods, which contribute to the satisfaction of the security objectives. Some of these methods are able to prevent security attacks, whereas others are able only to detect security breaches.

In the following, we introduce some mathematical notation that helps to formalise the above Secure Tropos concepts. Assume $\mathcal{C}$ a set of security constraints, and $\mathcal{O}$ a set of security objectives. Each security constraint can be satisfied by one or more security objectives. A security objective j contributes to the satisfaction of a constraint i at some degree $w_{ji} \in [0, 1]$, which is called *satisfiability weight*, with the property that $\sum_j w_{ji} = 1$. For example, when objective j does not satisfy constraint i (i.e. no `Satisfies` link exist between j, i), then $w_{ji} = 0$.

Each objective can be implemented by different mechanisms or *combination of security mechanisms*. In order to represent a combination of security mechanisms that are required for the implementation of a security objective we introduce the notion of a *security package*. This consists of either one security mechanism or a set of mechanisms connected with an AND decomposition. For a set $\mathcal{M}$ of mechanisms, any package z is modelled by the vector $\mathbf{p}_z := [p_{qz}] \in \{0, 1\}^{|\mathcal{M}|}$, where p_{qz} equals 1 when mechanism q is included in package z, and 0 otherwise. We define the set $\mathcal{P} := \{\mathbf{p}_z\}$ of π security packages that exist in the model. A security package z contributes to the implementation of a security objective j, and we define its degree of contribution as follows:

Definition 1 (Benefit). *Benefit is defined as the degree of implementation of a security objective by a security package.*

We model the benefit of package z to objective j, by $b_{zj} \in [0, 1]$. For example, if package z does not implement objective j then $b_{zj} = 0$. In this case, there is no `Implements` link between z and j.

Definition 2 (Satisfiability). *We define the satisfiability of a security constraint i as $s_i := \sum_j \sum_z w_{ji} b_{zj}$.*

As a security constraint mitigates one or more security threats, the satisfiability of a security constraint determines the *mitigation degree* of these *threats.* It is intuitive that the higher the satisfiability the higher the system protection against these threats. Furthermore, each security package comes also with a cost value, defined as follows:

Definition 3 (Financial Cost). *Each security package z has a financial cost value f_z, which refers to potential monetary expenses for acquiring, developing, maintaining, and operating its security mechanisms.*

Definition 4 (Non-functional Requirements Cost). *Each security package z has a non-functional requirements cost value η_z, which is the cost incurred to non-functional system requirements by the implementation of security mechanisms that comprise this package. This cost can be seen as the negative impact of the security package to, for example, usability, performance, and scalability* [38].

In the rest of this section, we discuss the newly defined security-aware process, which extends the Secure Tropos process. The extended process supports security requirements engineers with the selection of a set of security packages that fulfil identified security constraints. Given the fact that most of the security packages have different benefits and costs, there are multiple combinations of them that might satisfy the identified security requirements. As such, the aim of the engineer is to derive a set of security packages that: (i) meet a minimum satisfiability and a maximum NFR cost, which are set by the requirements engineer during the Secure Tropos modelling process; (ii) its financial cost can be covered by an available budget; (iii) is "optimal", based on a cost-benefit analysis, given the different satisfiability weights.

As part of the new process, after eliciting the security constraints following the traditional Secure Tropos process [3,7], the requirements engineer, with input from the system stakeholders, sets a *minimum satisfiability* α_i, and a *maximum acceptable non-functional requirements cost* β_i for each constraint i, and the different satisfiability weights. Furthermore, the requirements engineer, with the support of a security engineer, identifies the set $\mathcal{P}$ of available security packages that implement the system security objectives $\mathcal{O}$, along with the benefit values b_{zj} of each package z to each objective j. It is worth stressing here that, the process assumes the selection of only one security package per objective. This assumption does not restrict the number of security mechanisms that can be selected for the implementation of an objective, as a security package can be the composition of any security mechanisms. Finally, the requirements engineer, with input from the system stakeholders, provides a maximum available financial budget Φ to cover the financial cost of the selected security packages.

To correlate a security objective j with only one of the security packages that implement this objective, representing a possible *solution* for the implementation of this objective, we define the vector $\mathbf{x}_j := [x_{zj}] \in \{0,1\}^{\pi}$, s.t. $\sum_z x_{zj} = 1$. When package z is selected to implement objective j, then $x_{zj} = 1$, and hence $\mathbf{x}_j = [\underbrace{0,\ldots,0}_{j-1},1,\underbrace{0,\ldots,0}_{\pi-j}]$. A *complete solution*, denoted by $\mathbf{X}$, consists of combinations of different $\mathbf{x}_j$ covering the entire range of objectives. We formally denote a solution by $\mathbf{X} = [\mathbf{x}_1, \mathbf{x}_2, \ldots, \mathbf{x}_\rho]$. The goal of the requirements engineer is to select an $\mathbf{X}$ such that:

(**C-I**) for each constraint $i \in \mathcal{C}$, α_i and β_i are satisfied by packages in $\mathbf{X}$;
(**C-II**) the sum of costs of all selected packages, which comprise $\mathbf{X}$, are within the available budget Φ;
(**C-III**) $\mathbf{X}$ is optimal according to a cost-benefit analysis, which considers the non-functional requirements costs of packages that comprise $\mathbf{X}$, and their benefit values.

To support the aforementioned security-aware process of Secure Tropos, and utilise the newly defined modelling language, we must solve a multi-objective optimisation problem using the OptiMathSAT [39] tool. The solution satisfies criteria **C-I**, **C-II**, and **C-III**, mentioned in the previous section. To facilitate the cost-benefit analysis, which is part of **C-III**, we introduce the notion of the *utility of a security constraint.*

Definition 5 (Utility). *For a given* $\mathbf{X}$, *we define the utility* $u_i(\mathbf{X})$ *of a constraint* i *as* $u_i(\mathbf{X}) := \frac{s_i(\mathbf{X})}{\eta_i(\mathbf{X})}$.

In the following we discuss the computation of $s_i(\mathbf{X})$ and $\eta_i(\mathbf{X})$. From Definition 2 we can deduce that $s_i(\mathbf{X}) := \sum_j \sum_z w_{ji}\, x_{zj}\, b_{zj}$. In order to represent the objectives that satisfy each security constraint we define the latter as the vector $\mathbf{c_i} := [c_{ji}] \in \{0,1\}^{\rho}, \forall\ i \in \mathcal{C}$. By having this, we can now define the total non-functional requirements cost for a specific constraint as $\eta_i(\mathbf{X}) := \sum_j \sum_z c_{ji}\, x_{zj}\, \eta_z$. We can also derive the financial cost of a solution $\mathbf{X}$ as $f(\mathbf{X}) := \sum_j f(\mathbf{x}_j) = \sum_j \sum_z x_{zj}\, f_z$. We finally compute the optimal solution $\mathbf{X}^*$ by solving the following optimisation problem:

$$\begin{aligned}
&\max_{\mathbf{X}} \sum_i I_i\, u_i(\mathbf{X}) \\
&\text{s.t.} \sum_i I_i = 1 \\
&f(\mathbf{X}) \leq \Phi \\
&s_i(\mathbf{X}) \geq \alpha_i, \forall i. \\
&\eta_i(\mathbf{X}) \leq \beta_i, \forall i,
\end{aligned}$$

where I_i signifies the importance of a security constraint to the system, and it is defined by the requirements engineer, in each case.

5 Case Study

In order to exhibit the applicability of our approach, this section describes how our approach can be applied on the real life case study of the established Greek national e-prescription system [40]. This is a cloud-based system, which is currently used by Greek *healthcare professionals* to handle patients' electronic medication and clinical tests prescriptions. *Medical practitioners*, regardless of specialty, can create an electronic prescription document, which can then be fulfilled, by using the same platform, by any pharmacist or clinic staff. The healthcare professionals access the e-prescription system via an online portal. The back-end of the system has been created, and it is also maintained, by a non-profit organisation, which is in charge of the e-governance infrastructure of the Greek Ministry of Health. The system was introduced in October 2010, as a pilot, for one healthcare provider. By May 2012, the system was fully released, and it supported all registered Greek healthcare providers. It is estimated that the system handles over 500 thousand prescriptions on a daily basis, accommodating over ten thousand pharmacists and thirty eight thousand medical practitioners [41].

It is worth noting that in this paper, we focus on the main functionalities of the e-prescription system and its security requirements, as described in the relevant act of the Greek parliament [40]. Following the extended Secure Tropos modelling language and security-aware process we have elicited the main security requirements, in terms of security constraints, of the system along with security mechanisms as depicted in Fig. 2. To help with the creation of the model, we have used the SecTro tool. SecTro is a tool for the Secure Tropos methodology based on the ADOxx meta-modelling platform [42], which supports the requirements engineer in creating Secure Tropos models, according to the language metamodel, and it provides a set of analysis functionalities such as identifying security constraints that are not satisfied, and threats that are not mitigated. The rest of this section, describes the application of our work to the case study.

As shown in Fig. 2, for a healthcare professional to get access to the system, a user registration process must be completed. To this end, the users must provide a number of personal information, before they are given their login credentials. This fulfils the system goal of "*Register system users*". The main functionality of the e-prescription system is the handling of the prescription documents from their creation to their fulfilment, as indicated by the goal "*Handle prescription documents*". This process is initiated when a patient visits a medical practitioner, and the latter decides to prescribe some medical treatment, in the form of medication or clinical tests. *Patient Information* is accessed from the system via a unique patient identification number and it is included in each *Prescription Document* along with the prescribed treatment. A prescription is fulfilled when a patient receives consultation or treatment by a pharmacy or a clinic. Each prescription document that a healthcare professional handles can later be accessed via a personal archive. This is maintained by the system, and it generates the system goal "*Archive prescription documents*".

The security requirements of the e-prescription system are described in the legal framework of the e-prescription system [40] and modelled in our approach

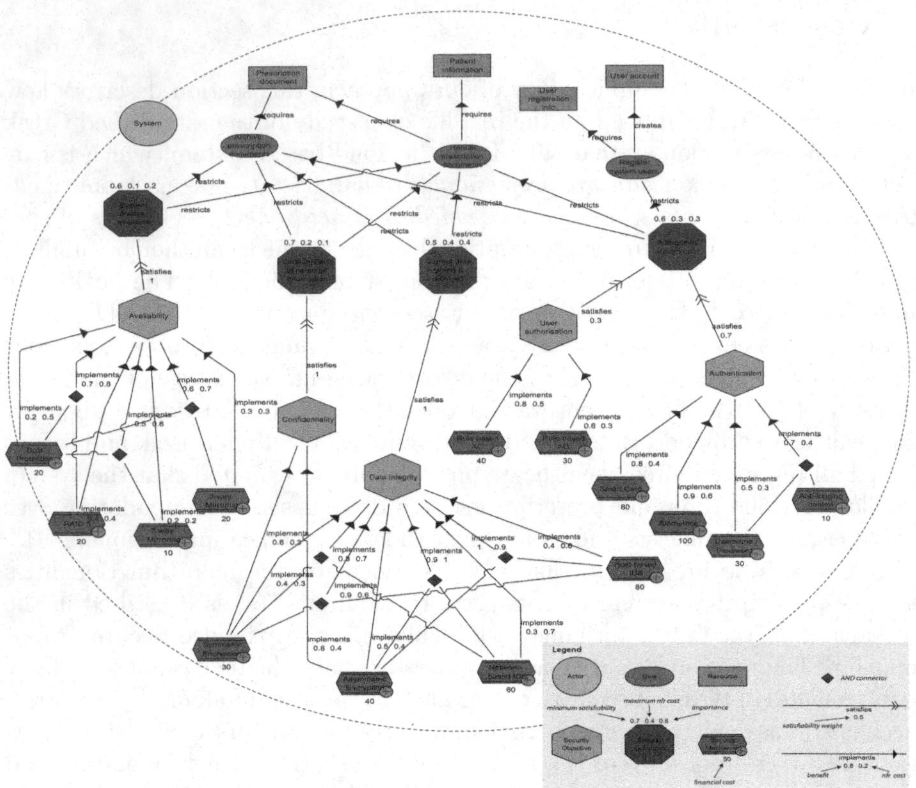

Fig. 2. Security analysis of part of the Greek national e-prescription system

as security constraints. These constraints are satisfied through the implementation of security objectives as shown in Fig. 2. In particular, the security constraint "*Authorised access only*" aims to ensure that only registered users access and operate the system. This constraint is satisfied by the security objectives "*Authentication*" and "*User Authorisation*". Similarly, the security constraint "*Correct data received and stored*" restricts the creation, fulfilment and access to prescription documents, aiming to ensure the integrity of the information stored in the system. This is satisfied by the implementation of the "*Data Integrity*" security objective. "*Confidentiality of personal information*" requires that the sensitive and personal patient information contained in a prescription document must be accessed only by authorised system users, and it is satisfied by the implementation of the security objective "*Confidentiality*". Finally, the security constraint "*System always available*", satisfied by the "*Availability*" security objective, ensures the uninterrupted functionality of the e-prescription system, regardless of potential infrastructure technical issues or targeted attacks launched against it.

In our work, the aforementioned security objectives are implemented by an optimal set of security packages derived solving a multi-objective optimisation problem. As there is an one-to-one mapping between packages and mechanisms, the afore optimal set can be translated to a set of optimal security mechanisms. Starting from the "*Authentication*" objective, this can be implemented by the use of "*Username/Password*" mechanism. A security package can contain this mechanism along with an "*Anti-logging control*" mechanism. Other alternative security packages that provide user authentication could implement the use of "*Smart card*" or "*Biometrics*" mechanisms. Similarly, for the "*User Authorisation*" security objective, there is a choice between "*Role-based Access Control*" (RBAC) or "*Rule-based Access Control*" (RAC). According to this, each user has access only to specific system information and functionalities.

Different encryption mechanisms (i.e. "*Symmetric*" or "*Asymmetric Encryption*") can be implemented in security packages to contribute towards the achievement of both "*Data Integrity*" and "*Confidentiality*" security objectives. These security packages can contribute towards both objectives, as they can protect transmitted information from being accessed and modified by unauthorised users. In addition to encryption, "*Intrusion Detection Systems*" (IDS) can be deployed for the implementation of the "*Data Integrity*" objective. Thus, "*Host-based IDS*" or "*Network-based IDS*" can be standalone security packages or they can be combined with encryption mechanisms.

Finally, the security objective "*Availability*" can be achieved by creating redundancy at the system infrastructure. Therefore, different types of disk mirroring can be implemented (e.g. "*2-way mirroring*", "*3-way mirroring*" or "*RAID 5*") to ensure the uninterrupted functionality of the system and the availability of the stored data. Alternative to disk mirroring solutions, can be packages that offer protection against denial of service attacks ("*DoS Protection*"). This mechanism can be implemented along with redundancy mechanisms to form security packages able to enforce the "*Availability*" objective.

To set the different costs and benefits of the security packages we have combined information found in scientific literature, technical reports, and pricing of commercial security solutions. As an example, literature suggests that while solutions using biometrics are the most secure as opposed to simple passwords or smart card authorisation, they lack in usability and deployability [43]. However, commercial applications used for managing biometric authorisation entail a high financial overhead, due to the infrastructure required at each end-user's terminal. Based on these insights, appropriate values are assigned to these packages resulting in the highest benefit values for "Biometrics" among the 3 available packages, followed by "Smart Cards" and finally "Username/Password". Similarly, due to the high financial and NFR costs associated with them, "Biometrics" also receive the highest cost value compared to the alternative mechanisms. Similar value assignment activities were followed for each of the security packages.

We have undertaken simulations to derive the optimal set of security packages for different financial budgets, as presented in Table 2. The format of the solution in this table is given by the tuple $[\mathbf{p}_x, \ldots, \mathbf{p}_y]$, where its i-th element represents the security package that implements the security objective i, where $i \in [1, 5]$. In the same table, we see that for each financial budget more than

Table 1. Security packages.

Package	Mechanism	Package	Mechanism
$\mathbf{p}_1$	m_1 (DoS protection)	$\mathbf{p}_2$	m_2 (2-way mirroring)
$\mathbf{p}_3$	m_3 (3-way mirroring)	$\mathbf{p}_4$	m_4 (RAID5)
$\mathbf{p}_5$	$m_1 \wedge m_2$	$\mathbf{p}_6$	$m_1 \wedge m_3$
$\mathbf{p}_7$	$m_1 \wedge m_4$	$\mathbf{p}_8$	m_5 (Symmetric encryption)
$\mathbf{p}_9$	m_6 (Asymmetric encryption)	$\mathbf{p}_{10}$	m_7 (Network-based IDS)
$\mathbf{p}_{11}$	m_8 (Host-based IDS)	$\mathbf{p}_{12}$	$m_5 \wedge m_7$
$\mathbf{p}_{13}$	$m_5 \wedge m_8$	$\mathbf{p}_{14}$	$m_6 \wedge m_7$
$\mathbf{p}_{15}$	$m_6 \wedge m_8$	$\mathbf{p}_{16}$	m_9 (Role-based AC)
$\mathbf{p}_{17}$	m_{10} (Rule-based AC)	$\mathbf{p}_{18}$	m_{11} (Username/Password)
$\mathbf{p}_{19}$	m_{12} (Smart card)	$\mathbf{p}_{20}$	m_{13} (Biometrics)
$\mathbf{p}_{21}$	$m_{11} \wedge m_{14}$: (m_{14} Anti-logging)		

Table 2. Simulation results

Budget	Solution	Utility	Satisf. values	NFR costs	Utilities	Cost
190	$[\mathbf{p}_7, \mathbf{p}_9, \mathbf{p}_9, \mathbf{p}_{16}, \mathbf{p}_{21}]$	2.324	0.7, 0.8, 0.5, 0.67	0.4, 0.2, 0.2, 0.35	1.75, 4, 2.5, 1.914	190
	$[\mathbf{p}_6, \mathbf{p}_9, \mathbf{p}_9, \mathbf{p}_{16}, \mathbf{p}_{21}]$	2.317	0.6, 0.8, 0.5, 0.67	0.35, 0.2, 0.2, 0.35	1.714, 4, 2.5, 1.914	190
230	$[\mathbf{p}_7, \mathbf{p}_9, \mathbf{p}_9, \mathbf{p}_{16}, \mathbf{p}_{19}]$	2.38	0.7, 0.8, 0.5, 0.74	0.4, 0.2, 0.2, 0.35	1.75, 4, 2.5, 2.114	230
	$[\mathbf{p}_6, \mathbf{p}_9, \mathbf{p}_9, \mathbf{p}_{16}, \mathbf{p}_{19}]$	2.38	0.6, 0.8, 0.5, 0.74	0.35, 0.2, 0.2, 0.35	1.714, 4, 2.5, 2.114	230
	$[\mathbf{p}_7, \mathbf{p}_9, \mathbf{p}_9, \mathbf{p}_{16}, \mathbf{p}_{21}]$	2.324	0.7, 0.8, 0.5, 0.67	0.4, 0.2, 0.2, 0.35	1.75, 4, 2.5, 1.914	190
260	$[\mathbf{p}_7, \mathbf{p}_9, \mathbf{p}_{13}, \mathbf{p}_{16}, \mathbf{p}_{21}]$	2.524	0.7, 0.8, 0.9, 0.67	0.4, 0.2, 0.3, 0.35	1.75, 4, 3, 1.914	260
	$[\mathbf{p}_6, \mathbf{p}_9, \mathbf{p}_{13}, \mathbf{p}_{16}, \mathbf{p}_{21}]$	2.517	0.6, 0.8, 0.9, 0.67	0.35, 0.2, 0.3, 0.35	1.714, 4, 3, 1.914	260
	$[\mathbf{p}_7, \mathbf{p}_9, \mathbf{p}_9, \mathbf{p}_{16}, \mathbf{p}_{19}]$	2.38	0.7, 0.8, 0.5, 0.74	0.4, 0.2, 0.2, 0.35	1.75, 4, 2.5, 2.114	230
300	$[\mathbf{p}_7, \mathbf{p}_9, \mathbf{p}_{13}, \mathbf{p}_{16}, \mathbf{p}_{19}]$	2.584	0.7, 0.8, 0.9, 0.74	0.4, 0.2, 0.3, 0.35	1.75, 4, 3, 2.114	300
	$[\mathbf{p}_6, \mathbf{p}_9, \mathbf{p}_{13}, \mathbf{p}_{16}, \mathbf{p}_{19}]$	2.577	0.6, 0.8, 0.9, 0.74	0.35, 0.2, 0.3, 0.35	1.714, 4, 3, 2.114	300
	$[\mathbf{p}_7, \mathbf{p}_9, \mathbf{p}_{13}, \mathbf{p}_{16}, \mathbf{p}_{21}]$	2.524	0.7, 0.8, 0.9, 0.67	0.4, 0.2, 0.3, 0.35	1.75, 4, 3, 1.914	260

one set of packages are given; the optimal, the second optimal, and the third optimal, whenever available. This is because we believe that the requirements engineer, might want to have an idea of the alternative solutions if he wishes, for instance, to reduce the financial budget. We have restricted our results to the best 3 sets, because these might be indicative of the available alternatives. It is obvious that, if the requirements engineer desires to reduce the budget further, then another execution of the program is required. Table 1 facilitates the results discussion by summarising all security packages, of our case study, along with the mechanisms that constitute them. It is worth noting that as mechanisms represent the fundamental notion of security implementations, they are the building blocks of security packages. Hence, there is no sense in combining different alternative packages that implement a security objective, when instead we can combine different mechanisms, by using an AND relationship, to form a new security package.

In our simulations, we have varied the financial budget from very low values and we were increasing this, by using a step of 10 units, until we reach a point where an additional budget provides no improvement in the optimal set of the packages. By using Fig. 2 and Table 1, it is trivial to see the exact security mechanisms that constitute each solution. First, we observed that the minimum financial budget required to satisfy the system security requirements, was 190. This allows two solutions with the same financial cost but with the $[\mathbf{p_7}, \mathbf{p_9}, \mathbf{p_9}, \mathbf{p_{16}}, \mathbf{p_{21}}]$, to perform better. The next financial budget that allows a new solution, i.e. $[\mathbf{p_7}, \mathbf{p_9}, \mathbf{p_9}, \mathbf{p_{16}}, \mathbf{p_{19}}]$, is 230. In this case, we notice a 7% improvement of the satisfiability of the fourth security constraint, as opposed to the case where the budget was 190. It is worth noting here that this improvement comes with no increment to any of the non-functional requirements costs. The next budget level that introduces a different solution, and improves security, as determined by its 2.524 utility value, is the $[\mathbf{p_7}, \mathbf{p_9}, \mathbf{p_{13}}, \mathbf{p_{16}}, \mathbf{p_{21}}]$. This solution costs 30 extra financial units, but improves the satisfiability of the third security constraint by 40%. Finally, the highest performance is achieved when the budget equals 300, where the optimal solution is $[\mathbf{p_7}, \mathbf{p_9}, \mathbf{p_{13}}, \mathbf{p_{16}}, \mathbf{p_{19}}]$. In other words, the simulation results show that any budget value higher than 300 does not improve security.

6 Conclusion

The selection of appropriate security mechanisms that satisfy the security requirements under a limited budget is an important task, as it determines the final security level of a system. Furthermore, a major consideration when selecting security mechanisms is to maximise the satisfaction of security requirements while minimising their negative side effects to other non-functional requirements. Despite its importance, the computation of an optimal set of security mechanisms is not a straightforward task due to the large decision space. This paper presents a twofold extension of Secure Tropos methodology. First, the relationship between security requirements and security mechanisms is explicitly shown to enable a better understanding and alignment. To this end, the modelling language was enriched with the new concepts so that requirements engineers have a clear understanding of the relationship between what the system needs to do in terms of security, i.e. security requirements, and how they system will do it, i.e. security mechanisms. Second, the Secure Tropos process was enriched with a selection process that enables requirements engineers to derive an optimal set of security packages, which, in effect, is a set of preferable security mechanisms. This set maximises the overall satisfaction of the system's security requirements while respecting a set of criteria, which the engineer sets during the analysis of the system, and a given financial budget. For this purpose, the relevant modelling concepts were defined mathematically to support formal analysis. In this paper, the optimal set of security mechanisms corresponds to a baseline security solution. In the future, we aim to undertake a risk assessment to inform selection. In this way, the requirements engineer will perform threat and vulnerability analysis, update the Secure Tropos model, and then execute selection to derive the set of security mechanisms that maximise the overall system security.

References

1. McDermott, J., Fox, C.: Using abuse case models for security requirements analysis. In: 15th Annual Computer Security Applications Conference, (ACSAC 1999) Proceedings, pp. 55–64. IEEE (1999)
2. Basin, D., Doser, J., Lodderstedt, T.: Model driven security for process-oriented systems. In: Proceedings of the Eighth ACM Symposium on Access Control Models and Technologies, pp. 100–109. ACM (2003)
3. Mouratidis, H.: Integrating Security and Software Engineering: Advances and Future Visions: Advances and Future Visions. IGI Global, Hershey (2006)
4. Haley, C.B., Laney, R., Moffett, J.D., Nuseibeh, B.: Arguing satisfaction of security requirements. Integr. Secur. Softw. Eng. Adv. Future Vis. 16–43 (2006)
5. Fabian, B., Gürses, S., Heisel, M., Santen, T., Schmidt, H.: A comparison of security requirements engineering methods. Requir. Eng. **15**(1), 7–40 (2010)
6. Dubois, E., Mouratidis, H.: Guest editorial: security requirements engineering: past, present and future. Requir. Eng. **15**(1), 1–5 (2010)
7. Mouratidis, H., Giorgini, P.: Secure tropos: a security-oriented extension of the tropos methodology. Int. J. Softw. Eng. Knowl. Eng. **17**(2), 285–309 (2007)
8. Chung, L., Nixon, B., Yu, E., Mylopoulos, J.: Non-Functional Requirements in Software Engineering. International Series in Software Engineering. Springer, Heidelberg (2000). doi:10.1007/978-1-4615-5269-7
9. Hatebur, D., Heisel, M.: Problem frames and architectures for security problems. In: Winther, R., Gran, B.A., Dahll, G. (eds.) SAFECOMP 2005. LNCS, vol. 3688, pp. 390–404. Springer, Heidelberg (2005). doi:10.1007/11563228_30
10. Hatebur, D., Heisel, M., Schmidt, H.: Security Engineering Using Problem Frames. In: Müller, G. (ed.) ETRICS 2006. LNCS, vol. 3995, pp. 238–253. Springer, Heidelberg (2006). doi:10.1007/11766155_17
11. Gupta, M., Rees, J., Chaturvedi, A., Chi, J.: Matching information security vulnerabilities to organizational security profiles: a genetic algorithm approach. Decis. Support Syst. **41**(3), 592–603 (2006)
12. Neubauer, T., Pehn, M.: Workshop-based risk assessment for the definition of secure business processes. In: Second International Conference on Information, Process, and Knowledge Management, eKNOW 2010, pp. 74–79. IEEE (2010)
13. Viduto, V., Maple, C., Huang, W., López-Peréz, D.: A novel risk assessment and optimisation model for a multi-objective network security countermeasure selection problem. Decis. Support Syst. **53**(3), 599–610 (2012)
14. Sawik, T.: Selection of optimal countermeasure portfolio in it security planning. Decis. Support Syst. **55**(1), 156–164 (2013)
15. Giorgini, P., Mylopoulos, J., Nicchiarelli, E., Sebastiani, R.: Formal Reasoning Techniques for Goal Models. In: Spaccapietra, S., March, S., Aberer, K. (eds.) Journal on Data Semantics I. LNCS, vol. 2800, pp. 1–20. Springer, Heidelberg (2003). doi:10.1007/978-3-540-39733-5_1
16. Amyot, D., Ghanavati, S., Horkoff, J., Mussbacher, G., Peyton, L., Yu, E.: Evaluating goal models within the goal-oriented requirement language. Int. J. Intell. Syst. **25**(8), 841–877 (2010)

17. Letier, E., Van Lamsweerde, A.: Reasoning about partial goal satisfaction for requirements and design engineering. In: ACM SIGSOFT Software Engineering Notes, vol. 29, pp. 53–62. ACM (2004)
18. Bryl, V., Giorgini, P., Mylopoulos, J.: Designing cooperative is: exploring and evaluating alternatives. In: On the Move to Meaningful Internet Systems 2006: CoopIS, DOA, GADA, and ODBASE, pp. 533–550. Springer, Heidelberg (2006)
19. Kaiya, H., Horai, H., Saeki, M.: Agora: attributed goal-oriented requirements analysis method. In: IEEE Joint International Conference on Requirements Engineering, Proceedings, pp. 13–22. IEEE (2002)
20. Bencomo, N., Belaggoun, A.: Supporting decision-making for self-adaptive systems: from goal models to dynamic decision networks. In: Doerr, J., Opdahl, A.L. (eds.) REFSQ 2013. LNCS, vol. 7830, pp. 221–236. Springer, Heidelberg (2013). doi:10.1007/978-3-642-37422-7_16
21. Feather, M.S., Cornford, S.L., Hicks, K., Kiper, J.D., Menzies, T., et al.: A broad, quantitative model for making early requirements decisions. Software **25**(2), 49–56 (2008). IEEE
22. Heaven, W., Letier, E.: Simulating and optimising design decisions in quantitative goal models. In: 2011 19th IEEE International Requirements Engineering Conference (RE), pp. 79–88. IEEE (2011)
23. Mellado, D., Fernández-Medina, E., Piattini, M.: A common criteria based security requirements engineering process for the development of secure information systems. Comput. Stan. Interfaces **29**(2), 244–253 (2007)
24. Mead, N.R., Stehney, T.: Security quality requirements engineering (square) methodology. SIGSOFT Softw. Eng. Notes **30**(4), 1–7 (2005)
25. Sindre, G., Opdahl, A.L.: Eliciting security requirements with misuse cases. Requir. Eng. **10**(1), 34–44 (2005). http://dx.doi.org/10.1007/s00766-004-0194-4
26. Liu, L., Yu, E., Mylopoulos, J.: Security and privacy requirements analysis within a social setting. In: 11th IEEE International Requirements Engineering Conference, Proceedings, pp. 151–161 (2003)
27. Paja, E., Dalpiaz, F., Giorgini, P.: Managing security requirements conflicts in socio-technical systems. In: Ng, W., Storey, V.C., Trujillo, J.C. (eds.) ER 2013. LNCS, vol. 8217, pp. 270–283. Springer, Heidelberg (2013). doi:10.1007/978-3-642-41924-9_23
28. Van Lamsweerde, A.: Elaborating security requirements by construction of intentional anti-models. In: Proceedings of the 26th International Conference on Software Engineering, pp. 148–157. IEEE Computer Society (2004)
29. Franqueira, V.N., Tun, T.T., Yu, Y., Wieringa, R., Nuseibeh, B.: Risk and argument: a risk-based argumentation method for practical security. In: 2011 19th IEEE International Requirements Engineering Conference (RE), pp. 239–248. IEEE (2011)
30. Asnar, Y., Giorgini, P., Mylopoulos, J.: Goal-driven risk assessment in requirements engineering. Requir. Eng. **16**(2), 101–116 (2011)
31. Lee, S.W.: Probabilistic risk assessment for security requirements: a preliminary study. In: 2011 Fifth International Conference on Secure Software Integration and Reliability Improvement (SSIRI), pp. 11–20. IEEE (2011)
32. Houmb, S.H., Georg, G., Jürjens, J., France, R.: An integrated security verification and security solution design trade-off analysis approach. Integrating Security and Software Engineering: Advances and Future Visions/Mouratidis, Haralambos pp. 190–219 (2007)

33. Tsigkanos, C., Pasquale, L., Menghi, C., Ghezzi, C., Nuseibeh, B.: Engineering topology aware adaptive security: Preventing requirements violations at runtime. In: 2014 IEEE 22nd International Requirements Engineering Conference (RE), pp. 203–212. IEEE (2014)
34. Van Lamsweerde, A.: Goal-oriented requirements engineering: a guided tour. In: Fifth IEEE International Symposium on Requirements Engineering, Proceedings, pp. 249–262. IEEE (2001)
35. Bresciani, P., Perini, A., Giorgini, P., Giunchiglia, F., Mylopoulos, J.: Tropos: An agent-oriented software development methodology. Auton. Agent. Multi-Agent Syst. **8**(3), 203–236 (2004)
36. Sommerville, I., Kotonya, G.: Requirements Engineering: Processes and Techniques. Wiley, Hoboken (1998)
37. Haley, C.B., Laney, R., Moffett, J.D., Nuseibeh, B.: Security requirements engineering: a framework for representation and analysis. IEEE Trans. Softw. Eng. **34**(1), 133–153 (2008)
38. Cysneiros, L.M., Sampaio do Prado Leite, J.C.: Nonfunctional requirements: from elicitation to conceptual models. IEEE Trans. Softw. Eng. **30**(5), 328–350 (2004)
39. Sebastiani, R., Trentin, P.: Optimathsat: a tool for optimization modulo theories
40. Greek-Parliament: Act 3892: Electronic registration and fulfilment of medical prescriptions and clinical test referrals. FEK **189**(1), 4225–4232 (2010)
41. Sfyroeras, V.: The electronic prescription system. Pharmacy management and communications, pp. 68–69, September 2012. http://www.idika.gr/files/synenteyxeis/arthro_pharmacy_management_09.12.pdf
42. Adoxx Meta-modeling platform. http://www.adoxx.org
43. Bonneau, J., Herley, C., van Oorschot, P.C., Stajano, F.: The quest to replace passwords: a framework for comparative evaluation of web authentication schemes. In: Proceedings of the 33rd IEEE Symposium on Security and Privacy. San Francisco, CA, USA, May 2012

Improving Fuzzy Searchable Encryption with Direct Bigram Embedding

Christian Göge(✉), Tim Waage, Daniel Homann, and Lena Wiese

Institut für Informatik, Georg-August-Universität Göttingen,
Goldschmidtstraße 7, 37077 Göttingen, Germany
{christian.goege,waage,homann,wiese}@informatik.uni-goettingen.de

Abstract. In this paper we address the problem of fuzzy search over encrypted data that supports misspelled search terms. We advance prior work by using a bit vector for bigrams directly instead of hashing bigrams into a Bloom filter. We show that we improve both index building performance as well as retrieval ratio of matching documents while providing the same security guarantees. We also compare fuzzy searchable encryption with exact searchable encryption both in terms of security and performance.

Keywords: Searchable encryption · Similarity search · Fuzzy search · Semantic security · Locality sensitive hashing

1 Introduction

For several applications, users prefer virtual machines on cloud platforms instead of maintaining expensive hardware at their premises. Furthermore, many applications – such as databases – are available *as a service*, where cloud providers facilitate and maintain also the software at their sites. Prominent providers for database-as-a-service products are Amazon Web Services and Microsoft Azure.

In conjunction with outsourcing of private or sensitive data to remote servers comes the need of protecting the data, not only from outside attackers, but also from the service provider, because it might try to learn information from its customers' data and data flow. The simplest solution is to encrypt all data before outsourcing it to a remote location. However, this prevents even simple processing in the cloud. In order to search through the encrypted data, one would have to download the whole database, decrypt it and then run the search on the decrypted data, which obviously ridicules the idea of outsourcing the database in the first place. The solution here is searchable encryption (SE). An SE scheme enables a server to search in encrypted data while preventing it from gaining information about the plaintext data.

Most SE schemes involve a preprocessing step on the data to build an *index*. The index can be built in two shapes: A *document-based*, also called *forward* index [3], relates documents or their unique identifiers to the keywords they contain. This allows a search time of $\mathcal{O}(n)$, where n is the number of documents,

J. Lopez et al. (Eds.): TrustBus 2017, LNCS 10442, pp. 115–129, 2017.
DOI: 10.1007/978-3-319-64483-7_8

because each document's index is processed during a query. Sublinear query time can be achieved with a *keyword-based* index, also called *inverse* index [3] or *collection-based* index [5]. It relates a keyword to the documents it is contained in. Then, the optimal query time to be achieved is $\mathcal{O}(D(w))$, where $D(w)$ is the number of documents which contain the query term [3]. Updates in a document-based index are easier because the new index entry can simply be added, while in the keyword-based index, updates will require more effort. The choice of the index type depends on the use case: In a write-heavy scenario the former performs better, while in a read-heavy scenario the latter should be chosen [20].

A client can query an encrypted index using a *trapdoor* (an encrypted form of a query). The server can run a *search* algorithm given a trapdoor, and decide which documents contain the query term belonging to the trapdoor. It can then return the encrypted documents without having to see any plaintext. A searchable encryption scheme will however always *leak* some information from the index and the queries. [3] divide the leaked information in three groups:

- *Index information* is the information leaked directly from the stored ciphertexts of the index, as well as the documents. It may include the number of keywords in a document or the database, the total number of documents, their length, identifiers and possibly the similarity between them.
- The *search pattern* captures the information held by two queries returning the same result. With a deterministic trapdoor-generating function, this information is directly leaked, because a query will always compute to the same trapdoor. With non-deterministic trapdoors, the search pattern will at least give the possibility to determine whether two trapdoors were generated from the same query. The search pattern allows the server to possibly gain information about the keywords through statistical analysis. It might also leak similarity between two queries [12].
- The query results yield the *access pattern*, showing which query returned which documents. If a query q returns document x and a second query w returns x and several other documents, the server can learn that q is more restrictive than w.

Most SE schemes choose to leak the search and access pattern on purpose in order to be computationally efficient. A scheme not leaking either of them can be built using *oblivious RAM* [10]; but it requires $\log n$ rounds of communication for one query, where n is the number of documents stored, which is not scalable for large databases [5]. With some inverted indexes like [12], a client can hide the access pattern by outsourcing the index and the encrypted data to two different servers. A query to the index server will return the encrypted set of document identifiers which can then be decrypted and queried from the second server. However, this will always require two rounds of server communication and superior security is only provided if the two servers do not collaborate.

Depending on the use case, SE schemes can be built using symmetric or public key encryption. Symmetric searchable encryption (SSE) [17] is used when one data owner wants to outsource his data collection. Access to the data can be granted to other trusted parties by sharing the secret key among all data users. In a public key encryption scheme (PEKS) [2], users can add encrypted keywords to an index with a public key and only the private key holder can search on the encrypted data. This is useful to make public-key encrypted documents like emails searchable for the recipient. This paper focuses on a symmetric searchable encryption scheme that additionally allows *fuzzy search*. Fuzzy search is the ability to find documents containing terms the spelling of which is similar to a query term – a key feature known from web search engines like Google. Taking the scheme in [12] as our baseline we make the following contributions:

- When embedding bigrams into a metric space, we replace the hash-based approach of [12] by a direct bigram vector.
- We show that our approach achieves better query performance and retrieval success for misspelled queries.
- In addition, we make a comparison between our scheme, the original fuzzy searchable encryption scheme in [12] and the exact searchable encryption scheme in [18], and hence analyze the impact of the fuzzy search functionality in a unified framework.

The paper is outlined as follows: Sect. 2 presents related work. Our approach is based on the work of Kuzu et al. [12]; this scheme is described in detail in Sect. 3. Our own contribution is described in Sect. 4. The security of our approach is analyzed in Sect. 5. Section 6 provides details of the implementation and presents the comparative results based on our implementations of the schemes in a common framework. Section 7 concludes the paper.

2 Related Work

A recent survey of the field of searchable encryption can be found in [3]. Here, we will concentrate on important approaches for exact symmetric searchable encryption as well as encrypted fuzzy search.

The first approach addressing searchable encryption was proposed by Song et al. [17]. They use a two-layered encryption construct that makes a sequential search of the ciphertext possible and hence does not require an index. Because both, encryption and search, need to iterate over the whole collection, this scheme does not scale for large databases. It also relies on fixed-size words.

Goh [9] was the first to introduce a *secure index* built on individual documents. For each document, it uses a Bloom filter that holds all keywords extracted from the document. A query has to check set membership of a string in each index Bloom filter, which leads to a constant lookup time for one document and results in a linear query time on the document collection.

Curtmola et al. [5] developed a keyword-based index consisting of an array of linked list nodes. It allows for optimal query time but the encryption is costly, because it has to encrypt all nodes separately.

Stefanov et al. [18] use a keyword-based index stored in a set of exponentially growing hashmaps. The main advantage of the scheme is that its leakage is considerably lower than the leakage of other schemes – the authors call this "forward security". The disadvantages of the scheme are the complexity of the data structure as well as the search time which is, although sublinear, quite high.

The above approaches only find exact matches. We now move on to the topic of *fuzzy* encrypted search. The term fuzzy or similarity search is used in the literature with two different meanings. The first meaning covers search schemes which return documents which contain a subset of a given keyword set. Schemes for this direction of research are given by [8, 19, 23]. In contrast, we use the term similarity search as the search for a single keyword, which may be misspelled, but nevertheless can be resolved to the correct documents.

Several fuzzy search schemes are based on the idea of considering all keywords in a certain edit distance of a keyword [11, 13, 14, 22]. In order to decrease the required storage space, they do not generate all possible keywords but introduce a special wildcard character which stands for any single letter of the alphabet.

Wang et al. [21] achieve fuzzy queries for multiple keywords at once. Their index is a Bloom filter for each document. Keywords are inserted into the index with locality-sensitive hashing (LSH) functions, which makes similar words likely to hit the same indices in the Bloom filter. Since the Bloom filters are large, encrypting them and computing their score without decrypting them involves a large matrix and matrix-vector multiplication. In order to allow multiple fuzzy keyword search, this scheme pays with a large asymptotic constant to the $\mathcal{O}(n)$ query time.

Boldyreva and Chenette [1] provide two formal definitions of fuzzy search which are very strict with regard to result quality and leakage. They show that there can not exist a space-efficient scheme fulfilling the first definition and give a fuzzy scheme for fingerprint data satisfying the second definition.

Chua et al. [4] also use Bloom filters for the encoding of the keywords and store them in a special tree structure for efficient search.

3 Background

Formally, a searchable encryption scheme (SE) provides the key functions

- *Keygen(s):* Computes the master key K_{priv} given the security parameter s.
- *Trapdoor(*K_{priv}, q*):* Computes the trapdoor T_q for query q with the key K_{priv}.
- *BuildIndex(*D, K_{priv}*):* Computes the index I_D for the document collection D.
- *Search(*I_D, T_q*):* Outputs a set of document identifiers, for which the documents contain the query term q.

Our approach is based on prior work by Kuzu et al. [12]. The *search* is relaxed such that it allows retrieval of documents within a certain distance to the query.

- *FuzzySearch:* Let D be a collection of documents consisting of features f. A query for a feature f_q returns a document $D_i \in D$ with high probability if $\exists f \in D_i : dist(f, f_q) < \alpha$. Furthermore, the query will not return documents if $\forall f \in D_i : dist(f, f_q) > \beta$.

We now formally describe the fuzzy search approach in [12].

Locality Sensitive Hashing. Locality sensitive hashing (LSH) is used to efficiently approximate distances between two terms. Let M be a metric space with distance function $d : M \rightarrow \mathbb{R}$. A family $\mathcal{H}$ of hash functions $h : M \rightarrow S$ is called (r_1, r_2, p_1, p_2)-sensitive, if for all $h \in \mathcal{H}$ and arbitrary $x, y \in M$:

$$d(x, y) \leq r_1 \Rightarrow Pr[h(x) = h(y)] \geq p_1$$
$$d(x, y) \geq r_2 \Rightarrow Pr[h(x) = h(y)] \leq p_2$$

with $r_1 < r_2$, $p_1 > p_2$. Given a similarity function $\phi : U \times U \rightarrow [0, 1]$ between elements x, y of a universe U, a LSH family has the property $Pr[h(x) = h(y)] = \phi(x, y)$. The probabilities can be amplified to match the *FuzzySearch* thresholds α, β by combining several uniformly chosen functions $h \in \mathcal{H}$. Let $Pr[h(x) = h(y)] = p$. Kuzu et al. form a $(r_1, r_2, (1 - p_1^k)^\lambda, (1 - p_2^k)^\lambda)$-sensitive family $\mathcal{F}$ (as in [15]) by combining the basic hash functions with logical AND and OR:

$$g_i(x) = h_{i_1}(x) \wedge \cdots \wedge h_{i_k}(x) \quad (1)$$
$$f(x) = g_1(x) \vee \cdots \vee g_\lambda(x), \quad (2)$$

in the sense that $g_i(x) = g_i(y)$ iff $\forall j : h_{i_j}(x) = h_{i_j}(y)$ and $f(x) = f(y)$ iff $\exists i : g_i(x) = g_i(y)$.

Metric Space Embedding ρ. The set F of features of a document consists of all the words it contains. The use of LSH to efficiently approximate the distance between two words requires a distance function for which such approximation functions are known. This is not the case for the well known Levensthein or Edit distance [12]. Therefore the documents' features have to be embedded in a metric space first. Kuzu et al. [12] embed them in the metric space of sets with an embedding function ρ, that is presented in [16]: The strings are identified by their bigrams, that are the continuous substrings of length two extracted from the string. For the word "john", the bigram set is {jo, oh, hn}. The bigrams are then inserted into a Bloom filter of length $m = 500$ with $k = 15$ cryptographic hash functions. The Bloom filters are interpreted as sets and the distance is measured using Jaccard distance $J_d(A, B) = 1 - \frac{|A \cap B|}{|A \cup B|}$ (see Fig. 1).

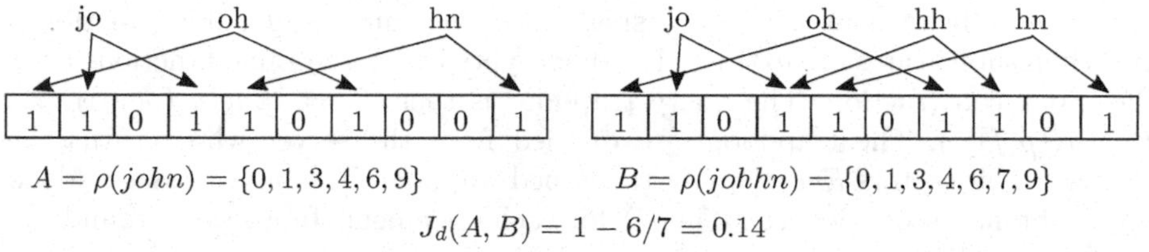

Fig. 1. Hashed bigram embedding of length 10 with 2 hash functions

Minhash. The minhash functions form a $(r_1, r_2, 1 - r_1, 1 - r_2)$-sensitive LSH family for the Jaccard distance. Let Δ be the ordered domain of the set, i.e. $\Delta = \{1, \ldots, m\}$. A minhash function is defined with a random permutation $P(\Delta)$ on the domain Δ. Let $X \subset \Delta$. The minhash of X is then

$$h_P(X) = \min_{i=0,\ldots,m} \{i \mid P[i] \in X\}. \tag{3}$$

For example, let $\Delta = [0, \ldots, 9]$, $P(\Delta) = \{3, 4, 1, 5, 2, 6, 7, 9, 8, 0\}$ and $X = \rho(\text{john}) = \{0, 1, 2, 4, 5, 8, 9\}$. Then, the first index i in P that is a member of X is $P[1] = 4$, hence $h_P(X) = 1$. For two sets X, Y, the probability that $h_P(X) = h_P(Y)$ equals the Jaccard similarity $J = \frac{|A \cap B|}{|A \cup B|}$. In practice, a permutation on Δ can be defined with a simple hash function $h_\Delta : [1, m] \rightarrow [1, m]$ that pseudo-permutes the domain. The minhash can then be efficiently computed as

$$h(x) = \min_{x \in X} h_\Delta(x). \tag{4}$$

Index. The index is built with keyword subfeatures extracted with the LSH functions g as described by Eqs. (1) and (2). The LSH parameters k, λ are chosen beforehand and the λ subfeatures sort the documents into buckets. If two documents appear in the same bucket (i.e. have a keyword subfeature in common), they are likely to both contain the keyword. All documents D_i to be inserted into the index are labelled from 1 to n. For each document, the features are the words contained in it. The features are embedded into the metric space of sets with the embedding ρ. Its λ subfeatures are extracted using the LSH functions $(g_1(\rho(f)), \ldots, g_\lambda(\rho(f)))$; each subfeature is a bucket identifier in the index: $B_k = g_i(\rho(f))$. For each bucket, a bit vector V_{B_k} of length n is stored. If the feature f that yielded the bucket B_k was extracted from document D_i, then $V_{B_k}[i] = 1$. Both the bucket identifiers and the bit vectors are encrypted with two different secret keys to form the encrypted index, where $\pi_{B_k} = Enc_{K_{id}}(B_k)$ is a pseudorandom permutation and $\sigma_{V_{B_k}} = Enc_{K_{pay}}(V_{B_k})$ is PCPA-secure[1]. In the end, a number of random fake records (R_1, R_2) with $|R_1| = |\pi_{B_k}|$ and $|R_2| = |\sigma_{V_{B_k}}|$ are inserted to keep the index at the constant size $MAX \cdot \lambda$, where MAX is the maximum number of features.

Query. A query requires two rounds of server communication. The query feature f is embedded in the metric space with the same embedding function ρ and then subfeatures are extracted and encrypted with the same functions as in the index construction. The query trapdoor is then $T_q = (Enc(g_1(\rho(f))), \ldots, Enc(g_\lambda(\rho(f))))$. The trapdoors are queried from the server who returns the encrypted bit vectors $Enc(V_{B_k})$ for the issued trapdoor. The bitvectors are added up to obtain a score between 0 and λ for each document. In a second round, we can request the top t scored documents from the server via their ids.

[1] PCPA-security: An encryption scheme is PCPA secure (pseudo–randomness against chosen plaintext attacks) if the ciphertexts are indistinguishable from a random [5].

4 Direct Bigram Embedding

Using the original embedding of [12], there is always the possibility of collisions in the Bloom filter, meaning that because of the involved hashing two different bigrams can yield the same position to be 1 in the representing set and hence making strings similar even if they are not. The security of this scheme does not rely on the cryptographic properties of the embedding, since the output is encrypted again, so we can replace this embedding with a new one.

We found that we can improve the retrieval of misspelled documents significantly by using another metric space embedding. We adopt the approach of Wang et al. [21] who also use LSH for string distance but use a bigram vector instead of a Bloom filter. The bigram vector has the maximum size 26^2; every position in the vector accounting for one bigram. If a bigram is present in the string, the vector is set to one at the according position.

More formally we proceed as follows: The keywords are converted to lower case. Letters are identified by their alphabetical order with $ord(\text{'a'}) = 0$ to $ord(\text{'z'}) = 25$. The position of a bigram $\alpha_1\alpha_0$ in the vector is then $pos(\alpha_1\alpha_0) = ord(\alpha_1)\cdot 26 + ord(\alpha_0)$. Finally, we set the bigram vector at the according position to one: $v[pos] = 1$. Most importantly, we represent the vector as the set of indices set to 1, making the representation as compact as possible. That makes our embedding also smaller in memory than Kuzu's, who has to store (at most) $k \cdot n$ positions while we store n positions. (k is the number of hash functions Kuzu uses, n the number of bigrams of the word).

While Wang et al. [21] use euclidean distance between the bigram vectors, we can clearly interpret the bigram vector as the set of indices which are set to one. This allows us to keep using the Jaccard distance. Figure 2 pictures the bigram vector. Note that in comparison to the Bloom filter embedding (see Fig. 1), the distances between the words become larger. This allows us to choose smaller LSH parameters k and λ (see Eqs. (1) and (2)), resulting in fewer LSH functions to be computed per keyword.

As mentioned before, the original embedding can produce collisions in the Bloom filter and thus can make non-similar strings look similar. This has indeed a great impact on the minhash LSH subfeatures that form the buckets in the index construction. We found that with our bigram embedding without such collisions, we produce twice as many distinct subfeatures from the keywords as

$$\overset{\text{hn}}{\downarrow}\quad \overset{\text{jo}}{\downarrow}\quad \overset{\text{oh}}{\downarrow}\qquad\qquad \overset{\text{hh}}{\downarrow}\quad \overset{\text{hn}}{\downarrow}\quad \overset{\text{jo}}{\downarrow}\quad \overset{\text{oh}}{\downarrow}$$

$$(0, ..., 0, 1, 0, ..., 0, 1, 0, ..., 0, 1, 0, ..., 0) \quad (0, ..., 0, 1, 0, ..., 0, 1, 0, ..., 0, 1, 0, ..., 0, 1, 0, ..., 0)$$

$$A = \rho(john) = \{195, 248, 371\} \qquad B = \rho(johhn) = \{189, 195, 248, 371\}$$

$$J_d(A, B) = 1 - 3/4 = 0.25$$

Fig. 2. Hashed bigram embedding of length 10 with 2 hash functions

with the original embedding. With this we achieve an increase in the search success, because in our larger index the subfeatures of different terms have less collisions. More details are provided in Sect. 6.

5 Security Analysis

The server is assumed to be *honest-but-curious*, meaning that it will carry out its tasks as it is expected, but tries to learn about the data it hosts. Note that when assuming more malicious attackers, the security of our or any other searchable encryption scheme might not be maintainable. For example, Zhang et al. [24] consider a server that sometimes injects files in the index. This leads to attacks in which the server can quite easily figure out the content of the user's files.

Our scheme has still the same security properties as the original scheme: it has the adaptive semantic security property (see Definition 7). Informally this definition means, that exactly the following information is leaked to an adversary:

- Search pattern: Hashes of searched keywords
- Access pattern: Document identifiers matching queries and document identifiers of added or deleted documents
- Similarity pattern: Similarity between the encrypted queries

5.1 Leaked Information

In an optimal world, the query process will not leak any information, not even which item corresponds to which query. While this can be achieved by *Oblivious RAM* [10], it is computationally expensive and not suitable for large databases. Secure indexes leak some information on purpose, in order to achieve linear or constant query times [5] in the number of documents contained in the database.

The trapdoor generating function is a deterministic function, that means a query q will always compute to the same trapdoor T_q. That allows the adversary to see the search pattern, e.g. which trapdoors are requested how often.

Definition 1. ***Search Pattern*** π *([12], III-B.1): Let* $\{f_1, \dots, f_n\}$ *be the feature set for* n *consecutive queries. The search pattern* π *is a binary symmetric matrix with* $\pi[i, j] = 1$ *if* $f_i = f_j$ *and* 0 *otherwise.*

The deterministic trapdoors also yield the connection between a query trapdoor T and the returned documents. This is captured by the access pattern.

Definition 2. ***Access Pattern*** A_P *([12], III-B.2): Let* $D(f_i)$ *be a collection that contains the identifiers of data items with feature* f_i *and* $\{T_1, \dots, T_n\}$ *be the trapdoors for the query set* $\{f_1, \dots, f_n\}$*. Then, the Access Pattern is defined as the matrix* $A_p(T_i) = D(f_i)$*.*

Kuzu's [12] FuzzySearch algorithm extracts subfeatures from a query feature via LSH, making a query for feature f consist of λ subfeatures. The number of shared subfeatures for two queries is an indicator for the similarity between them. This information is also leaked and captured in the similarity pattern. Note that this definition naturally includes the search pattern π.

Definition 3. ***Similarity Pattern*** S_P *([12], III-B.3): Let* $\{f_i^1, \ldots, f_i^\lambda\}$ *be the subfeatures of feature* f_i*. For n queries,* $\{(f_1^1, \ldots, f_1^\lambda), \ldots, (f_n^1, \ldots, f_n^\lambda)\}$ *is the feature set. Let* $i[j]$ *define the* j^{th} *subfeature of feature* f_i*. Then, the similarity pattern is* $S_P[i[j], p[r]] = 1$ *if* $f_i^j = f_p^r$ *and 0 otherwise for* $1 \leq i, p \leq n$ *and* $1 \leq j, r \leq n$*. In other words, it contains all matrices* $S_{i,p}$ *capturing the similarity between features* f_i *and* f_p *by setting* $S_{i,p}[j, r] = 1$ *if* f_i *and* f_p *share subfeatures* f_i^j *and* f_p^r*.*

The similarity pattern is derived from the queries posed to the encrypted index. The server is not able to deduce similarity between documents from the index alone, nor can he see if the returned documents were a fuzzy or exact hit for a query. Therefore, this fuzzy scheme makes it harder to deduce document similarity from queries than an exact scheme with comparable index structure does, because in an exact scenario, the link between (encrypted) query and returned document (the *access pattern*) is present, while in our fuzzy scheme it is covered with the uncertainty whether the returned document *really* includes the query. The access pattern can be hidden completely by using two different (non-collaborating) servers to store the index and the document collection.

In order to capture the information an adversary has, we first define a sequence of n consecutive queries as an n*-query history*. The *trace* $\gamma(H_n)$ captures the maximum amount of data that is purposely allowed to leak from the secure index scheme, meaning the maximum amount of information that should be computable from what an adversary sees from an n-query history. The data visible to the attacker is called the *view*.

Definition 4. ***History*** H_n *([12], III-B.4): Let D be the data collection and* $Q = \{f_1, \ldots, f_n\}$ *the features for n consecutive queries. Then* $H_n = (D, Q)$ *is an n-query history.*

Definition 5. ***Trace*** $\gamma(H_n)$ *([12], III-B.5): Let C be the collection of encrypted documents,* $id(C_i)$ *the identifiers and* $|C_i|$ *the size of the encrypted documents. The trace* $\gamma(H_n) = \{(id(C_1)...id(C_l)), (|C_1|, \ldots, |C_l|), S_p(H_n), A_p(H_n)\}$ *is the maximum amount of information that is allowed to leak.*

Definition 6. ***View*** $v(H_n)$ *([12], III-B.6): Let C be the collection of encrypted documents,* $id(C_i)$ *the identifiers, I the secure index and T the trapdoors of the history* H_n*. All the information seen by an adversary is captured by the view* $v(H_n) = \{(id(C_1), \ldots, id(C_l)), C, I, T\}$*.*

In contrast to the scheme of Kuzu, the scheme of Stefanov et al. [18] does not allow for similarity search. As the authors show, only the search pattern and the access pattern as defined above are leaked. The fact that their scheme allows dynamic updates does not affect the leakage; they call this forward security.

5.2 Semantic Security

The general idea of the security definition is to play a game against the attacker, who is modelled as a probabilistic polynomial time (p.p.t.) algorithm. If the attacker has a probability of winning not better than a coin toss win ($\frac{1}{2}$), then the scheme is secure. This is formulated as a simulator based definition, where a p.p.t. simulator can generate a random *view* $v_S(H_n)$ to the real query view $v_R(H_n)$ only using information available in the *trace* $\gamma(H_n)$ and the adversary again has a probability not greater than $\frac{1}{2}$ of deciding which view is the real one.

The definition was given by Curtmola et al. [5] and widely adopted afterwards (e.g., [12,21]). They distinguish between two types of adversaries: non-adaptive (IND-CKA1) and adaptive (IND-CKA2). The non-adaptive adversary generates queries (the *history*) without taking into account information he might have learned from previous queries. This is of course rarely the case in a real world scenario where the secure index scheme is running on a server, and the server is the adversary. The adaptive adversary can generate his queries adaptively during his examination.

Definition 7. ***Adaptive Semantic Security*** *([5], 4.1): An SSE scheme is secure if for all p.p.t. adversaries A there is a p.p.t. simulator S which can adaptively construct a view $v_S(H_n)$ from the trace $\gamma(H_n)$ such that the adversary cannot distinguish between the simulated view $v_S(H_n)$ and the real view $v_R(H_n)$.*

More formally, the scheme is secure according to the security definition if one can define a simulator S such that for all polynomial time attackers A holds $\Pr(A(v(H_n)) = 1) - \Pr(A(S(\gamma(H_n))) = 1) < p(s)$, where s is a security parameter and $p(s)$ a negligible function.[2] The probability is taken over all possible H_n and all possible encryption keys.

5.3 Security Proof

The proof that our adaptation of Kuzu et al.'s algorithm is still secure according to the given definition is analogous to the original paper. Let $v_R(H_n)$ and $\gamma(H_n)$ be the real view and the trace. Then a p.p.t. simulator S can adaptively generate the simulated view $v_S(H_n) = \{(id(C_1)^*, \ldots, id(C_l)^*), (C_1^*, \ldots, C_l^*), I^*, (T_{f_1}^*, \ldots, T_{f_n}^*)\}$ as follows:

- Identifiers of documents can simply be copied since they are available in the trace. Hence, both identifier lists in v_S and v_R are identical.
- S can choose n random values $\{C_1^*, \ldots, C_l^*\}$ with $|C_i^*| = |C_i|$. Since the C_i result from an encryption scheme which is pseudo-random against chosen-plaintext attacks (PCPA) [5], they are computationally indistinguishable from random values.
- Let π_{B_k} and $\sigma_{V_{B_k}}$ be the encrypted bucket id and encrypted bucket content of the index. S chooses $MAX \cdot \lambda$ random pairs (R_{i_1}, R_{i_2}) with $|R_{i_1}| = |\pi_{B_k}|$ and $|R_{i_2}| = |\sigma_{V_{B_k}}|$ and inserts them into I^*, where MAX is the maximum number of features and λ is the number of components of a trapdoor. Since π_{B_k} is a pseudorandom permutation and $\sigma_{V_{B_k}}$ is PCPA-secure, pairs in I^* are computationally indistinguishable from pairs in I. Since both contain $MAX{\cdot}\lambda$ records by construction, I^* is computationally indistinguishable from I.

[2] p is negligible if for all positive polynomials f holds: $p(x) < 1/f(x)$ [5].

- The trapdoors $(T^*_{f_1}, \ldots, T^*_{f_n})$ can be constructed from the similarity pattern S_p. They are filled such that $T_i[j]^* = T_p[r]^*$ if $S[i[j], p[r]] = 1$ and otherwise $T_i[j]^* = R_{i_j}$, where R_{i_j} is a random value with $|R_{i_j}| = |\pi_{B_k}|$ and $R_{i_j} \neq R_{p_r} \forall 1 \leq p < i$ and $1 \leq r < \lambda$. Again, the simulated trapdoors are indistinguishable from the real encrypted trapdoors because they are computed by pseudorandom permutation. Also they show the same similarity pattern as the real trapdoors by construction.

Since the components of v_S and v_R are computationally indistinguishable, the scheme satisfies the security definition.

6 Implementation and Results

Even if the cloud databases use encryption at the server side, the plaintexts would be sent to the server, which undermines our goal of security. Therefore, the index generation and encryption of documents has to take place at the client side. While this burdens all computation to the client, it has the advantage that we can easily connect to all existing databases in the cloud without the need of altering one of the database's implementation. We can also seperate index and the data storage to two different servers. Provided that the servers do not collaborate, this also hides the access pattern.

We implemented the scheme of Kuzu et al. [12] and our improvements in Java 1.8[3]. For keyword extraction, we used the Apache Lucene (6.2.1) classes *StandardTokenizer* together with *Standard-*, *Stop-* and *EnglishPossessiveFilter*. We continued filtering all remaining words containing numbers. The minhashes were computed using the implementation available at [6]. In the implementation of the LSH algorithm, we define g_i by $g_i(x) = \sum_{j=1}^{k} h_{i,j}(x) \cdot m^{j-1} \mod 2^{64}$, with $h_{i,j}$ being the jth minhash function of g_i and m the length of the metric space embedding. For encryption we used the AES-128 implementation available in *javax.crypto*.

To achieve similar results as in the original paper [12], the same testing setup was applied. 5000 mails were randomly selected from the publicly available Enron email dataset [7]. The features describing a mail are chosen as the words in the mail's body. In Kuzu et al.'s paper, they are embedded into Bloom filters of length 500 using 15 hash functions by hashing the bigrams of a feature (the authors adopt these settings from [16]). To determine the fuzzy search thresholds for LSH, Kuzu et al. measured the distances between keywords and possible misspellings. Their resulting minhash LSH algorithm uses $\lambda = 37$ stages of length $k = 5$, building a $(0.45, 0.8, 0.85, 0.01)$-sensitive LSH family.

For keyword misspells, we randomly introduced one of the following errors with equal probability: (1) deleting a random letter, (2) doubling a random letter and (3) switching two adjacent letters. Analyzing the keyword–misspell distances with the new bigram embedding shows that dissimilar words are further apart than in Kuzu et al.'s original embedding. To account for that, we choose

[3] The implementation can be found at https://github.com/dbsec/FamilyGuard.

$k = 4$, $\lambda = 25$ to build a $(0.5, 0.85, 0.85, 0.01)$-sensitive family. This also has the advantage of a smaller number of minhashes $(k \cdot \lambda)$ to be computed.

The performance results were obtained by running the schemes on a PC with an Intel i5-6500 CPU with 16 GB RAM and a Samsung EVO 840 SSD.

6.1 Retrieval

For retrieval evaluation we choose *precision* and *recall* as a metric, which is often used in information retrieval. Let w denote a keyword. A query for w is denoted with w'. If the query introduces a spelling error, then $w' \neq w$. Let $D(w)$ be the number of documents containing word w. A document D_i is correctly retrieved for a query w' if $w \in D_i$. Let $R^{D(w')}$ be the retrieved set of documents for query w' and $R^{D(w)}$ the subset that was correctly retrieved. Then precision and recall are defined as

$$prec(w') = \frac{|R^{D(w)}|}{|R^{D(w')}|}, \quad rec(w') = \frac{|R^{D(w)}|}{|D(w)|}. \tag{5}$$

Kuzu et al. [12] misspell 25% of 1000 randomly chosen queries and return the t top-scored documents, while changing t. We believe that this approach has two problems: First, since not misspelled queries will always compute to a maximum score of λ, it is easy to return all exact hits with a precision of 0.99. (There might be two different words having the same bigrams, therefore it is not exactly 1). Second, the recall will depend on the choice of t. If we fix t too low, there might be much more relevant documents than we requested.

Because of these reasons, we choose in our evaluation to misspell all queries. We uniformly selected a total of 10,000 queries from the set of all extracted keywords and introduced one random spelling mistake mentioned above. We then measured precision and recall not depending on a fixed t, but by returning all documents with a score greater than x for $x \in \{\lambda, \dots, 1\}$. The result in Fig. 3 shows the results. On average, a query had 13 relevant documents to it. With our Bigram embedding, we achieve at best a precision of 0.36 with a recall of about 0.5, which is achieved returning all documents with a score greater than 6. Compared to Kuzu et al.'s embedding this is a significant improvement.

6.2 Performance and Comparison

First, we wanted to compare the time needed to compute the query trapdoors for our bigram embedding compared to Kuzu's. Therefore, for words with n bigrams for $n = 1$ to 20, we computed 100,000 trapdoors each. Figure 4 shows the averaged time needed to compute one trapdoor. As said before, our embedding is smaller in size, because we only compute one position for a bigram instead of k hashes. Also, our embedding lets us choose a LSH family with fewer functions. The Kuzu measurement shows a slight curve, this can be explained by collisions in the bloom filter: The more bigrams we hash, the more collisions happen and therefore the number of ones in the filter does not grow linearly.

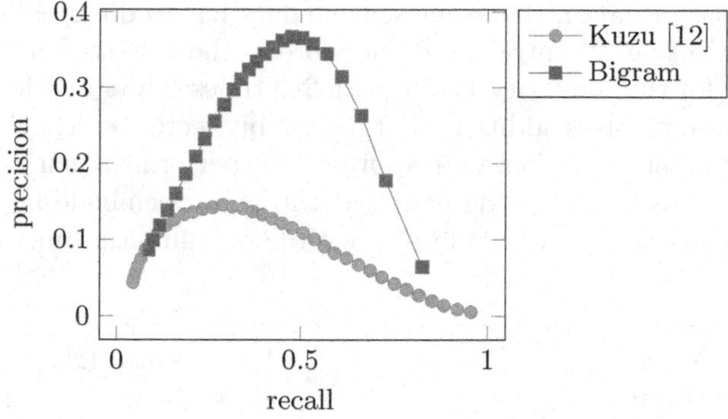

Fig. 3. Retrieval success

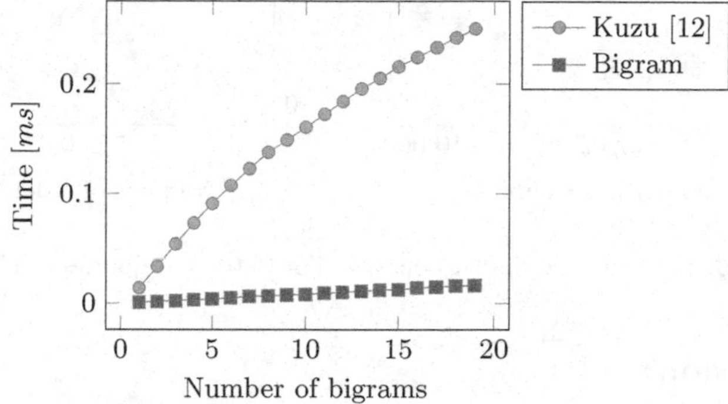

Fig. 4. Performance: trapdoor computation

We then measured the time needed to construct the index for 1,000 to 10,000 mails taken randomly from the Enron dataset [7]. The times are averaged over three index constructions each. We then query the indexes with 1000 keywords randomly selected from the documents. We compare the performance of our contribution to Kuzu et al.'s original scheme. Additionally, we compare the performance to an exact-keyword matching scheme of Stefanov et al. [18].

The results are shown in Fig. 5. All schemes build an inverted index. Comparing our scheme to Kuzu et al.'s original, we find that the index construction performs slightly worse. Because of the properties of the embedding (see Sec. 4), we find that our index is larger than Kuzu's. Therefore we have to encrypt about twice as many index entries. Since this index construct is built to be computed only once and performs badly with updates anyway, this increase is insignificant. The scheme of Stefanov et al. [18] builds the index such that online updates are still possible, but follows the same assumption that updates are infrequent. This flexibility leads to larger index creation times. The scheme partially rebuilds the index on updates (with an amortized cost of $\mathcal{O}(\log^2 N)$); the decryption of the entries, oblivious sorting and reencryption introduce large constants in this asymptotic runtime. The scheme hence needs more time than [12].

For query performance, the exact scheme only has to do a lookup operation followed by collecting all entries and therefore is the fastest. The fuzzy search algorithms pay for the similarity search with 2–3 times slower queries because the query process also involves addition of at most λ bit vectors of length equal to the size of the document collection. Our approach outperforms Kuzu et al.'s scheme by about 20%. This is due to the fact that the bigram embedding is computed faster and we can choose an LSH family with fewer minhash functions.

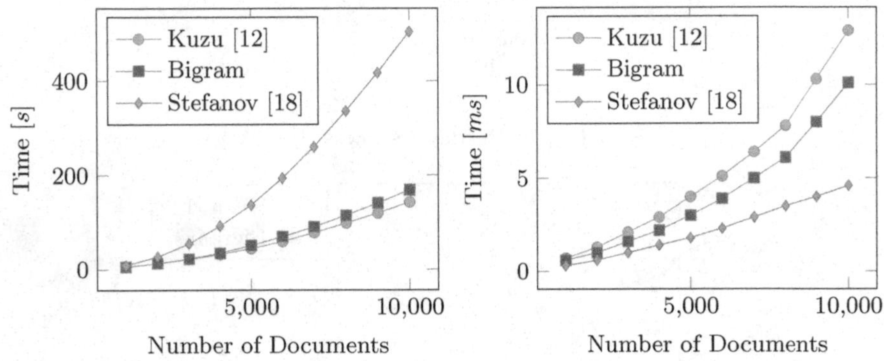

Fig. 5. Performance: index construction (left) and queries (right)

7 Conclusion

We provided an improvement to the encrypted fuzzy search scheme of Kuzu et al. [12] by replacing the metric space embedding for strings based on a Bloom filter with a direct bigram embedding used in [21]. We showed that this improves the retrieval success of misspelled queries significantly, and makes the queries 20% faster. The performance of both the original and the modified fuzzy search scheme was also compared to the performance of an exact searchable encryption scheme [18]; the results show that there is only a modest overhead for the additional feature of fuzzy search.

Acknowledgement. This work was partially funded by the DFG under grant number Wi 4086/2-2.

References

1. Boldyreva, A., Chenette, N.: Efficient fuzzy search on encrypted data. In: Cid, C., Rechberger, C. (eds.) FSE 2014. LNCS, vol. 8540, pp. 613–633. Springer, Heidelberg (2015). doi:10.1007/978-3-662-46706-0_31
2. Boneh, D., Di Crescenzo, G., Ostrovsky, R., Persiano, G.: Public key encryption with keyword search. In: Cachin, C., Camenisch, J.L. (eds.) EUROCRYPT 2004. LNCS, vol. 3027, pp. 506–522. Springer, Heidelberg (2004). doi:10.1007/978-3-540-24676-3_30

3. Bösch, C., Hartel, P., Jonker, W., Peter, A.: A survey of provably secure searchable encryption. ACM Comput. Surv. (CSUR) **47**(2), 18 (2015)
4. Chuah, M., Hu, W.: Privacy-aware bedtree based solution for fuzzy multi-keyword search over encrypted data. In: ICDCS, pp. 273–281. IEEE (2011)
5. Curtmola, R., Garay, J., Kamara, S., Ostrovsky, R.: Searchable symmetric encryption: improved definitions and efficient constructions. IACR Cryptology ePrint Archive 2006 (Rep. 210) (2006)
6. Debatty, T.: Java-LSH. https://github.com/tdebatty/java-LSH
7. Enron email dataset (2015). https://www.cs.cmu.edu/~./enron/
8. Fu, Z., Shu, J., Wang, J., Liu, Y., Lee, S.: Privacy-preserving smart similarity search based on simhash over encrypted data in cloud computing. J. Internet Technol. **16**(3), 453–460 (1971)
9. Goh, E.J.: Secure indexes. IACR Cryptology ePrint Archive 2003 (Rep. 216) (2004)
10. Goldreich, O., Ostrovsky, R.: Software protection and simulation on oblivious RAMs. J. ACM (JACM) **43**(3), 431–473 (1996)
11. Hu, C., Han, L.: Efficient wildcard search over encrypted data. Int. J. Inf. Sec. **15**(5), 539–547 (2016)
12. Kuzu, M., Islam, M.S., Kantarcioglu, M.: Efficient similarity search over encrypted data. In: Data Engineering (ICDE) 2012, pp. 1156–1167. IEEE (2012)
13. Li, J., Wang, Q., Wang, C., Cao, N., Ren, K., Lou, W.: Fuzzy keyword search over encrypted data in cloud computing. In: INFOCOM, pp. 441–445. IEEE (2010)
14. Liu, C., Zhu, L., Li, L., Tan, Y.: Fuzzy keyword search on encrypted cloud storage data with small index. In: IEEE CCIS, pp. 269–273 (2011)
15. Rajaraman, A., Ullman, J.D., Lescovec, J.: Mining of Massive Datasets, vol. 1. Cambridge University Press, Cambridge (2010)
16. Schnell, R., Bachteler, T., Reiher, J.: Privacy-preserving record linkage using Bloom filters. BMC Med. Inform. Decis. Mak. **9**(1), 41 (2009)
17. Song, D.X., Wagner, D., Perrig, A.: Practical techniques for searches on encrypted data. In: IEEE Symposium on Security and Privacy, pp. 44–55. IEEE (2000)
18. Stefanov, E., Papamanthou, C., Shi, E.: Practical dynamic searchable encryption with small leakage. In: NDSS, vol. 14, pp. 23–26 (2014)
19. Sun, W., Wang, B., Cao, N., Li, M., Lou, W., Hou, Y.T., Li, H.: Privacy-preserving multi-keyword text search in the cloud supporting similarity-based ranking. In: ACM SIGSAC, pp. 71–82. ACM (2013)
20. Waage, T., Jhajj, R.S., Wiese, L.: Searchable encryption in apache cassandra. In: Garcia-Alfaro, J., Kranakis, E., Bonfante, G. (eds.) FPS 2015. LNCS, vol. 9482, pp. 286–293. Springer, Cham (2016). doi:10.1007/978-3-319-30303-1_19
21. Wang, B., Yu, S., Lou, W., Hou, Y.T.: Privacy-preserving multi-keyword fuzzy search over encrypted data in the cloud. In: INFOCOM, pp. 2112–2120. IEEE (2014)
22. Wang, C., Ren, K., Yu, S., Urs, K.M.R.: Achieving usable and privacy-assured similarity search over outsourced cloud data. In: INFOCOM, pp. 451–459. IEEE (2012)
23. Yuan, X., Cui, H., Wang, X., Wang, C.: Enabling privacy-assured similarity retrieval over millions of encrypted records. In: Pernul, G., Ryan, P.Y.A., Weippl, E. (eds.) ESORICS 2015. LNCS, vol. 9327, pp. 40–60. Springer, Cham (2015). doi:10.1007/978-3-319-24177-7_3
24. Zhang, Y., Katz, J., Papamanthou, C.: All your queries are belong to us: the power of file-injection attacks on searchable encryption. In: USENIX, pp. 707–720 (2016)

Modeling Malware-driven Honeypots

Gerardo Fernandez(✉), Ana Nieto, and Javier Lopez

Network, Information and Computer Security (NICS) Lab,
Department of Computer Science, University of Malaga, Malaga, Spain
{gerardo,nieto,jlm}@lcc.uma.es
http://www.nics.uma.es

Abstract. In this paper we propose the Hogney architecture for the deployment of *malware-driven honeypots*. This new concept refers to honeypots that have been dynamically configured according to the environment expected by malware. The adaptation mechanism designed here is built on services that offer up-to-date and relevant *intelligence information* on current threats. Thus, the Hogney architecture takes advantage of recent *Indicators Of Compromise* (IOC) and information about suspicious activity currently being studied by analysts. The information gathered from these services is then used to adapt honeypots to fulfill malware requirements, inviting them to unleash their full strength.

Keywords: Honeypot · Malware · Adaptive · Dynamic · Intelligence · IOC

1 Introduction

According to the report issued by Symantec last year, there was an increase of 36% in the collection of unique malware samples compared to the previous year [1]. In 2016, ransomware grew considerably, affecting almost half of businesses worldwide [2]. Infections via e-mail, phishing and botnet nodes remain the most commonly used methods to compromise computers in the business environment. As a consequence, one of the biggest concerns today is how to respond effectively to malware dissemination campaigns.

Honeypot systems are designed to capture attacks by simulating real services and/or applications. They employ deception techniques that try to satisfy the attacker's demands, providing him/her with valid responses to service requests and apparently accepting modifications they want to make on the system. There are two main scenarios commonly used for deploying honeypots that differ depending on the objective pursued:

- *Replicate live services of the production environment*: showing a footprint similar to that of the services offered in the production network.
- *Research environments*: showing a configuration of honeypots that enables attacks to be captured, to later analyze new techniques used.

J. Lopez et al. (Eds.): TrustBus 2017, LNCS 10442, pp. 130–144, 2017.
DOI: 10.1007/978-3-319-64483-7_9

This paper focuses on the second scenario, specifically on the design of a capture system that can respond to attacks performed automatically. The main issue when designing this type of solution is the lack of information prior to the attack. Currently, there are principally two approaches to the problem; studying only specific scenarios (web servers, SSH/Telnet protocols, etc.), or implementing specialized trap systems for a reduced set of malware families (eg. Mirai) [3]. However, new malware attacking these honeypots will not necessarily activate all stages of the attack, due to an unfulfilled requirement.

The main contribution of this paper is the design of the Hogney architecture to capture evidence and acquire knowledge about new malware activities by using malware intelligence services. These services are designed to distribute knowledge about compromised IP addresses (for filtering systems), or serve as a platform for the exchange of information about characteristics and operation of malware. One of Hogney's goals is to integrate this type of service into the dynamic adaptation process of honeypots, designed according to the requirements of the malware.

This article is structured as follows. Section 2 details related work. A brief introduction to malware intelligence services is described in Sect. 3. Section 4 describes the components of the proposed architecture, whose interaction is analyzed in Sect. 5 using a specific attack example. Section 6 discusses the feasibility of implementing and deploying the proposed solution. Finally, the conclusions and future work are presented.

2 Related Work

There have been previous works for adapting services offered in honeypots to attackers' requests [4]. Honeytrap implements a connection interception service that dynamically selects which services to offer as stated by a pre-set configuration file. Honeyweb is able to emulate Apache, Microsoft IIS and even Netscape servers. The decision of which one to serve is taken after analyzing the URL requested and then the HTTP headers are configured according to the needs of the attacker.

Moreover, there are honeypots for the TELNET protocol that can simulate that they are running under up to 8 processor architectures [5]. The decision of which architecture to use depends on the type of command sent by the attacker. Similar work has been done with SSH [6,7] whose adaptability mechanism focuses on the interaction with the attacker through an established SSH session. SIPHON [8] focuses on the construction of honeypots using physical devices interconnected through wormholes that redirect attacks towards a set of trap devices.

With a broader scope of application, the work in [9] shows a dynamic management system of high and low interaction honeypots, deployed in a virtualized way according to the honeybrid decision engine. Decision making in this case is focused on detecting interesting traffic using pre-established rules triggered by intrusion detection engines such as Snort.

However, these approaches do not take into account specific aspects of malware behavior. In some cases it is because the scope is not intended for automatic propagation malware, but rather for manual attacks. In other cases the area of study is focused on specific replication of devices, protocols or services based on prior knowledge of attack vectors.

The Hogney architecture is intended to highlight the benefits of incorporating existing live information about current malware campaigns, recent indicators of compromise (IOCs), or/and intelligence information available through projects such as *Malware Information Sharing Platform* (MISP) [10] or *Virus Total Intelligence* (VTI) [11], in order to build an environment as close as possible to malware needs, in such a way that its whole load is unleashed and can be analyzed.

3 Malware Intelligence

We use the term *malware intelligence* [12] to refer to *malware behavior and threat information*. Sometimes the terms *threat intelligence* and *cyber threat intelligence* are also used when there is a need to describe how malware spreads, which nodes are been used and who is behind that code. Nevertheless, we think the term *malware intelligence* better represents the kind of information we need for the architecture described in Sect. 4.

Depending on the information requested, different types of malware intelligence services can be used. We classify them in three levels (L1–L3, Table 1):

- L1. Services that offer lists of compromised IP addresses belonging to botnets or that are part of any current malware deployment campaign.
- L2. Services that allow information about malware files or malicious URLs to be obtained, discovering the malware family, architecture and target operating system, and in many cases information related to the implementation: linked libraries, anti-analysis or anti-virus techniques, processes to which it injects code, etc.
- L3. Malware information sharing services. These services will provide the most up-to-date information regarding the dissemination activities of malware. They allow access to published IOCs and to information about incidents currently under investigation, so none of the information collected has been published.

Regarding L1 services, there is a wide range of projects that list IP addresses, URLs or domains used by malware. For instance, a search for the domain *wrcwdxjh.org* produces an output similar to the following:

```
wrcwdxjh.org Intel::DOMAIN
from malwaredomains.com,locky
via intel.criticalstack.com F
```

This reveals that the domain is related to *Locky* ransomware.

L2 services provide detailed information about files and URLs linked to malware. By submitting a file to these services we get an overview of what kind of malicious activities it performs, what processes are launched, what services are used and what traces it leaves behind.

Table 1. Common information obtained from malware intelligence services

Level	Domain	Information provided
L1	IP/Domains/URL	ip-src, ip-dst, port, url, malware name
L2	File	processor, architecture, mail, PE/ELF/MACH-O executables, document specific, traffic generated by sample, ...
L3	Threat intelligence	private/public info about current threats, IOCs, correlation of incidents, ...

A common query is to search the hash of a suspicious file in order to obtain a report that contains, between other things, information about the architecture and operating system needed to run the file, communications with a domain or IP, files read or modified, libraries and methods used, file format and anti-analysis techniques implemented. If the search request does not provide result, the file is sent for a complete analysis that will generate the information needed.

L3 services are useful when there has been no information collected by L1 and L2 services or this information is inconclusive. L3 services provide access to intelligence information, shared by incident response teams or malware analysts, among different organizations. Sometimes this type of service gives access to information about active campaigns of malware not yet published, because they are currently being studied by analysts and are therefore only labelled as *suspicious activities*.

For instance, searching the hash value *64973870ed358afec07b0ebb1b70dd40* of a file produces a response in which that hash is related to a current propagation campaign of Locky ransomware. The code below shows part of the response obtained when searching that hash. In addition to the information related to that file, several IPs belonging to Locky command and control nodes are also present.


```
<Attribute>
    <id>3367</id><org_id>2</org_id>
    <info>Malspam (2016-03-16)</info>
    <value>http://188.127.231.116/main.php</value>
</Attribute>
<Attribute>
    <id>366617</id><type>md5</type>
    <category>Payload delivery</category>
    <to_ids>1</to_ids>
    <uuid>56e6c1a6-3b5c-457e-9443-473402de0b81</uuid>
```

```
    <event_id>3354</event_id>
    <distribution>5</distribution>
    <timestamp>1457963430</timestamp>
    <comment>- Xchecked via VT</comment>
    <sharing_group_id>0</sharing_group_id>
    <deleted>0</deleted>
    <value>64973870ed358afec07b0ebb1b70dd40</value>
    <ShadowAttribute/>
    <RelatedAttribute>
        <Attribute><id>3355</id><org_id>2</org_id>
            <info>Malspam (2016-03-14)</info>
            <value>64973870ed358afec07b0ebb1b70dd40</value>
        </Attribute>
    </RelatedAttribute>
</Attribute>
```


4 The Hogney Architecture

The purpose of the Hogney platform is to create trap environments to capture activity performed by malware, adapting them progressively as new evidence is generated to determine which action will be triggered next. Therefore, it is necessary to design an architecture that allows analysis according to the three stages of malware: (1) exploration, (2) infection and (3) execution of the payload.

During the *exploration* phase the attacker tries to discover which services are running, checking them for vulnerabilities. An attacker succeeds if he finds a vulnerable service for which he has an exploitation mechanism. Hogney tries to deduce the type of service that the attacker is looking for, offering a honeypot that meets his needs.

In the case the exploration is successful, the attacker moves on to the second stage, *infection*, where the infection code is launched against a vulnerable service for a wide range of reasons. At this point it is important to analyze the infection vector to discern what kind of action the attacker wishes to unleash on the honeypot: inject code, upload a file, leave code, manipulate files, send an email, login to the system, etc. As far as possible it should be made clear to the attacker that such action has been successfully carried out.

Thus, we reach the third stage: *execution of the payload*. This is where, depending on the type of activity, the execution of the code is simulated, the downloaded file is executed in a controlled environment, or the e-mail is sent. However it is important to note that all the modifications executed in the victim's environment have to be logged.

These three phases are managed by the control components shown in Fig. 1: the interception module (IM), dynamic configuration module (DCM) and monitoring of the generated evidence (EM). These three modules are fed with information that allows the next step that malicious code intends to carry out to be predicted.

A key element of the Hogney architecture is the use of malware intelligence services. There are a multitude of services that can be used to obtain information about malware activity, either through searching IP addresses belonging to malware campaigns, querying known infection vectors, signatures or search patterns, or by the explicit execution of malware samples and observation of the actions and changes made. Hogney orchestrates this information, adapting honeypots to the three aforementioned stages. To this end, there are two different trap environments: (i) honeypots specializing in certain protocols and/or services, and (ii) highly interactive environments in which to execute files generated by malware.

The relationship between the components is detailed in the following subsections.

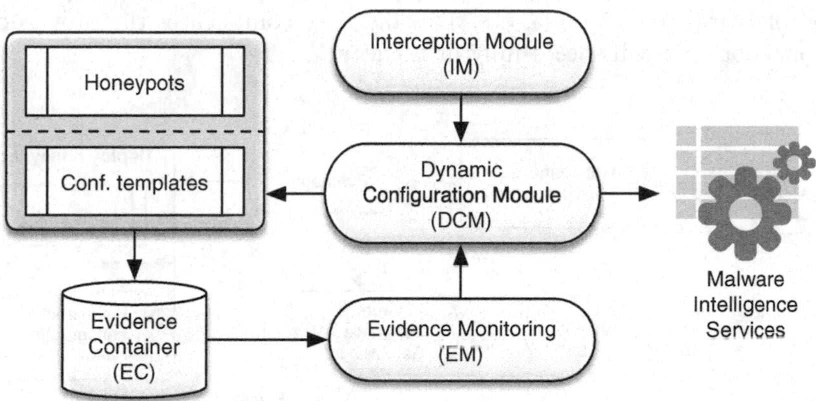

Fig. 1. Architecture diagram

4.1 Interception of Connections

A typical honeypot is configured to listen to a series of predefined ports. When a connection is established with one of them, it responds as described in its configuration. Some low-interaction honeypots only receive requests and store them (e.g. honeyd) while medium interaction honeypots (Inetsim [13]) are able to operate at the service level, responding to sender requests in accordance with the behaviour configured by the operator.

The component for the *interception of connections* (IM) will (i) listen to all ports studied, (ii) receive and accept connections and (iii) send service requests to the DCM component for the configuration of honeypots (Fig. 1). Such requests should include all the information that may have been collected at the time of establishing the connection (IP, destination/source ports, protocol headers, etc.) so that the DCM can more accurately estimate the honeypot with the highest probability of success for this connection.

4.2 Configuring Trap Services

This service is called the *Dynamic Configuration Module* (DCM) and is able to dynamically discern which honeypot is the most suitable for the type of malware involved. To achieve this objetive it is be necessary to have a repository of pre-configured honeypots, set up in such a way that it is easy to switch from one to another depending on the malware's requirements, or to modify its configuration.

For instance, the SMTP protocol is frequently used by malware to send e-mails with attachments containing some kind of malicious code. If a request is received at port 25 it will be redirected to a honeypot capable of handling the reception of the e-mail. However a request to the HTTP/HTTPS port can have very different objectives: it could be an attack on the Apache web server (Windows, Linux, ...), on IIS, etc. It could additionally be an attack on a particular version of WordPress, Joomla, etc. This diversity complicates the provisioning of a honeypot that will successfully fit the attack.

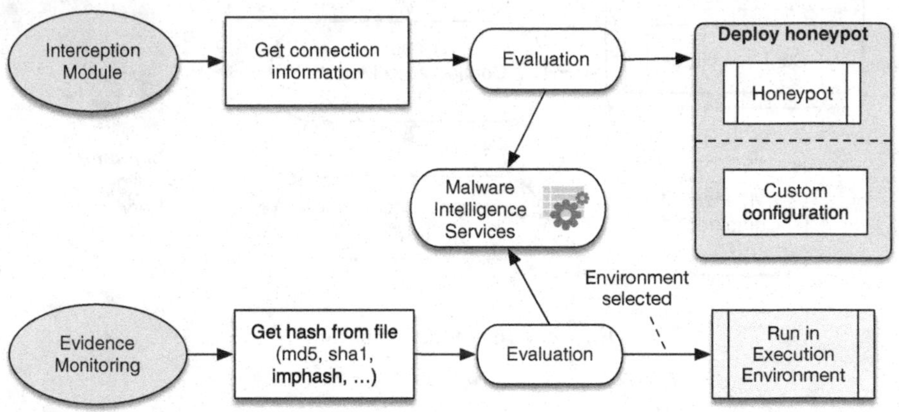

Fig. 2. Two different execution flows of the DCM module

Consequently, this component must process the connection requests in order to choose a honeypot, to initiate or adapt, for the malware in question. This decision is based on the data gathered about the characteristics of the connection:

- **Source IP:** check whether this IP address belongs to a malware campaign currently in progress. In this case, information must be retrieved about the malware family and what services and applications it affects.
- **Destination IP:** if a file has been executed and it is trying to establish an external connection, firewall rules must be adapted to allow this traffic. At the same time, all traffic generated must be recorded for further analysis.
- **Protocol headers:** first packets of many service level protocols contain information about the type of service expected. This must be monitored in order to decide which honeypot, offering that service, could be set up and run.

- **Service information:** destination IP addresses, file and folders, running processes, DNS entries, etc. This information facilitates the configuration of suitable honeypots.
- **Related files:** downloaded files contain useful information about the target operating system, required libraries, resources needed, etc., which can later be used to select a suitable execution environment.

To illustrate, Fig. 2 shows a graph of the execution flow of this component in two specific cases: (i) a service request is received from the interception module, and (ii) the request is received from the evidence monitoring component upon detection of a file created in the evidence container.

In the first case, the information about the received connection (source/destination IP address, protocol, service data, destination files/folders, etc.) must be analyzed. This information will then be used to try to find out which malware is behind that connection. Hence, queries to *external intelligence services* are launched to look for any evidence of malware based on the information collected. As a result, the information obtained from these services is used to adapt a honeypot, already pre-configured, so that it is as close as possible to the scenario that the attacker expects to find. The inquiry process is shown in Fig. 3, where the diagram shows the process which determines whether the IP is linked to malware activities. L1 services are used to determine whether or not the IP is part of any current malware campaign. If there are not results, a query to L2 and L3 services is launched.

The second case reflected in Fig. 2 corresponds to a scenario in which the attacker has managed to download some type of file, either within a honeypot or when running in an execution environment configured by DCM. The monitoring process (EM) will detect the existence of any new evidence, in the form of a new file stored in EC, and will ask DCM to deploy an execution environment for it. Again, this will initiate another request to malware intelligence services to obtain information about that file, in order to gather information about how to build a suitable environment for it. This process is reflected in Fig. 4.

4.3 Evidence Monitoring

The architecture designed includes a container of evidence to store any type of content generated during the attack, regardless of whether it is an executable, interpreted code, binary code, images, documents, etc. The objective of this container is twofold: to gather as much information as possible about the actions carried out by malware, as well as to facilitate the continuity of the attack process, by activating the different stages implemented in the malware.

The *evidence monitoring* (EM) component is continuously monitoring the creation of new evidence. When a new piece is detected, a request is sent to the DCM containing the characteristics of the evidence (file type, operating system, etc.). Then, a new execution environment is set up to analyze this evidence.

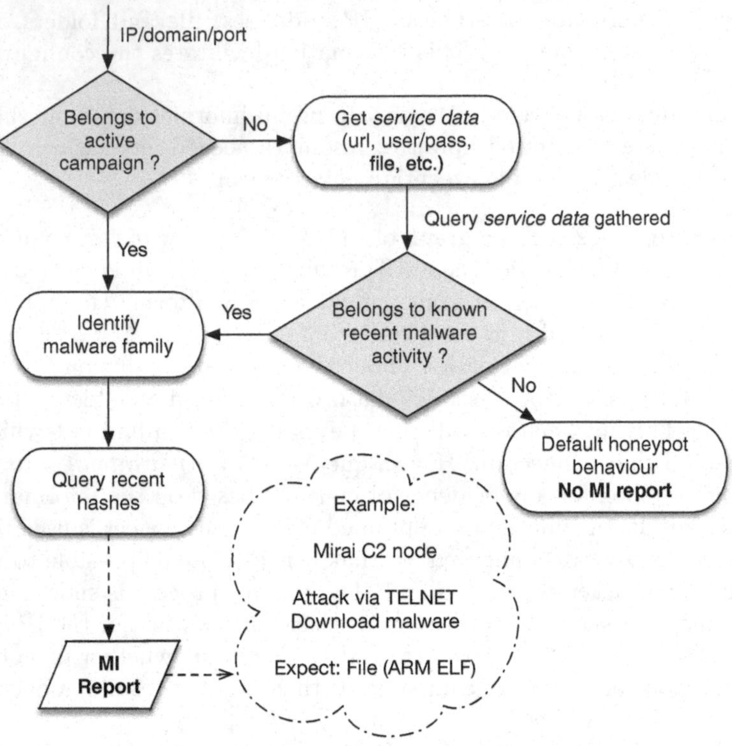

Fig. 3. Requesting information about an IP address

4.4 Provisioning of Honeypots

Thus far, each element of the architecture described corresponds to a controlling or monitoring process. Hogney also needs a set of preconfigured honeypots for common scenarios susceptible to attack. Fortunately, there are a multitude of honeypots specialized in certain environments [4] (Cowrie for ssh, glastopf for HTTP, conpot for PLCs, jackpot for SMTP, elastichoney for elasticsearch, etc.) and others of more general scope (inetsim). Hogney includes them as the basis for our current set of preconfigured honeypots.

However, for a honeypot to be used by DCM, it needs to fulfill some requirements:

- Easily configurable by modifying text files.
- Provide options for configuring banners, service folders, responses to protocol commands, etc.
- Allow configuration of the listening network interface.
- Include capabilities for recording activities performed by attackers.

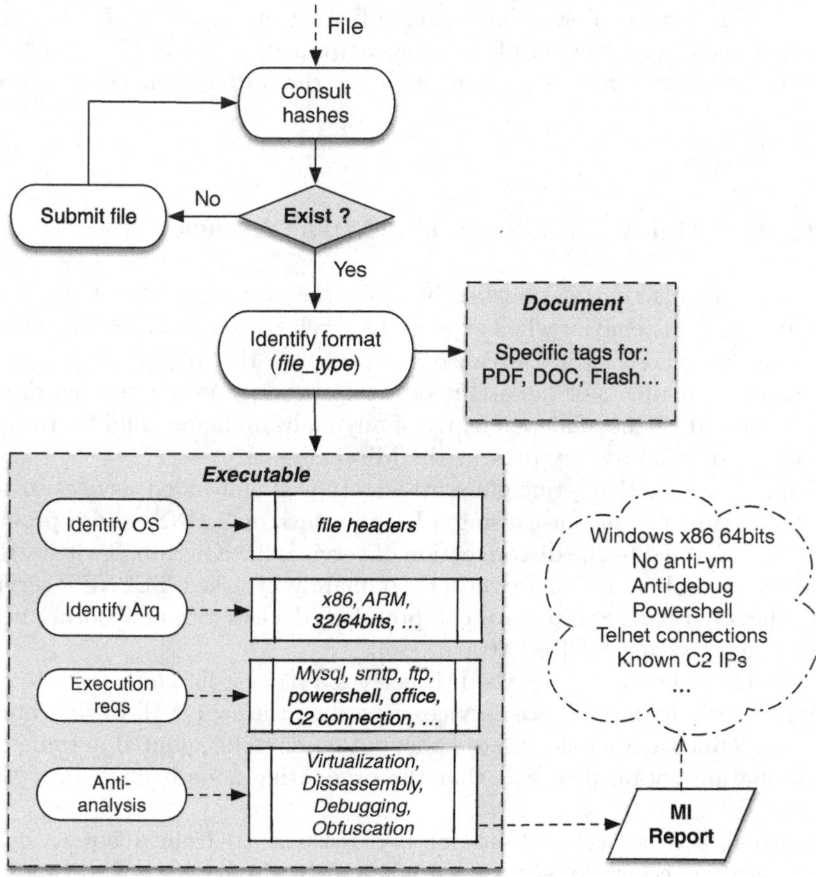

Fig. 4. Requesting information about a downloaded file

Compliance with these requirements will allow DCM to modify the configuration files according to the parameters received in a request for service (which folders should be available, which applications, which protocol banners are expected to be found, etc.).

In addition to specific honeypots of low, medium or high interaction it is necessary to have execution environments where the evidence obtained can be processed. These environments, also considered as high-interaction honeypots, comprise both virtualized and physical machines managed by an orchestrator process. *Cuckoo Sandbox* [14] has been selected for the deployment of the execution environments, largely because it covers our main needs:

- It provides an API that can be used to send files to preconfigured analysis environments.
- It issues an activity report after the execution of files, which is easy to process automatically.

- Good escalation capabilities, offering different mechanisms of adaptation where an increasing number of analysis environments is needed.
- The analysis performed is good enough for the automation needed in our platform.
- Freely available.

5 Hogney Behavior Under the Mirai Attack

This section details the relationship between the components of the Hogney architecture and its behavior when exposed to a well known malware propagation attack. We have chosen Mirai because it produces a rich relationship between the different components of the architecture. However, we want to remark that we have designed Hogney independently of any malware family, and for the sake of brevity we decided to only present the Mirai case.

Mirai is a botnet that principally attacks typical embedded devices in IoT. In 2016 it became famous for causing a DDoS attack on a DNS service provider named DYN that led to the disconnection of services like GitHub, Twitter, Reddit, Netflix, Airbnb among many others. It mainly attacked TELNET services through dictionary attacks, to turn compromised devices into new botnet nodes to be used in subsequent DDoS attacks [15].

Under this scenario (Fig. 5), the IM receives a request for connection to port 23. Next, it consults intelligence services regarding the source IP of the connection to determine whether the telnet honeypot needs to be adapted in some way. The information obtained reveals that the originating node belongs to a Mirai botnet.

Mirai makes telnet connections for two reasons: (i) from a bot to detect that this service accepts known credentials and (ii) from a *loader* to cause the download of a malware file. Since Mirai has malware versions for different architectures, the default configuration of the honeypot can be modified by the DCM to show one of the architectures determined by the intelligence service (ARM in this case).

In the use case modeled in Fig. 5 we depicted the second case, where Hogney is receiving a connection from a Mirai loader. Here, the honeypot deployed records the commands to be executed and even the files that the *loader* has specified to be installed. There are several honeypot implementations of the telnet services (such as Cowrie) that are able to correctly interpret regular file download commands like *curl* or *wget*. The files downloaded are stored in the evidence container.

Once the creation of the downloaded file has been detected, the monitoring process sends a request to the DCM to prepare a honeypot for it. It uses the intelligence obtained from the analysis of the file (e.g. malware for ARM 32-bit architectures in the Linux environment), to create an emulation environment to execute the file (like QEMU [16]).

After executing the file in an environment deployed by the DCM, a connection is made to an external IP address that, after contrasting it with the intelligence available, could reveal a new C2 node of Mirai, or confirm that this is already

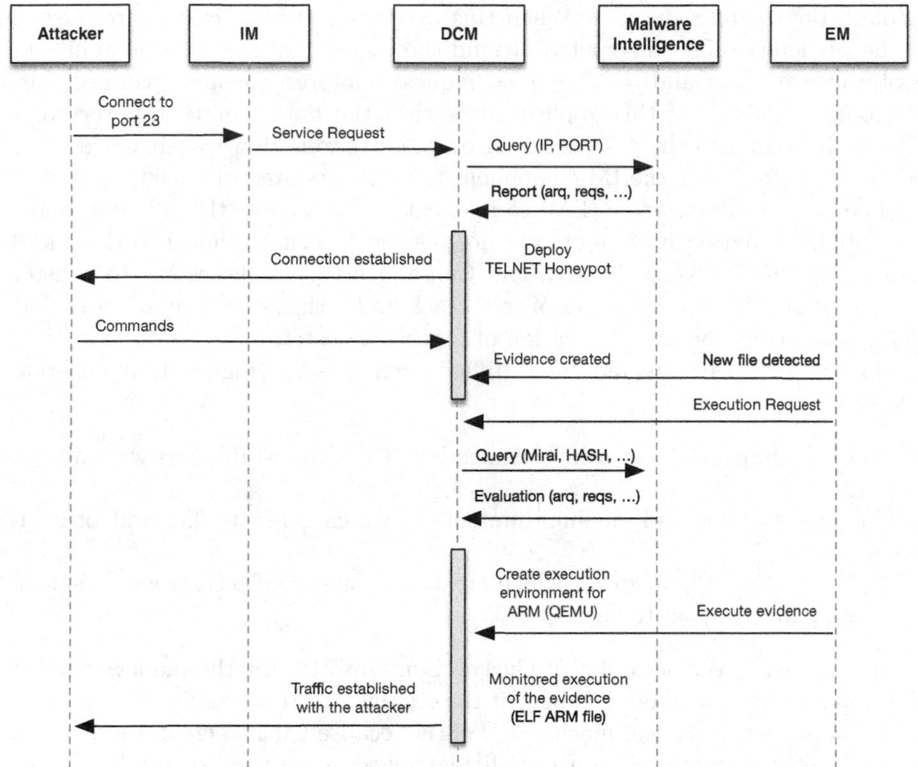

Fig. 5. Hogney components interaction under the Mirai attack

known. Keeping a honeypot acting as a bot node of Mirai allows access to the information about how the C2 node operates, such as the execution of DDoS attacks (and the IP addresses affected).

6 Implementation Discussion

The proposed architecture will eventually employ a multitude of available honeypots, some for generic use and others focused on certain protocols, all together offering a wide range of solutions for the capturing of evidence. However, the construction of a malware capture and analysis platform, like the one designed in this paper, involves overcoming a number of obstacles, some related to design criteria and others regarding implementation. In this section, the implementation of the main components (IM, DCM and EM) of the Hogney architecture will be discussed.

With respect to the *interception module* (IM) there are currently applications, such as *honeytrap*, which work in a similar way as that described for IM in Hogney. Honeytrap is a process that remains listening on all ports, waiting for a connection to be requested. When this happens the connection is redirected to the predetermined honeypot to attend the request. It also has the ability to apply reverse proxy and *mirroring* techniques to address incoming connections. The only drawback of this application is that the honeypot that is served is defined according to the port accessed by the attacker. However, it could serve as a basis for building the IM component that the architecture needs.

The *evidence monitoring* (EM) component must correlate the different events generated, so that each piece of evidence obtained must be linked to the initial connection that triggered its creation. Consequently, it is necessary to register the execution of the three stages of the attack under the same case in a way that facilitates correlation and generation of reports a posteriori.

So far, we have detected three different engines in Hogney that generate evidence:

- The IM component, recording connections that are established with honeypots.
- Honeypots of low and medium interaction, which generate files and/or commands.
- High-interaction honeypots, which create files and connections as a result of running malware on them.

In this sense, the selection of Cuckoo Sandbox [14] for the management of high interaction honeypots will benefit the organization of the evidence executed in virtualized and physical machines. This is because Cuckoo creates a different structure of folders and files for each file launched on an analysis machine. This structure contains all the collected evidence provoked by the execution of the file.

The logic behind the choice of which trap environment to launch is one fundamental aspect to be developed for the DCM component. It must decide, depending on the information gathered, which is the most appropriate environment to serve to the attacker. For this purpose, it will use information available through malware information services, grouped into the three levels described in the Sect. 3.

With regard to L1 services, there is a wide range of projects that offer specific malware information: indicators of compromise (IOCs), types of devices affected, sources of IP used, etc. Perhaps the most convenient way to maximize results when searching, is to use platforms that allow the user to launch queries using several combined sources. For instance, to date the *Critical Stack Intel* [17] includes 118 feeds and offers an application to query them externally.

There are several alternatives for L2 services, although we have selected two solutions that, a priori, can cover our the needs with respect to file/URL analysis:

- *Virus Total Intelligence* (VTI) [11]: this service allows searches with a multitude of parameters. In addition to the hash of a file, it is possible to consult IPs or URLs linked to malware, as well as search for characteristics of the file/URL itself (operating system, architecture, resources contained in the file, system resources used, etc.). Although Virus Total offers free access to its core service for antivirus evaluation, VTI is a paid service.

- *Hybrid Analysis de PAYLOAD Security* [18]: similar to VTI but with fewer options for searching and a smaller base sample base. Nevertheless, the analysis performed on the files adds some interesting features not provided by VTI, such as the anti-analysis techniques implemented. This service, unlike the previous one, offers free access to its intelligence database by limiting the number of queries a user can make.

Hogney will use the MISP platform [10] to access malware intelligence information (L3 services). MISP offers different ways of sharing information, providing an API for querying and obtaining events in different formats (MISP XML, MISP JSON, STIX, STIX JSON, CSV, etc.). Hogney will use a custom installation of MISP connected to an external community for accessing shared data. We will add some custom attributes to our own community created in MISP to improve the interoperability between Hogney and MISP for configuring honeypots.

7 Conclusions and Future Works

The ability of malware intelligence services to provide early recognition of malware traces is noteworthy. It is no surprise therefore, that this is why they are widely used in many defense systems such as IDS and firewalls. Even services like proxies and DNS use the information they provide to avoid leading the user to malicious sites.

Until now, these services have not been used for the dynamic deployment of honeypots. The Hogney architecture, proposed in this paper, shows the versatility that they can provide to configure honeypots in the initial stages of an attack. This functional architecture provides a set of components for the automatic deployment of honeypots according to the intelligence information obtained.

The next steps will be taken towards analyzing the convenience of adopting machine learning techniques for the core of the DCM component. There has been some progress made in creating a machine learning dataset [19] implementing the MIST representation [20] of malware behavior. As stated by MIST's authors, "*the representation is not restricted to a particular monitoring tool and thus can also be used as a meta language to unify behavior reports of different sources*". We could integrate the information gathered from malware intelligence services to quickly create an up-to-date dataset for the DCM component.

Acknowledgments. This work has been funded by Junta de Andalucia through the project FISICCO (TIC-07223), and by the Spanish Ministry of Economy and Competitiveness through the project IoTest (TIN2015-72634-EXP/AEI).

References

1. Internet security threat report: vol. 21, Symantec, Technical report, 2016, April 2016

2. SentinelOne: Sentinelone ransomware research data summary (2017). https://go.sentinelone.com/rs/327-MNM-087/images/Data%20Summary%20-%20English.pdf
3. Cymmetria: Mirai open source iot honeypot (2016). http://blog.cymmetria.com/mirai-open-source-iot-honeypot-new-cymmetria-research-release
4. Nawrocki, M., Wählisch, M., Schmidt, T.C.: A Survey on Honeypot Software and Data Analysis. arXiv.org, vol. 10, pp. 63–75 (2016)
5. Pa, Y.M.P., Suzuki, S., Yoshioka, K., Matsumoto, T., Kasama, T., Rossow, C.: IoTPOT - a novel honeypot for revealing current IoT threats. JIP **24**(3), 522–533 (2016)
6. Pauna, A., Patriciu, V.V.: CASSHH – case adaptive SSH honeypot. In: Martínez Pérez, G., Thampi, S.M., Ko, R., Shu, L. (eds.) SNDS 2014. CCIS, vol. 420, pp. 322–333. Springer, Heidelberg (2014). doi:10.1007/978-3-642-54525-2_29
7. Wagener, G., State, R., Engel, T.: Adaptive and self-configurable honeypots. In: Integrated Network Management (IM) (2011)
8. Guarnizo, J., Tambe, A.. Bhunia, S.S., Ochoa, M., Tippenhauer, N.O., Shabtai, A., Elovici, Y.: SIPHON - Towards Scalable High-Interaction Physical Honeypots. CoRR, vol. cs.CR (2017)
9. Fan, W., Fernández, D., Du, Z.: Adaptive and flexible virtual honeynet. In: Boumerdassi, S., Bouzefrane, S., Renault, É. (eds.) MSPN 2015. LNCS, vol. 9395, pp. 1–17. Springer, Cham (2015). doi:10.1007/978-3-319-25744-0_1
10. Wagner, C., Dulaunoy, A., Wagener, G., Iklody, A.: Misp: the design and implementation of a collaborative threat intelligence sharing platform. In: Proceedings of the 2016 ACM on Workshop on Information Sharing and Collaborative Security, pp. 49–56. ACM (2016)
11. G. Inc.: Virus total intelligence (2017). https://www.virustotal.com
12. Porcello, J.: Navigating and Visualizing the Malware Intelligence Space, pp. 1–7, November 2012
13. Hungenberg, T., Eckert, M.: Internet services simulation suite (2014). http://www.inetsim.org
14. Guarnieri, C., Tanasi, A., Bremer, J., Schloesser, M.: The cuckoo sandbox (2012)
15. Angrishi, K.: Turning internet of things (IoT) into internet of vulnerabilities (IoV): Iot botnets, February 2017
16. Bellard, F.: Qemu, a fast and portable dynamic translator. In: USENIX Annual Technical Conference, FREENIX Track, pp. 41–46 (2005)
17. Critical Stack Inc.: Critical stack intel // feed (2017). https://intel.criticalstack.com
18. Payload Security.: Free automated malware analysis service (2017). https://www.hybrid-analysis.com
19. Ramilli, M.: A machine learning dataset for everyone (2016). http://marcoramilli.blogspot.com.es/2016/12/malware-training-sets-machine-learning.html
20. Trinius, P., Willems, C., Holz, T., Rieck, K.: A Malware Instruction Set for Behavior-Based Analysis. Sicherheit (2010)

Cloud - IoT Security and Privacy

Modelling Cloud Forensic-Enabled Services

Stavros Simou[1(✉)], Christos Kalloniatis[1], and Stefanos Gritzalis[2]

[1] Privacy Engineering and Social Informatics (PrivaSI) Laboratory, Department of Cultural Technology and Communication, University of the Aegean, University Hill, 81100 Mytilene, Greece
{SSimou, chkallon}@aegean.gr

[2] Information and Communication Systems Security Laboratory, Department of Information and Communications Systems Engineering, University of the Aegean, 83200 Samos, Greece
sgritz@aegean.gr

Abstract. Cloud forensics assist investigators on solving cloud-based cyber-crimes. Although investigators use forensic methods and tools to cope with incidents, there are other aspects that put barriers to the whole investigation process. One of these aspects is the way cloud services are designed and implemented. Software engineers are responsible for the design and implementation of them but in many cases, cloud services are not designed nor implemented as cloud forensic-enabled, introducing issues to the outcome of the potential investigation. To design cloud services capable of assisting investigators to solve an incident is a challenge. To overcome this issue, in this paper we present a requirements engineering framework to support software engineers in the elicitation of forensic requirements and the design of forensic-enabled cloud services. The framework considers a set of cloud forensic constraints and a modelling language for the successful collaboration of them with the rest of the requirements engineering concepts. The main advantage of the proposed model is the correlation of cloud services' characteristics with the cloud investigation while providing software engineers the ability to de-sign and implement cloud forensic-enabled services via the use of process patterns.

Keywords: Cloud forensic framework · Cloud forensic constraints · Cloud forensic meta-model · Cloud forensic requirements · Cloud forensics

1 Introduction

Cloud computing provides end-users the ability to use cloud services with minimal management effort and avoiding infrastructure costs. Due to its rapid development and high adoption by consumers and organizations the need to develop cloud services increased dramatically over the past years. These services have been developed in many cases without taking into consideration the cloud forensic needs, resulting in a huge impact in respective cloud forensic investigation processes. In order to investigate an incident in cloud computing, Law Enforcement Agents (LEAs) need to rely on different aspects such as forensic processes, resources, assets, etc. A major help to assist LEAs is to develop a reliable cloud forensic-enabled service/system.

J. Lopez et al. (Eds.): TrustBus 2017, LNCS 10442, pp. 147–163, 2017.
DOI: 10.1007/978-3-319-64483-7_10

A number of perpetrators use cloud computing to gain access to information by exploiting vulnerabilities or they use cloud resources to distribute illegal context, keeping their anonymity behind this "complex" environment. To protect end-users from perpetrators, information system designers should be able to design cloud forensic-enabled services that could assist investigators solve cloud-based cyber-crimes. Designing and implementing trustworthy cloud forensic-enabled services is a great challenge for software engineers. The concept of designing a cloud forensic-enabled service is to provide investigators with all the necessary capabilities to investigate an incident in a forensically sound manner. In order to do so, designers need to explore those forensic requirements and processes that will identify a cloud service or a sys-tem as forensicable (in this paper the term forensicable is used to describe a service of being forensic-enabled).

After a thorough analysis of the respective literature, we concluded that there is a literature gap in supporting software engineers so as to elicit and model forensic-related requirements [1]. Thus, to fill the aforementioned gap we present a requirements' engineering framework to support a way for reasoning about forensic requirements. The framework consists of a set of cloud forensic constraints and a modelling language expressed through a conceptual meta-model. The meta-model presented in this paper not only includes the concepts that make a system forensic-enabled, but also the concepts for cloud forensic investigation identified in [1], raising the importance of the relation between a forensic-enabled system and an investigation process and how the latter is assisted when an incident occurs. In this way an integrated meta-model is produced to assist designers in a way that they will be able to design forensicable cloud services.

The paper is organized as follows. Section 2 presents the set of the cloud forensic constraints considered in the proposed framework. Also for every constraint, an activity diagram is presented describing the applicability of the constraint in the organizational processes in the form of process patterns. In Sect. 3, a modelling language is presented in terms of a meta-model, based on the concepts and the forensic constraints identified in Sect. 2 for supporting the design of a cloud forensic-enabled system. Finally, Sect. 4 provides conclusions and discusses future work.

2 Cloud Forensic-Enabled Framework

This section presents a list of concepts that should be realized in order for a cloud-service to be characterized as cloud forensic-enabled service. The main question answered here is what are those elements that make a system or a service to be characterized as forensic-enabled. To answer this question, a list of concepts is presented following our previews review on the respective field [2]. The concepts presented are defined as constraints since their implementation forces the mandatory use of specific technologies in addition to the existing functionality of the services.

2.1 Cloud Forensic Constraints

For a system or a service to be characterized as cloud forensic-enabled (meeting specific criteria) a dependence should exist between the people using the particular sys-tem or service and, from a technical point of view, the way the service has been implemented. From the people's perspective NIST [3] highlights that the actors involved in the cloud are: consumers, providers, auditors, brokers and carriers. Actors interact with one another depending on their roles in the cloud. The technical perspective focuses on the procedures, forensic mechanisms, security and private policies that are used to implement a cloud service in order to make it reliable and trustworthy to the people.

Seven cloud forensic constraints have been identified from the respective literature based on the cloud characteristics and the forensic properties [4–10]. These forensic constraints have a lot in common with security and privacy concepts identified in various research works [11–14]. Some of the concepts are identical in both worlds, especially when they are examined under a technical point of view. This is due to the fact that the cloud forensic process relies on the privacy and security capabilities to help resolve forensic issues. To clarify the role of the constraints identified in the forensic process, a definition has been given for every single constraint to address its relationship with cloud forensics. Cloud forensic constraints have been also categorized according to the cloud forensic stages that they belong to, the challenges and the solutions that apply to, as well as the actors involved and the respective cloud layers (service models). Stages, challenges and solutions are derived from our previous work in the respective field [2, 15, 16].

Accountability.

Definition: Accountability is the Cloud Service Provider's (CSP) obligation to protect and use consumer's data with responsibility for its actions and liability in case of an issue.

Stages: Identification, Preservation-Collection, Examination-Analysis, Presentation.

Challenges: Access to evidence in logs, Dependence on CSP-Trust, Service Level Agreement, Chain of custody, Documentation, Compliance issues.

Solutions: CSPs should ensure that policies and standards are met with great responsibility and any problems arising from their actions are remedied promptly. They should be able to monitor data and logs with appropriate tools in order to satisfy the policies and demonstrate compliance [4]. Develop assurance methodologies to resolve problems. Obtain assurance of the services by using vulnerability assessment and penetration testing approaches [5].

Actors: Consumer, Cloud Service Provider, Cloud Broker, Cloud Auditor.

Layers: SaaS, PaaS, IaaS.

Transparency.

Definition: Transparency is the condition where an entity can have full access and freedom to manage and control its own data in the cloud at any given time and allow feedback from the entities that accommodate it.

Stages: Identification, Preservation-Collection, Presentation.

Challenges: Access to evidence in logs, Dependence on CSP, Physical inaccessibility, Service Level Agreement, Volatile data, Imaging, Documentation, Compliance issues.
Solutions: CSPs should provide the freedom to consumers to handle and control their own computation and data according to their usage. CSP should implement the obligations (organizational, technical and legal) in order to be transparent about their procedures and functions. Strong SLAs should be signed. On the other hand, trusted mechanisms should be implemented to help establish a better relationship between parties and increase mutual trust.
Actors: Consumer, Cloud Service Provider, Cloud Broker.
Layers: SaaS, PaaS, IaaS.

Internal Disciplinary Procedures.
Definition: Internally disciplinary procedure is the process through which a cloud provider or broker deals with its employees in order to ensure that its employees follow certain norms of discipline.
Stages: Identification, Preservation-Collection, Examination-Analysis.
Challenges: Internal staffing-Chain of custody, Integrity and stability-Multitenancy and privacy, Service Level Agreement.
Solutions: Frequent personnel surveillance to prevent turning rogue and intentional or accidental compromise users' data. Well-trained and accredited staff to undertake the sensitive parts of the investigation. Access rights both on physical equipment and digital data. Enforce legal contracts in employee behavior policy. Access to critical equipment management is restricted.
Actors: Cloud Service Provider, Cloud Broker, Cloud Carrier.
Layers: SaaS, PaaS, IaaS.

Access Rights (Policies).
Definition: Access rights is the permissions that are assigned by an administrator to grand users and applications access to specific operations. Security (data protection) mechanisms for authentication, authorization, access controls, and auditing should be considered in this concept.
Stages: Preservation-Collection, Examination-Analysis.
Challenges: Internal staffing-Chain of custody, Integrity and stability-Multitenancy and privacy, Time synchronization-Reconstruction, Identity.
Solutions: Use security checkpoints. Enforce stringent registration and validation process. Make sure important updates are installed on-time. Prohibit user credentials sharing among users, applications, and services.
Actors: Consumer, Cloud Service Provider.
Layers: SaaS, PaaS, IaaS.

Isolation.

Definition: Isolation is the mechanism to ensure that each consumer's data is sealed and cannot be seen by other tenants.
Stages: Preservation-Collection.
Challenges: Integrity and stability-Multitenancy and privacy.
Solutions: Separate data through partitioning. Ensure that the memory, storage, and network access are isolated.
Actors: Cloud Service Provider.
Layers: SaaS, PaaS, IaaS.

Legal Matters (Regulatory).

Definition: Legal matters are the procedures and actions that need to be undertaken related to jurisdiction issues, international law, contractual terms, legislative frameworks and constitutional issues.
Stages: Identification, Preservation-Collection.
Challenges: Access to evidence in logs, Service Level Agreements, Multi-jurisdiction-Distribution-Collaboration.
Solutions: Global unity must be established. New regulations and international laws should be developed to prevent a breach under any jurisdiction. Accessing and handling data by third parties should be ensured and should be structured in a manner consistent with the provider's policies.
Actors: Cloud Service Provider, Cloud Broker.
Layers: SaaS, PaaS, IaaS.

Traceability.

Definition: Traceability is the ability, for the data to be traced or not by the user [11] and the capability of keeping track of the actions taken at any given point. It also refers to the ability to trace the activities of a consumer in order to lead to him/her.
Stages: Identification, Preservation-Collection, Examination-Analysis.
Challenges: Client side identification, Volatile data, Identity, Time synchronization-Reconstruction.
Solutions: Enterprises should track deployment options to make sure the value chain is uncompromised. Traceability through logs from the user's perspective involving the lifecycle of a file. Track and store all the users' actions through logs. Data and client's traffic should be monitored at all times. Monitor Quality of Service for SLAs regularly to determine any vulnerabilities. Users' activities and accounts should be monitored at all times in order to link users to their logs. Their actions should be stored in the CSP's servers and should be kept ready to be processed by trusted personnel.
Actors: Consumer, Cloud Service Provider.
Layers: SaaS, PaaS, IaaS.

Trust in the cloud is a very important notion; it is the customer's level of confidence in using the cloud. It could be identified as another forensic constraint besides the seven previously described. Due to the fact that trust is fulfilled through the identified forensic constraints such as accountability, transparency, etc., we excluded it from our list. Implementing the forensic constraints and using them with cloud services automatically increases the customer's level of confidence and assists towards the implementation of trustworthy services. In order for a cloud service to be characterized as forensic-enabled all the aforementioned seven cloud forensic constraints should be realized. The implementation of a service consists of numerous actions that need to be carefully examined to prevent malicious activities. These actions can be implemented using one or more forensic constraints. On the other hand, one forensic constraint can be used to implement more than one action in a cloud service. For example, the authorization access, which is part of the access rights forensic constraint, can be used in different activities of a storage cloud service.

2.2 Cloud Forensic Process Patterns

For each forensic constraint identified in the previous section, a process pattern is introduced and explained in the form of an activity diagram. In order to implement these constraints an activity diagram template is introduced as shown in Fig. 1. The template presents the activities that need to be undertaken in order to realize that service. In the case where an activity is not fulfilled, software engineers should seek and implement those techniques that solve the issue and make the service ready for use.

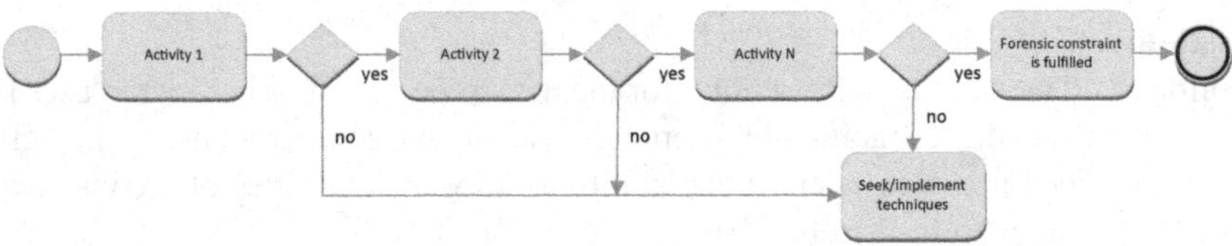

Fig. 1. Template of forensic implementing activity diagram

The proposed patterns (following the activity diagram) describe the actions a cloud provider should produce/take in order to make a cloud service forensic-enabled. The forensic constraints focus on the cloud provider side since it is the entity that owns the infrastructures and provides the cloud services to consumers. The activities shown in the diagrams refer to the cloud provider's activities and the order in which they will be implemented, which in most cases, is not mandatory. Thus, the constraints and the patterns presented are fulfilled on the provider's side. On the other hand, whenever a cloud service is implemented by a third party and a contract agreement is signed between the provider and the third party for using the service, it is the latter's obligation to comply with the forensic constraints and process patterns and implement techniques so as to make the cloud service forensic-enabled. The same applies for the cloud brokers or any other entity involved. The cloud provider is entitled to reject any third party that refuses to comply with the fulfillment of the forensic constraints and can seek for another party who is willing to do so. For instance, if a provider gives a service to a consumer ensuring there is no problem with jurisdictions, the third party the provider relies on, should also ensure that no issues will arise.

The activity diagram for accountability constraint, shown in Fig. 2, presents the activities that need to be fulfilled to ensure that the constraint is successfully implemented. Cloud providers should ensure that strong SLAs will be signed between third parties/consumers and on the other hand, policies and standards are put in practice. Assurance is obtained by providing security certification or validation exercise such as ISO 27001 certification and the results of a SAS70 Type II audit [7]. All the actions undertaken by the provider, third parties, and the consumers should be monitored to ensure that a prompt solution will be given in case of an incident. Attributability is provided in revealing which system element or actor is responsible in case of a deviation from the expected behavior [7]. In the case that one or more of the previous actions/activities have not been fulfilled, the provider should seek or implement techniques that resolve the issue. The same applies for all the constraints listed in the paper.

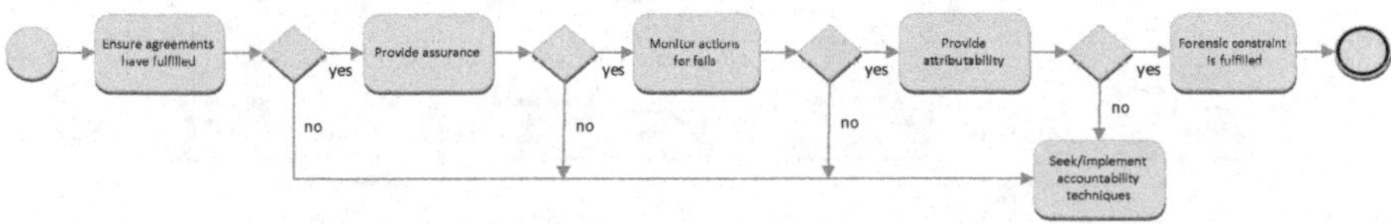

Fig. 2. Accountability activity diagram

For the transparency activity diagram in Fig. 3, CSPs need to ensure visibility of the applications by providing information about them at any time and inform consumers about the location/s of their data. They also need to notify the consumers about their procedures and policies on how the data is being treated and finally, CSPs need to be transparent. Notifications about the policy violations should be used to notify consumers in case of an incident.

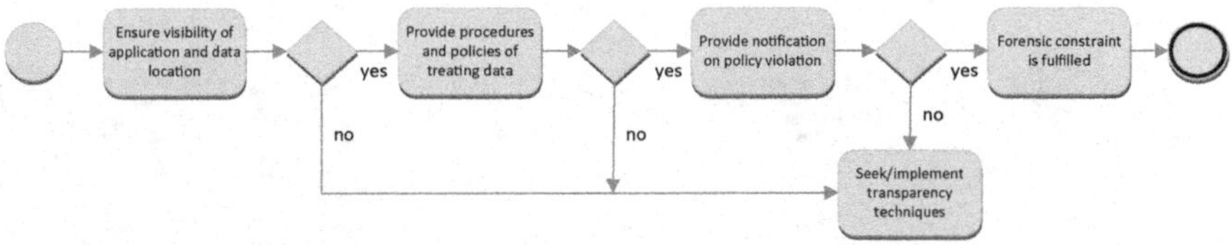

Fig. 3. Transparency activity diagram

The steps a CSP needs to undertake to fulfill internal disciplinary procedures constraint are presented in Fig. 4. Discipline rules need to be implemented and all the personnel should follow them. In case of any deviations, CSP should be able to

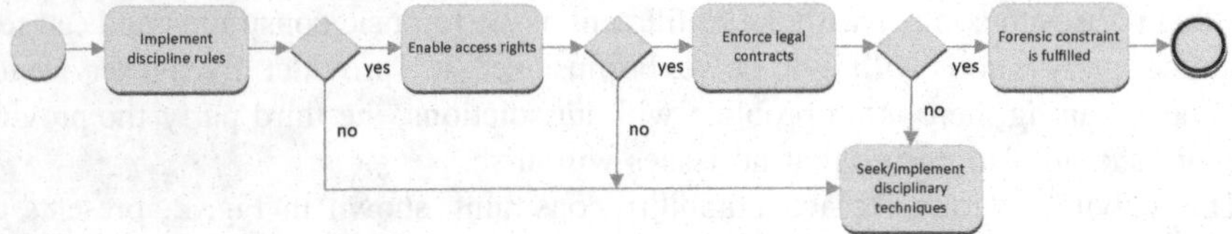

Fig. 4. Internal disciplinary procedures activity diagram

discipline the responsible party without harming its interests. Access rights, both physical and digital should be categorized and their allowance should be granted accordingly. Contracts between the CSP and its personnel should be signed, stating all the details about misuse of information and the penalties.

The access rights activity diagram in Fig. 5 shows the steps a CSP needs to undertake to use the constraint. First, registration should provide all the necessary user's details and a control mechanism should validate the registration form to link as much information as possible with the user's true ID. Authentication and authorization control should be used to verify and determine the level of access of the users. Finally, access control should be implemented to enforce resources' required security.

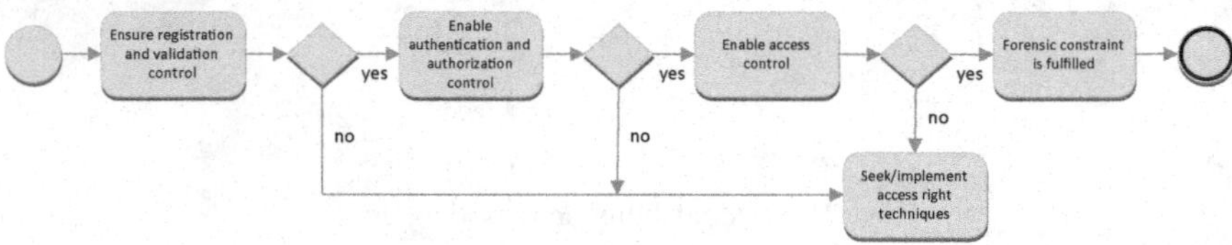

Fig. 5. Access rights activity diagram

The isolation activity diagram in Fig. 6 ensures that a user does not have the right to access other users' data and the data is securely stored. User's virtual machines are separated from the rest of the VMs and in case of an incident, contamination of other users is prevented. Privacy and confidentiality should be maintained at all times in such multi-tenant environment.

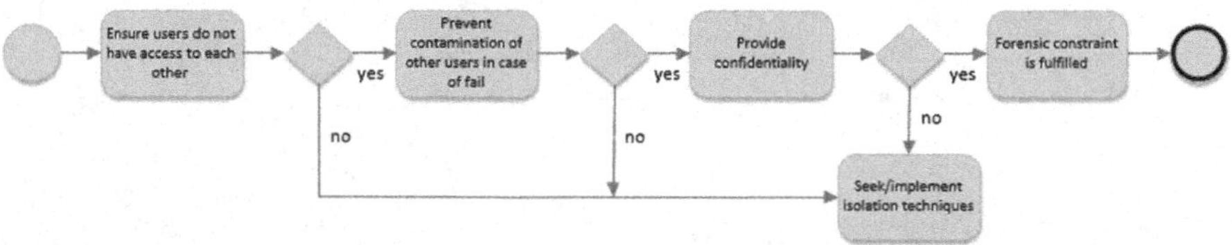

Fig. 6. Isolation activity diagram

Legal matters activity diagram in Fig. 7 is of vital importance since it is the most difficult to implement with all the different people, countries and laws involved. First, a

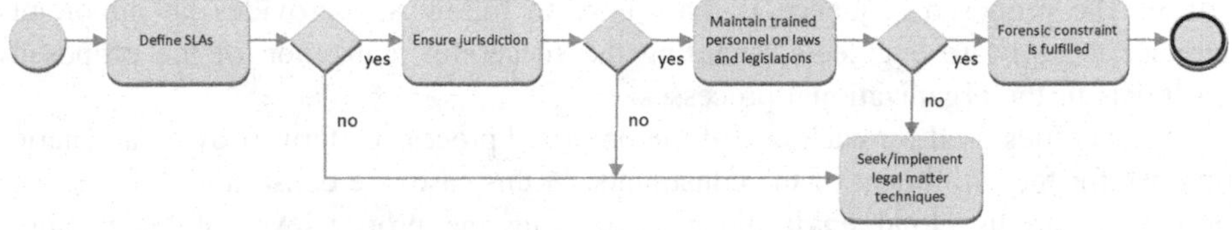

Fig. 7. Legal matters activity diagram

strong and detailed SLA should be presented to ensure the terms of using cloud infrastructures. Then, ensure that a consumer's data should remain within the geographical boundaries of the country the user belongs to, remain under the same jurisdiction and also ensure that the consumer's data will not be distributed around the world. Finally, CSPs should hire and maintain specialized personnel on international laws and legislations related to cloud computing and data handling. The personnel should be trained on a regular basis to be brought up-to-date with new technologies.

Traceability activity diagram in Fig. 8 concerns users and their data. Monitoring users' actions is important in order to reveal any faults. On the other hand, monitoring data logs and taking regular backups can reduce time and effort that is required to resolve malicious incidents. All logs should be stored and secured in places with limited access. The CSP should implement procedures to link data logs with a specific user and his/her activities.

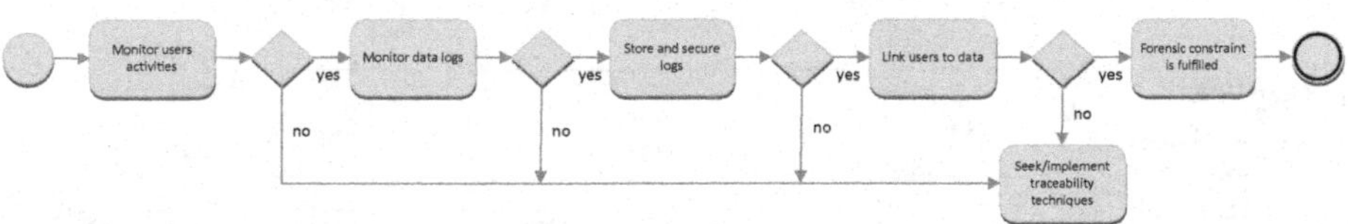

Fig. 8. Traceability activity diagram

The seven forensic constraints described in this section can be divided into four sequential categories. The first one is the *preliminary procedures* and includes the internal disciplinary procedures constraint. This constraint should be implemented before all others, since companies need to establish and implement strong disciplinary procedures for internal usage. The second category is the *organizational agreements*, where the three forensic constraints of accountability, transparency and legal matters are included. This category deals with the agreements need to be signed and clarified between the provider and the clients or third parties. The next category is the *implement technical procedures*. This one includes two forensic constraints, the access rights and the isolation. The specific forensic constraints need to be implemented after the contracts are signed between the parties in order to know on which terms they will be implemented. Finally, the fourth category is the *monitoring*, in which the traceability forensic constraint is included. This is the last constraint in sequence that needs to be established since monitoring occurs after the implementation of the whole system or service. The proposed sequence is mandatory to follow and provides an important guidance to software engineers regarding the successful realization of the proposed constraints in the organizational processes.

The activities used for each one of the proposed process patterns provide a generic approach for the fulfillment of the constraints. In this case, the constraints can be also applied in various cloud environments providing the proper level of technicality without being narrowed for one specific field.

3 Modelling Language for Designing Cloud Forensic-Enabled Services

In order to produce a requirements engineering framework to support the elicitation and modeling of the aforementioned forensic constraints, a common modelling language is introduced. The modelling language is presented in terms of a meta-model, based on the concepts and the forensic constraints identified for designing a cloud forensic-enabled system. The meta-model presented in this paper not only includes the concepts that make a system forensic-enabled but also the concepts for a cloud forensic investigation process from our previous work [1]. In this way, an integrated meta-model is produced to assist designers in creating cloud forensic-enabled services.

Taking under consideration the forensic constraints identified, we proceed in identifying the concepts from the software engineer's perspective in order to develop a cloud forensic-enabled meta-model. The model illustrated in Fig. 9 shows the

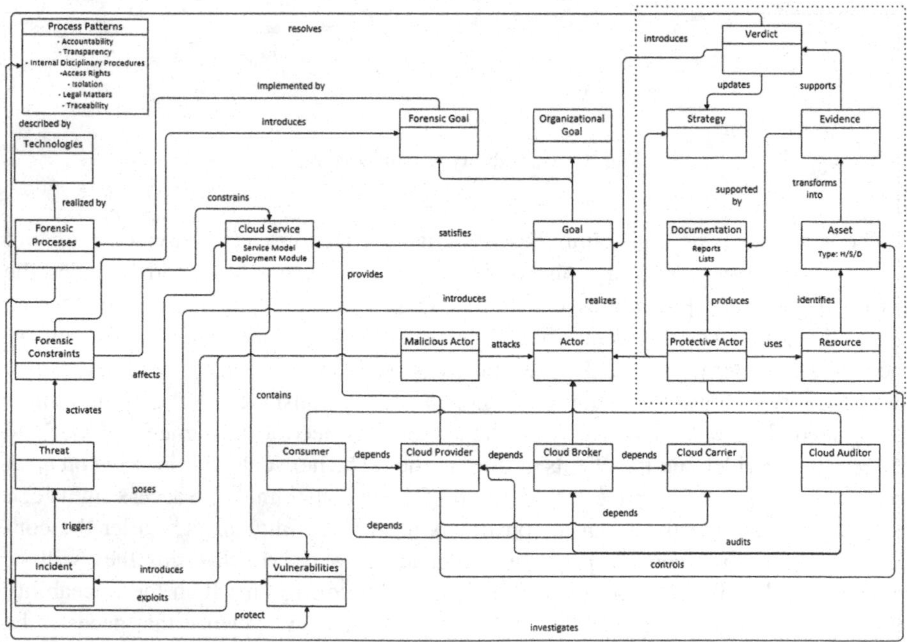

Fig. 9. Meta-model for assisting a cloud forensics process

relationships among critical components through the modelling language. The meta-model is based both on the concepts that make a system forensic-enabled and the concepts that form a cloud forensic investigation process. In the model, the two different groups of concepts are clearly defined and separated from each other since they are used differently in the cloud forensics. On the other hand, some concepts that form the two groups are related to each other, thus the relationships between them must be clarified.

The first group (located in the main area of the meta-model) shows the concepts related to a cloud forensic-enabled service. The second group (located on the upper right corner of the meta-model, separated with dots) shows the concepts related to the investigation of an incident. The two groups have a common goal; the design of cloud forensic-enabled services in order for the investigators to solve an incident in a forensically sound manner. Once the process of making a system forensic-enabled is implemented and the cloud forensic investigation process is developed, then, protective actors just need to follow the steps.

In the next paragraphs, a detailed presentation of the two groups of concepts is introduced describing all the aspects that will assist software engineers in designing a cloud forensic-enabled system/service and investigators to solve an incident in a forensically sound manner.

3.1 Concepts Related to Cloud Forensic-Enabled System

As mentioned earlier in the paper, there are two different groups of concepts concerning the cloud forensic process. The first group assists software engineers in designing and implementing trustworthy cloud services. It describes all those concepts a designer needs to include in his/her design to produce a forensic-enabled service. The list of the concepts is as follows:

Actor. According to NIST [3] the actors involved in the cloud are: consumers, providers, auditors, brokers and carriers. The definitions given for the five actors are as follows:

Cloud Consumer. "Person or organization that maintains a business relationship with, and uses service from Cloud Providers" [3]. A consumer can be any person that uses the cloud either as a common user or as a malicious user. The malicious actor is the one who introduces an incident and he/she is responsible for attacking any other actor involved in the cloud. He/she uses CSPs' services to launch his/her attacks exploiting vulnerabilities hidden behind anonymity. Consumers have dependencies on both cloud providers and cloud brokers.

Cloud Service Provider. "Person, organization or entity responsible for making a service available to interested parties" [3]. CSPs are responsible for offering multiple services to consumers through their deployment modules and service models. Their services should be supplied with responsibility and reliability according to service level agreements signed between actors. CSPs depend mostly on cloud carriers.

Cloud Broker. "An entity that manages the use, performance and delivery of cloud services and negotiates relationships between Cloud Providers and Cloud Consumers"

[3]. The broker helps the consumer to find the suitable cloud providers and negotiate contracts with them. The brokers' main dependencies are on CSPs and cloud carriers.

Cloud Carrier. "An intermediary that provides connectivity and transport of cloud services between Cloud Providers and Cloud Consumers" [3]. Cloud carriers are mostly traditional telecommunication providers responsible for delivering cloud services over their own network and other access devices. The carrier's main objective is to provide CSPs with secure and dedicated connections through service level agreements.

Cloud Auditor. "A party that can conduct independent assessment of cloud services, information system operations, performance and security of the cloud implementation" [3]. Auditors are responsible for evaluating cloud providers' and brokers' services by performing audits in order to verify if their performance and security mechanisms are acceptable to the consumers.

Goal. The concept of goal introduced in this model focuses on the realization and achievement of specific objectives, such as the way the system is designing, implementing, and operating. A goal can be either organizational or forensic. "*Organizational goals express the main organization objectives that need to be satisfied by the system into consideration*" [17]. Forensic goals are generated by forensic constraints. In cloud computing, when system engineers develop a service, they need to realize different forensic goals in order to make the service forensic-enabled. These forensic goals are being introduced by specific forensic constraints and are implemented within the use of forensic processes (explained in the next paragraphs).

Cloud Service. A cloud service describes any kind of resource made available to users over the Internet. Cloud Service Providers are responsible to provide those services through service models and deployment models. Attackers exploit vulnerable services, thus is the most important asset along with the respective resources providing this asset. Cloud services are satisfied by goals.

Vulnerabilities. A vulnerability is a weakness in design, implementation or operation of a system/service that allows malicious actors to exploit the system/service, and create an incident in order to take control, breach, or violate the system. Cloud services may have one or more vulnerabilities that may compromise the integrity or privacy and security of the service. In order to be able to design forensic-enabled services and mitigate the respective vulnerabilities appropriate forensic processes need to be implemented.

Incident. "*A breach of security or a loss of integrity that has impact on the operation of network and information system core services, which public administrations and market operators provide*" [18]. The malicious actor is responsible for introducing an incident in order to exploit vulnerabilities of cloud services. On the other hand, the incident triggers threats for the system. Protective mechanisms should be implemented based on previous incidents to assist software engineers to develop forensic-enabled services.

Threat. A threat is an action that might cause harm to a system/service. Malicious actors pose threats to a system/service and these threats are triggered by their incident. Depending on the type of threat, specific forensic constraints are activated to deal with. The threat aims to affect cloud services in order to gain control of specific assets.

Forensic Constraints. Forensic constraints are non-functional requirements that relate to a system's ability to be forensic-enabled and specify the system's or service's quality attributes. Forensic constraints identified and presented in the previous section allow software engineers to develop forensic-enabled systems/services; systems/services whose architecture supports forensic investigation. These constraints are being activated by the threats triggered by an incident and their main objective is to introduce and produce forensic goals.

Forensic Processes. A forensic process is a sequence of steps where they are applied on the goals that describe a cloud service. When all the forensic processes are applied successfully on the respective goals the cloud service is characterized as forensic-enabled. Forensic processes are described by process patterns (process models that include activities and flows). Specifically, the proposed framework defines seven forensic process patterns, one for each identified forensic constraint. Forensic processes are realized with the help of technologies.

Technologies. Technologies are these techniques and solutions used to handle digital evidence (identify, collect, preserve, analyze and present) and achieve protection in cloud systems. Techniques such as registration and validation that allow us to have accurate information about users, or logging and monitoring mechanisms that provide us information at all-time about users' activities. These procedures will be automatically performed to eliminate potential threats.

3.2 Concepts Related to Cloud Investigation

The second group of concepts provides LEAs with the ability to understand all those concepts that are involved in a cloud forensic investigation and the importance of their roles. This is of vital importance since the cloud forensic-enabled service should be designed in a matter that the identified information will assist the investigator when an incident occurs. Thus, the concepts describing the proposed meta-model should be able to fulfill and collaborate with the information required during an investigation. The list of the concepts related to the investigation process that are considered in the proposed meta-model are the following:

Protective Actors. Protective actors are the people (team) responsible for investigating an incident. They conduct the investigation "*by utilizing and managing the forensic capabilities within the cloud environment adding their own forensic capabilities*" [10]. Protective actors use resources and develop strategies concerning decisions they have to take, based on the training, planning and preparation activities. Planning and organizing an actor's next moves in case of an incident, is very productive when the time comes.

Resources. Protective actors use resources (personnel, tools, methods, etc.) to resolve an incident. The resources that can be used related to personnel are the technicians (provider, protective or victim), the law officers and everyone else working on the case. Using the resources in a proper way the investigation can move forward since the resources can identify all the assets (especially data) hidden in the cloud environment.

Assets. CSP is the one who controls all the assets during a forensic investigation. There are three types of assets; hardware, software and data. Investigators extract data from media and identify traces in data. According to [19] the forensic investigation process transforms media into evidence in three steps. Initially, data is extracted from media and is transformed into a new format, then data is transformed into information and finally, information is transformed into evidence. The types of assets that can be transformed to evidence include, but are not limited to, remote computers, hard discs, deleted files, computer names and IP addresses, usernames and passwords, logs, registry entries and temporary files, browser history, temporary internet files and cache memory, etc. Assets related to cellular phones could be SIM cards, call logs, contacts, SMS and MMS, calendar, GPS locations and routes, etc.

Evidence. Evidence is the most important concept of the legal system. Depending on the way evidence have been acquired and handled in order to maintain chain of custody it can be admissible or not, in a legal proceeding. Examining and analyzing the assets investigators can find evidence and build a case in a court. Documentation supports the evidence and the strongest type of evidence obtained can support an assertion and pursue a positive verdict.

Documentation. The main objective of documentation is to keep the investigation properly documented in order to increase the probabilities of winning a case in a court of law or in an internal investigation. Any risk analysis or assessment tests performed during the training and preparation should be documented to assist the team. All tools, processes, methods and principles performed should be documented properly in order to maintain the chain of custody. Any changes made to the evidence should be also recorded. To present the evidence in a court as admissible, all the parties that have conducted the investigation should record their actions through logs.

Strategy. Strategy is developed both by protective actors and consumers. As far as protective actors are concerned, this concept deals with the methods and policies they use to proceed in an investigation. Protective actors have to take decisions about the acquisition of evidence or the presentation. The outcome of the trial depends on their decisions. On the other hand (consumers way), strategy plays a vital role on the preparation and planning of the system in order to meet the organizational goals. Training is also part of an organization's strategy in order to support forensic services and be prepared to handle an incident.

Verdict. This concept is related to the evidence and particularly to its presentation. When the verdict is announced, the incident is either resolved or an appeal follows. Either way, the strategy should be revised and updated to identify areas of improvement and review methodologies and procedures. Even though verdict as a concept does not belong to a cloud forensic investigation (a verdict is a judgment in a court of law, not a protective actor's action) we strongly believe that it must be illustrated in the meta-model. This is due to the fact that the decision of a jury concludes (closes) a forensic investigation. It is the outcome of the investigation whether it is positive or negative.

An instantiation of all the concepts is presented in Table 1. The scenario where the instantiation is based is as follow:

An executive member (consumer) of an organization stores sensitive data in the cloud using Microsoft Azure as a CSP. A malicious actor who uses the same provider exploits vulnerability in the system and steals the data from the consumer. LEAs have been called to trace and find the malicious actor in a forensically sound manner.

Table 1. Instantiation of concepts

Concepts	Instantiation of concepts
Malicious actor	User who wants to steal information
Consumer	Member of the organization
Cloud provider	Microsoft Azure
Cloud broker	Netskope
Cloud carrier	AT&T
Cloud auditor	StarAudit
Goal	Provide storage capabilities to organization's members
Cloud service	Data storage platform in cloud
Vulnerabilities	Failure to provide isolated storage service to consumers
Incident	Sensitive data have been stolen from consumer
Threat	Data leakage
Forensic constraint	Traceability
Forensic processes	Store data in the cloud providing monitoring capabilities
Technologies	Data and operation logs tracing
Protective actor	Law Enforcement Agents
Resources	Forensic tools, LEA's and CSP's personnel
Assets	Card payment information, CSP's subscriber id, logs, virtual machine and storage data, usernames and passwords
Evidence	IP address, username and password, logs
Documentation	Action plan report, methodology report, resource report, assets report, evidence report
Strategy	LEA acquires evidence through monitoring and snapshots
Verdict	Strong evidence brought a conviction

4 Conclusion

Cloud services used by consumers have been increased rapidly. There is an urgent need for these services to be developed in a way to assist protective actors to resolve cloud incidents. In order to do so, cloud services should be implemented to be used as cloud forensic-enabled. This paper focuses on this direction and introduces a cloud forensic-enabled framework that identifies the forensic constraints and the forensic process patterns for each one of them. Then, it presents a modelling language for designing cloud forensic-enabled services in terms of a meta-model, based on the concepts and the forensic constraints requirements identified for designing a cloud forensic-enabled system. This paper is an initial step towards the construction of a Cloud Forensic-Enabled Framework (CFEF) that will contain the proposed forensic constraints, the process patterns and the meta-model as well as a process based on the constraints and concepts for assisting designers to develop cloud forensic-enabled services. Our intention is to present the framework process in our next work.

References

1. Simou, S., Kalloniatis, C., Mouratidis, H., Gritzalis, S.: Towards a model-based framework for forensic-enabled cloud information systems. In: Katsikas, S., Lambrinoudakis, C., Furnell, S. (eds.) TrustBus 2016. LNCS, vol. 9830, pp. 35–47. Springer, Cham (2016). doi:10.1007/978-3-319-44341-6_3
2. Simou, S., Kalloniatis, C., Kavakli, E., Gritzalis, S.: Cloud forensics: identifying the major issues and challenges. In: Jarke, M., Mylopoulos, J., Quix, C., Rolland, C., Manolopoulos, Y., Mouratidis, H., Horkoff, J. (eds.) CAiSE 2014. LNCS, vol. 8484, pp. 271–284. Springer, Cham (2014). doi:10.1007/978-3-319-07881-6_19
3. Liu, F., Tong, J., Mao, J., Bohn, R., Messina, J., Badger, L., Leaf, D.: NIST cloud computing reference architecture. NIST Special Publication, vol. SP 500-292, p. 35 (2011)
4. Cloud Accountability Project. http://www.a4cloud.eu/cloud-accountability. Accessed Mar 2017
5. Newcombe, L.: Securing Cloud Services: A Pragmatic Approach to Security Architecture in the Cloud. IT Governance Publishing, UK (2012)
6. NIST Cloud Computing Security Working Group: NIST cloud computing security reference architecture, Working document. NIST, vol. Draft SP 500-299, p. 204 (2013)
7. Catteddu, D., Felici, M., Hogben, G., Holcroft, A., Kosta, E., Leenes, R., Millard, C., Niezen, M., Nuñez, D., Papanikolaou, N., Pearson, S.: Towards a model of accountability for cloud computing services. In: Paper Presented at the Proceedings of the DIMACS/BIC/A4Cloud/CSA International Workshop on Trustworthiness, Accountability and Forensics in the Cloud (TAFC) (2013)
8. Zawoad, S., Hasan, R.: A trustworthy cloud forensics environment. In: Peterson, G., Shenoi, S. (eds.) DigitalForensics 2015. IAICT, vol. 462, pp. 271–285. Springer, Cham (2015). doi:10.1007/978-3-319-24123-4_16
9. Ruan, K., Carthy, J., Kechadi, T., Crosbie, M.: Cloud Forensics. In: Peterson, G., Shenoi, S. (eds.) DigitalForensics 2011. IAICT, vol. 361, pp. 35–46. Springer, Heidelberg (2011). doi:10.1007/978-3-642-24212-0_3
10. Ruan, K., Carthy, J.: Cloud forensic maturity model. In: Rogers, M., Seigfried-Spellar, Kathryn C. (eds.) ICDF2C 2012. LNICST, vol. 114, pp. 22–41. Springer, Heidelberg (2013). doi:10.1007/978-3-642-39891-9_2
11. Kalloniatis, C., Mouratidis, H., Vassilis, M., Islam, S., Gritzalis, S., Kavakli, E.: Towards the design of secure and privacy-oriented information systems in the cloud: identifying the major concepts. Comput. Stand. Interfaces **36**(4), 759–775 (2014)

12. Chang, C., Ramachandran, M.: Towards achieving data security with the cloud computing adoption framework. IEEE Trans. Serv. Comput. **9**(1), 138–151 (2016)
13. Kalloniatis, C., Kavakli, E., Gritzalis, S.: Addressing privacy requirements in system design: the PriS method. Requir. Eng. **13**(3), 241–255 (2008)
14. Shei, S., Kalloniatis, C., Mouratidis, H., Delaney, A.: Modelling secure cloud computing systems from a security requirements perspective. In: Katsikas, S., Lambrinoudakis, C., Furnell, S. (eds.) TrustBus 2016. LNCS, vol. 9830, pp. 48–62. Springer, Cham (2016). doi:10.1007/978-3-319-44341-6_4
15. Simou, S., Kalloniatis, C., Kavakli, E., Gritzalis, S.: Cloud forensics solutions: a review. In: Iliadis, L., Papazoglou, M., Pohl, K. (eds.) CAiSE 2014. LNBIP, vol. 178, pp. 299–309. Springer, Cham (2014). doi:10.1007/978-3-319-07869-4_28
16. Simou, S., Kalloniatis, C., Gritzalis, S., Mouratidis, H.: A survey on cloud forensics challenges and solutions. Secur. Commun. Netw. **9**(18), 6285–6314 (2016)
17. Kavakli, E., Kalloniatis, C., Loucopoulos, P., Gritzalis, S.: Incorporating privacy requirements into the system design process: the PriS conceptual framework. Internet Res. **16**(2), 140–158 (2006)
18. ENISA: Cloud computing incident reporting: framework for reporting about major cloud security incidents (2013)
19. Kent, K., Chevalier, S., Grance, T., Dang, H.: Guide to integrating forensic techniques into incident response. NIST Special Publication, vol. SP 800-86, p. 121 (2006)

An Exploratory Analysis of the Security Risks of the Internet of Things in Finance

Carlton Shepherd[1(✉)], Fabien A.P. Petitcolas[2], Raja Naeem Akram[1], and Konstantinos Markantonakis[1]

[1] Information Security Group, Royal Holloway, University of London, Surrey, UK
{carlton.shepherd.2014,r.n.akram,k.markantonakis}@rhul.ac.uk
[2] Vasco Data Security, Wemmel, Belgium
fabien.petitcolas@vasco.com

Abstract. The Internet of Things (IoT) is projected to significantly impact consumer finance, through greater customer personalisation, more frictionless payments, and novel pricing schemes. The lack of deployed applications, however, renders it difficult to evaluate potential security risks, which is further complicated by the presence of novel, IoT-specific risks absent in conventional systems. In this work, we present two-part study that uses scenario planning to evaluate emerging risks of IoT in a variety of financial products and services, using ISO/IEC 20005:2008 to assess those risks from related work. Over 1,400 risks were evaluated from a risk assessment with 7 security professionals within the financial industry, which was contrasted with an external survey of 40 professionals within academia and industry. From this, we draw a range of insights to advise future IoT research and decision-making regarding potentially under-appreciated risks. To our knowledge, we provide the first empirical investigation for which threats, vulnerabilities, asset classes and, ultimately, risks may take precedence in this domain.

Keywords: Internet of Things · Risk assessment · Finance · Security

1 Introduction

The Internet of Things (IoT) – the notion that everyday objects will act on the environment and gain Internet connectivity – is projected to transform various sectors, such as agriculture [24], logistics [11], manufacturing [32] and healthcare [35]. The vision that IoT will be adopted into most business processes necessitates the development of technologies to secure it. Managing potentially sensitive data from an unprecedented number of sources, malware, and designing infrastructures with hugely heterogeneous devices are widely-recognised security challenges [38]. The IoT is projected to significantly impact the financial sector in particular [13]. The abundance of business- and consumer-held IoT devices – whether in the home, on business premises, or held personally – may enable novel payment methods, finer customer profiling and more accurate pricing of

J. Lopez et al. (Eds.): TrustBus 2017, LNCS 10442, pp. 164–179, 2017.
DOI: 10.1007/978-3-319-64483-7_11

financial products. The concept of pricing insurance from sensing devices, e.g., for home [27] and life [8] products, is long-standing. Vehicle telematics have, most notably, been deployed widely for pricing motor insurance premiums more accurately from driving style [28,35]. Enterprise analysis products, like IBM's Watson IoT for Insurance [16], are becoming deployed for computing insurance risks at scale from customer IoT data. Salesforce IoT Cloud [29], similarly, aggregates customers' IoT data – behavioural and contextual information from personal devices – for user profiling. Additionally, IoT devices have been targeted for interacting with financial data more conveniently, e.g., stock tickers and trading platforms for smartwatches [14]; building energy budgeting models using ambient data from the home [5]; and conditioning smart contracts using in-transit environmental data [12]. Tata Consultancy predicts that, by 2018, over $207m will spent by financial firms on IoT-related product development [33].

Despite the growing number of applications, however, little academic work exists to assess the risks it poses to users and providers. In insurance, malicious customers may offer fraudulent data to providers to falsely achieve cheaper premiums. Alternatively, the value and volume of data produced by IoT devices may complicate customer data protection, potentially exposing businesses to significant reputational and legal risks. In this work, we address this space by methodically quantifying the risks involved with plausible IoT financial situations, using scenario planning scenarios and ISO/IEC 27005:2008 [1]. We examine a cross-section of consumer-centric financial products and services, such as insurance, in-branch banking and frictionless payments, to formulate scenarios in which IoT could be applied. The risks are evaluated using a detailed internal risk assessment with 7 financial security professionals with 55 combined years experience, before comparing them with a survey with 40 external security professionals in industry and academia. The contributions of this paper are as follows:

- Systemically quantifying the potential risks of IoT on a range of financial products and services, across a range of situations, with the assistance of scenario planning and ISO/IEC 27005:2008. To our knowledge, this is the first work that methodically grounds the potential risks of IoT in finance.
- Categorising and ranking these risks and a comparative analysis with existing opinions on IoT security from 40 security professionals.
- Recommended areas of focus, based on empirical analysis, for where IoT may impact most significantly in finance.

2 Related Work

While little work has been conducted on IoT in finance, academic risk assessments have been published in related domains, namely in mobile [20,34] and cloud computing literature [30], and RFID/NFC in air travel [2]. Theoharidou et al. [34] present a smartphone-based risk assessment methodology to address the shortcomings of traditional assessments (which typically consider smartphones as a single entity). Smartphone-specific assets – device hardware, operating systems and mobile applications of varying classes, e.g., finance and transport – are used alongside application permissions and threat likelihood to derive risk values. The authors illustrate the methodology using an Android-based device and a test user with a managerial position in the pharmaceutical industry. The resulting risk values are intended to be incorporated with a regular ISO/IEC 27005:2008 assessment.

In healthcare, Lewis et al. [20] propose a methodology for assessing the risk of mobile applications by professionals, such as drug-dose calculators, reference and educational resources, and stored patient records. The authors focus on applications that may violate patient rights, e.g., health data remaining confidential and integral, and applications that may bring harm to parents. Healthcare-specific threats are incorporated in the risk analysis, e.g., whether clinical harm is reversible, in addition to typical threats, e.g., the loss of patient data. Such threats are subsequently paired with their associated vulnerabilities, e.g., absence of rigorous fail-safes and data encryption. These are combined with the physical capability of the application, such as a BMI calculator (low capability) or drug control device (high capability), to evaluate whether the application ought to undergo formal regulatory approval.

Saripalli et al. [30] propose the QUIRC framework for evaluating the security risks of cloud computing platforms. The work defines an impact factor, the effect of a security event on an organisation's assets and operations, and the probability of that event occurring to derive a risk value. An event's impact factor is drawn from its effect on six attributes – confidentiality, integrity, availability, trust, accountability and usability – and combined using a weighted sum as function of its probability. Event probability is determined from known statistics, such as the number of XSS and SQL injection attack reports. The authors also present a list of cloud and web security threats relevant to a QUIRC-based assessment.

Distinctively, our work assesses the risks of IoT in consumer-centric finance using technologies gaining traction in emerging academic and industrial research, e.g., car-based commerce [4] and smart contracts [12], as well as more mature technologies, e.g., vehicle telematics. The European Network and Information Security Agency (ENISA) conducted similar work in forecasting the risks of RFID on air travel [2,3]. Scenario planning – discussed in Sect. 4 – is used to examine these from a variety of demographics and applications, such as using programmable RFID tags placed in luggage to track whereabouts and to expedite check-in and boarding. Three scenarios are constructed in total covering a variety of such situations. The threats, vulnerabilities and assets involved in these are used to calculate risks using ISO 27005:2008, and a range of research and policy recommendations are proposed.

3 High-Level Methodology

Based on existing work by ENISA [2,3], we opted for a scenario-based methodology to plan IoT applications in consumer finance. Scenario planning is used routinely in the military [18], corporate planning [6] and governmental policy making [7,9,36] to evaluate emerging risks of plausible, but not yet realised, scenarios. Schoemaker describes scenario planning as the telling of realistic stories about plausible future events based on extrapolation from present trends, and *"helps expand the range of possibilities we can see, while keeping us from drifting into unbridled science fiction"* [26]. Each scenario was constructed with input from a base of seven professionals in the financial security sector, and the risks in each were evaluated in accordance with ISO 27005:2008. This was contrasted with the results of a survey with 40 external information security professionals, sourced from academia and industry. The forecasting process comprises six stages, shown in Fig. 1, and described as follows:

1. **Plausible Scenario Formulation:** Formulate various situations that explore IoT applications in consumer-centric finance with scenario planning (using the process and scope described in Sect. 4).
2. **Formalisation:** Identify and categorise threats, vulnerabilities and assets in those scenarios, as per ISO 27005:2008, via the process in Sect. 5.
3. **Value Assignment:** Assign integers that reflect the likelihood and impact of threats and vulnerabilities, and the value of assets involved.
4. **Internal Risk Evaluation:** Review and evaluate the values in the last step, and computing risk values using the process in Sect. 5.2.
5. **External Evaluation:** Establish existing judgements relating to IoT security using a survey with external participants, as described in Sect. 6.1.
6. **Insights and Conclusions:** Produce insights via comparative analysis and formulate recommendations.

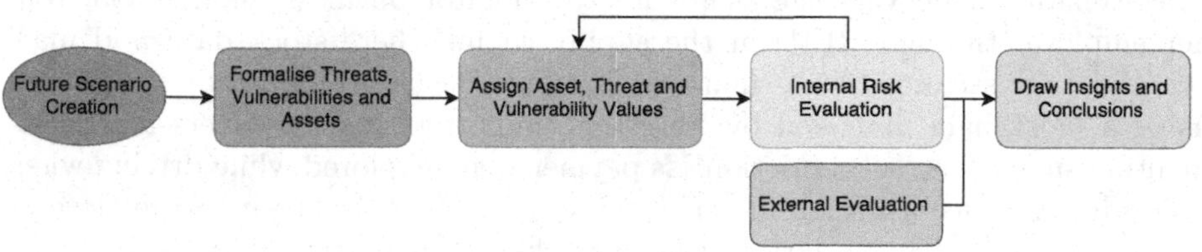

Fig. 1. High-level risk analysis process.

4 Scenario Formulation

The focus of this work is consumer-oriented financial products. We concentrate on end-users and their relationship with financial institutions; we do not directly consider bank personnel or the internal workings of financial institutions. While these too are likely to be impacted by IoT, we believe that this will be shared by most service industries. The timeframe for our investigation is limited to the present to near-future (approximately 5 years) to incorporate emerging IoT technologies that may become mainstream. Where available, we refer to real-life examples of emerging IoT products explored by financial services, e.g., as demonstrations or in white papers.

Similar to [2], three scenarios were created using an iterative approach that, firstly, identified locations where IoT could be applied, e.g., while in-store, at home or in a bank's branch; secondly, listing plausible and relevant IoT technologies in such locations; and, thirdly, identifying financial products that could leverage such technologies in those locations. The locations, actors, IoT technologies and chosen financial products were revised between scenario creators and reviewers. This cycle was repeated until all implausible IoT applications were removed, before formalising the associated assets, threats and vulnerabilities. Note, however, that security threats regarding a smartphone owned by other entities in the scenario, such as a fellow shopper in a supermarket, for example, were not considered. The scenarios are summarised in the following sub-sections. We explicitly list the financial products and the IoT applications in each scenario in Table 1. Given the timeframe of the scenarios, we made the conservative assumption that communication and architectural methods would not change radically. We make regular use of current, standardised methods of short-range communication (e.g., Bluetooth, RFID and NFC), long-range communication (WiFi and 4G) and architectures (e.g., client-server model mediated by an HTTP API).

Scenario A. Follows a technically-adept international businesswoman suffering from a chronic health condition. The scenario explores the use of sensor-equipped pillboxes that monitor drug consumption to assist with adherence[1]. Her adherence is used to price her health insurance premiums by streaming the data through her smartphone, via Bluetooth, to a remote service via 4G or WiFi. The scenario also covers the use of IoT to monitor business information from her employer through RFID in the supply chain, where stock data and market prices are streamed to a smartwatch client. Business shipments are tracked using a blockchain managed by freighters, importers and exporters for implementing smart contracts. Frictionless payments are explored while driving when pre-ordering coffee using an in-car, Internet-connected dashboard to retrieve at a roadside store. The scenario captures tracking lost or stolen insured items by placing GPS/location modules into valuables, such as a watch or necklace, that streams coordinates to a remote recovery service.

Scenario B. Observes a family supermarket trip, exploring the use of product recommendation using a system that learns past behaviour; frictionless payments with RFID-equipped items, avoiding the need to queue at checkouts; and targeted advertising using in-store beacons, which push discounts via Bluetooth LE[2]. The scenario examines emerging budgeting methods that monitor energy consumption from smart home appliances. This is enabled by streaming data to

[1] AdhereTech is one example of sensor-enabled pillboxes (https://adheretech.com).

[2] Beacons track users' in-store location and push notifications to connected mobile devices. Beaconstac is one such example (http://www.beaconstac.com/retail).

Table 1. Investigated IoT technologies and products and services.

Product/Service	IoT applications & related work
Scenario A	
Health insurance	Personalised pricing from physiological sensor data [19]
	Drug adherence monitoring [23]
Business analytics	RFID in financial supply chains [17]
	Sensor-equipped warehouses [39]
	Smart contracts in international trade [12]
Motor insurance	Premium pricing from vehicle telematics [28]
Frictionless payments	Car-based commerce[a] [4]
	Ubiquitous contactless payments[b]
Targeted advertising	Localisation with Bluetooth beacons [10]
Insurance forensics	Tracking sensor-equipped valuable items [25]
Scenario B	
Price comparison	RFID-tagged store items [22]
Product recommendations	Learning from in-store item interactions [37]
Frictionless payments	Automated item replenishment from appliances [15]
	Automated checkout with RFID-tagged items [22]
Budgeting services	Adapting home energy consumption to budget [5]
Frictionless payments	Car commerce [4]
Targeted advertising	In-store beacon technology [10]
Scenario C	
Bank account management	Centralisation of retail banking services on wearable devices
	Continuous, sensor-based authentication [31]
	NFC access control for 'smart' bank safety deposit boxes
In-branch experience	Beacon technology [10]
Motor insurance	Vehicle telematics [28]

[a]Car commerce is the ability to initiate in-vehicle financial transactions.
[b]Ubiquitous payments refer to NFC-type contactless payments in public places, e.g., purchasing advertised goods on digital signage using a nearby terminal.

a LAN-connected hub, which is accessible to a mobile client. The owner may control these appliances by activating eco-/power-saving modes to reduce operating cost. In-vehicle commerce is also explored to pay for charging points with electric cars using a credit account stored on the driver's phone, as well as proposing optimal loan terms from past spending behaviour.

Scenario C. Observes a retired man and the effects of evolving demographics on banking with respect to technological resistance and technical illiteracy. The scenario captures managing multiple bank accounts from a single wearable device (service centralisation) and in-branch Bluetooth beacons for displaying offers, assessing customer footfall, and clerk/appointment notification. Vehicle telematics is investigated for accurately pricing motor insurance, where sensor data – car location, speed and driving aggression – is streamed to a remote insurance server over a 4G mobile network. Additionally, continuous authentication and NFC-based access control is explored for accessing bank accounts and in-branch safety deposit boxes with improved usability.

5 Risk Assessment Methodology

The scenarios were formalised into explicit lists of assets, security threats and vulnerabilities, as defined in the following section.

5.1 Definitions

In our assessment, the definitions of assets, vulnerabilities and threats were drawn from ISO/IEC 27005:2008 [1] as follows. Note that typical risk assessments include existing controls; as per [2], we assume their existence and are reflected in the threat, asset and vulnerability values.

Threats are events that endanger an asset via criminal actions, e.g., the interception of network traffic; the environment, e.g., fire and floods; or accidental actions, such as through human error. Each was given a value between 1–5 representing its likelihood and noted whether it impacts confidentiality, integrity and availability. Human threats, e.g., criminal behaviour, were approximated from the likely capability and motivation of the threat agent, while the remaining threats were estimated from their perceived likelihood and damage potential.

Assets comprise physical devices, online/corporate services, software applications and data that supports business processes or relate to personal information. Assets were categorised into the following groups: *physical devices*, e.g., wearable devices and smartphones; *data*, such as transaction information, sensor data and access credentials; *services*, i.e. applications required to conduct and support business activity, such as customer databases; and *consumer applications* used by users to interact with business services. Each asset was assigned its owner and an value of 1–5 (low to high) representing its likely value. This value was approximated by considering its replacement value and the following areas based on Marinos et al. [21]: *convenience*, *economic benefit to users*, *time saved*, *energy saved* and *security benefit*. Assets may also be comprised of smaller sub-assets: a smartphone, for example, that contains multiple applications.

Vulnerabilities comprise circumstances that enable a threat to be realised and were categorised into the following groups: *hardware*, *network*, *organisational/governance* (e.g., compliance with regulations), *personnel* (e.g., poor employee awareness) and *software* flaws. Each vulnerability was paired with its relevant assets and assigned an integer between 1–5 denoting the *exposure* of the asset to the vulnerability and the degree to which it may harm an asset (*severity*). A single value was produced by computing the mean of these.

5.2 Risk Calculation

Asset, threat and vulnerability combinations were assessed manually for their plausibility, before discarding illogical triples, e.g., power outages disrupting the confidentiality of passive RFID tags. The final risk list was aggregated from the remaining combinations of assets, vulnerabilities and threats. Following this, the exposure, severity and value numbers for the vulnerabilities, threats and assets were reviewed and revised once more. A single risk value was calculated using the risk formula in Eq. 1, as used in [1]. The matrix shown in Table 2 depicts the range of possible risk values from 1–13, reflecting the ENISA classification system (1: lowest; 13: highest risk) [1,2]. Finally, the mean risk and standard deviation was computed for each asset, threat and vulnerability category in Sect. 5.1.

$$\text{Risk} = \text{Asset Value} + \text{Vulnerability Value} + \text{Threat Value} - 2 \tag{1}$$

Table 2. Risk score matrix derived from asset, threat and vulnerability values.

Vuln. value		1					**2**					3					**4**					5				
Threat value		1	2	3	4	5	**1**	**2**	**3**	**4**	**5**	1	2	3	4	5	**1**	**2**	**3**	**4**	**5**	1	2	3	4	5
	1	1	2	3	4	5	2	3	4	5	6	3	4	5	6	7	4	5	6	7	8	5	6	7	8	9
	2	2	3	4	5	6	3	4	5	6	7	4	5	6	7	8	5	6	7	8	9	6	7	8	9	10
Asset value	3	3	4	5	6	7	4	5	6	7	8	5	6	7	8	9	6	7	8	9	10	7	8	9	10	11
	4	4	5	6	7	8	5	6	7	8	9	6	7	8	9	10	7	8	9	10	11	8	9	10	11	12
	5	5	6	7	8	9	6	7	8	9	10	7	8	9	10	11	8	9	10	11	12	9	10	11	12	13

6 Evaluation

We conducted a survey with 40 participants from the security profession to contrast the results of our internal assessment with existing IoT security opinions.

6.1 Survey Methodology

An online survey was conducted comprising 48 questions that requested participants to judge and rank various assets, threats and vulnerabilities using in-context examples from the scenarios. Given the detail of the internal assessment – over 1,400 risks in total – the survey questions were formed by taking a random sample of assets, vulnerabilities and threats from the scenarios. At least one item was taken from each class sub-group, while remaining within a 10 min time limit to maximise participation. For threats and vulnerabilities, participants were asked to predict their importance in the context of the scenario, while clearly stating the specified timeframe of the scenarios. For assets, users were presented with a random subset of scenario assets and asked to rank their perceived value to their respective owners. All responses used a 10-point Likert scale, from lowest to highest value. Survey participants were recruited by email invitation via mailing lists for Ph.D. students, alumni and staff of the Information Security Group at Royal Holloway, University of London. Postings to social media networks for security professionals were also made and no further incentive was offered for participation. Users were asked to input their current occupation and their experience – both academic and industrial – within the security profession in years, and their current position.

7 Results

In total, 1,429 risks were analysed across all three scenarios. Scenario A comprised **515** risks with a mean risk $\mu = 8.50$ and standard deviation $\sigma = 1.44$. Scenario B comprised **604** risks ($\mu = 8.24$; $\sigma = 1.45$), while Scenario C contained **310** risks ($\mu = 8.68$; $\sigma = 1.09$). Table 3 summarises the risks across all three scenarios based on asset, threat and vulnerability classes, while Fig. 2 illustrates the distribution of risks across all scenarios. Furthermore, we present the top 10 items with the highest risk for each class – assets, vulnerabilities and threats – in Table 4, along with the proportion of these in each scenario in Fig. 3.

Forty security professionals responded to our survey, with a mean of $\mu = 6.33$ years experience ($\sigma = 6.78$) in the field, both industrial and academic security experience combined. The survey results were standardised to the risk range in Table 2 (1–13), before conducting a two-sample t-test with the difference of means to determine statistical significance between the assessments. We present this in Table 4. Many concerns found in our work coincide with those previously known; our findings suggest, however, that particular areas are potentially over- and undervalued, and we analyse these forthwith.

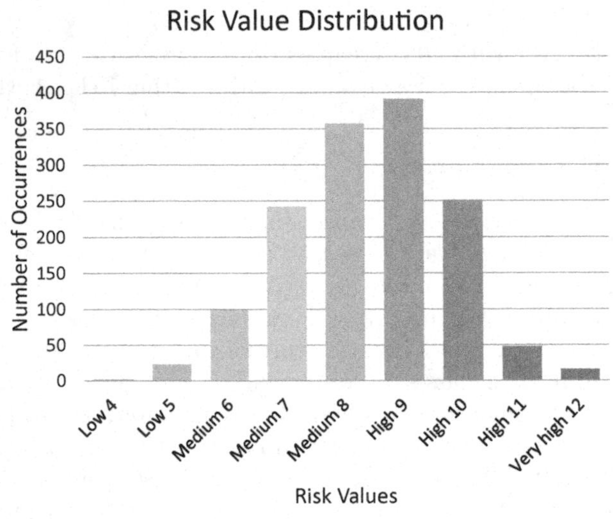

Fig. 2. Distribution of risks across all scenarios.

Table 3. Summary of asset, vulnerability and threat classes across all scenarios.

Class	Mean risk	Std. dev	Occurrences
Assets			
Services	9.40	1.26	233
Applications	8.54	1.15	280
Hardware	8.14	1.35	795
Data	7.97	1.35	121
Vulnerabilities			
Network	9.07	1.43	193
Software	8.55	1.24	649
Organisational	8.24	1.34	432
Hardware	7.19	1.33	155
Threats			
Nefarious activity	8.85	1.06	136
Outages (non-malicious)	7.79	1.12	121
Device reliability	7.88	1.17	129
Data interception and modification	8.78	1.09	546
Organisational	8.43	0.88	215
Physical security	8.42	0.99	101
Unintentional damage and loss	7.52	1.36	181

Untrusted Sensing Data. Acting on potentially untrustworthy data from remote, unattended devices was a recurring theme in our findings. IoT offers opportunities in automating financial payments and optimising services using sensor data, but the findings suggest this correlates with high risk. Three of the top identified risks concerned trusting sensor data, i.e. (1) improper integrity checks, (2) unreliable sensors, and (3) poor verification/auditing of sensing data to ensure its veracity. Using data from remote devices at face value is likely to impose significant risk. Data could itself be poor at source: low-cost sensing systems, for example, may simply return inaccurate or unreliable data, but may also be the result of tampering, e.g., a reckless driver tampering with telemetric firmware to transmit 'safer' values to mislead insurers. If systems become largely automated without adequate human oversight and auditing procedures, the consequences may be more severe. Our survey findings illustrate that external experts tended to show a small but statistically significant bias (for $p < 0.05$) towards undervaluing the risk imposed by untrusted sensing data (-0.93; $p = 0.04$). This is further exhibited by assets that receive and transmit such data – asset 2: *investment database*, and asset 4: *freight communication device* – both of which were significantly under-appreciated in the expert survey (-3.13 and -2.37 respectively; $p < 0.01$). Consequently, we recommend particular attention be given to oversight when trusting data from remote, unattended devices at scale.

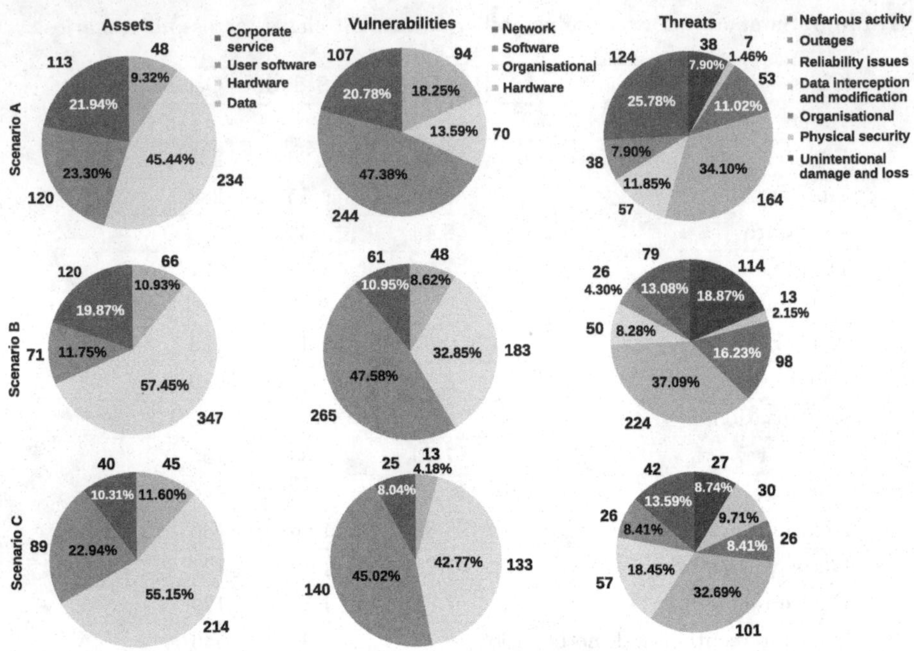

Fig. 3. Distributions of asset, vulnerability and threat classes.

Authentication. Unsurprisingly, authentication issues – both user and device authentication – consistently yielded the highest risk for both vulnerabilities and threats across our studies (9.22–10.67), comprising aspects such as unauthorised device pairing, permitting weak passwords, and the absence of multi-factor authentication. Consequences of poor authentication vary widely, from obvious examples of unauthorised use of banking and shopping applications, to allowing unauthorised users to pair with sensitive devices, such as for health-care. Evidently, IoT authentication is complicated by the need for providers to authenticate both customers, their devices and any intermediary services, e.g., cloud providers, which may operate with a large degree of autonomy.

Hardware and Physical Protection. A related observation is the correlation of poor device hardware security with high risk. Remote IoT devices, potentially under users' control, gives rise to the opportunity for adversaries (who could be users themselves) to interrogate devices without the deterrent of human detection. Noticeably, this contributes directly to the first theme. Inadequate physical protection may enable attackers to access the device PCB to tamper with sensing hardware, such as through unauthorised firmware flashing via unsecured interfaces, e.g., UART or JTAG; replacing hardware with purposefully defective components; and adding unauthorised components to bypass existing security controls ('modchip' attacks). Such vectors could be exploited to deliver inaccurate measurements to an insurer or other receiving financial entity. Concurrently,

Table 4. Comparison of top ten mean risks from assets, vulnerabilities and threats of the internal assessment with the user survey, with mean differences and t-test p-values.

Class	Internal	Survey	μ-Difference	t-test$_p$
Assets				
1. Card payment data	11.00	11.79	+0.79	0.35
2. Investment database	10.58	7.71	−3.13	<0.01
3. Online banking service	10.05	11.88	+1.83	<0.01
4. Freight communication device	9.50	7.13	−2.37	<0.01
5. Customer location data	9.25	5.83	−3.42	<0.01
6. Coffee store purchasing service	9.22	9.92	+0.70	0.08
7. Investment mobile app	9.15	8.21	−0.94	0.09
8. Remote insurance service	9.14	8.34	−0.80	0.16
9. Smart safe	9.05	9.75	+0.70	0.32
10. Car operating system	9.00	10.58	+1.58	0.03
Vulnerabilities				
1. Poor user authentication	9.22	10.58	+1.36	<0.01
2. Software network vulnerabilities[a]	9.27	11.29	+2.02	<0.01
3. Poor auditing of remote data	9.11	8.58	−0.53	0.22
4. Poor data integrity protection	9.04	9.54	+0.54	0.16
5. Poor logical access control	8.86	10.50	+1.64	<0.01
6. API vulnerabilities	8.76	10.79	+2.03	<0.01
7. Unreliable sensors	8.60	7.67	−0.93	0.04
8. Poor self-correction mechanisms[c]	8.55	8.50	−0.05	0.91
9. Unfriendly user interface	7.88	9.92	+2.04	<0.01
10. Poor Physical Security	7.08	8.13	+1.05	<0.01
Threats				
1. Authentication issues	10.10	10.67	+0.57	0.13
2. Transaction data modification	9.64	10.75	+1.11	0.01
3. Denial of Service	9.38	10.25	+0.97	0.03
4. Privacy violations[b]	9.19	11.54	+2.35	<0.01
5. Physical theft	9.18	8.42	−0.76	0.04
6. Data and identity theft	9.00	10.92	+1.92	<0.01
7. Use of inaccurate of data	8.89	8.58	−0.31	0.37
8. Service unavailability (non-malicious)	8.78	8.38	-0.40	0.33
9. Malware	8.67	11.63	+2.96	<0.01
10. Hardware tampering	7.38	9.83	+2.45	<0.01

[a]Software network vulnerabilities comprises risks such as exposed and unprotected networking ports and services running on a device.

[b]Privacy violations comprise unauthorised customer profiling and tracking.

[c]Self-correction refers to users' ability to undo/reverse automated transactions.

devices themselves may be of significant value (including the data they hold) and hence a target for theft, e.g., smartwatch. Both hardware tampering and poor physical security ranked in the top 10 threats and vulnerabilities (7.38 and 7.08 respectively). Survey participants marginally undervalued physical theft as a threat (−0.76; p=0.04), but somewhat overvalued hardware tampering (+2.45; $p < 0.01$). We recommend giving physical security high prominence in an IoT system design, particularly when placed remotely.

Data Governance. One significant theme expectedly surrounded data protection and adequate measures for disposing obsolete and superfluous data. The access to potentially sensitive data enabled by IoT devices may lead to abuse, whether intentional or unintentional, such as through unauthorised profiling and tracking via beacons and other location techniques. Moreover, with potentially large volumes of data, customer data may be retained longer than necessary or over-collected without adequate oversight – exposing firms to risks surrounding over-sharing, loss and theft. IoT also has the potential to exacerbate existing data protection concerns: valuable data initially collected for one purpose, e.g., self-monitoring home energy consumption, may easily be used for another without consent, e.g., targeted advertising of new, energy-efficient appliances. Participants undervalued the risks posed by customers' location data (−3.13; $p < 0.01$), but appreciated the risks imposed by privacy violations, such as unauthorised profiling (11.54), and identity theft (9.00–10.92).

Interception/Modification of Transaction Data. Expectedly, interception of transaction data from IoT devices yielded high risk (9.64–10.75). While paying for RFID-equipped goods without waiting sounds attractive, or smart appliances automatically replenishing items, these transactions make obvious targets for attackers. Such attacks – the result of inadequate encryption, integrity protection and secure credential storage – are neither new nor specific to IoT, and are known widely by the community. The risks, however, could be exacerbated when considering limited, smaller-scale devices manufactured at a minimal price per unit (<$0.05), which may be incapable of secure tamper-proof credential hosting, or secure encryption at acceptable speeds.

7.1 Limitations

A number of assumptions were made to scope scenario creation: cryptocurrencies, e.g., Bitcoin, were not sufficiently captured. Such currencies typically eliminate or replace financial services altogether; for this study, focus was concentrated primarily on the role of IoT in traditional services. Importantly, we do not claim that our scenarios are exhaustive of all financial services, and our work should be treated with caution in other domains. Moreover, our results should not be over-interpreted as a definitive risk assessment; rather, we aim to provide indications of potential areas of focus. Like with any risk assessment work, comes uncertainty: biases may be present from the professionals in this work, but we attempted to mitigate this through a large user-base with input restricted to informed professionals. Note that risk assessments take intense effort to conduct correctly, and a survey is not sufficient to digest the described scenarios entirely; we reiterate that the external survey was used to capture and contrast opinions on IoT in finance and was not a fundamental component of the assessment itself.

8 Conclusion

In this work, we introduced the need to robustly assess potential security risks associated with use of IoT in financial products and services. This was succeeded by an examination of related work in mobile and cloud computing, healthcare, and RFID in air travel, before describing a high-level framework using scenario planning and ISO 27005:2008 from past work. A range of related scenarios were developed with consultation from domain experts, which incorporated a variety of emerging IoT technologies and financial applications. After formalising the threats, vulnerabilities and assets in each scenario, a total of 1,429 risks were identified. We contrasted these results with an external survey with 40 security professionals, both in academia and industry, with the aim of capturing existing opinions on IoT security. From this, we identified and analysed several areas of concern that are likely to take precedence in the field. The results are presented in order to assist future research, policy formulation and decision making.

8.1 Future Research

Subsequent to this work, we hope to pursue the following avenues of research:

- Investigating the potential security risks associated with cryptocurrency use in IoT deployments.
- Capturing the risks of machine-to-machine payments and unconventional technologies for frictionless payments, such as implantable devices.
- Incorporating unique financial interactions with multiple actors, such as group payments and peer-to-peer lending.

Acknowledgements. The authors would like to thank those at Vasco Data Security, who initiated and supported this work; the participants of the user survey for their time and consideration; and the anonymous reviewers who provided their insightful and helpful comments. Carlton Shepherd is supported by the EPSRC and the UK government as part of the Centre for Doctoral Training in Cyber Security at Royal Holloway, University of London (EP/K035584/1).

References

1. BS ISO/IEC 27005:2008 Information technology - Security techniques - Information security risk management. British Standards (BSI), June 2008
2. Flying 2.0 - Enabling automated air travel by identifying and addressing the challenges of IoT & RFID technology. Technical report. European Network and Information Security Agency (ENISA) (2010)

3. ENISA EFR Framework - Introductory Manual. Technical report. European Network and Information Security Agency (ENISA) March 2013
4. Accenture: Connected commerce hits the road (2016). https://www.accenture.com/be-en/success-visa-connected-commerce-car
5. Alahakoon, D., Yu, X.: Smart electricity meter data intelligence for future energy systems: a survey. IEEE Trans. Industr. Inf. **12**(1), 425–436 (2016)
6. Bodwell, W., Chermack, T.J.: Organizational ambidexterity: integrating deliberate and emergent strategy with scenario planning. Technol. Forecast. Soc. Chang. **77**(2), 193–202 (2010)
7. Cairns, G., Wright, G., Bradfield, R., van der Heijden, K., Burt, G.: Exploring e-government futures through the application of scenario planning. Technol. Forecast. Soc. Chang. **71**(3), 217–238 (2004)
8. Capgemini: Wearable Devices and their Applicability in the Life Insurance Industry. April 2014. https://www.capgemini.com/resource-file-access/resource/pdf/wearable_devices_and_their_applicability_in_the_life_insurance_industry.pdf
9. Chang, M.-S., Tseng, Y.-L., Chen, J.-W.: A scenario planning approach for the flood emergency logistics preparation problem under uncertainty. Transp. Res. Logistics Transp. **43**(6), 737–754 (2007)
10. Chawathe, S.S.: Beacon placement for indoor localization using bluetooth. In: 11th International IEEE Conference on Intelligent Transportation Systems, pp. 980–985. IEEE (2008)
11. DHL: Internet of Things in Logistics (2016). https://www.scribd.com/document/285437514/DHL-TrendReport-Internet-of-Things
12. Franklin, R., Metzger, A., Stollberg, M., Engel, Y., Fjørtoft, K., Fleischhauer, R., Marquezan, C., Ramstad, L.S.: Future internet technology for the future of transport and logistics. In: Abramowicz, W., Llorente, I.M., Surridge, M., Zisman, A., Vayssière, J. (eds.) ServiceWave 2011. LNCS, vol. 6994, pp. 290–301. Springer, Heidelberg (2011). doi:10.1007/978-3-642-24755-2_27
13. Gartner, Inc.: 6.4 Billion Connected 'Things' Will Be in Use in 2016, Up 30 Percent From November 2015. http://www.gartner.com/newsroom/id/3165317
14. Gren, M.: Finance stock watch on Google play (2016). https://play.google.com/store/apps/details?id=com.mathck.android.wearable.stoc
15. Gu, H., Wang, D.: A content-aware fridge based on RFID in smart home for home-healthcare. In: 11th International Conference on Advanced Communication Technology. ICACT 2009, vol. 2, pp. 987–990. IEEE (2009)
16. IBM: IBM Watson IoT for Insurance (2016). http://www.ibm.com/internet-of-things/iot-solutions/iot-insurance/
17. Inaba, T.: Impact analysis of RFID on financial supply chain management. In: IEEE International Conference on Service Operations and Logistics, and Informatics, pp. 1–6 (2007)
18. Karvetski, C.W., Lambert, J.H., Linkov, I.: Scenario and multiple criteria decision analysis for environmental security of military and industrial installations. Environ. Assess. Manag. **7**(2), 228–236 (2011)
19. Kumara, S., Cui, L., Zhang, J.: Sensors, networks and internet of things: research challenges in health care. In: Proceedings of the 8th International Workshop on Information Integration on the Web, p. 2. ACM (2011)
20. Lewis, L., Wyatt, J.: mHealth and medical apps: a framework to assess risk and promote safer use. J. Med. Internet Res. **16**(9), e210 (2014)
21. Marinos, L.: ENISA threat taxonomy - a tool for structuring threat information. Technical report. European Union Agency for Network and Information Security (ENISA) (2016)

22. Melià-Seguí, J., Pous, R., Carreras, A., Morenza-Cinos, M., Parada, R., Liaghat, Z., De Porrata-Doria, R.: Enhancing the shopping experience through RFID in an actual retail store. In: Proceedings of the 2013 ACM Conference on Pervasive and Ubiquitous Computing, pp. 1029–1036. ACM (2013)
23. Morak, J., Schwarz, M., Hayn, D., Schreier, G.: Feasibility of mhealth and near field communication technology based medication adherence monitoring. In: 2012 IEEE International Conference on Engineering in Medicine and Biology, pp. 272–275. IEEE (2012)
24. Nadimi, E.S., Jørgensen, R.N., Blanes-Vidal, V., Christensen, S.: Monitoring and classifying animal behavior using ZigBee-based mobile ad hoc wireless sensor networks and artificial neural networks. Comput. Electron. Agric. **82**, 44–54 (2012)
25. NXP Semiconductors, FreeScale and ARM. What the Internet of Things (IoT) needs to become a reality (2013). http://www.nxp.com/assets/documents/data/en/white-papers/INTOTHNGSWP.pdf
26. Schoemaker, P.J.H.: Scenario planning: a tool for strategic thinking. Sloan Manag. Rev. **36**(2), 25–40 (1995)
27. PwC: Connected insurance (2016). https://www.pwc.com/it/it/publications/assets/docs/connected-insurance.pdf
28. RAC Limited: Black box car insurance (2017). http://www.rac.co.uk/insurance/car-insurance/black-box-insurance
29. Salesforce: Introducing Salesforce IOT Cloud (2016). http://www.salesforce.com/uk/iot-cloud/
30. Saripalli, P., Walters, B.: Quirc: a quantitative impact and risk assessment framework for cloud security. In: 3rd International Conference on Cloud Computing, pp. 280–288. IEEE (2010)
31. Shepherd, C., Akram, R.N., Markantonakis, K.: Towards trusted execution of multi-modal continuous authentication schemes. In: Proceedings of the 32nd ACM Symposium on Applied Computing, pp. 1444–1451. ACM (2017)
32. Shrouf, F., Ordieres, J., Miragliotta, G.: Smart factories in industry 4.0: a review of the concept and of energy management approached in production based on the internet of things paradigm. In: IEEE International Conference on Industrial Engineering and Engineering Management, pp. 697–701. IEEE (2014)
33. Tata Constultancy: Banking, Financial Services: Pleasing Customers, Fighting Fraud (2016). http://sites.tcs.com/internet-of-things/industries/banking-and-financial-services/
34. Theoharidou, M., Mylonas, A., Gritzalis, D.: A risk assessment method for smartphones. In: Gritzalis, D., Furnell, S., Theoharidou, M. (eds.) SEC 2012. IAICT, vol. 376, pp. 443–456. Springer, Heidelberg (2012). doi:10.1007/978-3-642-30436-1_36
35. Varshney, U.: Pervasive healthcare and wireless health monitoring. Mobile Netw. Appl. **12**(2–3), 113–127 (2007)
36. Volkery, A., Ribeiro, T.: Scenario planning in public policy: understanding use, impacts and the role of institutional context factors. Technol. Forecast. Soc. Change **76**(9), 1198–1207 (2009)
37. Von Reischach, F., Guinard, D., Michahelles, F., Fleisch, E.: A mobile product recommendation system interacting with tagged products. In: Pervasive Computing and Communications, pp. 1–6. IEEE (2009)
38. Yan, Z., Zhang, P., Vasilakos, A.V.: A survey on trust management for IoT. J. Netw. Comput. Appl. **42**, 120–134 (2014)
39. Zhang, Z., Pang, Z., Chen, J., Chen, Q., Tenhunen, H., Zheng, L.-R., Yan, X.: Two-layered wireless sensor networks for warehouses and supermarkets. In: 3rd International Conference on Mobile Ubiquitous Computing, Systems, Services, and Technologies, pp. 220–224 (2009)

A New Sharing Paradigm for the Personal Cloud

Paul Tran-Van[1,2,3(✉)], Nicolas Anciaux[2,3], and Philippe Pucheral[2,3]

[1] Inria Saclay-Île-de-France, 1 rue d'Estienne d'Orves, 91120 Palaiseau, France
paul.tran-van@inria.fr

[2] DAVID Lab., University of Versailles, 45 av. Etats-Unis, 78035 Versailles, France
{nicolas.anciaux,philippe.pucheral}@inria.fr

[3] Cozy Cloud, 158 rue de Verdun, 92800 Puteaux, France

Abstract. Pushed by recent legislation and smart disclosure initiatives, personal cloud solutions emerge and hold the promise of giving the control back to the individual on her data. However, this shift leaves the privacy and security issues in user's hands, a role that few people can properly endorse. Considering the inadequacy of existing sharing models, we advocate the definition of a new sharing paradigm dedicated to the personal cloud context. This sharing paradigm, called SWYSWYK (Share What You See with Who You Know), allows to derive intuitive sharing rules from the personal cloud content, to self-administer the subjects and the sensitive permissions, and to visualize the net effects of the sharing policy on the user's personal cloud. We then propose a reference architecture providing the users tangible guarantees about the enforcement of the SWYSWYK policies. An instance of this architecture has been implemented on top of an existing personal cloud platform to demonstrate the practicality of the approach.

Keywords: Personal data sharing · Personal cloud · Self-administered policies

1 Introduction

Today, *smart disclosure* initiatives are pushed by legislators (e.g., EU General Data Protection regulation [1]) and industry-led consortiums (e.g., Blue Button for medical records in the US, Midata in the UK, MesInfos in France) in order to enable individuals to get back their personal data from companies or administrations that collected them. The Personal Cloud paradigm emerges (e.g., Cozy Cloud, ownCloud, SeaFile, Databox) and holds the promise of a Privacy-by-Design storage and computing platform where each individual can gather her complete digital environment in one place and share it with applications and users under her control.

However, this gravity shift of data management from organizations to individuals raises new fundamental issues. One of the founding principles of the Personal Cloud paradigm is to enable individuals making sovereign decisions about the sharing of their data, i.e., administering sharing rules to regulate data dissemination. This task is difficult for regular users who are not database administrators nor security experts. Indeed,

J. Lopez et al. (Eds.): TrustBus 2017, LNCS 10442, pp. 180–196, 2017.
DOI: 10.1007/978-3-319-64483-7_12

the main existing access control models are not adapted to the personal cloud context. Existing solutions are either geared towards central authorities, allowing them to properly define users, roles and privileges thanks to robust models (e.g., RBAC, MAC, ABAC or TBAC [2]) or suggest decentralized tools to let individuals manually define their sharing preferences (e.g., thanks to PGP, Web of Trust models or Friend of a Friend (FOAF) dissemination rules [3]). The former approach is adapted to a centralized database and requires a deep expertise in terms of administration and security. The latter puts all the cognitive load of defining sharing rules to the user while providing tools of limited expressive power (privileges are declared manually on a user-resource case-by-case basis). Some solutions like [4, 5] try to exploit machine learning techniques to automatically infer the best sharing policies but they can lead to unexpected data leakage when the classification goes wrong.

We thus advocate the definition of a new sharing paradigm dedicated to the personal cloud context. How could regular users share the recent information obtained from their quantified-self appliances with medical practitioners of their acquaintance? How photos of an excursion can be shared with the relatives appearing in these same photos? How to avoid personal pictures to be shared with working colleagues?

Our proposal builds upon the transversal nature of the content of a personal cloud and makes easy and intuitive the definition and administration of sharing policies. The personal cloud content intrinsically describes the individual's acquaintances under different forms (e.g., contact files, agendas, identity pictures, address book entries, etc.). Conversely, acquaintances are associated with pieces of information in the user's space (e.g., photos on which a friend appears). New sharing models should be able to map personal data to acquaintances (or subjects) and exploit their links with the stored documents (or objects) to produce authorizations satisfying users' sharing desires such as those expressed above. Interesting and common sharing rules could also be published and adopted by the members of a community of interest. Beyond the definition of the sharing policy, the sharing paradigm must provide means to the personal cloud owner to easily understand the net effects of a sharing policy, identify suspicious permissions and sanitize the sharing policy accordingly, and finally, to trust the way the policy is practically enforced.

In this paper, we make the following contributions:

- We propose a new sharing paradigm called SWYSWYK (*Share What You See with Who You Know*) which allows to automatically derive intuitive sharing rules from a personal cloud content, to let each user visualize the net effects of these rules on her own personal cloud and to finely customize data sharing according to their own privacy concerns,
- We introduce a reference architecture for the SWYSWYK paradigm which helps the user to administer her sharing policy and provides tangible guarantees about its enforcement, and show the feasibility of our approach with an implementation combining an existing personal cloud platform and a secure personal device.

The rest of the paper is organized as follows. Section 2 presents related works and Sect. 3 derives from them a problem statement. Sections 4, 5 and 6 are devoted to the aforementioned contributions, and Sect. 7 concludes.

2 Related Works

This section positions existing access control approaches with respect to the personal cloud context, in order to introduce our problem statement in the next section.

2.1 Traditional Database Access Control Models

The access control management in databases is well established and models like DAC, RBAC and MAC [2] are widely supported. The question is whether or not such models can apply to the personal cloud context. These models actually share the following characteristics: (1) the access control administration is a complex and critical task usually handled by a security expert; (2) the applicative logic, the users and their roles are identified at an early stage of the information system design, so that the access control policy is part of the database schema definition and (3) these models are integrated in standards like SQL and benefit from the expressive power of such languages. However, in a personal cloud context, nothing of the above still holds. First, the administrator of a personal cloud is the owner herself and, apart from rare exceptions, is not a technical expert. Second, usages are difficult to predict because new appealing apps are produced at a high rate and so are the interactions between users. Third, no central authority delivers a common framework to identify unambiguously subjects and objects in a potential access control rule and no universal standard exist to define and manipulate them. These reasons make traditional access control models not suitable for the personal cloud context.

2.2 Access Control in a Decentralized Setting

The decentralization aspect raises new challenges starting with users' identification and authentication. To avoid any confusion between users, let us call *owner*, the owner of a personal cloud and *subjects*, the users willing to interact with the personal cloud owner. Web of Trust (WoT) models have been investigated, allowing subjects to authenticate thanks to their public key and are identified through social attestations [6] or public profiles [7], to which access rights are associated and defined by the owner. It requires the owner to manually assign the authorizations, for each subject and for each object, which can quickly become tedious and error-prone. [8] relies on a centralized trusted party for the authentication. A second challenge is enforcing the access control rules, meaning preventing confidentiality attacks over data to be shared. [9–11] focus on data encryption in untrusted clouds, while [12] presents a decentralized alternative to social networks based on ABE encryption. [13, 14] use obfuscation schemes, where data is scrambled for the former and substituted for the latter. Access control policies are implemented here by means of encryption but, again, this requires the owner to manually define who can access which data on a case-by-case basis. Thus, the cognitive load on the owner is such that it often leads to consider access control as an intractable burden, letting desperate owners define far too permissive policies [15].

2.3 User-Friendly AC Administration

Several contributions have been proposed to ease the access control administration by allowing the declaration of logic-based sharing rules. [16, 17] propose rule frameworks based on fixed attributes, but do not cope well with the versatile personal cloud context. Negative policies are also supported to deal with exceptions that can occur in sharing policies. [18] defines an SQL-based language to let applications create queryable views on the shared data, and transmit capabilities to granted subjects. Some works propose to use existing user's social relationships as a convenient way to facilitate policies declaration. In [19], subjects are granted access depending on their FOAF relationship properties, such as type, graph depth, and a computed trust value. [20] adds web scraping on social networks to retrieve common social events attendance. Finally, [4, 5] focus on machine learning techniques to automatically infer the best sharing policies. [4] takes small manual input from the user and exploits its data on social networks, including profile characteristics and relationships, to extract sharing communities patterns. [5] uses an image classification module based on content and metadata from large images set, and analyze the owner privacy preferences to predict the sharing policy for each of her uploaded photos. These works both claim a good accuracy in the predicted policies and can greatly ease the access control administration, but they can also lead to unexpected data leakage when the classification goes wrong. It is also not certain that owners would accept to let an opaque algorithm scrutinize their data and their social relationships.

3 Problem Formulation

This state of the art highlights two major difficulties that need to be circumvented when designing a sharing model for the personal cloud context: (1) *The owner is the weakest link of the security chain*: she is de facto the administrator of her personal cloud platform, but it is illusory to expect her gaining expertise and spending time to administer subjects, secure her personal cloud against all forms of attacks or use tricky protocols to exchange cryptographic secrets with partners; and (2) *personal cloud usage is versatile and volatile*: while traditional information systems are built to support well identified services invoked by well identified users and applications, the personal cloud world favors opportunistic usages and unpredictable interactions between users. We derive from these statements three major requirements for a sharing model dedicated to the personal cloud:

- *Enlighten empowerment*. User's empowerment should be enlightened, meaning that the effects of all owner's decisions must be perceivable and understandable by herself. We advocate the integration of a SWYSWYK (pronounce Swiss-week) principle (Share What You See with Who You Know) in the definition of access control policies. Roughly speaking, this means that the model should provide means to derive intuitive sharing rules from the content of personal cloud documents and let the owner visualize the net effects of these rules on her personal cloud.
- *Self-sustaining administration*. In the line of the SWYSWYK principle, the administration of subjects must be intuitive and (quasi) automatic, derived from the

content of personal cloud documents and from regular actions performed by the owner on these documents. As well, the owner should be offered simple means to finely administer the effects of the sharing rules according to her own privacy concerns.

- *Tangible enforcement.* To give substance to the SWYSWYK principle, the logic of the reference monitor enforcing the sharing policy must itself be perceivable and understandable by the owner and the platform implementing this logic must be trusted by her. Typically, we don't believe that a regular user can figure out the results of neither a powerful solver taking as input a set of positive and negative sharing rules nor that she can trust a remote machine or her vulnerable computer to run this logic. A side effect of the expected extreme simplicity of our model is that the reference monitor could be embedded in a tamper-resistant personal device kept in user's hand, thereby providing a physical element of trust.

Of course, these requirements are not enough to solve all the problems identified above, but we believe they can lead to a more affordable and trusted sharing process.

4 SWYSWYK Model

As many existing proposals, SWYSWYK is a rule-based model, but our goal is not to propose yet another more expressive rule-based access control model. The originality of SWYSWYK lies in a few elementary core principles, which can be summarized as follows: *documents are rules* and *subjects and objects are documents*. The combination of these principles gives birth to an access control model tackling important requirements of the personal cloud context. We introduce here the model baselines and semantics. Operational aspects are discussed in the next section.

4.1 Model Baseline

Let us first illustrate the impact of *enlightened empowerment* in the access control declaration. Sharing a picture with people appearing on it, sharing a document minutes with the meeting attendees or an agenda entry with the corresponding relatives should be straightforward to express. Subsequent permissions can be "derived" from the documents' content, leading to our first core principle: *documents are rules*. The subjects directly concerned with a document, also called *identifiees* [21], should also be extracted from the document content and be identifiable as such to enter in the rule definition. We call "reflexive sharing rules" the rules based on this principle. A corollary of this is that each subject should correspond to a viewable personal cloud document (i.e., *subjects are documents*), e.g., contact record, resume or picture. As well, whether the result of a complex treatment over a set of documents needs to be shared (e.g., an unintelligible computation over a set of smart meter measurements), this treatment must output a viewable shared document (e.g., a curve of consumption). The combination of *documents are rules* and *subjects and objects are documents* gives substance to the '*Share What You See with Who You Know*' paradigm. The impact of *self-sustaining administration* is also paramount, automating the subject declaration and maintenance (e.g., sharing meeting minutes with attendees could automate the creation/updates of subjects). Regarding the *tangible enforcement* requirement, the decision process must remain as simple as possible. And in any case the administration of the sharing rules must remain in line with the privacy concerns of the owner.

We show next how these principles can be integrated in a simple sharing model, and let open the discussion of their integration in a more powerful/expressive model or in traditional existing ones. Hence, we do a set of simplifying assumptions. First, our model relies on a closed policy (every action not explicitly granted is denied). Actions are CRUD operations on documents in the personal cloud. The model supports only authorizations (positive rules) and allows the owner to post-filter the Access Control List (ACL) produced when exceptions need to be declared. Consequently, there is a direct translation between sharing rules and sets of ACLs. An action a is granted to subject s on document d iff $(s, d, a) \in ACL$ and is denied otherwise. The model is by construction *consistent* (the decision is unique), *complete* (the decision always exists) and can finally be evaluated in *logarithmic time*.

4.2 Sharing Model Semantics

Reflexive sharing rules implement the *documents are rules* principle, and are thus considered as first-class citizen rules in SWYSWYK. Such rules express the sharing of documents with subjects directly concerned with those documents. We introduce below a set of notations required to define the semantics of reflexive sharing rules.

D: set of all documents in a personal cloud (by extension, set of all *DocId*).
S: set of all subjects in a personal cloud (by extension, set of all *SubjectId*).
A: set of actions which can be performed on elements of D.
Q: set of qualifications which can be expressed on elements of D with the host language of the personal cloud (we do not make any assumption on this language).
IT: set of identification traits uniquely linked to any element of S (e.g., ssn, <lastname, {firstname}>, pseudo, phone n°, docId of a contact entry...).

Let us now consider the following relations and functions:

$ACL \subseteq S \times D \times A$: set of Access Control Lists.
Allowed: $S \times D \times A \rightarrow \{true, false\}$: characterizes the access control
Allowed (s, d, a) $= true$ iff $(< s, d, a > \in ACL)$
$= false$ otherwise
SI: $S \rightarrow IT$: delivers all known identification traits of any element of S.
MatchS: $P(IT) \times P(IT) \rightarrow \{true, false\}$ where P is the powerset of a set. *MatchS* evaluates the pairwise correspondence between subjects by comparing *ITs*.
MatchS(*ident1*, *ident2*) $= true$ iff $(ident1 \cap ident2 \neq \emptyset)$
$= false$ otherwise
IsS: $D \rightarrow S \cup \Phi$: gives the unique element of S characterized by a document or Φ (absence of value) if the document does not correspond to any subject. *IsS* is surjective, i.e., $(\forall s \in S, \exists d \in D \,/\, IsS(d)=s)$, meaning that each subject is represented by an existing (viewable) document in the personal cloud.

Two additional functions are independent of the access control logic and could be provided by communities or personal cloud providers. For the sake of genericity, they are considered as user-defined functions (UDFs) in the model:

DI: $D \rightarrow \mathcal{P}(IT) \cup \Phi$: delivers the identification traits (potentially from multiple subjects) contained in a document or Φ. Example of a *DI* could be a facial recognition function for pictures or a function extracting identification traits (e.g. email addresses, phone numbers) from a text document.

Filter: $D \times Q \rightarrow \{true, false\}$: evaluates whether $d \in D$ matches a qualification Q. *Filters* are used to form subsets of documents satisfying a given criteria. Filters are personal cloud platform dependent. They are assumed to select documents either based on their content or on metadata (e.g., type, creator, date, tags) attached to each document by the personal cloud.

Reflexive Sharing Rules. Thanks to the above notations, reflexive sharing rules can be expressed as follow:

$$\text{ACL} \leftarrow \{(s,d,a) \in S \times D \times A \; / \; Filter_1(d,Q) \wedge MatchS(DI(d), SI(s))\}$$

Examples of reflexive sharing rules follow for illustration purpose:

Example 1. Share the minutes of meetings with the corresponding attendees:

Q: docName like '../Meetings/minutes-%.doc'
DI: extract attendee names from a minute document

Example 2. Share the photo gallery 'MyBirthday 2016' with people who appear in the pictures:

Q: docType = '.jpg' ∧ tagGallery = 'MyBirthday 2016'
DI: face recognition function from.jpg files

For this example, profile pictures linked to contact forms could be used to recognize the faces with a trained model.

It is likely that reflexive rules apply additional restrictions over the subjects identified in documents, leading to the following more complete definition of reflexive rule:

$$ACL \leftarrow \{(s,d,a) \in S \times D \times A \; / \; Filter_1(d,Q) \wedge MatchS(DI(d), SI(s)) \wedge \exists d' \in D, Filter_2(d',Q') \wedge (IsS(d')=s)\}$$

Example 3. Share the minutes of a meeting held in Paris on March 12th 2017 with the members of my team attending the meeting:

Q: docId = /lib1/lib2/minutes-Paris-120317.doc
Q': docType = '.vcf' ∧ tagStatus = 'Team member'
DI: extract attendee names from a minute document

Basic Sharing Rules. Non reflexive rules can also easily be supported by the model. In particular, the usual rules sharing a selection of documents ($Filter_1$) with a selection of subjects ($Filter_2$), called basic rules, are expressed as follows:

$$| \ ACL \leftarrow \{(s,d,a) \in S{\times}D{\times}A \ / \ \exists d' \in D, \ Filter_2(d',Q') \wedge IsS(d')=s \wedge Filter_1(d,Q)\}$$

Example 4. Share document PCloud/MedicalFolder/Myheartbeat with doctors:

Q: docId = PCloud/MedicalFolder/Myheartbeat
Q': docType = 'contact' ∧ tagStatus = 'Physician'

Example 5. Share the photo gallery 'MyNewPaintings' with my friends:

Q: docType = 'photo' ∧ tagGallery = 'MyNewPaintings'
Q': docType = 'contact' ∧ tagStatus = 'Friend'

Example 6. Share my calorie intakes of the last 3 months with my family doctor:

Q: docType = '.xls' ∧ tagContent = 'calorie' ∧ Date ≥ 'CurrentDate - 3 month'
Q': docType = '.vcf' ∧ tagStatus = 'Family doctor'

4.3 Administration Model

The subject declaration and maintenance must be (quasi) automatic and the owner should be able to apply her own privacy concerns while administrating rules and permissions. We first introduce the notion of *rule consistency*, which concretizes the fact that the effects of all rules can be visualized. Then, we show how owner's specific privacy concerns are supported by means of *exceptions* without introducing any complexity. Third, we explain how *subject administration* can be performed transparently as a constituent part of the sharing rules.

Rules Consistency. A SWYSWYK sharing rule is said well-formed iff it produces only ACLs involving viewable documents shared with recognizable subjects. More notations are introduced here related to the SWYSWYK-like administration.

$DV \subseteq D$: the subset of documents being viewable (in the interpretable sense) by the owner. In other words, $DV = \{d \in D \,/\, \exists Viewer(d)\}$ with *Viewer* an application trusted by the owner (e.g., certified by an authority or a community of users) which delivers an interpretable view of the document to the owner (e.g., potentially transforms a binary format into a text, an image or a graphic).

$DS \subseteq DV$: set of viewable documents characterizing a unique subject (e.g., a vCard file, a resume, a photo labeled with a subject ID).

$DI \subseteq D$: set of documents containing identification traits of subjects or identifiees (e.g., an agenda, a photo of a group of people, the meeting minutes).

SR: set of all sharing rules defined by the owner.

Based on these notations, the SWYSWYK sharing rules are well-formed iff $\forall sr \in SR, \forall acl \in ACL, acl.d \in DV \wedge acl.s \in DS$. Any *acl* which does not satisfy this condition will be filtered out.

Rules Exceptions. We enacted as a design principle the fact to consider a closed policy and to allow only the declaration of positive rules (i.e., authorizations). We exclude negative rules (i.e., interdictions) because we consider that a common owner cannot easily figure out the output of a policy mixing potentially conflicting positive and negative rules, making the cognitive cost of administering his policy out of reach. Thus, instead of enriching the model semantics to capture authorizations and interdictions, we simply give the owner the ability to filter out a posteriori some permissions which may hurt her privacy (considered as exceptions). Hence, the resulting logic of the reference monitor remains straightforward, thereby complying with the *tangible enforcement* property. As explained below, an administration GUI is devoted to this task.

An ACL can be considered suspicious either because it involves a sensitive subject (e.g., my manager) or a sensitive object (e.g., a compromising picture or a part of my medical folder) or because the association between a particular subject and object may itself be compromising (e.g., I'm not ready to share all my holiday pictures with my colleagues, even if I trust them and if most of these pictures are not sensitive). Based on such information, we consider three types of enquiry queries, respectively targeting sensitive subjects, sensitive objects and sensitive associations between them, where $ACL^?$ denotes a set of newly generated ACLs:

$What(Q_S, A) \rightarrow \{(s, \{(d,a)\}) \,/\, (s,d,a) \in ACL^? \wedge s \in Q_S(S) \wedge a = A\}$: identifies, for each selected (sensitive) subject, the new set of action *a* they are granted to perform on which documents *d* (e.g., "which new documents can be seen by my boss?").

$Who(Q_D, A) \rightarrow \{(d, \{(s,a)\}) \,/\, (s,d,a) \in ACL^? \wedge d \in Q_D(D) \wedge a = A\}$: identifies, for each sensitive document *d*, the new set of subjects *s* with granted action *a* on them (e.g., "which new subjects have a read access to my medical records?").

$Which(Q_S, Q_D, A) \rightarrow \{(s,d,a) \,/\, (s,d,a) \in ACL^? \wedge s \in Q_S(S) \wedge d \in Q_D(D) \wedge a = A\}$: identifies new ACLs combining a selection of (sensitive) subjects and documents (e.g., "which new authorizations my colleagues have on my family photos?").

An administration GUI lets the data owner declare *suspicion clauses*, that is select sensitive subjects (i.e., $Q_S(S)$ clauses), sensitive documents (i.e., $Q_D(D)$ clauses) and compromising association (i.e., pairs of ($Q_S(S)$, $Q_D(D)$) clauses). The inquiry queries *What, Who* and *Which* based on these clauses are *watchdog triggers* evaluated on any new set of ACLs produced by sharing rules. Certain suspicious ACLs are then identified and need the owner's validation that can be easily done through the GUI. This guarantees that no unwanted disclosure will be done on sensitive data.

Subjects Administration. The administration of subjects is usually one of the most cumbersome task for a owner. The objective here is to make this task as transparent as possible, extracting the subject definition from the documents themselves and from the rules declaration. Let us first detail the structure of *S*. *S* can be represented by a table of schema (*Sid*: *S*, *Did*: *P*(*DS*), *It*: *P*(*IT*), [*Ct*: *CONTACT*], [*Auth*: {(*AUTH*, *credential*)}]), where *Sid* is the subject identifier, *Did* is a (set of) document identifier(s) referencing document(s) representing this unique subject on personal cloud, *It* is the (set of) identification trait(s) of this subject, *Ct* and *Auth* are optional -personal cloud dependent- information required to notify and authenticate the granted subjects. New subjects are registered in *S* as side-effects of the function *IsS*(*d*) (algorithm below).

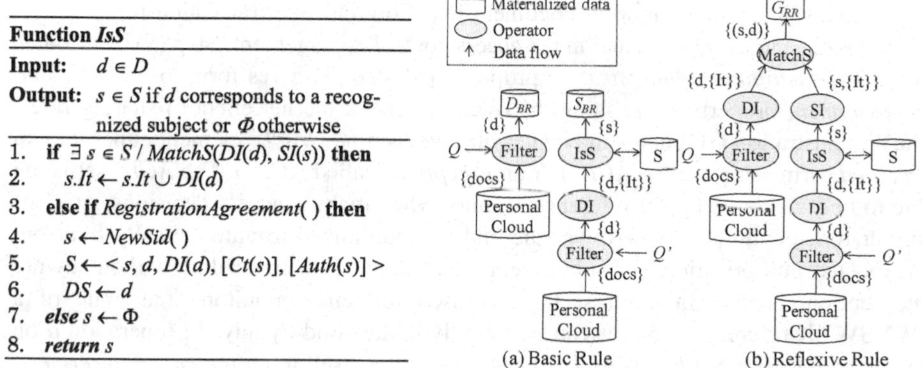

```
Function IsS
Input:   d ∈ D
Output:  s ∈ S if d corresponds to a recog-
         nized subject or Φ otherwise
if ∃ s ∈ S / MatchS(DI(d), SI(s)) then
   s.It ← s.It ∪ DI(d)
else if RegistrationAgreement( ) then
   s ← NewSid( )
   S ← < s, d, DI(d), [Ct(s)], [Auth(s)] >
   DS ← d
else s ← Φ
return s
```

Algorithm 1. Function IsS

Fig. 1. ACL production.

IsS is automatically invoked (1) each time *DS* documents are created or updated in the personal cloud (e.g., contacts documents, resumes, etc., as determined by the personal cloud platform) and (2) each time a new rule invoking *IsS* is defined. If at least one identification trait present in document *d* matches an existing subject *s*, *s* is returned and *s.It* is potentially enriched with the other identification traits present in *d*. If no correspondence is found, the owner may be asked on the fly to accept the registration of a new subject based on *d* content. Otherwise, *IsS* fails and *Φ* is returned. Hence the set of subjects automatically grows along document insertions and rule declarations with minimal owner interaction. The owner may however wish to disambiguate from time to time the content of *S* through an administration GUI (e.g., merge duplicates in situations like *'John Doe'*$\in$*s.It* and *'john@doe.io'*$\in$*s'.It*). Smart mechanisms may help, like relying on FOAF [3] and trying to parse the public pages of friend users to discover their identification traits, but this is let for future works.

5 Operational Semantics

We discuss here operational and architectural baselines in SWYSWYK, which are critical to enable a secure implementation of the model.

5.1 SWYSWYK Operational Baselines

The creation, maintenance and evaluation of a set of SWYSWYK permissions is as follows: (1) the owner creates sharing rules and *suspicion clauses* to be applied on her personal cloud; (2) a *rule translator* translates the selected rules into candidate and suspicious ACLs; (3) the owner checks the produced ACLs at will and accepts or rejects the suspicious ones using the *administration GUI*; (4) the *reference monitor* authenticates subjects and evaluates *Allowed(s, d, a)* calls to *true* or *false* and delivers the requested documents accordingly; and (5) new subjects are automatically integrated in the owner's personal cloud at document insertion and rule translation time.

Steps (3) and (5) are unusual in the access control management. Step (5) contributes to the *self-sustaining administration* property and step (3) gives form to the *enlighten empowerment* property by pushing the owner to check the net effect of sharing rules. The administration GUI helps the owner turning each new $ACL^?$ element either into an *accepted* permission (called ACL^+) or an *exception* (called ACL^-). The ACL^+ set is the sole to be considered by the reference monitor when making access decisions. ACL^- is similar to exceptions of a positive rule and is materialized to automatically filter out unexpected authorizations in subsequent runs of the rule translator, without owner intervention. Hence, in contrast to rule-based reference monitors, the logic of a SWYSWYK reference monitor can be trivially understood by anyone (operation *a* on *d* is granted to *s* iff $(s, d, a) \in$ ACL +) and contributes itself to *enlighten empowerment*.

5.2 Sharing Rules Constructs and Management

Our model is based on the materialization of all ACLs, which makes the evaluation of the *Allowed* function trivial and enables the user to visualize and filter the reference monitor effects. As shown on Fig. 1, five physical operators are required to express any basic or reflexive sharing rule, namely *Filter*, *DI*, *SI*, *IsS*, *MatchS*. The semantics of these operators are equivalent to their functional counterparts presented in Sect. 3 and thus are not recalled. The main difference is that each operator implements the corresponding function in a set-oriented way. For instance, *Filter* operator applies to all documents of *D* and returns the subset of documents satisfying condition *Q*. The flow of data consumed and produced by the operators is presented in Fig. 1 for the translation of basic and reflexive rules into ACLs.

At declaration time, the rule translator must evaluate a new sharing rule over all documents of the personal cloud. For a basic rule, it applies a filter at the leaf of each branch (i.e., selection of targeted subjects on the right branch and of targeted documents on the left branch). Then *DI* operator extracts the list of *ITs* from the targeted subject documents while *IsS* tries to match these *ITs* with the subjects already registered in *S*. As discussed in Sect. 4.3, *IsS* operator may have side-effects to dynamically populate *S* when unknown subjects are encountered. Finally, for a basic rule *BR*, the right branch feeds the S_{BR} structure while the left branch feeds the D_{BR} structure registering the produced (candidate) ACLs. The operator tree of reflexive rules follows the same logic, except that left and right branches must be joined on subject *ITs* and produce (candidate) ACLs on the G_{RR} structure.

Each time a new document *d* is inserted into the personal cloud, the filters of each branch of all rules are evaluated against *d* to check whether new candidate ACLs can be produced. While this cost is rather low for basic rules, the *MatchS* operator at the root of the reflexive rule tree may incur a full re-scan of the left branch on personal cloud (e.g., a subject *s* inserted at time t_2 may match with a document *d* inserted at time $t_1 < t_2$, while this association was not detectable at time t_1). We introduce an additional structure registering pending reflexive associations between subjects and documents to alleviate this cost (see Sect. 6). Whether a document *d* is deleted from the personal cloud, any entry referencing *d* in S_{BR}, D_{BR} and G_{RR} must be removed.

5.3 Reference Architecture and Enforcement

Although formally proving the security of an architecture for SWYSWYK is out of the scope of this paper, this section introduces an abstract architecture implementing the model while providing the *tangible enforcement* property. We consider an architecture made of (1) an *untrusted environment* (*UE*) on which no security assumption is made, (2) an *isolated environment* (*IE*) on which code can run with the guarantee that its execution is isolated from UE and (3) a *Secure Execution Environment* (*SEE*) which protects data and code against snooping and tampering.

Since no specific security assumption can be made on the personal cloud platform, it is part of the UE. All the documents of the personal cloud are thus stored encrypted and can be decrypted only by the reference monitor, which acts as an incorruptible doorkeeper for the personal cloud. Whenever an *Allowed(s, d, a)* request is evaluated to *true*, document *d* is decrypted in the SEE before being delivered to subject *s*. The reference monitor resides in the SEE and given its simplicity, can be hosted in many kinds of tamper-resistant SEE (e.g., SIM cards in smartphones, secure personal tokens [22, 23]). Data structures like *SR*, the set of sharing rules activated by the owner, *S*, the set of subjects in relation with the owner, and $ACL^?$, ACL^+ and ACL^- are stored in the SEE.

The rule translator updates these internal data structures. *IsS*, *MatchS* and *SI* are internal operators running inside the SEE. *Filter* and *DI* must be extensible (e.g., integrate existing libraries) and thus cannot be stored in the SEE. However, they need to access large portions of the personal cloud, leading to potential risks of information disclosure if observed or corrupted. Thus, *Filter* and *DI* are running in *isolated containers*[1] in the IE. The *Administration GUI* and the document *viewers*, which involve interactions with the owner, also run in IE.

Several physical instances of this architecture are possible. The experimental platform presented in the next section is an extreme case, but other target architectures could be envisioned. For example, a certified hypervisor running on top of an Intel SGX processor [24] on the personal computer itself can provide a logical implementation of IE. Smart devices equipped with a SIM card (embedding the reference monitor), a flash memory card (embedding the encrypted internal data structures) and an ARM Trustzone processor [25] (running UDFs and administration tools) are other interesting options.

6 Experimental Platform

We consider here a specific instance of the SWYSWYK architecture combining Cozy (open-source personal cloud, see: https://cozy.io/) and PlugDB (developed at Inria, see: https://project.inria.fr/plugdb/). The personal device has a 3 GHz Intel Xeon E5-1660 CPU, 8 GB of RAM and a 500 GB 10.000 RPM hard drive. PlugDB uses a STM32F417GH6 MCU with a 168 MHz ARM Cortex M4 CPU, 192 KB of RAM and 1 MB of NOR storage. The Raspberry Pi 3 has a 1.2 GHz ARMv8 CPU and 1 GB of RAM. We use an external UHS-I microSD card of 16 GB for both SEE and IE. A video of the experimental platform and its usability is available[2] (Fig. 2).

Environmental Cost. The environmental cost to insert a new document in the personal cloud is pictured in Fig. 3(left). The 4 components of this cost are: (1) transfer cost of the document between UE and SEE (in cleartext from UE to SEE and in encrypted form back), (2) document encryption cost in SEE, (3) insertion of the

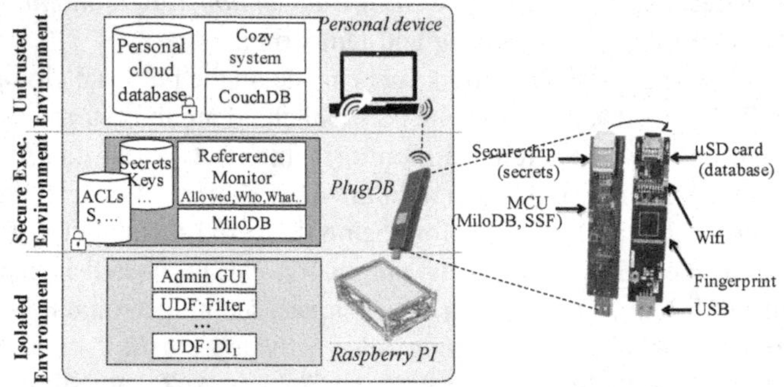

Fig. 2. Experimental platform: software and hardware (right).

---

[1] In practice, isolated containers can be implemented using a dedicated hardware platform (physical isolation), an hypervisor or a microkernel. Recent hardware advances propose an hardware support for running isolated code, e.g., using ARM Trustzone [2] or SGX processors [9].

[2] http://wanda.inria.fr/CIKM/cikm.ogg.

encrypted document in Cozy and (4) transfer cost of the cleartext document from SEE to IE (which applies *Filter* and *DI* on sharing rules). Step 4 (USB transfer) can be performed in parallel with the other steps, explaining why we isolate that cost in Fig. 3.

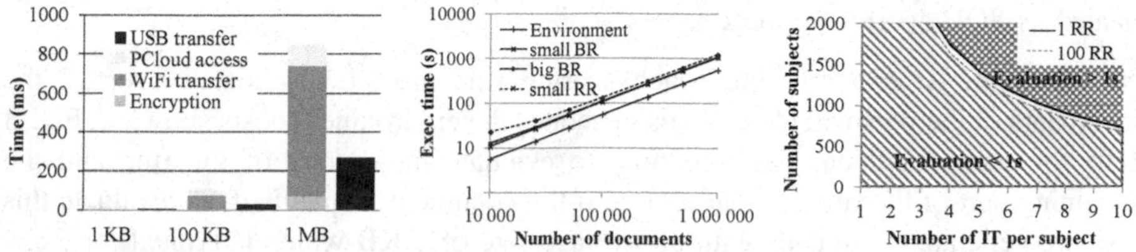

Fig. 3. Environmental costs for one document (left curve), rule initialization costs (middle) and rule maintenance costs in function of the subjects cardinality (right).

Rules and Data Sets. In Table 1, we introduce the rules and data sets used in the experiments to measure the performance at rule translation time (i.e., initialization cost incurred by a rule creation and maintenance cost of a rule when new documents are inserted). We define four different rules representative of *basic* and *reflexive* rules, with *Big* and *Small* output sizes in terms of the number of produced ACLs.

Table 1. Sharing rules considered in the experiments. E.g., Big BR is a big basic rule qualifying 1.000 documents on the predicate *type* = '*cardio*' and 10 subjects on *type* = '*health community*' resulting in 10 K ACLs (this rule corresponds to a quantified-self context).

Rule name	Filter on D	Filter on S	#Results: D, S, ACLs
Small BR	Type = 'directory' & name = 'team'	Type = 'contact' & group = 'team'	10, 5, 50
Big BR	Type = 'cardio'	Type = 'health community'	1.000, 10, 10.000
Small RR	Type = 'note'	Type = 'contact' & group = 'lab'	10, 30, 50
Big RR	Type = 'album' & tag = 'holidays'	Type = 'contact' & group = 'friends'	1.000, 200, 5.000

Rule Translation. In Cozy, documents are formatted in JSON with a set of key-values, potentially associated to a binary file. Simple implementations of *Filter* and *DI* check a set of filtering conditions and extract the *ITs* needed to subsequently identify the subject(s) based on the document key-value pairs. More complex implementations deal with the binary part of the document, e.g., image recognition or classification. *SI*, *IsS* and *MatchS* are implemented in PlugDB on the MiloDB [3] RDBMS. The S_{BR}, D_{BR}, G_{RR} and G_{except} data structures used to materialize ACL^+, ACL^- and $ACL^?$ are mapped in MiloDB relational tables. Tables *BRD*(*Rid int*, *Did char*(*32*), *A char*(*1*)) and *BRS*(*Rid int*, *Sid int*) materialize the union of S_{BR} and D_{BR} for all basic rules *BR*, with *Rid* the identifier of a basic rule granting authorization *A* on document *Did* (ids in Cozy are 32 bytes) to subject *Sid*. Tables *RR* and *Except*, of schema (*Sid int*, *Did char(32)*, *A char(1)*), respectively materialize G_{RR} and G_{Except}. The set of $ACL^?$ are stored in 3 tables *BRD?*, *BRS?* and *RR?* with the same schema as respectively *BRD*, *BRS* and *RR*. The subjects and their identification traits are stored in table *SIT* (*Sid int*, *IT varchar*). *SI*, *IsS*, *MatchS,* as well as *Allowed* and *Who*, *What*, *Which* can trivially be implemented as SQL queries on these tables.

Initialization. At creation time, each sharing rule must be evaluated over all the documents of the personal cloud. This generates the environment costs shown in Fig. 3 (left) for each document plus the time to evaluate the *Filters* of the rule and the remaining part of the rule evaluation tree if the document is qualified. To evaluate this cost, we generate documents with an average size of 1 KB which is typical for Cozy documents with no binary part. We assume large binary files don't impact the overall cost as the *Filters* first check the metadata and rule out the files without the expected type. Figure 3(middle) plots the time spent to run the initialization process for each rule of Table 1, depending on the number of considered documents. Conclusions are as follows: (i) the initialization cost of rule creation is acceptable; (ii) the environmental cost represents half of the total cost and is mainly due to communications between SEE, IE and UE which could largely be saved with other settings (e.g., Trustzone or SGX); and (iii) apart from environment costs, the cost of evaluating *Filters* is predominant because of the number of iterations (1 evaluation per document and rule) but not because of the cost of an elementary filter.

Maintenance. Each time a document *d* is inserted, the *Filters* of all rules are evaluated against *d* to check whether new ACLs can be produced. This is not an issue for basic rules, but may lead to a rescan of the personal cloud for reflexive rules if pending reflexive associations between subjects and documents are not maintained. To this end, we create table *RD*(*Rid int*, *Did char(32)*, *IT varchar*) to record the rules and doc id pairs along with any identification trait which did not match an existing subject at the current time. Conversely, table *HR*(*Rid int*, *Sid int*) records the subjects ids qualified by that reflexive rule in order to detect an association with a future inserted document referencing one of these subjects. Given the shape of the operator trees (Fig. 1) the maintenance cost is determined by (1) the *Filters* evaluation for all active rules and (2) the cost of *IsS* when the document is qualified by *Filter*. Indeed, *IsS* cost depends on the cardinality of *S* and on the number of *ITs S* holds. Figure 3(right) indicates the number of subjects and *ITs* per subject which remains compatible with the insertion of a document in less than 1 s for a given number of rules. To vary the number of rules, we generate new rules having the same characteristics as the ones shown in Table 1. The maintenance cost for *BR* rules (not reported) always remains under 2.5 ms per document, as it is independent of the number of subjects. Given Fig. 3(right), there is no performance issue linked to ACL maintenance (with 100 *RR* rules and without resorting on indexes, we can manage more than 1.000 subjects with 7 ITs for a maintenance cost of less than 1 s per inserted document.

7 Conclusion

This paper introduces a new sharing paradigm for the personal cloud, called SWYS-WYK (*Share What You See with Who You Know*), empowering individuals with new means to regulate by themselves the dissemination of their data with tangible enforcement guarantees. The model allows the expression of intuitive reflexive rules and lets the owner visualizes the net effects of these rules. Subjects are self-administered by design at rule translation and document insertion. We proposed an architecture to enforce the model and shown its feasibility through a performance evaluation performed on a secure DB engine (PlugDB) linked to an existing personal cloud platform (Cozy). While the personal cloud paradigm is pushed by recent legislation and smart disclosure initiatives, finding new ways to intuitively and securely share personal data is paramount. We hope that this work actively contributes to this challenge.

References

1. Regulation (EU) 2016/679 on the protection of natural persons with regard to the processing of personal data and on the free movement of such data, 27 April 2016
2. Bertino, E., Ghinita, G., Kamra, A.: Access control for databases: concepts and systems. Found. Trends Databases **3**(1-2), 1–148 (2011)
3. Brickley, D., Miller, L.: FOAF vocabulary specification 0.91. TR ILRT Bristol (2007)
4. Fang, L., LeFevre, K.: Privacy wizards for social networking sites. In: ACM WWW (2010)
5. Squicciarini, A.C., Sundareswaran, S., et al.: A3P: adaptive policy prediction for shared images over popular content sharing sites. In: ACM Hypertext and Hypermedia (HT) (2011)
6. Tootoonchian, A., Saroiu, S., Ganjali, Y., Wolman, A.: Lockr: better privacy for social networks. In: Conference Emerging Networking Experiments and Technologies (CoNEXT) (2009)
7. Van Kleek, M., Smith, D.A., Shadbolt, N., Schraefel, M.C.: A decentralized architecture for consolidating personal information ecosystems: the WebBox. In: PIM (2012)
8. Seong, S.-W., Seo, J., Nasielski, M., Sengupta, D., et al.: PrPl: a decentralized social networking infrastructure. In: ACM Mobile Cloud Computing & Services (MCS) (2010)
9. Ali, M., et al.: SeDaSC: secure data sharing in clouds. IEEE Syst. J. **11**(2), 395–404 (2015)
10. Thilakanathan, D., Chen, S., Nepal, S., Calvo, R.A.: Secure data sharing in the cloud. In: Nepal, S., Pathan, M. (eds.) Security, Privacy and Trust in Cloud Systems, pp. 45–72. Springer, Heidelberg (2014). doi:10.1007/978-3-642-38586-5_2
11. Wang, F., et al.: Cryptographically enforced access control for user data in untrusted clouds. In: USENIX Symposium on Networked Systems Design and Implementation (NSDI) (2016)
12. Baden, R., Bender, A., Spring, N., et al.: Persona: an online social network with user-defined privacy. In: ACM SIGCOMM Computer Communication Review, vol. 39(4) (2009)
13. Guha, S., Tang, K., Francis, P.: NOYB: privacy in online social networks. In: ACM Workshop on Online Social Networks (2008)
14. Yuan, L., et al.: Privacy-preserving photo sharing based on a secure JPEG. In: CCC (2015)
15. Liu, Y., Gummadi, K.P., Krishnamurthy, B., Mislove, A.: Analyzing facebook privacy settings: user expectations vs. reality. In: ACM SIGCOMM (2011)

16. Mazurek, M.L., Liang, Y., et al.: Toward strong, usable access control for shared distributed data. In: USENIX Conference on File and Storage Technologies (FAST) (2014)
17. Wang, L., Wijesekera, D., Jajodia, S.: A Logic-based framework for attribute based access control. In: ACM Workshop on Formal Methods in Security Engineering (FMSE) (2004)
18. Geambasu, R., Balazinska, M., Gribble, S.D., Levy, H.M.: Homeviews: peer-to-peer middleware for personal data sharing applications. In: ACM SIGMOD (2007)
19. Carminati, B., Ferrari, E., Perego, A.: Rule-based access control for social networks. In: Meersman, R., Tari, Z., Herrero, P. (eds.) OTM 2006. LNCS, vol. 4278, pp. 1734–1744. Springer, Heidelberg (2006). doi:10.1007/11915072_80
20. Mori, J., Sugiyama, T., Matsuo, Y.: Real-world oriented information sharing using social networks. In: ACM SIGGROUP (GROUP) (2005)
21. Park, J., Sandhu, R.: The UCON ABC usage control model. ACM TISSEC **7**(1), 128–174 (2004)
22. Anciaux, N., Bouganim, L., Pucheral, P., Guo, Y., Le Folgoc, L., Yin, S.: MILo-DB: a personal, secure and portable database machine. DAPD **32**(1), 37–63 (2014)
23. Anciaux, N., Lallali, S., Popa, I.S., Pucheral, P.: A scalable search engine for mass storage smart objects. PVLDB **8**(9), 910–921 (2015)
24. Costan, V., Devadas, S.: Intel SGX explained. IACR Cryptology ePrint Archive (2016)
25. Alves, T., Felton, D.: Trustzone: integrated hardware and software security. ARM White Pap. (2004)

Security Awareness and Social Engineering -Policy Languages

Don't Be Deceived: The Message Might Be Fake

Stephan Neumann[1], Benjamin Reinheimer[1](✉), and Melanie Volkamer[1,2]

[1] Technische Universität Darmstadt, Darmstadt, Germany
[2] Karlstad University, Karlstad, Sweden
{stephan.neumann,benjamin.reinheimer,melanie.volkamer}@secuso.org

Abstract. In an increasingly digital world, fraudsters, too, exploit this new environment and distribute fraudulent messages that trick victims into taking particular actions. There is no substitute for making users aware of scammers' favoured techniques and giving them the ability to detect fraudulent messages. We developed an awareness-raising programme, specifically focusing on the needs of small and medium-sized enterprises (SMEs). The programme was evaluated in the field. The participating employees demonstrated significantly improved skills in terms of ability to classify messages as fraudulent or genuine. Particularly with regard to one of the most widespread attack types, namely fraudulent messages with links that contain well-known domains as sub-domains of generic domains, recipients of the programme improved their recognition rates from 56.6% to 88%. Thus, the developed security awareness-raising programme contributes to improving the security in SMEs.

Keywords: Usable security · Education concept · User studies · SME · Awareness

1 Introduction

The boundary between our physical and digital worlds is increasingly blurred. It is inevitable that fraudsters ply their trade in both worlds. One of their most common strategies is sending digital messages that appear to be genuine. These messages tempt users to take an action which will allow the fraudsters to achieve their nefarious aims. The transmitted message is often difficult to spot since purports to come from a trusted party and looks genuine because it replicates the expected layout, style and format. Sometimes a malicious link is included, in the hope that the recipient will click on it. If victims click on these links, they are redirected a genuinely-looking website, on which they are required to provide their secret credentials. Once entered, these credentials are directly forwarded to fraudsters. Other times, fraudsters call on their victims to reply to their messages with sensitive data or to open malicious attachments, which will compromise the computer if activated. The consequences of successful deception range from identity theft to blackmail or sabotage, potentially resulting in severe reputational and/or financial loss. Estimations of the U.S. Federal Bureau

J. Lopez et al. (Eds.): TrustBus 2017, LNCS 10442, pp. 199–214, 2017.
DOI: 10.1007/978-3-319-64483-7_13

of Investigation quantify the damage caused only by fraudulent emails at 2.3 billion dollars between October 2013 and February 2016 [9]. Fraudulent messages particularly constitute a growing threat for small and medium-sized enterprises (SMEs) as research shows [15]. A number of technical measures can mitigate these security threats to a certain extent. Popular technical measures include whitelists or blacklists. However, technical measures generally do not offer sufficient protection on their own; e.g., it takes on average of 30 h for automated detection mechanisms to identify and block malicious websites [11]. It is therefore of fundamental importance to teach Internet users how to protect themselves. Security awareness-raising programmes are widely considered to be an essential component of an IT-security resilience programme. Programmes exist in a variety of formats, each with their own advantages and disadvantages: Instructor-based, computer-based, and text-based programmes h [13,16]. Here we focus on text-based programmes as it is well suited for the needs of small and medium-sized enterprises (SMEs). This approach has the benefit of offering self-paced, individualized learning, to be engaged in as and when the employee has the time and inclination.

Contribution: We iteratively developed and improved an awareness-raising educational programme (Sect. 2) and knowledge-application assessment test (Sect. 3). The awareness-raising programme comprises four education modules: introduction into fraudulent messages, implausible fraudulent messages, plausible fraudulent messages with dangerous links and with malicious attachments. After iteratively refining the modules, the programme was evaluated in the field by three SMEs (Sect. 4). The results show that participants significantly improved their skills in correctly identifying both fraudulent and genuine messages (Sect. 5). Identification rates were raised from 63.3% (fraudulent messages) and 82.4% (genuine messages) to 84.3% (fraudulent messages) and 87.1% (genuine messages) respectively. In terms of implausible fraudulent messages, participants improved their detection rates from 71.1% to 92%. Detection of plausible fraudulent messages with dangerous links improved from 48.6% to 74.3%, detection of plausible fraudulent messages with malicious attachments from 82% to 94.4%. We discuss these results (Sect. 6) and conclude that the developed programme can significantly contribute to the security in SMEs.

2 Awareness-Raising Programme

In developing the awareness-raising programme, we followed the main principles of learning (*i.e.*, readiness, exercise, effect, intensity, and primacy) and a human-centred design approach. Furthermore, meetings with IT-security consultants revealed the need that besides being effective and efficient, the programme shall be applicable in a flexible manner, *i.e.* employees shall have reasonable breakpoints and the intensity should depend on the pre-knowledge. To address these requirements, we decided to split the programme into four distinct modules.

2.1 Structure

According to the primacy learning principle, the programme commences with the information that is likely to make the strongest impact:

Message Types, Attack Types, and Consequences: The first module provides an introduction to the fact that messages can contain dangerous content and that any type of message can be sent by a fraudster. Examples are cited, including email (widely-known), text message, a Facebook post, or a WhatsApp message. An explanation follows that anybody can be targeted by fraudulent messages as many fraudsters address as many people as possible. Furthermore, it is pointed out that sender information is an unreliable indicator. To that end, our programme is in line with the recommendations elaborated by Kirlappos and Sasse [12], *i.e.* to address first the misconceptions. The consequences of unwisely acting are outlined to increase motivation.

Implausible Fraudulent Messages: The second module helps employees to identify fraudulent messages by providing the means to conduct plausibility checks on incoming messages. After this module, they ought to be able to detect those fraudulent messages that are relatively easy to detect.

Plausible Fraudulent Messages with Dangerous Links: The third module helps employees to detect fraudulent messages that look plausible at first glance but which actually contain a dangerous link. The module explains how to check the genuineness of these links.

Plausible Fraudulent Messages with Malicious Attachments: The fourth module helps employees to detect fraudulent messages that look plausible at first glance but actually contain a malicious attachment. The module explains how to check the genuineness of attachments.

The three main modules (2–4) follow the same internal structure:

Teaser: At the beginning of each module, two messages are shown, one of which is fraudulent. Employees are encouraged to identify the fraudulent message by posing the question: *Which message is fraudulent?* The differences between messages is deliberately subtle, in order to motivate employees further to engage with the content of the upcoming module (while following the readiness principle). At the end of each module, both messages are shown once again and employees are encouraged, once more, to judge which is the fraudulent message, before the correct answer is provided. This approach makes it possible for learners to gauge their learning success.

Instructions: Each module is sub-structured by fundamental instructions that allow those engaging with the programme to detect fraudulent messages either based on their plausibility or because the link or the attachment is malicious. The content is structured taking into account the trade-off between enabling early success (effect principle) and starting with the most important content (primacy principle). Instructions are either about identifying relevant information or checking this information. The instructions are to be followed until one check fails, *i.e.* reveals that the considered message is fraudulent. In this case, it is recommended to delete the message. Note, we also provide information how to proceed if one is not certain about the outcome of any check.

Fraudster Strategies: Instructions are accompanied by fraudster strategies that make applying the instructions difficult. Modules raise awareness of these strategies in order to decrease the likelihood to fall for them.

Examples: Instructions and fraudster strategies are accompanied by illustrative fraudulent messages, including explanations how to detect that the corresponding message is fraudulent. Examples are used to make the programme more attractive, thus following the principle of intensity.

Exercises: Employees are invited to apply the gained knowledge by doing exercises for each instruction and fraudster strategy. Each exercise asks to decide whether a message is genuine or fraudulent. According to the exercise learning principle, the exercises contain repetition and immediate feedback is provided.

Due to the lack of space, only the content of the three main modules is outlined in the following subsections. We use plain language in order to provide the concise and accurate information, as recommended by Bauer *et al.* [3] and Furnell *et al.* [10]. Note, the programme as well as the knowledge-application assessment test were developed for the German context. The programme is available online.

2.2 Implausible Fraudulent Messages

This module explains how to conduct plausibility checks on incoming messages.

Teaser: The plausibility module is motivated by two emails that appear to come from Amazon and purport to be raising an issue related to the receiver's Amazon account. The message encourages the recipient to click on an embedded link. Emails differ with respect to the sender address. The genuine email was supposedly sent by the address `order@amazon.com`, while the fraudulent message used `amazonorder@forsur.ru`.

Instructions and Fraudster Strategies: The plausibility modules contains the instruction to conduct a variety of checks, such as "Does the sender name match the message content?", "Do you know the sender?", "If the sender is a web service, do you have an account with them?", "Do you know the language the message is written in?", "Does the content of the message match the supposed sender?", "Does the message style, topic, and salutation match up to previous messages?", "Does the message contain promises, threats of punishment, or upsetting news?", "Does the message attempt to persuade you to reveal sensitive information?". If none of these checks indicate fraud, the employee is advised to apply the instructions given in the next module before following any links or opening/saving an attachment. The plausibility module captures the following fraudster strategy: "Fraudsters create a sense of urgency, pressuring people to perform actions without due consideration." It is recommended that employees take their time, especially when a message urges haste.

2.3 Plausible Fraudulent Messages with Dangerous Link

If an incoming message turns out to be plausible and contains a link, employees should check the validity of the link as explained in this module.

Teaser: It is designed analogously to the previous one. Here, the fraudulent email can be identified by checking the embedded link's URL.

Instructions and Fraudster Strategies: The module contains four instructions and several fraudster strategies, which are presented in the following:

Identify the Actual Target URL Behind a Link. Explanations for different browsers, different mail clients, different mobile operating systems, and special-purpose software (*e.g.* Skype) are provided as sometimes the actual URL is displayed in the status bar, sometimes in a tooltip, sometimes in the text within the message (*e.g.* several social networks), and sometimes after softly clicking and holding a link (*e.g.* on mobile devices). This first instruction is complicated by two popular fraudster strategies, namely "The actual URL is hidden behind a feign URL within the message itself." And "Tooltips with fake URLs are encoded into the message that appears as soon as the user hovers over the link. This does not represent the actual URL (shown in the status bar)."

Identify the Most Relevant Part of a URL (Referred to as the Who Section). Different constituent parts of URLs are introduced as well as the most relevant parts that signal malicious links, *i.e.* the domain and top level domain[1]. The second instruction is complicated by two fraudster strategies, namely "Trustworthy *who* sections are placed in the sub-domain or the path of the URL." (*e.g.* http://amazon.de.home-shopping.cc) and "SSL certificates are generated for fraudulent websites to generate trust in the URL." (*i.e.* `https://...`).

Check Whether the Who Section is Related to the Supposed Sender and/or Content of the Incoming Message. This third instruction is complicated by three fraudster strategies, namely "Fraudsters generate trust by using trustworthy terms (*e.g.* secure, trust) in their *who* sections.", "Fraudsters generate *who* sections that are visually hardly distinguishable from known *who* sections." (*e.g.* http://arnazon.com), and "Fraudsters generate *who* sections that are cognitively hardly distinguishable from known *who* sections." (*e.g.* http://mircosoft.com). While the first strategy exploits humans' positive association to trustworthy terms, the latter strategies confront employees with the fact that humans generally read texts by perceiving whole words rather than reading letter-by-letter.

If a Who Section Cannot be Evaluated Conclusively, Gather Further Information. Examples of such *who* sections might be http://amazonshopping.com for a message supposedly originating from Amazon. Explanations are provided on how to check the genuineness of the URL under investigation, *e.g.* the employee might navigate to the supposed service provider by using the known *who* section, the

[1] Note, that the content of this module might need to be adapted for other contexts, *e.g.* the U.K. provides second level domains in addition to top level domains.

employee might check whether the *who* section appeared in previous messages from the service provider, or use a search engine.

If any of these checks indicate fraud, the employee should delete the message.

2.4 Plausible Fraudulent Messages with Malicious Attachments

The fourth module shall provide support to evaluate a plausible message with attachment(s). To the best of our knowledge, there is no reliable source about the criticality of different file formats. We decided to classify executable file formats and macro file formats as very dangerous. Furthermore, we classify encrypted files[2] and compressed files as very dangerous, because of their potential to hide malicious code from anti virus scanners.

Teaser: The teaser is designed analogously to the plausibility module. In order to resolve a claimed problem, the employee is encouraged to open a document that contains further information. While the genuine email contains a PDF file, the fraudulent contains a EXE file with double ending (information.pdf.exe).

Instructions and Fraudster Strategies: The attachment module captures the following instructions:

Consider Whether Receiving a Corresponding File from the Supposed Sender, Using this Channel in this Particular Format was Announced Beforehand. The recognition of malicious attachments is complicated by the following strategy: "Fraudsters incorporate non-dangerous file formats into the file names in order to deflect users' attention from the actual file format."

If a Corresponding Message Was Not Announced, Check Whether the Attachments Has a Very Dangerous File Format. To conduct the check, employees receive a list of dangerous file formats, *i.e.* executable file formats, and file formats that may encode macros, as well as encrypted and compressed file formats.

If a Corresponding Message Was Not Announced and the Attachment Does Not Have a Very Dangerous Format, then Gather Further Information. It is explained that theoretically all files may be dangerous if client software to open these files is vulnerable. Employees therefore are advised to handle any type of attachment generally with care. Therefore, explanations are provided to gather further information, *e.g.* the employee may contact the supposed sender by other means or she/he may look for the sender on search engines if the sender is unknown.

2.5 Iterative Improvements

The development of the awareness-raising programme was characterised by considering the lessons learned from research published on security awareness raising, *e.g.* [2,12,18], as well as by regular and careful revisions informed by experts

[2] Note, we mean in particular encrypted containers rather than signed and encrypted emails with attachments while one is able to verify the signature.

(both from academia and industry including those doing security consulting for SMEs) and typical lay people. Exhaustive feedback was provided by a professional school. The awareness-raising programme was used as teaching unit in the classes and we were allowed to collect feedback from the notes the pupils took during the class and a discussion at the end of the class. Teaching units for two classes were held on the same day, for three days spread over a week. The arrangement made it possible for us to review student feedback and to incorporate this into the programme before the next teaching units were presented. The procedure was as follows: The teacher presented the invited author as a researcher in the field of IT security from the University of X, who were developing a new security awareness-raising programme. The presenter subsequently distributed printouts of the material and invited pupils to work through the educational material and to provide feedback whenever they felt the need to do so. Each page offered space for comments such that providing feedback was easy. Afterwards, a discussion was initiated where students were invited to discuss the content and to provide feedback. The presenter took notes of these discussions. Subsequently, the received feedback was discussed and integrated into the programme by the research team. The main challenge was to balance effectiveness and efficiency of the programme. Based on the received feedback, it was considered apposite to offer two options to SMEs: one with exercises, and one without, the latter being more suitable to those with very limited time to complete the programme.

3 Knowledge-Application Assessment Test

In addition to an awareness-raising programme, a knowledge-application assessment phase is important to know whether the employees actually take the time to work through the programme. This section explains the knowledge-application assessment we developed. In general, there are two options for such a test. One can either test declarative knowledge of fraudulent messages, strategies, consequences, or test the ability to judge the validity of messages. The second type is superior because it is important that they know how to apply their knowledge. In order to ensure that the test was realistic and employees do not discard supposedly plausible messages as implausible because they do for instance not use the respective service providers, we came up with a scenario. All messages seem to come from personal contacts (colleagues or the supervisor) or from well-known service providers. Ideally one would test at least one fraudulent message per (check-)instruction, fraudster strategy and message type – and of course at least as many genuine messages. This would require us to test responses to an unfeasible number of messages (more than 500). We had to reduce the number of messages while still covering a variety of attack types. The test will also be made available online[3]. SMEs might consider providing

[3] https://www.secuso.informatik.tu-darmstadt.de/de/secuso/forschung/ergebnisse/erkennung-betruegerischer-nachrichten-german-only/. Accessed 11 Apr 2017.

the knowledge-application assessment test to employees before the actual programme, if employees feel sufficiently confident on the topic, before receiving the actual programme.

Selected Messages for the Link-Related Module: We constructed the following seven attacks[4]:

- Three 'implausible' attacks: These attacks use domains unrelated to the actual *who*, *i.e.* for the messages considered implausible *who* sections, combined with fraudster strategies: (1) Implausible *who* section and actual *who* not in URL; (2) Implausible *who* section while the actual *who* section appears in the path of the URL; (3) Implausible *who* sections while the actual *who* section appears in the sub-domain of the URL.
- Three 'trust' attacks: These are attacks combining a generic domain with a trustworthy term and applying the same fraudster strategies as before.
- One 'obscure' attack: This attack is difficult to detect as the *who* section is visually and cognitively hardly distinguishable from the actual *who* sections.

After the attacks were constructed, we decided to use https for all URLs (both fraudulent and genuine). The alternatives were either to use only http (which could lead to a misleading message that dangerous links always use http and a conclusion that https is always trustworthy) or to combine each attack type applied with both (which would lead to twice as many test messages). Afterwards, we considered how to address the following fraudster strategies: fake tooltips and mismatch between URL in text and actual one. We decided to just add one message for the first and two for the second one (as this is more common in real world), *i.e.* the 'tooltip' strategy combined with the 'obscure' attack and the 'mismatch' strategy combined once with the 'implausible' and once with the 'trust' attack. This leads us to ten fraudulent messages with dangerous links. Finally, we decided to distribute the message types across the different ways of identifying URLs behind links (status bar, tooltip, within message, softly clicking). Consequently, to test the link module, ten fraudulent and ten genuine messages were generated.

Selected Messages for the Attachment-Related Module: Similar to the link-related module, the basis for the construction of test messages are the instructions and strategies provided within the module. As a result, we consider messages that may contain two types of malicious attachments: (1) Attachments with dangerous file formats, which are not hidden and (2) malicious attachments, with camouflaged file types. We selected only two attack types, as compared to the ten for the link related module. While the number of messages between the link-related and the attachment-related modules may appear unbalanced, this decision is justified by the fact that the link-related module contains many

[4] We did not include attacks where the actual *who* section is extended with a plausible term, as these can only be identified by using a search engine. The snag is that SME employees might have restricted Internet access while undertaking the programme.

more instructions and addresses more fraudster strategies. Similar to the link-related module, the number of fraudulent and genuine messages are equal. To summarise, the attachment-related module contains four messages.

Selected Messages for the Implausible Messages-Related Module: We tested the plausibility module in association with the other modules because implausible messages often encourage recipients to click on dangerous links or to download malicious attachments. For the link-related module, we decided to add three implausible messages, distributed over 'implausible', 'trust' and 'obscure' attacks. Furthermore, messages were distributed so that the URL can be identified from the status bar, in the tooltip, and within the message.

Since there were fewer fraudulent messages with attachments than those without, we added only one implausible fraudulent message with a malicious attachment. This message contained an attachment with a very dangerous file format, which is not hidden. To maintain a balance between fraudulent and genuine messages, four genuine messages (three with links and one with attachment) were included in the test. To summarise, the plausibility-related module requires employees to estimate the genuineness of eight messages.

Iterative Improvements: The test was iteratively improved by carrying out a pilot test with potential target persons in the authors' environments. These persons received the material and were invited to do the test after the programme, both either as PDF or printouts. In addition to estimating the genuineness of messages within the test, testers were asked to justify their decision in a few words. Having these justifications helped us to determine when information was missing, perhaps because the test scenario was underspecified or testers were faced with file formats which were not covered in the material.

4 Evaluation

We evaluated the awareness-raising programme's effectiveness, as a whole, as well as the efficacy of the main modules. We therefore posed the following hypotheses:

- **H-overall**: The programme leads to significant more correct decisions.
- **H-certainty**: The programme leads to significant improvements in employees' certainty when distinguishing fraudulent from genuine messages.
- **H-genuine**: The programme leads to significant improvements in identifying genuine messages.
- **H-attack**: The programme leads to significant improvements in recognising fraudulent messages.
- **H-module-2/3/4**: The programme leads to significant improvements in recognising implausible fraudulent messages/plausible but with dangerous links/plausible but with dangerous attachments.

4.1 Study Design

The study was conducted as within-subjects study using the following procedure:

Introduction and Pre-knowledge-Test: Participants received a PDF file. The file contained background information about the study and welcomed the participants. The PDF also contained the knowledge-application assessment test including the scenario to assume to be Martin Müller and the 32 messages (while the order of the messages was randomised and there was one message per page). In addition, to the question whether the displayed message is fraudulent (yes, no), participants were asked for their confidence in their decision (1–5 Likert scale). After completing the pre-test, participants returned the PDF.

Awareness-Raising: Once the first PDF was completed, participants worked through the awareness-raising programme. We decided to provide SMEs with the awareness-raising programme without exercises and with a fixed set of examples to get equal conditions for all study participants.

Post-knowledge-Test: Participants received and completed the knowledge-application assessment test (again the 'Martin Müller' scenario was presented first), *i.e.* they received the same 32 messages but in a different randomised order. Again two questions per message had to be answered. In addition, we asked them to provide their age and their gender.

4.2 Recruiting, Procedure, and Ethics

The evaluation was conducted at three small and medium-sized enterprises (SME) in Germany, each with several employees from a wide range of professions. In particular, we asked the contact persons to include a variety of employees that do not mainly work in the field of information security. The authors provided the contact person of each SME with the awareness-raising programme, PDFs with the pre-test and PDFs with the post-test. The contact person was advised to send out the pre-test PDFs, asking their employees to send it back within the next business day. Upon receiving a completed pre-test PDF, the corresponding employee got the awareness-raising programme and advice to take time to work through the programme. Upon receipt of confirmation, the contact person sent the post-test PDF and encouraged participants to return the completed test the next business day. The requirements for research that involves humans are defined by the ethics commission of Technische Universität Darmstadt and were respected: Each SME's contact person solely distributed and collected the pre- and post-knowledge-assessment tests, and subsequently returned the filled tests by encrypted means to the authors of the paper. The contact persons were not involved in the evaluation, such that participants' anonymity was ensured.

5 Results

In total 89 employees participated. The average age of the participants is 32.8 (median 30). The youngest was 18 and the oldest one 55. With 63 male participants, more than two third are male. The population of our evaluation covers a broad knowledge-spectrum with regard to fraudulent and genuine messages.

Table 1. Descriptive statistics

	Pre-test		Post-test	
	Correctness	SD	Correctness	SD
Overall	72.87	11.30	85.72	7.96
Certainty	3.91	.45	4.33	.41
Genuine	82.42	13.99	87.11	13.99
Fraudulent	63.32	20.01	84.34	11.28
Module-2	71.16	25.10	91.95	16.69
Module-3	48.59	24.67	74.30	17.71
Module-4	82.02	30.38	94.38	17.58

Hypotheses Tests: For the hypotheses tests, we exclude four participants that before the programme already had a recognition rate of 100%.[5]. The descriptive data for all hypotheses is depicted in Table 1. To test the hypotheses we conducted paired-samples t-tests. The requirements for the paired-samples t-tests were satisfied: paired samples and interval scaled variables. The paired-samples t-test results are supplemented with Cohen's d, *i.e.* an approximated effect size. The approximated effect size substantiates the practical relevance of the findings and provides researchers with benchmarks for future interventions. The boxplots corresponding to the hypotheses are shown in Fig. 1[6].

- **H-overall:** Our analysis shows a significantly improved rate for distinguishing fraudulent from genuine messages ($T = 14, 28, p < .001$, $d = 1.401$). The Cohen's d of 1.401 is above .8, *i.e.* a large effect size.
- **H-certainty:** Our analysis shows a significantly improved rate for distinguishing fraudulent from genuine messages ($T = 10, 93, p < .001$, $d = .955$). The Cohen's d of .995 is above .8, *i.e.* a large effect size.
- **H-genuine:** Our analysis shows a significantly improved detection rate for genuine messages ($T = 4, 24, p < .001$, $d = .319$). The Cohen's d of .319 is below .5, *i.e.* a small effect size.
- **H-attack:** Our analysis shows a significantly improved detection rate for fraudulent messages ($T = 13.82, p < .001$, $d = 1.257$). The Cohen's d of 1.257 is above .8, *i.e.* a large effect size.

---

[5] One of these four participants made one mistake after the programme in the recognition of a fraudulent message. This message was considered relatively easy. Due to the overall recognition rate, it is likely that this is an accidental clicking mistake.

[6] There is no bar shown for the module-4 (post) due to the small variance in answers.

- **H-module-2:** Our analysis shows a significantly improved detection rate for implausible fraudulent messages ($T = 8.23, p < .001$, $d = .919$). The Cohen's d of .919 is above .8, *i.e.* a large effect size.
- **H-module-3:** Our analysis shows a significantly improved detection rate for plausible fraudulent messages with dangerous links ($T = 13.60, p < .001$, $d = 1.273$). The Cohen's d of 1.273 is above .8, *i.e.* a large effect size.
- **H-module-4:** Our analysis shows a significantly improved detection rate for plausible fraudulent messages with malicious attachments ($T = 4.42, p < .001$, $d = .5$). The Cohen's d of .5 is equal to .5, *i.e.* a medium effect size.

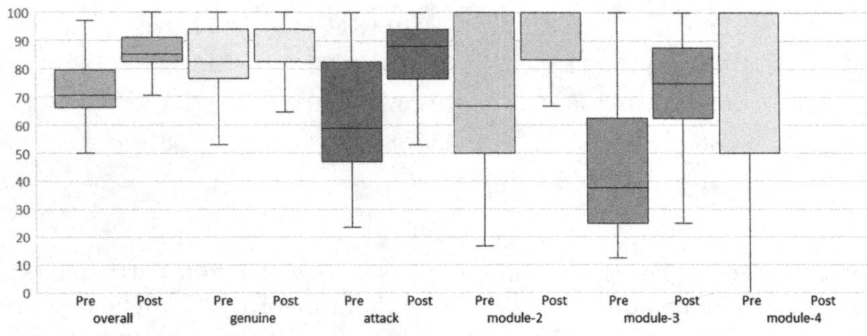

Fig. 1. Boxplots for hypotheses.

Further Findings: We want to point the reader's attention to three interesting findings: (1) The data shows that participants improved their abilities to recognize fraudulent messages with dangerous links that incorporate known *who* sections in the sub-domain of an URL from 56.6% to 88%. (2) After the programme, three fraudulent messages were incorrectly classified by more than one third of the participants. For these messages, detection rates of 13.5% (pre) $\rightarrow$ 37.1% (post), 22.5% $\rightarrow$ 48.3%, and 36% $\rightarrow$ 60.7% were identified. All of these messages incorporate *who* sections that were visually or cognitively hardly distinguishable from known *who* sections. (3) While the data shows a general improvement in the recognition of fraudulent and genuine messages, four participants did on average not improve their abilities to correctly recognize fraudulent or genuine messages. Three of these participants showed the same recognition rates before and after the programme. One of these three participants gave exactly the same answers in the pre- and post-tests (recognition rate: 87.5%). Two of these three participants (75%, 90.6%) improved their abilities to recognize either fraudulent or genuine messages, but showed lower performance with regard to the recognition of genuine messages after the programme. Furthermore, one participant showed lower overall recognition rates afterwards (recognition rates: 96.9% $\rightarrow$ 87.5%). That participant declared three genuine messages with links as fraudulent after the programme, which she/he declared genuine before.

6 Discussion

We note that the recognition of plausible fraudulent messages with dangerous links turned out to be the most challenging task for study participants, both before and after they undertook the awareness-raising programme. SMEs deploying the awareness-raising programme might therefore consider focusing on the link-related module, if their employees have time limitations. The results show that the programme is generally effective, because (1) over all message types, participants were confronted with, they made better decisions and (2) they were more confident in their decisions, (3) participants improved their ability to classify genuine messages as such, *i.e.* the programme did not over-sensitize participants.

(1) According to reports [11], the sub-domain attack proves to be very critical, as approximately 93.3% of all maliciously registered domains "*offered nothing to confuse a potential victim*", *i.e.* fraudsters increasingly choose to register sub-domains that correspond to *who* sections of known companies rather than domains that correspond to derivatives of known *who* sections, because companies more and more look for such domains. To that end, participants' large improvement in that regard is satisfactory. (2) As shown in the hypotheses tests, the link-related module poses a large challenge to study participants which lead to our recommendation to make exercises for that module compulsory. If time restrictions do not allow that, SMEs might consider making at least exercises for dangerous links compulsory that incorporate *who* sections that are visually or cognitively hardly distinguishable from known *who* sections. (3) It turned out that four participants did on average not improve their abilities to correctly recognize fraudulent or genuine messages. While the programme did not show a significant improvement on these four participants, *none* of these participants showed an endangering behaviour caused by the programme.

Limitations: (1) Study participants actively participated within the study by consciously indicating whether a shown message is fraudulent or genuine. The situation of estimating messages was certainly not natural and results may be affected by the triggered attention. (2) The study was conducted within three SMEs and was therefore out of the authors' control. Study participants passed through three main stages: (a) doing the pre-test, (b) receiving the programme, and (c) doing the post-test. Participants were unsupervised throughout these stages. Therefore, a number of limitations can be identified: Participants would have been able to look up details in the material when filling the post-test; they would have been able to fill the post-test without working through the material. Participants would also have been able to do the test (partially) together.

7 Related Work

Pre-click Detection: A number of researchers have focused on training users to spot fraudulent messages [1,12,13,17,18]. Canova *et al.* [4] proposed an anti-phishing education training, which comes in different flavours, *e.g.* as mobile game, web-based game or paper-based education materials. The training was evaluated and proved its effectiveness in different contexts [5,6,14] and aims at home users. The focus of previous NoPhish evaluations differed from ours. The herein presented study investigates the effectiveness of the education concept in the business context and previous evaluations obliged the education to study participants, which imposed an unnatural condition on participants. While certainly the game-based is appropriate in certain context, in the business context often more plain approaches turn out be more appropriate. The proposed concept does not restrict its focus to the recognition of dangerous links or malicious message attachments. Rather, the concept supports users in evaluating the plausibility of incoming messages. These approaches have been shown to improve phish detection but most of them address phish detection in a web browser context. Volkamer *et al.* [19] introduce the TORPEDO concept, which is implemented as Thunderbird AddOn. It supports users by providing in-time and in-place feedback: The AddOn emphasizes the actual domain of an URL and delays the user by disabling the link for three seconds. The AddOn's effect has also been tested in a field study [20].

Post-click Teaching Moments: Dodge *et al.* [8] and Volkamer *et al.* [21] report a different approach, post-click training. They send out fake fraudulent messages and then train people *who* click on the links. They report a positive effect. This approach is particularly helpful within organisations. There is an inherent flaw to post-click warnings. The human tendency to consistency makes it less likely for people to detect the deceptive nature of any site if they have already committed to the process [7]. They have judged the email to be genuine. Withdrawing at this stage is unlikely. This is amply demonstrated by a similar study by Wu *et al.* [22] *who* confronted study participants with security toolbars and other security indicators. Their results show that participants either were not able to interpret security indicators correctly or simply ignored them.

8 Conclusion

We developed and improved a security awareness-raising programme for the recognition of fraudulent messages in an iterative process while taking the needs of SMEs into account. The programme addresses a variety of aspects: it raises awareness for the problem and possible consequences (module 1); it raises awareness in recognizing fraudulent messages by simple plausibility checks (module 2) and by more advanced approaches of checking the genuineness of links (module 3) and message attachments (module 4). The effectiveness of this programme was validated in three SMEs. The developed education material and knowledge-test is freely accessible[7]. The company usd incorporated the material into their security awareness-raising platform[8], on which SME's can register free of charge for these modules. With the integration in their platform the organization of the awareness-raising programme is much easier as the platform allows the registration of employees as well as statistics about the success rates for all employees

[7] secuso.org/schulung.

[8] awareness.usd.de.

and reminders in case employees have not yet taken the time to consider the programme and the test. Furthermore, it enables employees to stop at any time and continue where they stopped in the modules which would also address the flexibility requirement raised during the requirement engineering phase. With this collaboration, the presented security awareness-raising programme will contribute to improving the security awareness in many SMEs.

Acknowledgement. This work was developed within the project KMUAWARE which is funded by the German Federal Ministry for Economic Affairs and Energy under grant BMWi-VIA5-090168623-01-1/2015. Authors assume responsibility for the content.

References

1. Alnajim, A., Munro, M.: ITNG. In: 6th International Conference on Information Technology: New Generations, pp. 405–410. IEEE (2009)
2. Anne, A., Angela, S.M.: Users are not the enemy. Commun. ACM **42**, 40–46 (1999)
3. Bauer, L., Bravo-Lillo, C., Cranor, L., Fragkaki, E.: Warning Design Guidelines. Carnegie Mellon University, Pittsburgh (2013)
4. Canova, G., Volkamer, M., Bergmann, C., Borza, R.: NoPhish: an anti-phishing education app. In: Mauw, S., Jensen, C.D. (eds.) STM 2014. LNCS, vol. 8743, pp. 188–192. Springer, Cham (2014). doi:10.1007/978-3-319-11851-2_14
5. Canova, G., Volkamer, M., Bergmann, C., Borza, R., Reinheimer, B., Stockhardt, S., Tenberg, R.: Learn to spot phishing URLs with the Android NoPhish app. In: Bishop, M., Miloslavskaya, N., Theocharidou, M. (eds.) WISE 2015. IAICT, vol. 453, pp. 87–100. Springer, Cham (2015). doi:10.1007/978-3-319-18500-2_8
6. Canova, G., Volkamer, M., Bergmann, C., Reinheimer, B.: NoPhish app evaluation: lab and retention study. In: USEC. Internet Society (2015)
7. Cialdini, R.B., Cacioppo, J.T., Bassett, R., Miller, J.A.: Low-ball procedure for producing compliance: commitment then cost. J. Pers. Soc. Psychol. **36**(5), 463 (1978). APA
8. Dodge, R.C., Carver, C., Ferguson, A.J.: Phishing for user security awareness. Comput. Secur. **26**(1), 73–80 (2007). Elsevier
9. Federal Bureau of Investigation. FBI warns of dramatic increase in business e-mail scams (2016). https://www.fbi.gov/contact-us/field-offices/phoenix/news/press-releases/fbi-warns-of-dramatic-increase-in-business-e-mail-scams. Accessed 11 Apr 2017
10. Furnell, S., Jusoh, A., Katsabas, D.: The challenges of understanding and using security - a survey of end-users. Comput. Secur. **25**(1), 27–35 (2006)
11. Greg, A., Rasmussen, R.: Global Phishing Survey: Trends and Domain Name Use in 2H2014 (2015). http://docs.apwg.org/reports/APWG_Global_Phishing_Report_2H_2014.pdf. Accessed 11 Apr 2017
12. Kirlappos, I., Sasse, M.A.: Security education against phishing: a modest proposal for a major rethink. IEEE Secur. Priv. **10**(2), 24–32 (2012)
13. Kumaraguru, P., Rhee, Y., Acquisti, A., Cranor, L.F., Hong, J., Nunge, E.: Protecting people from phishing: the design and evaluation of an embedded training email system. In: CHI, pp. 905–914. ACM (2007)

14. Kunz, A., Volkamer, M., Stockhardt, S., Palberg, S., Lottermann, T., Piegert, E.: Nophish: evaluation of a web application that teaches people being aware of phishing attacks. In: LNI, pp. 15–24. GI (2016)
15. Mansfield-Devine, S.: Securing small and medium-size businesses. Netw. Secur. **2016**(7), 14–20 (2016)
16. Sheng, S., Holbrook, M., Kumaraguru, P., Cranor, L.F., Downs, J.: Who falls for phish? A demographic analysis of phishing susceptibility and effectiveness of interventions. In: CHI, pp. 373–382. ACM (2010)
17. Sheng, S., Magnien, B., Kumaraguru, P., Acquisti, A., Cranor, L.F., Hong, J., Nunge, E.: Anti-Phishing Phil: the design and evaluation of a game that teaches people not to fall for phish. In: SOUPS, pp. 88–99. ACM (2007)
18. Stockhardt, S., Reinheimer, B., Volkamer, M., Mayer, P., Kunz, A., Rack, P., Lehmann, D.: Teaching phishing-security: which way is best? In: Hoepman, J.-H., Katzenbeisser, S. (eds.) SEC 2016. IAICT, vol. 471, pp. 135–149. Springer, Cham (2016). doi:10.1007/978-3-319-33630-5_10
19. Volkamer, M., Renaud, K., Reinheimer, B.: TORPEDO: tooltip-powered phishing email detection. In: Hoepman, J.-H., Katzenbeisser, S. (eds.) SEC 2016. IAICT, vol. 471, pp. 161–175. Springer, Cham (2016). doi:10.1007/978-3-319-33630-5_12
20. Volkamer, M., Renaud, K., Reinheimer, B., Kunz, A.: User experiences of TORPEDO: tooltip-powered phishing email detection. Comput. Secur. (2017)
21. Volkamer, M., Stockhardt, S., Bartsch, S., Kauer, M.: Adopting the CMU/APWG anti-phishing landing page idea for Germany. In: STAST, pp. 46–52. IEEE (2013)
22. Wu, M., Miller, R.C., Garfinkel, S.L.: Do security toolbars actually prevent phishing attacks? In: CHI, pp. 601–610 (2006)

On the Security Expressiveness of REST-Based API Definition Languages

Hoai Viet Nguyen(✉), Jan Tolsdorf, and Luigi Lo Iacono

Cologne University of Applied Sciences, Cologne, Germany
{viet.nguyen,luigi.lo_iacono}@th-koeln.de,
jan.tolsdorf@smail.th-koeln.de

Abstract. Modern software is inherently distributed. Applications are decomposed into functional components of which most are provided by third parties usually deployed as software services scattered around the network. Available services can be discovered and orchestrated by service consumers in a flexible and on-the-fly manner. To do so, a standardized specification of the service's functionalities is required. Apart from functional aspects, such an interface definition language needs to offer expressions for specifying important non-functional facets in addition, such as security. With WSDL and WS-Security such a standardized service description language and a mature security framework are available for the SOAP domain. For REST-based web services such standards are, however, missing. To overcome these shortcomings, many distinct sources propose service description languages and security schemes for REST-based web services. This paper provides a systematic analysis of these languages with a specific focus on their ability to express security policies. The obtained results reveal substantial limitations in all analyzed specification languages.

Keywords: REST · Service description language · Security · REST-Security

1 Introduction

The Service-Oriented Architecture (SOA) [1] paradigm defines an architectural principle for implementing interconnected software systems via service orchestration or service choreography respectively. Contemporary business applications [2] are greatly relying on this paradigm. It provides the foundation for a dynamic process management, in which service consumers and service provides are able to discover and bind themselves without knowing each other in advance. In this context, the service description –also known as the service contract– plays a central role when it comes to selecting and invoking services properly [2]. Such service invocations commonly involve the exchange of sensitive information across organizational boundaries and multiple distinct enterprises. The protection of such services and the incorporated datasets is henceforth a necessity, rendering tailored security safeguards mandatory for SOA-based business systems.

J. Lopez et al. (Eds.): TrustBus 2017, LNCS 10442, pp. 215–231, 2017.
DOI: 10.1007/978-3-319-64483-7_14

Distributed systems following the SOA principles have been most commonly realized by SOAP-based web services [3]. Here, a service contract is defined by means of the Web Service Description Language (WSDL) [4]. To declare security, the standardization body OASIS maintains the WS-SecurityPolicy specification [5]. This security framework includes extensions for describing security requirements and policies in WSDL. As WSDL and the extensions in terms of protection means provided by WS-SecurityPolicy represent a machine-readable data format for describing protected SOAP services, the interface definition language is often used by developers for automatic code generation. This facilitates the proper invocation of services as well as implementation of security properties. On the other hand, it reduces the likelihood of developers for making programming mistakes.

Over the last years, web services have been deployed following the architectural style Representational State Transfer (REST) [6]. One measure of how the architectural style influences contemporary service systems is an analysis of the platform ProgrammableWeb which has been conducted by the authors of this paper. This evaluation reveals that around 76% of 15,000 analyzed APIs are REST-based. In contrast to SOAP, the widespread usage of web services following the REST principles is, however, lacking on a standardized language for defining the service contract and security policies in particular. The missing technical foundation for describing REST-based web services in a machine-readable form, hinders the automatic discovery of services. Moreover, it increases the effort of implementing and testing the service invocations as automatic code generation is not supported. This induces a higher probability of producing insecure code as exemplified by Sun and Beznosov [7] in terms of the widely adopted authorization framework OAuth [8].

With the aim of establishing a REST-based counterpart to WSDL, several description languages for REST-based web services have been proposed. However, the languages' abilities to describe REST-based web services are very diverse. This paper analyzes the currently available description languages with the focus on the ability to declare required security policies and protection means. Section 2 lays the foundation for a basic understanding of the architectural style REST and thereby briefly recaps its key properties and constraints. Even though REST is still missing a standardized and mature security framework, a set of security mechanisms have become well-established and are presented in the Sect. 3. Based on this background, Sect. 4 evaluates the features and abilities of available service description languages for REST-based web services in respect to their security expressiveness. The findings are discussed in Sect. 5 and Sect. 6 concludes this paper with an outlook on future research challenges.

2 Representational State Transfer (REST)

REST [6] is a guideline for designing distributed systems. Adhering to the architectural constraints recommended by REST results in applications that are easy to use, maintain and scale. To ensure scalability the communication in REST must be stateless, cacheable and layered. Simplicity is realized by a uniform interface. This constraint governs that components within a REST architecture must communicate through a set of predefined actions enriched by meta data. The communication in REST is resource-oriented, meaning that each request targets a resource. In the context of REST, a resource can be any kind of information which maps to a static or varying set of values. Depending on the client's preference, a resource can be delivered in different resource representation. Moreover, each request must be self-contained, i.e., messages must include all required data elements describing the intention of the message, so that its semantic is self-explaining for every component within a REST architecture. This includes a resource identifier and action describing the target and intention of the request as well as further information including the state and resource representation meta data. The returned response may contain further resource identifiers which are embedded in the meta data and/or resource representation. These resource identifiers (links) and their description serve as a service description for clients to perform further requests to other resources. This property is known as Hypermedia As The Engine of Application State (HATEOAS).

The architectural principles of REST are fairly abstract and can be adopted with any suitable set of technologies. One technology which conforms to the REST principles is HTTP, since it is stateless, cacheable and contains a uniform interface which includes standard actions (methods) and meta data to express, e.g., the state and the cacheability. Moreover, HTTP is designed to transfer and obtain different resource representations including HTML [9], XML [10] or JSON [11]. HTTP represents the key technology of the web which is (arguably) the largest distributed system of the world [6]. By this, REST has proven of being an architectural style for building distributed systems that scale at large. Due to this and the other given arguments, REST gets adopted meanwhile in many other domains than the initial web applications. Among them are many driving environments for business applications including the Cloud and IoT systems [12, 13]. Consequently, security mechanisms for protecting REST-based application and services are becoming increasingly important.

3 Security Schemes for REST-Based Web Services

Only few standardized security technologies do exist for REST-based web services. The HTTP Basic and Digest Authentication [14] are the first two security schemes which have been published for web applications. HTTP Basic Authentication represents a login process to restricted resources via username and password embedded in a specifically defined *Authorization* header field. HTTP Digest Authentication requires a username and password as well, but does not transfer the cleartext password in the message header. Instead it deploys a challenge response scheme in form of a random number and a hash. The OAuth framework [8,15] is a standardized protocol for authorizing third party applications for accessing resources of end users. Two versions of OAuth have been proposed so far. OAuth provides a set of flows for retrieving tokens from an authorization server. Based on these tokens client are able to invoke information of end users from a resource server. OpenID Connect [16] extends OAuth by means of a standardized authentication. This specification enables the option for clients to validate the identity of end-users. Many identity providers apply OpenID Connect as a technical baseline. Beside HTTP Basic/Digest Authentication, OAuth and OpenID Connect, API-Keys are commonly used for authenticate requests. Usually, these keys are random generated tokens which must be saved by the service consumer and service provider. In each authenticated request, this API-Key must be included in the URL or in an HTTP header field.

These security schemes, however, merely provide authentication and authorization. Confidentiality, integrity and non-repudiation have not been covered by current standards yet. To protect the confidentiality and integrity of the communication, many REST-based web services utilize Transport Layer Security (TLS) [17]. As TLS only ensures transport-oriented security which does not provide an end-to-end protection in layered systems, many approaches targeting additional safeguards on the application layer have been published in the recent years. These approaches propose, e.g., HTTP message signature schemes protecting for the whole HTTP message [18]. This kind of authenticity and integrity protection is applied by the cloud storage services of Amazon [19], Google [20], HP [21] and Microsoft [22] as a complementary shield to TLS.

To gain an overview on the usage of protection schemes of other service providers, 11,500 REST-based web APIs listed in the web API directory ProgrammableWeb have been analyzed. The analysis reveals that 5,248 of the 11,500 REST-based web APIs require one or multiple authentication scheme for accessing their service. Table 1 gives an overview on the usage of authentication schemes of REST-based web APIs requiring authentication.

The directory distinguishes twelve authentication schemes from which service providers can select a subset to declare the protection scheme deployed for their API. Table 1 shows the most relevant ones which are sorted according their frequency of utilization. One observation is that the most frequently applied protection mechanisms are the ones which are not standardized. As no further security mechanism description apart from the name is specified by an API entry within the ProgrammableWeb directory, the actual security schemes declared as *Unspecified*, *Token*, *Other/Custom* and *Shared Secret* remain opaque for the user at the first glance. In most cases, users have to visit the web page of the API operated by the service provider in order to get further human-readable only information on the protection mechanism and details on implementing the client counterpart to it. Such security schemes can be any kind of safeguards ranging from proprietary approaches to not yet standardized technologies such as the HTTP message signature.

This current situation shows that the description of diverse security policies in a machine-readable form can be a great benefit for assisting developers in building security mechanisms properly.

Thus, the following section evaluates available REST-based web services description languages with a special focus on their ability to express standard and custom security mechanisms.

Table 1. AuthN schemes used by listed REST-based APIs in ProgrammableWeb

Authentication mechanisms	Total	Percentage of APIs using authentication
API-Keys	2711	52%
Unspecified	844	16%
Token	819	16%
HTTP basic authentication [14]	741	14%
OAuth 2 [8]	606	12%
OAuth 1 [15]	173	3%
App ID	163	3%
Other/custom	132	3%
Shared secret	99	2%

Only mechanisms with a usage ≥1% are considered. APIs may support multiple authentication schemes.

4 Description Languages for REST-Based Web Services

The previous section highlights the need for describing security policies in machine-readable manner in order to aid developers in implementing secure code. Moreover, the definition of security policies must be extensible as many service providers utilize custom or not standardized security schemes. This section therefore analyzes available service description language for REST-based Web Services according to the following criteria:

1. The ability to describe security schemes via native service description elements
2. The set of security schemes which can be defined by default
3. The ability to extend the default set of security schemes
4. The approach for defining the semantics of not natively supported security schemes
5. Available work extending the service description language with additional security description elements.

4.1 WSDL

The XML-based Web Service Description Language 2.0 (WSDL 2.0) [23] is a W3C Recommendation. In conjunction with the introduced HTTP adjunction [24] it has been the first approach providing a description language for REST-based web services. In contrast to its predecessor WSDL 1.1 [4], it offers a more general way of describing web services and it is not limited to SOAP anymore.

WSDL 2.0 considers the integration of security schemes. However only HTTP Basic and Digest Authentication are natively supported. Not supported security schemes can be integrated via the definition of new XML schema definitions. The drawback of WSDL 2.0 is the fact that it has not been widely accepted by developers for describing REST-based web services [25]. This might be the reason why no specification updates and XML schema definitions for REST-based security mechanisms have been presented so far.

4.2 WADL

Web Application Description Language (WADL) [26] is another XML-based interface definition language for REST-based web services.

WADL does not consider a native support for security mechanisms. But the description of security schemes is extensible via XML schema definitions and distinct child nodes for defining meta information such as header field as well as URL parameters. As with WSDL 2.0, WADL suffers from the problem that it is not widely adopted in the REST community [25]. Hence, neither XML schema definitions nor well-defined specification on security scheme do exist for WADL to date.

4.3 RSDL

RESTful Service Description Language (RSDL) [27] is an additional XML-based technology for defining REST-based web APIs.

The support of authentication schemes is provided by using the authentication element, which, however, is not defined any further. The RSDL specification shows only one example on describing HTTP Basic or Digest Authentication via the authentication element. As RSDL utilizes XML and XML schema, standard as well as custom security schemes can be integrated by defining new XML schema definitions. Unfortunately, it seems that the RSDL specification is not maintained anymore. The last version of RSDL stems from a paper [27] in 2013. Since then, no further work on this approach has been published. Therefore, there is a lack of XML schema definitions and tools for standardized and custom security mechanisms.

4.4 RADL

Similar to RSDL, RESTful API Description Language (RADL) [28] defines a documentation technology for REST-based web services which is based on XML as well.

Authentication mechanisms can be defined by an authentication element likewise. As with RSDL, the RADL specification does not specify the description of standard security mechanisms in the current version. Since RADL applies XML and supports XML schema, the missing security mechanisms can be included via XML schema definitions. As the current state of RADL is still a draft, a set of aspects are not completely defined. This is especially true for security schemes. Here, no XML schema definitions and examples about the definition on available security technologies are specified so far.

4.5 REST Chart

Another XML-based description language is REST Chart [29]. The aim of REST-Chart is to specify a REST-based web API over transitions which contain two input and one or multiple output elements. First input element defines the link to be invoked and the second one specifies required HTTP methods, meta data and an optional resource representation. The output elements describe resulting status codes of responses in conjunction with an optional embedded resource representation.

REST Chart does not provide a native support for security schemes. However, protection mechanisms can be specified via the aforementioned transitions. In case of a login process, the first input element contains link which refers to authentication endpoint. The other input element includes a control child element which specifies the HTTP method to start the transition. If the POST method is used, the input element may include a representation element which defines required media type and the schema of the credentials. The output indicates possible returning status codes and resource representations of responses. As REST chart does not specify an option for defining required header fields, this is the only way of describing a security process in the current state of REST Chart. The input element may include meta data nodes, but beside the fact that the meta data element can contain any kind of text-based XML attributes, the meta data element is not defined any further. Hence, the ability to describe an authentication scheme, which consider header fields for expressing the credentials, is therefore limited. Since REST Chart utilizes XML and therefore supports XML schema, this missing functionality can be included by new XML schema definitions. However, no specification and tools for such an extension have been proposed so far.

4.6 OAS/Swagger

The OpenAPI Specification (OAS) [30], formerly known as Swagger [31], represents a REST-based web service description languages which is not based on XML. The approach utilizes YAML [32] or JSON [11] as the technical foundation.

OAS provides a native description of security schemes. Security mechanisms are defined by the Security Definition Object which consists of multiple Security Scheme Objects. OAS supports HTTP Basic Authentication, API-Keys and OAuth 2.0 natively. Extensibility of not yet supported security mechanisms is, however, limited. Natively supported security schemes can only be extended by additional Security Scheme Object attributes. The integration of Security Scheme Objects defining new security schemes is not considered yet. Also, no work is available so far, which defines a definition approach for not supported security mechanisms.

The main strength of OAS is the wide range of tool support. Many technologies do exist for automatic testing and code generation which makes OAS well-established by developers.

4.7 RAML

RESTful API Modeling Language (RAML) [33] is another YAML-based description language for REST-based web services.

As with OAS, the RAML specification considers the integration of security mechanisms. This is realized by the securitySchemes element which comprise one or multiple security schemes. Each security scheme must contain a type attribute which is the identifier of the mechanism. RAML natively supports the types OAuth 1.0, OAuth 2.0, Basic Authentication, Digest Authentication and Pass Through. API-Keys are not supported by default. Custom or not defined security schemes can be described via the *x-<other>* type, where *<other>* represents the placeholder for the security mechanism name. In the current version, RAML does not provide the option for appending a semantic description of security schemes with *x-<other>* types. This shortcoming restricts the definition of custom and not specified safeguards which might be the reason why no work on describing other security schemes have been published so far.

Similar to OAS, RAML promotes a lot of tools for, e.g., testing and automatic code generation. Therefore, this approach is also widely used by developers.

4.8 API Blueprint

API Blueprint [34] is another widely used description language for REST-based web services alongside OAS and RAML. The syntax of this approach is based on MSON [35], which itself is based on Markdown [36].

The authors of API Blueprint attempt to establish the description language as an RFC. Here, an authentication framework in draft status is proposed. This draft depicts the general definition on authentication schemes as well as a description on concrete mechanisms including HTTP Basic Authentication and OAuth. Using this authentication framework, other authentication schemes can be included to an API Blueprint service description. Furthermore, API Blueprint's approach to utilize MSON for its description is different to previous concepts. As Markdown represents definition syntax for producing human-readable content such as HTML or readme documents, and MSON introduces conversion of Markdown to JSON or XML documents, API Blueprint may also addresses machine-readability of security extensions to some extent. However, it does not cover the complexity of describing the semantics of new defined elements such as provided by JSON or XML schema definitions.

As with OAS and RAML, developers using API Blueprint benefits from a set of tools which aid them in testing and implementing REST-based web services.

4.9 OData

OData [37] is an OASIS standard for describing REST-based web services. OData services are defined via an Entity Data Model (EDM). This model contains vocabularies for specifying the data model of the resource representation and their relationships. Additionally, the EDM includes elements for describing actions and URL queries and paths. A service description in OData can be defined either in JSON [38] or in ATOM [39]. The specification of the standard vocabulary is however defined in XML Schema. Similar to RAML, OAS and API Blueprint, OData provide a lot of libraries, SDKs and tools for implementing and testing services. Moreover, many service providers, among them also services of, e.g., Microsoft, IBM and SAP offer their service description via OData.

The OData specification recommends to use HTTP Basic authentication over TLS for securing REST-based OData services. Apart from the aforementioned authentication scheme no other security mechanisms are recommended or provided. To complement OData service descriptions with additional security policies, new XML Schema definitions can be used to extend OData. At the moment, no further security specification or work on integrating security in OData description do exist so far.

4.10 I/O Docs

I/O Docs [40] is a JSON-based approach for documenting REST-based web services. Currently, the specification of I/O Docs is only based on examples. A general definition on the I/O Docs elements is not defined yet. Also, no description on the definition of new service description elements does exist so far. This is especially true for defining security schemes. Only examples are available which show the definition on authentication schemes. Examples exist for HTTP Basic Authentication and OAuth, but other security mechanisms are not described. As with many aforementioned description languages, I/O Docs suffers from the low frequency of usage. This might be the reason why no extensions, tools and updates have been proposed recently.

4.11 hRESTS and RDFa

HTML for RESTful Services (hRESTS) [41] offers another approach as the aforementioned description languages. Instead of defining a new data format for describing REST-based web services, hREST augments HTML by including new HTML elements. The aim of this approach is to enrich HTML with machine-readable HTML elements, without modifying the visualization of the web page. These HTML elements provide additional information which can be processed by a machine-driven process. This has the advantage that a returned HTML contains human- and machine-readable description simultaneously. The semantics of new HTML elements for hRESTS is extensible via ontologies.

Resource Description Framework (RDF) is a model for describing machine-readable linked data structures and web APIs. The semantics of RDF elements and their relationships are defined by ontologies likewise. An RDF model can be implemented in various data formats such as XML. Resource Description Framework in Attributes (RDFa) [42] defines an adoption of RDF in HTML attributes. As with hRESTS, the goal of RDFa is to enhance the machine-readability of HTML.

Neither hRESTS nor RDFa provide a native support for security mechanisms. However, protection means can be incorporated via ontologies. Maleshkova et al. [43] propose an approach on defining a new ontology for authentication schemes. The authentication ontology of [43] comprises limitation, tough, as it is composed of three classes only. These classes define the authentication mechanisms name, the credentials form (e.g. API-Key, username and password or OAuth token) and the transmission medium which specifies whether the credentials are include in the header or in the URL. Following this concept, the definition more complex security mechanisms such as the HTTP message signatures can not be implemented in straightforward manner, as no ontology element for describing a signature other cryptographic mechanisms is specified. To do so, the authentication ontology of [43] must be redesigned by including security services and additional security definition elements. Beside this publication, no other security-related work has been presented so far.

4.12 ReLL

Resource Linking Language (ReLL) [44] is a REST-based web services description language that extends the vocabulary of RDF. ReLL utilizes XML to represent the RDF model.

ReLL does not consider a built-in support for security schemes. As it uses RDF, new elements and vocabularies can be added via ontologies in order to specify security schemes. Such an approach is presented by Bellido and Alarcon [45]. Here, the authors introduce an example description on defining OAuth in ReLL. Both authors continue the work on defining security schemes in [46] in which they propose ReLL-S, an ontology for describing security constraints and schemes. This ontology is more comprehensive than the ontology of [43]. It consists of a set of security goals which includes confidentiality, integrity, authentication and authorization. The security goals contain subclasses which defines cryptographic mechanisms (e.g. encryption and digital signatures) and authentication as well as authorization protocols. These subclasses include further subsubclasses referring to concrete security schemes such as OAuth, HTTP Basic/Digest Authentication as well as cryptographic algorithms such as AES, RSA or SHA. With the elements of ReLL-S, [46] introduces the definition of API-Keys, a simple username and password authentication, HTTP Basic/Digest Authentication, OpenID [47] as well as OAuth. As this ontology contains a comprehensive set of security elements, further security mechanisms can be deduced and included to a ReLL service description.

4.13 SERIN

Semantic RESTful Interface (SERIN) [48] is another description language for REST-based web services which is based on RDF. As with ReLL, SERIN also applies XML as the data format.

SERIN does not support any vocabulary for describing security policies by default. As SERIN is based on RDF, protection elements can be extended by introducing a new ontology. However, such extensions have not been proposed yet.

4.14 Hydra

Hypermedia-Driven API (Hydra) [49,50] represents a W3C community group which attempts to establish a vocabulary for defining the semantic of linked data and web APIs. This approach is based on JSON for linked data (JSON-LD) [51], a specification for defining machine-readable semantics of data and links included in JSON. The vocabulary of JSON-LD elements is defined by the Schema.org community. Hydra extends the vocabulary of JSON-LD by defining elements and a schema for describing REST-based web services properties such as entry points, supported HTTP methods, URL query parameters and the meaning of status codes. The current version of Hydra does not consider the integration security mechanisms yet. As the specification of Hydra is an early stage, the description of security properties may be considered in future work. Currently, no external work which approaches to resolve this shortcoming does exist so far. For the time being, the semantics of security mechanisms can be described by defining new JSON-LD vocabularies.

4.15 RESTdesc

RESTdesc [52] is an academic approach that utilizes Notation3 (N3) [53] for describing REST-based web APIs. N3 is an extension of RDF.

The current status of RESTdesc does not consider the description of security mechanisms. As with RDFa and hRESTS, missing security schemes can be extended by the integration of new RDF ontologies. However, such extensions have not been published so far.

5 Discussion

The analysis of the previous section highlights that a lot of approaches to describe a service contract for REST-based web services have evolved over time. This already emphasizes the huge demand of such technologies. Still to date, there is no standardized language available for developers. This situation allows, nonetheless, to analyze the current proposals in order to conclude whether there are already mature and comprehensive technologies available which could serve as a basis for a standard or if there still exist research challenges that need to be solved first.

Table 2 summarizes the available service description languages according to the five criteria defined in the previous section. Seven of the fifteen analyzed approaches consider the integration of security mechanisms. But only five evaluated technologies provide a native support for a set of standard security mechanisms. Most approaches offer the option to integrate missing security schemes by including or extending new schema and ontologies. Unfortunately, such security

Table 2. Security expressiveness of REST-based API definition languages

Description language	Native support for security mechanisms	Natively supported security schemes	Extension approach	Available security extensions
WSDL 2.0 [23,24]	AuthN	HTTP Basic and Digest	XML schema	-
WADL [26]	-	-	XML schema	-
RSDL [27]	AuthN	-	XML schema	-
RADL [28]	AuthN	-	XML schema	-
REST-Chart [29]	-	-	XML schema	
OAS [30,31]	AuthN, AuthZ	HTTP Basic, OAuth 2, OpenId Connect	-	-
RAML [33]	AuthN, AuthZ	HTTP Basic and Digest, OAuth 1 and 2, Pass Through	x-<other> type	-
OData [37]	-	-	XML schema	-
I/O Docs [40]	AuthN, AuthZ	API-Key, OAuth 1 and 2	-	-
API Blueprint [34]	AuthN, AuthZ	HTTP Basic, OAuth 2	-	-
hRESTS [41] and RDFa [42]	-	-	RDF ontology	[43]
ReLL [44]	-	-	RDF ontology	[45,46]
SERIN [48]	-	-	RDF ontology	-
Hydra [50]	-	-	JSON-LD schema	-
RESTdesc [52]	-	-	RDF ontology	-

extensions are only available for hRESTS, RDFa and ReLL so far [43,45,46]. The other technologies lack on further specification and work which extends these technologies by missing or additional security schemes. RAML and OAS support the description of many standardized security mechanisms. Driven by the global players of web technologies, both languages also provide a set of diverse tools for automatic code generation, testing and building REST-based applications and APIs. However, RAML and OAS do not provide the option for describing the semantics of other security schemes. This is also true for I/O Docs and API Blueprint. The former technology does not define a specification aspect for describing extensions. API Blueprint lacks on the functionality for defining the semantics of new service description elements due to the usage of Markdown. WSDL 2.0, WADL, RDSL, RADL, REST-Chart, OData, SERIN and RESTdesc provide only a definition for few authentication schemes or no security mechanisms. Missing security definition can, however, be included by XML schema definitions or ontologies. Such extensions have not been present so far, though.

Moreover, almost all API definition languages only consider authentication and authorization. Description elements for defining confidentiality, non-repudiation, integrity and further security mechanisms are not supported by default. Only ReLL-S, the extension of ReLL, supports all aforementioned security services except non-repudiation. However, for ReLL and ReLL-S, no tools which support developers in implementing REST-based web applications do exist so far.

Also, no analyzed technology provides a description on the invocation properties of TLS. All approaches are only able to describe whether TLS is used or not. Properties such as supported cipher suites or the TLS version is not specified by any approach at all. As it has been shown that the implementation of transport-oriented security can cause many critical vulnerabilities [54,55] due to the high complexity, such a description could serve as basis for automatic code generation and testing. This set of tooling could assist developers in implementing proper TLS connections and may reduce the likelihood to make programming mistake.

Another missing aspect of all evaluated service description languages is the absent ability for describing security policies for the resource representation. A demand for such a security description is, for instance, needed in some OAuth and OpenID Connect environments, where JavaScript Object Signing and Encryption (JOSE) [56] is utilized for securing the tokens and other sensitive information. All service description languages supporting the description of resource representations only provide the declaration of the media type. These approaches can merely define that a resource representation embodies the media type application/jose+json, but the context and the semantics of the security policies can not be specified by any service description technology.

An additional shortcoming of all analyzed service descriptions is that they only provide a definition on REST-based services which use HTTP as the transfer protocol. None of them considers the description of services that utilize CoAP [12], RACS [57] or other REST-based protocols.

6 Conclusion and Outlook

Overall, the security expressiveness of the available REST-based web service description languages is still at its beginning. Besides authentication and authorization, there are no further security capabilities expressible by default and even these very basic protections are not provided by all of the analyzed languages (see Table 2). ReLL in conjunction with ReLL-S is the only approach which consider the integration of all standardized authentication and authorization schemes. Also, the ontology of ReLL-S provides service description elements for all security mechanisms except non-repudiation. The other evaluated service description technologies lack on a native definition of standard protection means or have restrictions in terms of extending and defining security mechanisms. Moreover, none of the evaluated approach provide a comprehensive description on TLS and the protection of the resource representation.

One reason for this current situation may lie in a lacking overall REST-Security framework [58]. As current research activities are enhancing this field [18,59,60], new REST-Security components may be evolved in the future. Hence, REST-based service description languages need to cope with this by an increased extensibility in respect to security-related expressiveness.

This shows that a bunch of research and development challenges still exist in order to find a service description language and a security policy framework for REST-based systems which can serve as a standard such as WSDL and WS-SecurityPolicy for the SOAP domain. As many service definition technologies have been proposed, further work will therefore focus on enhancing available languages in terms of security expressiveness and extensibility, instead of proposing a new approach. Also, future studies will analyze REST-based service description languages for other REST-based protocols including CoAP and RACS.

References

1. Erl, T.: SOA Principles of Service Design (The Prentice Hall Service-Oriented Computing Series from Thomas Erl). Prentice Hall PTR, Upper Saddle River (2007)
2. Leymann, F., Roller, D., Schmidt, M.T.: Web services and business process management. IBM Syst. J. **41**(2), 198–211 (2002)
3. Gudgin, M., Hadley, M., Mendelsohn, N., Moreau, J.J., Nielsen, H.F., Karmarkar, A., Lafon, Y.: SOAP Version 1.2 Part 1: Messaging Framework (2nd edn.). W3C Recommendation, W3C (2007). http://www.w3.org/TR/soap.12-part1/
4. Christensen, E., Curbera, F., Meredith, G., Weerawarana, S.: Web Services Description Language (WSDL) 1.1. W3C Note, W3C (2000). http://www.w3.org/TR/2001/NOTE-wsdl-20010315
5. Nadalin, A., Goodner, M., Gudgin, M., Turner, D., Barbir, A., Granqvist, H.: WS-SecurityPolicy 1.3. Standard, OASIS (2012)
6. Fielding, R.T.: Architectural styles and the design of network-based software architectures. Ph.D. thesis, University of California, Irvine (2000)
7. Sun, S.T., Beznosov, K.: the devil is in the (implementation) details: an empirical analysis of OAuth SSO systems. In: 19th ACM Conference on Computer and Communications Security (CSS) (2012)
8. Hardt, D.: The OAuth 2.0 Authorization Framework. RFC, IETF (2012). https://tools.ietf.org/html/rfc6749
9. Hickson, I., Berjon, R., Faulkner, S., Leithead, T., Navara, E.D., O'Connor, E., Pfeiffer, S.: HTML5 - a vocabulary and associated APIs for HTML and XHTML. Recommendation, W3C (2014). http://www.w3.org/TR/html5/
10. Bray, T., Paoli, J., Sperberg-McQueen, C.M., Maler, E., Yergeau, F.: Extensible Markup Language (XML) 1.0 (5th edn.). Recommendation, W3C (2008). http://www.w3.org/TR/2008/REC-xml-20081126
11. Bray, T.: The JavaScript Object Notation (JSON) Data Interchange Format. RFC 7189, IETF. https://tools.ietf.org/html/rfc7159

12. Shelby, Z., Hartke, K., Borman, C.: The Constrained Application Protocol (CoAP). RFC, IETF (2014). https://tools.ietf.org/html/rfc7252
13. Lo Iacono, L., Nguyen, H.V.: Towards conformance testing of REST-based web services. In: 11th International Conference on Web Information Systems and Technologies (WEBIST) (2015)
14. Franks, J., Hallam-Baker, P.M., Hostetler, J.L., Lawrence, S.D., Leach, P.J., Luotonen, A., Stewart, L.C.: HTTP Authentication: Basic and Digest Access Authentication. RFC, IETF (1999). https://tools.ietf.org/html/rfc2617
15. Hammer-Lahav, E.: The OAuth 1.0 Protocol. RFC, IETF (2010). https://tools.ietf.org/html/rfc5849
16. Sakimura, N., Bradley, J., Jones, M., de Medeiros, B., Mortimore, C.: OpenID Connect Core 1.0. Specification, OpenID Foundation (2014). http://openid.net/specs/openid-connect-core-1_0.html
17. Dierks, T., Rescorla, E.: The Transport Layer Security (TLS) Protocol Version 1.2. RFC, IETF (2008). http://tools.ietf.org/html/rfc5246
18. Lo Iacono, L., Nguyen, H.V.: Authentication scheme for REST. In: Doss, R., Piramuthu, S., Zhou, W. (eds.) FNSS 2015. CCIS, vol. 523, pp. 113–128. Springer, Cham (2015). doi:10.1007/978-3-319-19210-9_8
19. Amazon: Signing AWS Requests By Using Signature Version 4 (2017). https://docs.aws.amazon.com/general/latest/gr/sigv4_signing.html
20. Google: Migrating from Amazon S3 to Google Cloud Storage (2017). https://cloud.google.com/storage/docs/migrating
21. Hewlett Packard: HP Helion Public Cloud Object Storage API Specification (2014). https://docs.hpcloud.com/publiccloud/api/object-storage/
22. Microsoft: Authentication for the Azure Storage Services (2017). http://msdn.microsoft.com/en-us/library/dd179428.aspx
23. Chinnici, R., Moreau, J.J., Ryman, A., Weerawarana, S.: Web services description language (WSDL) version 2.0 part 1: core language. W3C Recommendation, W3C (2007). http://www.w3.org/TR/2007/REC-wsdl20-20070626
24. Lewis, A., Haas, H., Orchard, D., Weerawarana, S., Chinnici, R., Moreau, J.J.: Web Services Description Language (WSDL) Version 2.0 Part 2: Adjuncts. W3C Recommendation, W3C (2007). http://www.w3.org/TR/2007/REC-wsdl20-adjuncts-20070626
25. Verborgh, R., Harth, A., Maleshkova, M., Stadtmüller, S., Steiner, T., Taheriyan, M., Van de Walle, R.: Survey of semantic description of REST APIs. In: Pautasso, C., Wilde, E., Alarcon, R. (eds.) REST: Advanced Research Topics and Practical Applications, pp. 69–89. Springer, New York (2014). doi:10.1007/978-1-4614-9299-3_5
26. Headley, M.: Web Application Description Language (WADL). W3C Member Submission, W3C (2009). http://www.w3.org/Submission/2009/SUBM-wadl-20090831
27. Robie, J., Cavicchio, R., Sinnema, R., Wilde, E.: RESTful service description language (RSDL): describing RESTful services without tight coupling. In: Balisage: The Markup Conference 2013, Montréal, Canada, 6–9 August 2013
28. Robie, J., Sinnema, R., Zhou, W.: RESTful API Description Language (2016). https://github.com/restful-api-description-language
29. Li, L., Chou, W.: Design and describe REST API without violating REST: a petri net based approach. In: 18th IEEE International Conference on Web Services (ICWS) (2011)
30. Open API Initiative: OpenAPI Specification (2016). https://github.com/OAI/OpenAPI-Specification/blob/master/versions/2.0.md

31. SmartBear Software: Swagger Specification (2016). http://swagger.io/specification
32. Ben-Kiki, O., Evans, C., dot Net, I.: YAML Aint Markup Language Version 1.2. Technical report (2009). http://www.yaml.org/spec/1.2/spec.html
33. RAML: RAML Version 1.0: RESTful API Modeling Language (2016). https://github.com/raml-org/raml-spec/blob/master/versions/raml-10/raml-10.md/
34. API Blueprint: API Blueprint Specification (2016). https://apiblueprint.org/documentation/specification.html
35. Apiary Inc.: Markdown Syntax for Object Notation. Technical report (2016). https://github.com/apiaryio/mson
36. Leonard, S.: Guidance on Markdown: Design Philosophies, Stability Strategies, and Select Registrations. RFC, IETF (2016). https://tools.ietf.org/html/rfc7764
37. Handl, R., Jeyaraman, R., Pizzo, M., Zurmuehl, M.: OData Version 4.0. Part 1: Protocol Plus Errata 03. OASIS Standard, OASIS (2016). https://docs.oasis-open.org/odata/odata/v4.0/odata-v4.0-part1-protocol.html
38. Handl, R., Jeyaraman, R., Pizzo, M., Biamonte, M.: OData JSON Format Version 4.0 Plus Errata 03. OASIS Standard, OASIS (2016). https://docs.oasis-open.org/odata/odata-json-format/v4.0/odata-json-format-v4.0.html
39. Hartel, B., Jeyaraman, R., Zurmuehl, M., Pizzo, M., Handl, R.: OData Atom Format Version 4.0. OASIS Standard, OASIS (2013). https://docs.oasis-open.org/odata/odata-atom-format/v4.0/odata-atom-format-v4.0.html
40. TIBCA Software Inc.: I/O Docs community edition in Node.js. Technical report (2015). https://github.com/mashery/iodocs
41. Kopecký, J., Gomadam, K., Vitvar, T.: hRESTS: an HTML microformat for describing RESTful web services. In: IEEE/WIC/ACM International Conference on Web Intelligence and Intelligent Agent Technology (WI-IAT) (2008)
42. Adida, B., Birbeck, M., McCarron, S.: RDFa Core 1.1 - 3rd edn. W3C Recommendation, W3C (2015). http://www.w3.org/TR/2015/REC-rdfa-core-20150317
43. Maleshkova, M., Pedrinaci, C., Domingue, J., Alvaro, G., Martinez, I.: Using semantics for automating the authentication of web APIs. In: Patel-Schneider, P.F., Pan, Y., Hitzler, P., Mika, P., Zhang, L., Pan, J.Z., Horrocks, I., Glimm, B. (eds.) ISWC 2010. LNCS, vol. 6496, pp. 534–549. Springer, Heidelberg (2010). doi:10.1007/978-3-642-17746-0_34
44. Alarcon, R., Wilde, E.: Linking data from RESTful services. In: Third Workshop on Linked Data on the Web (2010)
45. Bellido, J., Alarcon, R., Sepulveda, C.: Web linking-based protocols for guiding RESTful M2M interaction. In: Harth, A., Koch, N. (eds.) ICWE 2011. LNCS, vol. 7059, pp. 74–85. Springer, Heidelberg (2012). doi:10.1007/978-3-642-27997-3_7
46. Sepulveda, C., Alarcon, R., Bellido, J.: QoS aware descriptions for RESTful service composition: security domain. World Wide Web **18**(4), 767–794 (2015)
47. Recordon, D., Reed, D.: OpenID 2.0: a platform for user-centric identity management. In: 2nd ACM Workshop on Digital Identity Management (DIM) (2006)
48. de Azevedo Muniz, B., Chaves, L.M., Lira, H.A., Dantas, J.R.V., Farias, P.P.M.: Serin an aproach to specify semantic abstract interfaces in the context of RESTful web services. In: IADIS International Conference WWW/Internet (2013)
49. Lanthaler, M.: Creating 3rd generation web APIs with hydra. In: 22nd International Conference on World Wide Web (WWW) (2013)
50. Lanthaler, M.: Hydra Core Vocabulary - A Vocabulary for Hypermedia-Driven Web APIs. Unofficial Draft, W3C (2017). http://www.hydra-cg.com/spec/latest/core/

51. Sporny, M., Longley, D., Kellogg, G., Lanthaler, M., Lindstrm, N.: JSON-LD 1.0 - A JSON-Based Serialization for Linked Data. W3C Recommendation, W3C (2014). https://www.w3.org/TR/json-ld/
52. Verborgh, R., Steiner, T., Van Deursen, D., Coppens, S., Vallés, J.G., Van de Walle, R.: Functional descriptions as the bridge between hypermedia APIs and the semantic web. In: 3rd International Workshop on RESTful Design (WS-REST) (2012)
53. Berners-Lee, T., Connolly, D.: Notation3 (N3): a readable RDF syntax. W3C Team Submission, W3C (2011). https://www.w3.org/TeamSubmission/n3/
54. Fahl, S., Harbach, M., Muders, T., Baumgärtner, L., Freisleben, B., Smith, M.: Why eve and mallory love android: an analysis of android SSL (in)security. In: 19th ACM Conference on Computer and Communications Security (CCS) (2012)
55. Georgiev, M., Iyengar, S., Jana, S., Anubhai, R., Boneh, D., Shmatikov, V.: The most dangerous code in the world: validating SSL certificates in non-browser software. In: 19th ACM Conference on Computer and Communications Security (CCS) (2012). http://doi.acm.org/10.1145/2382196.2382204
56. IETF JOSE Working Group: Javascript Object Signing and Encryption (JOSE) (2017). http://datatracker.ietf.org/wg/jose/
57. Urien, P.: Remote APDU Call Secure (RACS). Internet-Draft, IETF (2016). https://tools.ietf.org/html/draft-urien-core-racs-08
58. Gorski, P.L., Lo Iacono, L., Nguyen, H.V., Torkian, D.B.: Service security revisited. In: 11th IEEE International Conference on Services Computing (SCC) (2014)
59. Nguyen, H.V., Lo Iacono, L.: REST-ful CoAP message authentication. In: International Workshop on Secure Internet of Things (SIoT), in conjunction with the European Symposium on Research in Computer Security (ESORICS) (2015)
60. Nguyen, H.V., Lo Iacono, L.: RESTful IoT authentication protocols. In: u, M.H., Choo, K.R., (eds.) Mobile Security and Privacy - Advances Challenges and Future Research Directions. Advanced Topics in Information Security, 1st edn., pp. 217–234. Elsevier/Syngress (2016)

A Structured Comparison of Social Engineering Intelligence Gathering Tools

Kristian Beckers[1](✉), Daniel Schosser[1], Sebastian Pape[2], and Peter Schaab[1]

[1] Institute of Informatics, Technische Universität München (TUM), Boltzmannstr. 3, 85748 Garching, Germany
beckersk@in.tum.de

[2] Faculty of Economics and Business Administration, Goethe University Frankfurt, Theodor-W.-Adorno-Platz 4, 60323 Frankfurt, Germany

Abstract. Social engineering is the clever manipulation of the human tendency to trust to acquire information assets. While technical security of most critical systems is high, the systems remain vulnerable to attacks from social engineers. Traditional penetration testing approaches often focus on vulnerabilities in network or software systems. Few approaches even consider the exploitation of humans via social engineering. While the amount of social engineering attacks and the damage they cause rise every year, the defences against social engineering do not evolve accordingly. However, tools exist for social engineering intelligence gathering, which means the gathering of information about possible victims that can be used in an attack. We survey these tools and present an overview of their capabilities. We concluded that attackers have a wide range of intelligence gathering tools at their disposal, which increases the likelihood of future attacks and allows even non-technical skilled users to apply these tools.

Keywords: Social engineering · Threat analysis · Security awareness · Security tools

1 Introduction

"The biggest threat to security of a company is not a computer virus, an unpatched hole in a key program or a badly installed firewall. In fact, the biggest threat could be you [...] What I found personally to be true was that it's easier to manipulate people rather than technology [...] Most of the time organizations overlook that human element". These words from Kevin Mitnick [7] were made over a decade ago and are still of utmost importance today.

As security technology improves the human user remains the weakest link in system security. It is widely accepted that the people of an organization are therefore both the main vulnerability of any organization's security as well as

The original version of this chapter was revised: Modifications have made to Table 7. For detailed information please see Erratum. The Erratum to this publication is available online at https://doi.org/10.1007/978-3-319-64483-7_16

J. Lopez et al. (Eds.): TrustBus 2017, LNCS 10442, pp. 232–246, 2018.
DOI: 10.1007/978-3-319-64483-7_15

the most challenging aspect of system security [6,27]. Hadnagy [17] defines social engineering as "Any act that influences a person to take an action that may or may not be in their best interest". Numerous security consultants consider it a given for themselves as well as for genuine attackers to access critical information via social engineering [14,43].

The harm of social engineering attacks has been discussed in various reports. In 2003 Gulati [15] reported that cyber attacks cost U.S. companies $266 million every year and that 80% of the attacks are a form of social engineering. Although not being very recent assessments of the situation, it seems that little has changed until today. A study of 2011 from Dimensional Research [9] shows that nearly half of the considered large companies and a third of small companies fell victim of 25 or more social engineering attacks in the two years before. The study further shows that costs per incident usually vary between $25 000 and over $100 000. Furthermore, surveys, like Verizon's *Data Breach Investigation Report* [41,42] show the impact of social engineering. According to these studies the impact has grown from 7% of breaches in 2012 to 29% of breaches in 2013. These numbers should not be ignored and active support for mitigating these threats is needed.

Even though companies are aware of the social engineering problem, they have little tools available to even assess the threat for themselves. Hiring penetration testing companies that *attack* their clients and show weaknesses in their defences is one available option. However, these tests have a number of inherent problems. Particularly, to address legal issues high effort has to be invested upfront [44]. In addition, the test outcome is closely related to the limited scope of the test. A tester may find that some employees are violating security policies. While this is an important finding that lets a company improve the education of their employees, the completeness of these kind of tests is an issue. Only few employees can be tested on only few occasions. Moreover, experiments indicate that this approach is difficult, due to humans' demotivation when confronted with these testing results [10].

A number of tools are available that enable intelligence gathering. On one side using these tools a social engineer can gather information that help him attack persons or organizations. On the other side, these tools provide an organization with an excellent alternative to pen testing or awareness trainings, as they allow to analyse possible vulnerabilities. However, a structured survey on the tools' capabilities is missing so far.

We believe to improve the current situation by conducting a structured survey of social engineering intelligence gathering tools and contribute the following:

- A classification of existing tools regarding categories such as proposed purpose, price, perceived usability, visualization of results etc.
- A survey of information types retrieved by the tools regarding information about company employees and their communication channels, as well as related information e.g. company policies;
- A discussion of how even simple attacker types can use these tools for sophisticated social engineering attacks.

The remainder of our paper is organised as follows. Section 2 outlines the criteria for comparison, and Sect. 3 presents the results of our comparison. Section 4 concludes and provides directions for future research.

2 Social Engineering Basics and Tool Criteria

We acquire a basic understanding of social engineering and the general process attackers follow in Sect. 2.1. During the process various information is gathered about people, whom social engineers attack. Section 2.2 details our categorization of this *social engineering information* based on related work. Furthermore, we classify the tools on their *potential of applicability*, which describes the barriers that may or may not prevent an attacker from using them. For example, a tool that has a high price and poor usability will have little potential to be used by any attacker.

2.1 The Social Engineering Process

Various works report an underlying process to social engineering [17,21,27], which have recently been unified by Milosevic [26]. A social engineering attack consists of multiple phases as summarized in Table 1. In phase one the attacker conducts surveillance to identify a person within the inner circle of the targeted company. This person shall have access to the information the attacker desires. The next phase focuses on finding out as much about this person as possible. Every bit of information can help the attacker to manipulate the victim and her trust. During the pretexting phase the attacker starts building a relationship to the victim. Afterwards the attacker exploits the built up trust in the relationship and evaluates the gathered information in the post-exploitation phase.

Table 1. Overview of social engineering phases by Milosevic [26]

Phase	Description
Pre-engagement interactions	Find targets with sufficient access to information/knowledge to perform an attack
Intelligence gathering	Gather information on each of the valid targets. Choose the ones to attack
Pretexting	Use gathered information to build a relationship to the target. Gain victims' trust to access additional information
Exploitation	Use the built up trust to get the desired information
Post-exploitation	Analyze the attack and the retrieved information. If necessary return to a previous phase to continue the chain of attack until the final information has been retrieved

2.2 Social Engineering Information

This section focuses on types of information that can be gathered by a tool, in the following referred to as criteria. All criteria cover one or more essential information for social engineering attackers. The more criteria a tool covers, the more interesting it is for a social engineer during information gathering.

Communication Channels. Communication channels are one of the most relevant information for a social engineer. This category will list which channels can be found by a certain tool. Possible channels are "Telephone Numbers", "Social Media Accounts", "E-Mails", "Instant Messengers", "Friends", "Personal Information" and "Private Locations" [23,27].

User Credentials. Some tools have access to databases which contain leaked user credentials. If a social engineer gets access to login information of a certain employee, it simplifies the conduction of an attack. Firstly, he can directly access a victim's accounts. Secondly, the attacker could pose as someone else, e.g. an administrator from the IT department, and by having access to the target's data convince his victim to act in a certain way [18,27].

Locations. Some tools are especially designed to gather location data, while others provide them as a byproduct. Both, work addresses as well as an employee's private addresses can be useful for multiple purposes. Location data can be gathered from social media as it is embedded in photos and videos taken by cellphones. Also posts on social media can be tagged with a location. Other tools can convert IP addresses into physical locations and therefore find the physical locations of technical equipment [18,35].

Job Positions. By retrieving the job position of an employee the social engineer can figure out what kind of information someone has access to. Based on job title, the attacker can draw conclusions about whether an employee is new to a company, what the hierarchy within the company looks like and much more. Based on the organization's structure, it is possible to use techniques such as name-dropping, using the name of someone higher in the company's hierarchy, to pressure the target into revealing information [18,27].

Company Lingo. One of the easiest ways to convince someone of being authorized to access some information is by knowing the correct lingo [27]. Lingo means the words and abbreviations employees use within a company. Although this information is of great importance, it is very challenging to get access to. Knowledge about the lingo can be obtained by getting access to company manuals, internal reports or talking to employees.

Personal Information. The more personal information an attacker has on his target, the easier it is to find the correct angle and pressure points. One example would be well-defined spear-phishing e-mails using a person's interests. In case the e-mail contains enough private information to make it believable, the target is far more likely to open an attachment [19,35].

2.3 Potential for Applicability

This section presents the evaluation criteria to generally classify the software.

Proposed Purpose. Some of the tools are actually designed to gather information on a person or company in the context of social engineering. However, a user can also use tools for attacks which were designed for something completely different than social engineering.

Price. While some tools are free, others can be quite expensive and therefore might not be applicable for a quick self assessment. In some cases the tool itself is free, but for some features the user needs to have an API key that can be costly. This criteria focuses on the prices of each tool and its limitations coming with different price tiers.

Usability. Based on the user interface and the amount of documentation provided, this category assesses the ease of usage. The underlying question is if the usability of a tool allows a company to perform its own threat assessment.

Input Parameters. Some tools have a broad range of possible search arguments, but most tools need specific information to initiate a search. Depending on which specific piece of information is required by the tool, this might limit the social engineer in the decision what tools to use.

Visualize Output. Some tools print all information into tables while others have better ways of visualizing gathered information. For example location data can be illustrated by marking the positions on a map, instead of only providing GPS coordinates.

Ranking of Results. As the amount of gathered information grows, the more valuable an adequate selection and sorting becomes. Therefore, filtering irrelevant information is helpful in focusing on more promising targets/information. We did not find significant support for filtering in the analysed tools and therefore do not list this criteria in the following.

Suggesting Counter-Measures. Most of the tools are only designed to gather information and do not inform how to protect this information. While this is not relevant for social engineers, it is highly relevant for those who want to protect themselves against attackers and against information gathering in general. Note that none of the tools suggest countermeasures, therefore we did not list the category in the following.

3 Comparing Social Engineering Tools and Webpages

In the following section, we introduce and analyze relevant tools and webpages. In a second step we provide an overview over the types of information that can be gathered by them.

3.1 Social Engineering Tools and Webpages

We compiled the following list of social engineering tools by using the following words "social engineering and tool or application or script or webpage" in a Google[1] search and the list published by Hadnagy [17]. Three security researchers analysed the results independently and we included all tools and webpages that

[1] https://www.google.de.

they agreed on having the potential to help a social engineering attacker conduct the process outlined in Sect. 2.1. We identified the following tools and webpages that met our criteria.

Maltego (Kali Linux Edition, Version 3.6.1). Maltego [32] is an intelligence and forensics application. Before starting a search, the user can choose between different machines. Every machine has its own purpose and is designed for a particular attack vector. Maltego offers 12 default machines within the software such as: *Company Stalker* This machine tries to get all e-mail addresses at a domain to resolve them on social networks. It also gets documents and extracts meta data. As an input, it needs a company's domain. *Find Wikipedia Edits* This machine takes a domain and looks for possible Wikipedia edits. *Footprint L1* This module performs a level 1 (fast, basic) footprint of a domain. *Person - E-Mail Address* This machine tries to obtain someone's e-mail address and checks where it's used on the internet.

Maltego combines multiple modules to gather information from various sources and represents them in an easy to understand way in form of a bubble diagram. The user can start of with a domain name, a username, an IP address or the name of a person depending on which module he wishes to use. The gained information can be used for further research e.g. as input for other modules.

Recon-ng (Version 4.8.0). Recon-ng [40] is a full-featured Web Reconnaissance framework. It is based on a large list of modules which can be used to gather information about a specific target. The modules range from host information to social media. The user is free to chain these modules after each other and by starting with a single domain name, the database can be filled with employee names, their e-mail addresses, usernames, passwords and geolocations of all involved servers. The final reports can be exported in json, csv, xml, html or as a pdf. Similar to the Social Engineering Toolkit and Metasploit its user interface is console based.

Cree.py (Version 1.4). Cree.py [20] is a geolocation Open Source Intelligence (OSINT) tool. It is designed to gather geolocation related information from online sources like social networks. This information can be filtered by location or date and is presented on a map. Therefore, Cree.py is useful to follow the trace of where a person has been over the time of using certain social media platforms. Examples would be Instagram, Twitter or Tumblr which gather location data on where photos or posts have been created. These information can be displayed on a map and recreate a trace of places where a person has been.

Spokeo. Spokeo [38] is a search engine for people in the United States of America. There exist equivalent versions for other countries e.g. Pipl.com and PeekYou.com index people from all over the world. By entering the name, e-mail address, phone number, address or username of a person all related people matching the provided criteria are reported back. Depending on the wanted detail of the provided report, the price varies.

Social Engineering Toolkit (SET). SET [16] does not focus on finding information about a person. SET rather uses information on persons to e.g. send them phishing e-mails or gather information about company networks. The SET allows integration with other tools such as Metasploit that contain various scripts for vulnerability testing.

The Wayback Machine. The Wayback Machine [39] is an archive of the internet. The vendor claims to provide the history of more then 427 billion web pages (as of July 2015). The platform creates snapshots of websites and allows a user to go back to older versions of a website that have been replaced by newer ones.

theHarvester (Version 2.7). The Harvester [12] is designed to gather e-mail addresses, subdomains, hosts, and open ports from public sources. These sources contain search engines, PGP key servers and the SHODAN [36] computer database for internet-connected devices.

Whitepages. The *Whitepages* [5] website supports persons in finding people, their addresses and telephone numbers, private and from work. The service focuses on the U.S. and also provides reverse phone searches and similar means to identify a person based on technical information such as a phone number.

Background Checks. The *freebackgroundcheck.com* [1] website provides information about people that has been collected by background checks on them for e.g. a telecommunication provider. The intention is that people can get informed what information is available about them and most likely checked in situations such as job interviews. The website *Instant Checkmate* [2] on the other hand focuses on providing information to the public about people's arrest records and criminal behaviour.

Tax Records. Especially in the United States it is very easy to gain access to government information, as most data is publicly available [30]. Every person interested in the data can get access to arrest records, tax records and more for a small monetary fee per request. In addition, Ratsit in Sweden [34], Veroposi in Finland [4], Skatterlister in Norway [3] and recently the Federal Board of Revenue in Pakistan [31] also publish tax records online.

Company Related Information. As social engineers thrive to know as much about the social surroundings of a target as possible, there are a lot of tools, that help gathering social related information about a target. Websites like *KnowEm* [22] and *Namechk* [29] allow to search on more then 600 social media networks, if a username is already allocated or still available. While this is not the primary purpose of the website, an attacker can use this to track down social media networks, which a target is using. *SocialMention* [37] is a platform, that searches for user-generated content like posts, blogs, videos, etc. from a specific user. By gathering this kind of information the attacker learns a lot about the target and his behavior.

In most cases a social engineer is not after private information about a target, but work related information. This is due to an attacker generally trying to get access to work related sensitive information. Websites such as *Monster* [28],

LinkedIn [24] and *Xing* [45] are good sources for collecting CVs and current job positions of people related to the target. In addition platforms like *careerbuilder* [8] and *glassdoor* [13] provide information about open job offers and expected earnings. *Hoovers* [11], *MarketVisual* [25] and *LittleSis* [33] are useful to gain knowledge about the social networks of employees. Especially for larger companies, these websites offer information about who is connected to whom.

3.2 Analyzing the Social Engineering Attack Potential

After having established each tool's characteristics, it is important to know, what tool is able to retrieve which kind of information. Some tools are able to collect more information than others and some information can only be found with a specific tool. Table 2 provides an overview of the tools survey. Furthermore, Table 3 provides a refinement of the previous table considering the potential for applicability categories introduced in Sect. 2.3 for selected tools and webpages. For space reasons we do not show the information for all tools and websites.

Our goal is to show the utility of these tools for attackers. Therefore, we selected three attack types mentioned repeatedly [17,23,27]: *Phishing*, *Baiting*, and *Impersonation*. We describe these below including their needs of two essential information categories: *communication channels* and *company knowledge*. An attacker requires communication channels since the attacker has to communicate with a victim to exploit her trust. In addition, an attacker requires knowledge about the company to know whom to attack and how to get the companies employees' trust. The more details an attacker knows, the more likely people

Table 2. Social engineering tool comparison

	SET	Maltego	Recon-ng	Cree.py	Spokeo	Wayback Machine	theHarvester	knowem.com	Whitepages	Instant Checkmate	freebackgroundcheck.org
Search by Person/ Company	o	++	++	++	++	++	++	+	++	++	++
Retrieve E-Mail Address	o	++	++	o	o	o	++	o	o	o	o
Retrieve Username/ Password	o	o	++	o	o	o	o	o	o	o	o
Retrieve Job-Title	o	o	++	o	o	o	o	o	o	++	++
Retrieve Locations	o	+	+	++	+	o	o	o	++	++	++
Retrieve Personal Data	o	o	o	o	++	o	o	+	+	++	++
Usability	+	+	+	++	++	++	+	++	++	++	++
Visualize Output	+	++	+	++	++	++	+	++	++	++	++
Retrieve Company Lingo	o	o	o	o	o	o	o	o	o	o	o
Free to use	++	++	++	++	o	++	++	++	++	o	o

o Does not apply or cannot be used in this case
\+ Does apply in some cases, does collect limited information
++ Does fully apply, does gather the amount/quality of information needed

Table 3. Potential for applicability

Category	Maltego	Recon-ng	Cree.py	Spokeo	The wayback machine	The Harvester
Proposed purpose	Delivery of a threat picture of an organization's environment	Enables conduction of web-based reconnaissance	Provision of geolocation related information from social media	Provision of personal information	Archive for webpages and other media	Gather e-mails, subdomains, hosts and open ports from different public sources
Price	Free community edition, Full license $760first year, $320additional year	Free, API Keys up to $60,000	Free	Free basic information, $4.95month for detailed reports, $9.95 for court records	Free	Free
Usability	Easy to understand UI. Basic knowledge about structure and connection of information and available machines required	Terminal based tool. Basic knowledge about structure and connection of information and available modules required	Easy to use due to UI and step by step guidance	Easy to use due to step by step guidance	Easy to use due to centralization in single search field	Terminal based tool. Simple execution
Input parameters	Depending on the machine name, web domain, username, company name	Depending on the module domain name, URL, name	Username	Name, e-mail, phone, username, address	Web domain	Company name, web domain
Visualize parameters	Bubble diagram. Color coded data categories. Bubble sizes according to data amount	Local database exportable to various formats	Data listed, pins on map	Pins on map	Calendar based data entries. Available snapshots highlighted	Data tables
Relevant phases	Phase 1 - Pre-Engagement Interactions, Phase 2 - Intelligence Gathering	Phase 2 - Intelligence Gathering	Phase 2 - Intelligence Gathering	Phase 1 - Pre-Engagement Interactions, Phase 2 - Intelligence Gathering	Phase 1 - Pre-Engagement Interactions, Phase 2 - Intelligence Gathering	Phase 2 - Intelligence Gathering

believe he has a relation to the company. We detail these information needs for the attack types below and refine them in Table 4.

Table 4. Mapping of social engineering characteristics to attack types

	Attack type		
	Phishing	Baiting	Impersonation
Communication			
Telephone number	x		
Friends	x		x
Personal information	x		x
Private locations	x		x
EMail	x		
Instant messenger	x		
Co-workers: communication			x
Company knowledge			
Co-workers: new employee			x
Co-workers: hierarchies			x
Lingo	x		x
Facilities: security-measures		x	x
Facilities: company location		x	x
Websites	x		
Policies: software		x	
Policies: network		x	
Policies: organization		x	

Phishing refers to masquerading as a trustworthy entity and using this trust to acquire information or manipulating somebody to perform an action. This often appears in an unguided way via email to thousands of possible victims. Recently, spear-phishing attacks happen, which aim for a specific target instead of the broader mass. The social engineer gathers as much intelligence about the target as he can or needs and then prepares a tailored message for the victim.

Information Needs: Phishing attacks are mainly based on communicating with the victim, therefore the amount of information on communication channels is critical. The more channels an attacker has, the easier it is, to find one that can help bridge the gap between the engineer and the victim. In addition, the more company knowledge exist, the more targeted the attack can be.

Baiting is to leave a storage medium (e.g., a USB stick) inside a company location that contains malicious software (e.g., a key logger). The malicious software is executed automatically when the stick is inserted in a computer.

Table 5. Tool coverage for communication channels

	Cree. py	Gitrob	KnowEm	LinkedIn	Maltego	Namechk	Recon-ng	Spokeo	theHarvester	Wayback machine	Wire-shark	Xing
Telephone number							x					x
E-mail				x	x		x		x			x
Instant messenger			x		x	x		x				x
Friends			x	x	x	x						x
Personal information	x		x	x		x		x				x
Private locations	x							x				x

Table 6. Tool coverage for company knowledge

	Cree. py	Gitrob	KnowEm	LinkedIn	Maltego	Namechk	Recon-ng	Spokeo	theHarvester	Wayback Machine	Wire-shark	Xing
Company locations	x			x			x	x	x			x
Company lingo												
Special knowledge				x	x		x					x
New employees				x	x							x
Hierarchies				x	x							x
Websites					x		x		x	x		
Facility security measures		x									x	
Security policies		x							x		x	
Software policies		x					x				x	

Information Needs: Baiting is a passive attack vector, which does not need direct interaction with the victim. Therefore, the focus lies on gathering company knowledge. In particular, locations and walking routes of employees for placing the storage medium are essential.

Impersonation is to play the role of someone a victim is likely to trust or obey, e.g. an authority figure. The attacker fools the victim into allowing him access to the desired location or information. Usually, attackers prepare well for an impersonation and leverage vast amount of information.

Information Needs: For a successful impersonation attack company knowledge is a priority. The social engineer needs knowledge of numerous areas of the company. The more information he has on the persona he is playing, the more convincing he can be. Communication channels are of less importance, since the victim is approached in person.

We illustrate the degree to which the information needs of a social engineer can be covered for the discussed attack types. Tables 5 and 6 match tools with communication channels and company knowledge. Table 6 reveals that numerous tools cover information gathering for locations, websites, new employees etc. of

Table 7. Tools vs. AttackType knowledge with P for phishing, I for impersonation, and B for baiting

	Cree.py	Gitrob	KnowEm	LinkedIn	Maltego	Namechk	Recon-ng	Spokeo	theHarvester	Wayback Machine	Wireshark	Xing
Telephone Number							P					P
Friends			P,I	P,I	P,I	P,I						P,I
Personal Information	P,I		P,I	P,I		P,I		P,I				P,I
Private Locations	P,I							P,I				P,I
E-Mail				P	P		P		P			P
InstantMessenger			P		P	P		P				P
Co-Workers: NewEmployee				I	I							I
Co-Workers: Hierarchies				I			I					I
Lingo												
Facilities: Security-Measures		B,I									B,I	
Facilities: Company Location	B,I			B,I			B,I	B,I	B,I			B,I
Websites					P		P		P	P		

companies. However, the *Company Lingo* is not covered at all. Company lingo contains all abbreviations and specific terms used in a company and has been used by social engineers to bypass authentication mechanisms, e.g. personnel often thinks everyone knowing the company lingo belongs to the company [27].

For "Facility Security Measures", "Security Policies" and "Software Policies" there is a similar result. Besides *theHarvester* and *Recon-ng*, which can both only gather information concerning web-security like open ports or SSL-Encryption, all other tools are not directly suitable for social engineers. *Wireshark* needs physical access, which is not exactly what a social engineer prefers and *Gitrob* is one of the tools, with very slim chances of success. If the company has any security policies or hosts their sourcecode within the company, then *Gitrob* will most likely not be able to access it and therefore not gain any information.

To sum up, modern social engineers have a variety of tools at their disposal for information gathering, which they can use in numerous attacks. We provide an exemplary overview for phishing, baiting, and impersonation attacks and summarize in Table 7. The empty fields mean that three security researchers could not identify a use for that tool for any of the attacks above. Note that there are still some types of information that are difficult to gather for an attacker such as company lingo, but we have little doubt that in the future further tools and social media offers will fill this gap. Furthermore, our comparison showed that all tools have a good or great usability and provide easy to understand output. This means intelligence gathering can be used by an attacker with little technical knowledge such as script kiddies. Therefore, we have to take the threats arising from increased and easily available knowledge for social engineering seriously.

4 Conclusions

We conducted a structured survey of social engineering tools, which ease the attacker's effort of finding information about victims. We mapped the information to their usefulness for phishing, impersonation or baiting attacks. Our analysis revealed that the social engineering threat is more dangerous than ever before, due to the number of tools at an attacker's disposal and the significant amount of detail they provide. We propose the following.

Implications for Possible Victims. People in general, not only employees in companies, can fall victim to social engineering. Therefore, people should find out what is available about them in the web using the tools or websites listed here. Ideally, stories of new contacts and unusual requests to secret information should be checked and verified more carefully than in the past. Means of protection can include false information released such a bogus address or non-existing hobbies. Any requests using this information identify possible social engineers.

Implications for Security Practitioners. Chief information officers and consultants should integrate a demonstration of the tools in this publication to raise awareness of the social engineering threat in companies. Just when people see the ease of collecting information with the tools and websites and how these are used e.g. in phishing, they can understand the need for strict security policies with regard to the release of data in the web.

Suggestions for Law Enforcement has to operate under the assumption that criminals will get all information about their victims without ever leaving their home or having mature computer skills. Everyone can be a social engineer and is a possible perpetrator. Countermeasures have to include network traffic analysis of how an attacker gathered the information for his attacks.

Limitations of the Tools. The only information type that social engineering tools do not provide today is the so-called *company lingo*, the abbreviations and specific words used in a company or domain. However, we are certain that in the future, tools combining machine learning and big data analysis will fill this gap.

Limitations of our Study. We conducted the study using a previous survey of tools and a web search engine. These sources can be extended in particular to including sites that are not indexed by web search engines e.g. in the dark web. This work will require a collaboration with a law enforcement agency.

Acknowledgements. This research has been partially supported by the Federal Ministry of Education and Research Germany (BMBF) with project grant number 16KIS0240.

References

1. Freebackgroundcheck. https://mybackgroundcheck.preemploy.com
2. Instant checkmate. https://www.instantcheckmate.com
3. Norwegian register. http://skattelister.no/
4. Tax information. http://www.veroporssi.com/
5. Whitepages. http://www.whitepages.com
6. Barrett, N.: Penetration testing and social engineering: hacking the weakest link. Inf. Secur. Tech. Rep. **8**(4), 56–64 (2003)
7. BBC News. How to hack people, October 2002. http://news.bbc.co.uk/2/hi/technology/2320121.stm
8. CareerBuilder. Job search engine. http://careerbuilder.com/
9. Dimensional Research. The risk of social engineering on information security, September 2011. http://docplayer.net/11092603-The-risk-of-social-engineering-on-information-security.html
10. Dimkov, T., van Cleeff, A., Pieters, W., Hartel, P.: Two methodologies for physical penetration testing using social engineering. In: Proceedings of ACSAC, ACSAC 2010, pp. 399–408. ACM (2010)
11. Dun & Bradstreet. Sales acceleration platform. http://www.hoovers.com/
12. Edge-Security. theHarvester. http://www.edge-security.com/theharvester.php
13. Glassdoor. Recruiting website. https://www.glassdoor.de/
14. Gragg, D.: A multi-level defense against social engineering. SANS Reading Room, 13 March 2003
15. Gulati, R.: The threat of social engineering and your defense against it. SANS Reading Room (2003)
16. Hadnagy. Social engineering toolkit (set). http://www.social-engineer.org/framework/se-tools/computer-based/social-engineer-toolkit-set/
17. Hadnagy, C.: Social Engineering: The Art of Human Hacking. Wiley, Indianapolis (2010)
18. Hadnagy, C.: The Official Social Engineering Portal (2015)
19. Internetsafety 101. Social Media Statistics (2013). http://www.internetsafety101.org/Socialmediastats.htm
20. Kakavas. Geolocation OSINT Tool. http://www.geocreepy.com/
21. Kee, J.: Social Engineering: Manipulating the Source. GCIA Gold Certification (2008)
22. KnowEm LLC. Social media brand search engine. http://knowem.com/
23. Krombholz, K., Hobel, H., Huber, M., Weippl, E.: Social engineering attacks on the knowledge worker. In: Proceedings of Security of Information and Networks, SIN 2013, pp. 28–35. ACM (2013)
24. LinkedIn. Business social networking service. http://linkedin.com/
25. MarketVisual. Business search engine. http://www.marketvisual.com/
26. Milosevic, N.: Introduction to Social Engineering (2013)
27. Mitnick, K.D., Simon, W.L.: The Art of Deception: Controlling the Human Element in Security (2003)
28. Monster Wolrdwide Inc., Job search engine. http://monster.com/
29. Namechk. Username and domain search tool. https://namechk.com/
30. National Association of Counties. http://www.naco.org/
31. Pakistan Government. Federal board of revenue. http://www.fbr.gov.pk/
32. Paterva. Maltego clients and servers. https://www.paterva.com/web6/products/maltego.php

33. Public Accountability Initiative. http://littlesis.org/
34. Ratsit & Invativa. Credit business website. http://www.ratsit.se/
35. Regan, K.: 10 Amazing Social Media Growth Stats From 2015 (2015)
36. Shodan. Search engine for the internet of things. https://www.shodan.io/
37. Socialmention. Social media search platform. http://socialmention.com/
38. Spokeo. People search website. http://www.spokeo.com/
39. The Internet Archive. The wayback machine. https://archive.org/web/
40. Tomes, T.: Web reconnaissance framework. https://bitbucket.org/LaNMaSteR53/recon-ng
41. Verizon. Data Breach Investigations Report (2012). http://www.verizonenterprise.com/resources/reports/rp_data-breach-investigations-report-2012-ebk_en_xg.pdf
42. Verizon. Data Breach Investigations Report (2013). http://www.verizonenterprise.com/resources/reports/rp_data-breach-investigations-report-2013_en_xg.pdf
43. Warkentin, M., Willison, R.: Behavioral and policy issues in information systems security: the insider threat. Eur. J. Inf. Syst. **18**(2), 101–105 (2009)
44. Watson, G., Mason, A., Ackroyd, R.: Social Engineering Penetration Testing: Executing Social Engineering Pen Tests, Assessments and Defense. Syngress, Rockland (2011)
45. Xing. Business social networking service. http://xing.com/

Erratum to: A Structured Comparison of Social Engineering Intelligence Gathering Tools

Kristian Beckers[1(✉)], Daniel Schosser[1], Sebastian Pape[2], and Peter Schaab[1]

[1] Institute of Informatics, Technische Universität München (TUM), Boltzmannstr. 3, 85748 Garching, Germany
beckersk@in.tum.de

[2] Faculty of Economics and Business Administration, Goethe University Frankfurt, Theodor-W.-Adorno-Platz 4, 60323 Frankfurt, Germany

Erratum to: Chapter "A Structured Comparison of Social Engineering Intelligence Gathering Tools" in: J. Lopez et al. (Eds.): Trust, Privacy and Security in Digital Business, LNCS 10442, https://doi.org/10.1007/978-3-319-64483-7_15

The presentation of Table 7 was incorrect in the original version of this chapter. The correct version is given below:

Table 7. Tools vs. AttackType knowledge with P for phishing, I for impersonation, and B for baiting

	Cree.py	Gitrob	KnowEm	LinkedIn	Maltego	Namechk	Recon-ng	Spokeo	theHarvester	Wayback Machine	Wireshark	Xing
Telephone Number							P					P
Friends			P,I	P,I	P,I	P,I						P,I
Personal Information	P,I		P,I	P,I		P,I		P,I				P,I
Private Locations	P,I							P,I				P,I
E-Mail				P	P		P		P			P
InstantMessenger			P		P	P		P				P
Co-Workers: NewEmployee				I	I							I
Co-Workers: Hierarchies				I			I					I
Lingo												
Facilities: Security-Measures		B,I									B,I	
Facilities: Company Location	B,I			B,I			B,I	B,I	B,I			B,I
Websites					P		P		P	P		

The original chapter has been corrected.

The updated online version of this chapter can be found at https://doi.org/10.1007/978-3-319-64483-7_15

J. Lopez et al. (Eds.): TrustBus 2017, LNCS 10442, p. E1, 2017.
https://doi.org/10.1007/978-3-319-64483-7_16

Author Index

Printed in the United States
By Bookmasters